Formerly and today, monks, I teach but one thing: Suffering and the release from suffering.

AN INTRODUCTION TO BUDDHIST THOUGHT

A Philosophic History of Indian Buddhism

A.L. Herman

UNIVERSITY PRESS OF AMERICA

LANHAM • NEW YORK • LONDON

4720 Boston Way
Lanham, MD 20706

3 Henrietta Street
London WC2E 8LU England

Printed in the United States of America

Library of Congress Cataloging in Publication Data

Herman, A.L.
An introduction to Buddhist thought.

Bibliography: p.
Includes index.
1. Buddhism—Doctrines—History. 2. Philosophy, Buddhist—History. I. Title.
BQ4090.H47 1983 181'.043 83-16782
ISBN 0-8191-3594-1 (alk. paper)
ISBN 0-8191-3595-X (pbk. : alk. paper)

All University Press of America books are produced on acid-free paper which exceeds the minimum standards set by the National Historical Publications and Records Commission.

For Dan

Wendy

and Karl

ACKNOWLEDGEMENTS

For permission to reprint copyrighted material in excess of fair use I would like to thank the following: The American Oriental Society for *Viṁśatikā of Vasubandhu*, translated by Clarence H. Hamilton (New Haven: American Oriental Society, 1938); George Allen & Unwin, Ltd. for Edward Conze, *Buddhist Thought in India* (London: George Allen & Unwin, Ltd., 1962), and K.N. Jayatilleke, *Early Buddhist Theory of Knowledge* (London: George Allen & Unwin, Ltd., 1963); Oxford University Press for *Some Sayings of the Buddha*, translated by F.L. Woodward (Oxford University Press, 1973/1925); Viking Penguin, Inc., for *Buddhist Scriptures*, selected and translated by Edward Conze (Baltimore, MD: Penguin Books, 1959); the Theosophical Publishing House for H. Wolfgang Schumann, *Buddhism, An Outline of Its Teachings and Schools* (Wheaton, IL: The Theosophical Publishing House, 1973).

I am most grateful for the photograph of the seated Buddha located in the Japanese Tea Garden, San Francisco. It was made by Harold Flaaten and appears here by permission.

A number of people have generously aided in the preparation of the manuscript. In particular I wish to thank the following: My wonderful colleagues at the University of Wisconsin-Stevens Point, who helped me with various stages of the manuscript and who have kept me on straight philosophic paths during our long and very pleasant association; Douglas D. Daye, Barbara H. Flaaten and David J. Kalupahana who read the manuscript in its entirety and made extraordinary comments and criticisms that saved it and me from flagrant errors and conspicuous embarrassment; Carolee Cote, Barbara Herman, Sandra Misiewicz and Judy Opiola, who typed and word-processed their way through various versions of the work; and Helen Anne Herman, who proof-read the final version of the book and provided valuable comments to nearly every page of the finished manuscript.

The errors that this book contains, and there are many, are entirely my own. Whatever merit the work contains is due entirely to the collective kindness, wit and attention of all of the above extremely generous persons.

Arthur Herman
October, 1983

Table of Contents

Preface

This book is intended to be three things: First, an introduction to Buddhist thought in India; second, a philosophic history of that thought; and, third, an introduction to philosophy. Let me say something about each of these three intentions, and then conclude with two convictions that underlie them and this work.

First, as an introduction, this study of Buddhist thought is meant for the beginning student, academic or secular, professional or amateur, who is interested in philosophy, religious studies and the humanities. The only skills expected of such a student would be in his or her ability to read the English language, and to hear thunder, see lightning, and feel rain, i.e. to have a certain sensitivity to the world we all live in. It is not even necessary to have any sympathy for that world; sensitivity is enough.

As an introduction to Buddhist thought this work is about the philosophical interests and religious beliefs of Buddhists, as those interest and beliefs relate to such diverse topics as the nature of suffering and evil, the existence of God, the existence of the self and other minds, life after death, freedom of action, and the relationship between moral action and the good life; in addition, this work is concerned with the proof of an external world, the nature of language and its objects, questions about what is (or are) ultimately real, and whether that real is knowable or whether anything is knowable; finally, this work will investigate the paths to liberation or enlightenment, the nature of liberation and how to discover or uncover it, and the values found in enlightenment. These are exciting and perennial philosophical and religious concerns that touch thinking beings everywhere. This book merely provides the occasion, it is hoped, for thinking critically, plainly and clearly about such topics and concerns.

As an introduction to Buddhist thought in India this work attempts to present the chief philosophical and religious views of Buddhism during the first 1000 years of its existence. The years spanned are approximately from 500 B.C.E. (Before the Christian Era) to almost 500 C.E. (Christian Era). The literature from this era of Indian Buddhism is enormous, and the epoch is undoubtedly the most significant period for the development, growth and maturing of Buddhist thought. Though Buddhism will continue to grow in India for another 500 years, and flourish in the rest of the world up to the present day, all subsequent Buddhisms can be seen as simply a series of doctrinal footnotes to this earlier era. This is not to denigrate later Buddhism, e.g., Tantrism, Ch'an, Zen, or the myriad other Buddhisms of Tibet, China, Mongolia, Korea and Japan (or Paris, London and San Francisco) but, rather, it is to emphasize the enormous significance that early Indian Buddhism will have on those later and other Buddhisms.

The Indian Buddhism that the present work encompasses is divided into three periods, viz., the pristine, or original, Buddhism of the founder, Gautama the Buddha (563 B.C.E. to 483 B.C.E.); Hīnayāna (sometimes called "Theravāda") Buddhism (ca. 350 B.C.E. to 400 C.E.); and Mahāyāna Buddhism (ca. 100 C.E. to 400 C.E.).

Second, as a philosophic history of Buddhist thought in India, this work attempts to give a systematic account of the intellectual problems or puzzles of a particular historical period, and, whenever possible, it then attempts to solve or answer those problems in metaphysics, epistemology, value theory, and religion. The philosophic historian seeks to isolate and to state the problems, and then to propose and critically evaluate possible solutions to those problems.

The philosophic historian makes us aware of problems, even to the point of creating or drawing out problems from situations where none existed before, or where none was expected, or made explicit, before.

The philosophic historian is a trouble-maker who believes that good philosophy, like good thinking, is born out of the encounter with problems and that human beings can always be at their best under such confounding circumstances.

Philosophic histories exist primarily to provide an arena for problem solving wherein by insights into past problems and past solutions, present problems can be clarified and new and stronger solutions can be revealed.

Third, as an introduction to philosophy this work uses Buddhist thought in India to display three of this author's own prejudices that relate to philosophy: The methods of philosophy; the tools of the methodology; and a hypothesis concerning the role of philosophy in human affairs. Let me speak briefly to these three prejudices.

From what has been said above regarding the activity of the philosophic historian, it should come as no surprise that that activity exemplifies quite adequately the methodology and the techniques of philosophic pursuit. Philosophy ought principally to be concerned with only one thing, viz., solving philosophic problems. What happens afterward, e.g., building philosophic systems, writing books about vouchsafed visions, becoming an international wise man, appearing on radio and television, and so on, is all purely incidental to this central concern. The extensive use of translated, primary materials, and the commentaries on those materials that are employed in this work, are there for the single purpose of generating, and then attempting to solve, philosophic problems. Another aim of all this questioning, probing and analyzing is simply to condition and encourage the reader to continue using the methods of philosophy in his or her own life. The reader will, if all goes well, simply get into the philosophic habit of asking questions and posing problems and seeking solutions to those questions and problems.

Which brings me to my second prejudice regarding philosophy. The tools of the methodology with which the philosopher and the philosophic historian work are logic and common sense. Logic is merely the set of universally accepted rules of sound thinking which, when properly employed, help to impose order on disorder. The rules of logic help us all to think like human beings rather than like buffaloes, boobies or bullfinches. Common sense is simply the application of those logical rules of sound thinking to everyday, ordinary experience, i.e. common sense is the application of rules of thought that help us to order our world and avoid fallacies and other embarrassing ways of mucking up. That is why I said previously that the only skills needed to undertake the study of the present work are literacy and sensitivity; the other tools, viz., logic and common sense, should already be there, merely in virtue of our being human.

But philosophy has another purpose beyond raising and solving problems, another goal beyond that of producing questioning, and problem-wise and solution-wise readers. This brings me to a third and final prejudice couched as a hypothesis about philosophy. I want to put forth a hypothesis concerning the role of philosophy in human affairs. This hypothesis is grounded in, or justified by, two pragmatic theories. The first theory I shall call "the mythic theory of truth." It states that a myth is true if and only if hearing it and believing it can lead to liberation. The mythic theory of truth will be discussed and illustrated as our investigation of Buddhist thought proceeds, and it will lead to the hypothesis that philosophy, like myth, can lead to liberation. The route to this hypothesis lies in treating philosophy just as myth has been treated, i.e. as a yoga or way to be tested by the liberating results it produces. The Buddhist texts appear to provide ample evidence for this hypothesis, as we shall see.

The second theory that grounds this hypothesis is what I shall call "the theory of useful or skillful means." It states that any means to an end is right, true or useful if and only if it leads to liberation. The list of the useful means that instantiate this theory is lengthy and includes such diverse items as the law of karma, the law of dependent origination and the doctrine of saṁsāra, certain general or abstract words, e.g., the concepts of the self, heaven, emptiness and, finally, once again, philosophy, itself.

The hypothesis supported by both the mythic theory of truth and the theory of useful or skillful means is the hypothesis that philosophy, i.e. doing philosophic history, can lead to liberation. The two theories and the hypothesis are illustrated throughout the text.

Finally, two convictions have motivated this philosophic history of Buddhist thought in India. The first is the rather strong belief that intellectual delight always accompanies the exercise of reason or thinking. When we consider the kinds of intellectual activities that give human beings delight, surely problem solving must be among the first of such considerations. The ability to solve problems is an ability that we share with other members of the animal kingdom; and if "problem solving" were defined loosely enough it is even possible that the plant kingdom could be said to have some expertise in it as well.

Problem solving, whether it be that of a plant attempting to find nourishment for its roots in an arid landscape, or an animal stalking prey and avoiding enemies by craft and cunning, or a human being making a sharp skidding turn on an ice-slicked street, is known to living species and it serves to separate us, plants, animals and humans, from the nonliving species: Rocks, ponds and corpses don't solve problems.

Problem solving, furthermore, can be a grave and solemn undertaking, where life, itself, may depend on the solution sought; or it can be a game, where delight and fascination, alone, are at stake. Out of all living entities, human beings are probably the only problem solvers for whom delight alone is the sole incentive for solving problems. But even for many members of the human species problem solving of a very unique sort can be a deadly serious activity, and for none more so than for those Buddhists for whom the problem of suffering has become the major challenge of life.

It is in critically examining their rational and extra-rational attempts to solve the problem of suffering, however, that, I anticipate, our own intellectual delight will come. That delight is found in analyzing and testing their putative solutions to the problem, and in examining the questions, difficulties and puzzles which led to those solutions.

It was a belief of the Athenian philosopher, Plato, and one to which this book subscribes, that man is at his best when he is exercising his reason. In other words, the application of reason, of logic and common sense, to philosophic problems is the key to intellectual delight, as I hope the present study will happily attest.

The second conviction that has motivated this study of Buddhist thought is the equally strong belief that not only is the human mind wasted and misused if it is not engaged in doing what it does best, viz., solving problems, but similarly, the discipline of philosophy is wasted and misused if it is not engaged in doing what it does best, viz., solving philosophic problems. Therefore, the topics chosen for this volume were chosen both for the inherent interest which they generate for students of Buddhism, the quick and the not-so-quick, and for the ease with which these topics lend themselves to philosophic treatment, i.e. to examination in philosophic history, i.e. to problem identification, to critical analysis and to possible solution.

What is a philosophic problem? Most simply answered, it is the kind of problem that philosophers alone attempt to solve.

Philosophers, generally, don't attempt to solve such problems as how to find the value of x for "$x^2=8$", or how to repair a sluggish fuel injection system, or how to predict a lava blowout from Mt. St. Helens, or why Caesar crossed the Rubicon River in 44 B.C., or why pi messons and R H messons don't get along well together, or even why inflation and joblessness seem casually related, or why you can't get a plumber on weekends. These are not philosophic problems. But they are questions and problems to be answered by non-philosophers, by householders, by historians, by economists, by mathematicians, and so on, all of whom may employ reason, i.e. logic and common sense, in seeking their answers. The use of reason in problem solving, in other words, is not sufficient to identify a philosopher solving a philosophic problem.

Again, philosophic problems are problems that philosophers attempt to solve; and if a philosopher, *qua* philosopher, attempts to solve a problem, then it is, for that reason alone, a philosophic problem.

Philosophers do attempt to solve such problems as, how is myth related to enlightenment? or how can a philosophic argument lead to enlightenment? or how can something be said to be the cause of something else? or how do you know that God does not exist? or how does Buddhism solve the problem of suffering? and what do "enlightenment", "cause", "God" and "suffering" mean?

Our philosophic history will examine the philosophic problems found at the roots of Buddhism in the Hindu tradition of the *Vedas* and the *Upaniṣads*, and in the non-Hindu heterodoxies that sprang up during the middle of the 6th century B.C.E. Our philosophic history will focus on questions concerning the life of the founder of Buddhism and the great myth and the theory of truth that evolved out of, and attempted to explain, that life. Further, our philosophic history will concentrate on the puzzles generated by the two major traditions of Buddhist philosophic and religious thought in India, viz., Hīnayāna Buddhism and Mahāyāna Buddhism. Finally, our philosophic history will analyze the problems, questions and puzzles connected with the four major schools of philosophy that became attached to these two major traditions, viz., Sarvāstivāda and Sautrāntika in the Hīnayāna tradition, and Mādhyamika (Śūnyavāda) and Yogācāra in the Mahāyāna tradition.

Some of the philosophic problems relating to the *Vedas* and the *Upaniṣads*, to the life of the Buddha, to the Hīnayāna and Mahāyāna traditions and to their four schools, are solvable, and solutions will be attempted where the effort seems appropriate; some of the problems that we identify will be left for the reader to solve; while other problems that we isolate may prove to be so intransigent as to be seemingly insoluble.

It is hoped that this presentation of the philosophic history of Buddhism, together with the examination of the perennial philosophic problems which that history has engendered, will sufficiently justify yet another book about Buddhism.

A.L.H.
University of Wisconsin
Stevens Point, WI 54481

The Pronunciation of the Sanskrit (and Pāli) Alphabet

The technical vocabulary employed throughout this work is in Sanskrit (and Pāli), the philosophic languages of Indian Buddhism. To aid the student in the pronunciation of these languages I append below a brief guide to pronunciation. The Pāli language, which is a variant of Sanskrit, is the language of Hīnayāna Buddhism and the language in which the oldest canon of rules and laws of Buddhism are still maintained. Because of the similarity between Sanskrit and Pāli and because many of the texts from which I shall be quoting are in Pāli I shall, whenever it seems appropriate, give the Pāli form of a term in parentheses following the introduction of the Sanskrit term: arhat (Pāli arahat or arahant), dharma (Pāli dhamma), dhyāna (Pāli jhāna), Gautama (Pāli Gotama), nirvāṇa (Pāli nibbana), prajñā (Pāli pañña), Siddhārtha (Pāli (Siddhattha), skandha (Pāli khanda), sthavira (Pāli thera), sūtra (Pāli sutta) and so forth.

Sanskrit (and Pāli) may be pronounced according to the following phonetic rules:

The vowels with macrons, or lines, over them, ā, ī, ū, are long vowels and are pronounced as in *father*, *machine* and *rude*. The same vowels without macrons are short vowels and equivalent in sound to the vowels in *but*, *tin* and *full*. Vowel ṛ is sounded as in *rill* and is lightly trilled. The vowels *e*, *ai*, *o* and *au*, are considered long and are pronounced as in *grey*, *aisle*, *open* and *cow*.

All consonants with *h* after them are aspirated consonants and the breath should be slightly released when pronouncing them. Thus *kh*, *gh*, *ch*, *jh*, *ph* and so on sound like *rockhouse*, *doghouse*, *churchhouse*, *fudgehouse*, *tophouse*, respectively. Other consonants that one must watch out for are *c* as in *cheese*, *ś* and ṣ both as in *ship*, *s* as in *sip* and *jñ* as in *gyana*.

Sanskrit (and Pāli) words are stress-accented according to the following simple formula:

1. Words of two syllables are accented on the first syllable: Búddha, dhárma, śúnya.
2. Words of more than two syllables, where the penult (second syllable from the end) is either long (i.e. has a long vowel or diphthong, e.g., ā, ī, ū, e, o, au or ai) or

has a short vowel followed by two or more consonants (and where kh, gh, th, ph, bh count as one consonant), e.g., ān, addh, árm, are accented on the penult: Hīnayā́na, Subhádra, Abhidhárma.

3. Words of more than two syllables, where the penult is short and not followed by two consonants, as above, are accented on the antepenult (third syllable from the end): Mādhyámika, Himálaya, Upániṣad.

I. THE BIRTH OF BUDDHISM (563-483 B.C.E.)

Chapter One: The Birth of a Myth

Once it came to pass that a noble and beautiful woman was visited by the Holy Spirit. This Holy Spirit entered into her and she conceived. At this same moment, the elements of the ten thousand world-systems quaked and trembled as an unmeasurable light appeared. The blind received their sight. The deaf heard. The dumb spoke with one another. The crooked became straight. The lame walked. Prisoners were freed from their bonds and chains. In hell the fire was extinguished. In the heaven of the ancestors all hunger and thirst ended. Wild animals ceased to be afraid. The illnesses of the sick vanished. All men began to speak kindly to one another as this new being was conceived in his mother's womb.

And the fruit of her womb was conceived without sin or defilement. Her subsequent pregnancy was free of distress, fatigue and depression, for she was pure and virtuous, and completely unlike any other mortal woman. On a journey during the last days of her pregnancy, she noticed that the time of her delivery had come. Therefore, she retired to a quiet place and, as a star[1] shone brightly down from heaven, she gave birth to a son.

The child was not born in the usual way and the birth was a virgin birth, without pain or injury to the mother. The holy child's miraculous entrance into the world was like that of a God descending to earth from heaven. It seemed as if the sun itself had come down from the sky, and the place where the infant lay was filled with light.

Now there was a certain wise man who learned of the miraculous birth of this child who was to become the Savior of all mankind. And perceiving the star in the sky, he journeyed to the place where the child was born. Seeing the divine babe in his mother's lap, the wise man proclaimed the infant a Savior and wept for both joy and sorrow: For joy that the Savior had been born, but for sorrow because he, the wise man, would not hear him preach the miraculous message of salvation.

Seven days after the divine child's birth, his mother, the holy vessel of the Savior, was raised bodily, whole and pure, into heaven.[2]

Who was this future Savior of mankind whose undefiled mother received the annunciation from a messenger of the Holy Spirit, immaculately conceived the future Savior of the world, gave miraculous birth to this Savior and was then raised bodily and without defilement, into heaven? The child was Gautama Siddhārtha Śākyamuni, the future Buddha, and the Savior's mother was Māyā, a royal lady from the city of Kapilavastu in Northeastern India, and the birth described took place in Lumbini in Nepal around 563 B.C.E. (Before the Christian Era).

This particular account of the birth of the future Buddha has come down to us in a work called *Buddhacarita*, or "the acts of Buddha", and it was composed sometime in the first century C.E. (Christian Era) by an Indian poet, dramatist and philosopher called Aśvaghoṣa. The story that Aśvaghoṣa records is undoubtedly a good deal older than the first century, however, going back, perhaps, to a time at which miracles and other supernatural activities first began to be attributed to the Buddha and his life. Reading the *Buddhacarita* , as with all accounts of the lives of great men composed by adoring disciples, we can learn not so much what did occur as what these disciples believed ought to have occurred. And the believed account is much more significant for our purposes than any factual account could be unless, of course, the believed account and the factual account should happen to coincide.

1. Truth and Meaning

There are two important philosophical questions that can be raised with regard to such a believed account. The first question is, Is the account true? and the second is, What does the account mean? In what follows I want to suggest that the most fruitful place in which to search for answers to these questions is not in the realm of the factual but in the realm of what we shall refer to as "myth."

The reason for turning away from the factual as an approach to the questions of truth and meaning in the account of the birth of the future Buddha is that, quite frankly, the factual approach appears, *prima facie*, false, simplistic and limited. The empirical truth and cognitive meaning in such an account as the story gives is either false, non-existent or misleading: Holy Spirits, a critic of the story might point out, don't enter into people today and make them conceive, and there's no good reason to suppose that times have changed that much that Holy Spirits did things yesterday that they don't or refuse to do now. Virgin births don't occur nowadays, and there's no good reason to believe that today is any different from 563 B.C.E. Stars don't shine down over maternity hospitals, suns don't come down from skies to fill obstetrical delivery rooms with supernatural lights and there's no good reason to believe that they ever did, since times and the world probably have not changed that much. To deny a constancy or uniformity to nature and nature's laws between 563 B.C.E. and the present is to abrogate common sense; and to deny common sense is to give up sanity and reason altogether. So, on a factual approach, an approach which is afterall the best ground for judging historical or putative historical events, the story of the birth of the future Buddha is false, simplistic and limited.

But Buddhists and Buddhologists alike don't treat the story as factually false or even as a mere factual account. Rather, it is taken to be what is technically called a "myth" and as such it is not meant to be interpreted only or completely on the factual level. And it is because this story has been believed as a myth that we must turn to the nature of myth, itself, for an interpretation of the truth and meaning of the birth of the future Buddha.

It has been claimed that myths have a timeless and universal character wherever they arise, from whatever source, and in whatever culture or period of human existence. Joseph Campbell has spoken most eloquently of the nature and significance of the timeless vision that myth offers in his classic work on the origin of the world's mythology, *The Hero With A Thousand Faces*.

> Throughout the inhabited world, in all times and under every circumstance, the myths of man have flourished; and they have been the living inspiration of whatever else may have appeared out of the activities of the human body and mind.

Campbell continues, focusing on what he considers to be the special role of myth in human history:

> It would not be too much to say that myth is the secret opening through which the inexhaustible energies of the cosmos pour into human cultural manifestation. Religions, philosophies, arts, the social forms of primitive and historic man, prime discoveries in science and technology, the very dreams that blister sleep, boil up from the basic, magic ring of myth.[3]

Myths express truths, their defenders say, that cannot be stated in mere literal language alone. A myth carries a deep metaphoric structure that is untranslatable into cognitive, i.e. factual or logical, categories. And yet myths express truth and meaning, the argument continues, that produce consequences that can be tested and identified, even though the myths cannot be translated completely into some literal language.

2. The Mythic Theory of Truth

Defenders of this interpretation of myth might say that the story of Gautama's birth is true, but in a mythic sense, and that its meaning lies in exhorting those familiar with the cultural tradition in which the myth arises to imitate the hero of the story if they too would satisfy the goal for man prescribed by the culture. Thus the story is both true and meaningful for Buddhists in a Buddhist culture, and the point of departure for showing this lies in what we shall call "the mythic theory of truth."

The mythic theory of truth holds that a story, legend or account is true if and only if the recitation or the hearing or the reading of the story, legend or account leads to metaphysical realization or enlightenment. Furthermore, if a story, legend or account is true according to the mythic theory of truth then that story, legend or account is what we shall call a "myth."

Metaphysical realization would seem to be brought about through the functioning of three necessary elements in the myth: An expressive element, an evocative element and an untranslatable metaphor.

The first, the expressive element in the myth, reveals the basic metaphysical values of the culture in which the myth arises. In the myth of the birth of the future Buddha the expressive meaning of the myth is revealed during the recitation of the events of the future Buddha's miraculous conception and birth. What is revealed are the metaphysical values, i.e. those values that are regarded as ultimately real and worthy of highest interest and attention by the culture in which the myth originates. In other words, expressive meaning is found in the presentation and elucidation of those metaphysical values.

The second, the evocative element in the myth, incites the listener to bring his* life into conformity with the metaphysical, the ultimately real, values thus expressed. In the myth of the birth of the future Buddha the evocative meaning of the myth is found in the manner in which the myth calls upon everyone to imitate in their own lives the birth of the future Buddha and to be reborn in the same miraculous and metaphysical manner. In other words, the evocative meaning is found in the exhortation that the myth makes to the listener inciting him to make his life conform to the metaphysical values expressed in the myth. The evocative meaning of myth is familiar to religious persons the world over. In most traditions it is described as a call from the Holy Spirit or God, or from the Savior or Avatār or from Conscience or the sacred Ancestors to do something or other with one's life; and it is expressed most forcibly through the world's religious literature, the *Torah* , the *Bible* , the *Bhagavad Gītā* , the *Qur'an* , the Buddhist *Sūtras* , and so on.

The third element in the myth is the untranslatable metaphor which lies at the heart of the myth. In the myth of the birth of the future Buddha the untranslatable metaphor of the myth is experienced as the metaphoric meaning of the myth and it is that experience that constitutes, whether in whole or in part, metaphysical realization. One may say of that innermost meaning of the myth that it is *like* such and such or *similar to* so and so; one resorts to symbols, to metaphors, to describe the indescribable. The

*I still have not found a neutral way of rendering pronoun gender that does not sound either cumbersome or grotesque. I apologize to those whom I shall no doubt offend.

metaphysical meaning is revealed in the same way that a mandala or a piece of monumental sculpture reveal their meaning hidden in the paint of the stone.[4] The participant in the myth is one who lives within, accepts and meditates upon, the metaphysical values expressed by the culture through the myth. It is from this culture that the participant in the myth and its values have all emerged. And it is against this background that metaphysical realization will ultimately emerge, as well. The myth is used as a vehicle to carry the participant to enlightenment through contact with, and experience of, the untranslatable metaphor.

It is important to remember that myths are "culture relative." To those ignorant of the culture where the myth was born, and where it grew and matured and was used, myth becomes mere fairy story and legend, of interest to anthropologists, antiquarians and "outsiders," who view the myth as an antique and a curiosity. Without the metaphysical foundation that all traditional cultures have, myth dies, only to be resurrected ultimately as hedonic and fabulous amusement or romantic entertainment. Again, I don't wish to leave the impression that myths can't be entertaining and provocative, teaching mores and morality, providing an identity and a history and a *raison d'etre* for the culture or the people whose myths they are. But these characteristics are also the characteristics of legends, fables and romances, and they don't serve to set the myth apart from these other endeavors. The serious purpose of myth is lost when its metaphysics, its sense of what is ultimately real, is lost: Myths like fine clarets don't travel. They are culture relative and it is in a culture that both their meaning and their truth are to be found.

3. Three Problems With the Mythic Theory of Truth

But even if we accept the above analysis of truth and meaning in the mythic account of the birth of the future Buddha, several problems remain. In our role as philosophic historians we shall state three such problems and then attempt to answer them.

a. The Problem of Perception

One problem we might call "the problem of perception." The question arises, since my senses might deceive me or since I might misinterpret the data that my senses do give to me, then aren't mistakes in perception (i.e. sensation together with an interpretation of what is sensed) possible? and then can't I be misled by my perception of the myth in some way or other?

Suppose that I listen to the account of the birth of the future Buddha. Now, one of two things can happen: Either I am carried forward on the path to realization or I am not. Since mistakes in sensory perception are possible then I can make a sense-mistake and mis-hear; or I can make a misjudgment and misinterpret what I did hear. But then whether I am carried forward on the path or not is not due to what the myth really says at all but to something entirely different - my mistaking of it. But how can I ever be sure I haven't mis-heard or misinterpreted? For I can never check up on my mistake to see if it was a mistake.

In other words, since using the myth to reach realization, liberation or nirvāṇa depends on hearing and interpreting what I hear, and since hearing and interpreting are both fraught with the possibility of mistakes, then I can never know whether my success or failure in reaching nirvāṇa is due to the myth or due to my mis-perception of the myth. How would I check up on it to see whether I had misheard it? Could I have it repeated to me? But that merely compounds the risk of the same or a different mistake in perception recurring or occurring. It would seem, therefore, that the success or the failure to reach nirvāṇa through the myth, or through any art object for that matter, could never be attributed with certainty to the myth or art object used.

In reply to the problem of perception, the defender of the mythic theory of truth might point out that perceptual certainty with respect to the theory is too much to hope for or expect, to begin with; the mythic theory is more committed to probabilities than certainties in matters of perception. In other words, the problem of perception is admitted to be a problem only if one is looking for certainties in perception. But such a search, the defender concludes, is a vain and useless undertaking in any area where sensation and sensory interpretation are involved: The problem of perception is no more a problem in the area of mythology than it is in our ordinary day to day existence.

b. The Problem of Pragmatism

A second problem we might call "the problem of pragmatism." Since the mythic theory of truth identifies truth with usefulness or workability in getting the participant to liberation, the critic observes, then isn't the theory being unduly narrow, if not downright misleading, when it defines truth in that way? In other words, when we say that such and such is true, the pragmatic theory of truth would have us believe that this means "it works" or "it's useful to believe such and such." To state a doctrine of truth in this way, identifying "truth" with sheer usefulness, the critic continues, misrepresents the nature of truth. For example, it might be extremely useful for me to believe that all blondes are inferior; but that wouldn't make it true. Therefore, the pragmatic theory of truth, which is an essential part of the mythic theory of truth, is narrow, misleading or downright false: And so also, therefore, is the mythic theory of truth.

In reply to the problem of pragmatism, the defender of the mythic theory of truth might point out that the critic obviously wants to import into the mythic theory of truth an extension and an interpretation that it clearly doesn't have. The mythic theory is narrow but only in the sense that it is dealing with myths and works of art that have a metaphysical use or function in a culture. The mythic theory is not going to enable one to determine the truth or falsity of statements in physics, geology or mathematics and it never claimed that it could (though if meditating on "$s = 1/2\ gt^2$" led to nirvāṇa that might be a different matter). But neither can the so-called correspondence theory of truth nor the coherence theory of truth be properly applied to determine the truth or falsity of all statements, and no one suggests that they are for this reason, alone, either narrow, false or misleading theories of truth. The pragmatic theory of truth, and with it the mythic theory of truth, are applicable to limited, well-defined and well-recognized areas of human activity, and when they stay within those areas there is little or no reason for the problem of pragmatism to arise.

c. The Problem of Right Mood

A third problem we might call "the problem of right mood." Since using a myth to carry one along the path to nirvāṇa depends on the presence of the myth, and on the proper working of my perceptual paraphernalia when I am presented with the myth, what happens if I'm just not in the mood? And suppose that I'm very seldom in the mood. Then I would tend to reject the myth as unworkable and therefore as false.

Suppose that I hear and interpret the myth of the birth of the future Buddha and that the myth is a traditional myth of my culture. But suppose that every time I hear it I'm turned off by it; it bores me, sends me to sleep, makes me think of other things, and so on. Sooner or later, because it doesn't work or turn me on, I would have to conclude that the myth was not true. In other words, the mythic theory of truth doesn't merely depend on a story and a perceiver but it depends on a perceiver being in a certain mood. But this then relativizes the theory so much as to make it possible to deny truth to every traditional myth. Thus an entire culture's mythology could be labeled "false" and eventually relegated to the categories of fairy tale and legend, if enough people in that culture aren't, at some critical moment in their history, in the right mood to respond to the hearing of their myths.

In reply to the problem of right mood, the defender of the mythic theory might say two things, one in disagreement with the criticism and the other in agreement with it. First, the problem of right mood overlooks the fact that the myth is embedded in a culture where, by necessity, the members of the culture as a whole are always in the mood for metaphysical realization: That's what it means to be a member of a traditional culture. Therefore, while occasional lapses in mood, receptivity or sensitivity are possible and even inevitable, we're all human, it does not follow that rampant and unrestrained universal lapses in mood are possible or inevitable in a culture, unless that culture is disintegrating. Therefore, the problem of right mood neglects the general nature or the prevailing mood of the citizens of the traditional culture who, from birth onwards, have been prepared for the one ultimate metaphysical end and sensitized to the various means to it.

But, second, the problem of right mood has focused on an especially disturbing sociological problem: The gradual disintegration of the traditional cultures. As modern civilization, with its withering and eroding anti-metaphysical approach to the world and life, creeps further and further into the traditional cultures of the East, their survival seems problematic, their disintegration inevitable. From this point of view, the problem of right mood emerges more as a warning than an objection to the mythic theory of truth.

4. Conclusion

In conclusion, we might say that the story of the birth of the future Buddha may qualify as a myth, but whether it is a "living myth" or a "dead myth" might depend on one's reaction to the three problems mentioned above. The myth's truth and meaning are both bound to its function and use in leading men and women to metaphysical liberation, an ultimate goal for all Buddhists for nearly two thousand five hundred years. That goal, and its discovery and meaning, are topics for our next chapter as we look further into the account of the life of the future Buddha.

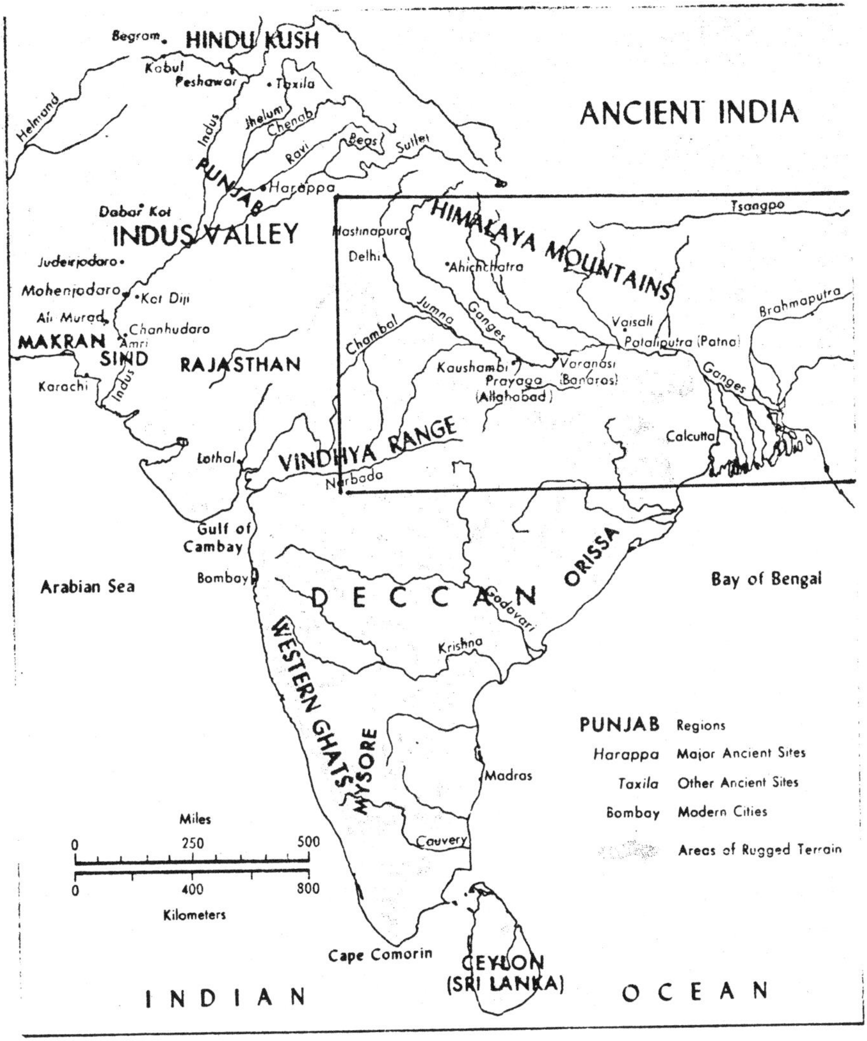
ANCIENT INDIA
Begram
HINDU KUSH
Kabul
Peshawar
Taxila
Helmand
Indus
Jhelum
Chenab
Ravi
Beas
Sutlej
PUNJAB
Harappa
Dabar Kot
INDUS VALLEY
Judeirjodaro
Mohenjodaro
Kot Diji
Ali Murad
Chanhudaro
MAKRAN
Amri
SIND
RAJASTHAN
Karachi
Lothal
Tsangpo
HIMALAYA MOUNTAINS
Hastinapura
Delhi
Ahichchatra
Jumna
Ganges
Chambal
Vaisali
Pataliputra (Patna)
Brahmaputra
Kaushambi
Varanasi
Prayaga
(Banaras)
(Allahabad)
VINDHYA RANGE
Narbada
Calcutta
Gulf of Cambay
Arabian Sea
Bombay
DECCAN
ORISSA
Godavari
Bay of Bengal
Krishna
WESTERN GHATS
MYSORE
Madras
Cauvery
PUNJAB Regions
Harappa Major Ancient Sites
Taxila Other Ancient Sites
Bombay Modern Cities
Areas of Rugged Terrain
Miles
0
250
500
400
800
Kilometers
Cape Comorin
CEYLON
(SRI LANKA)
INDIAN OCEAN

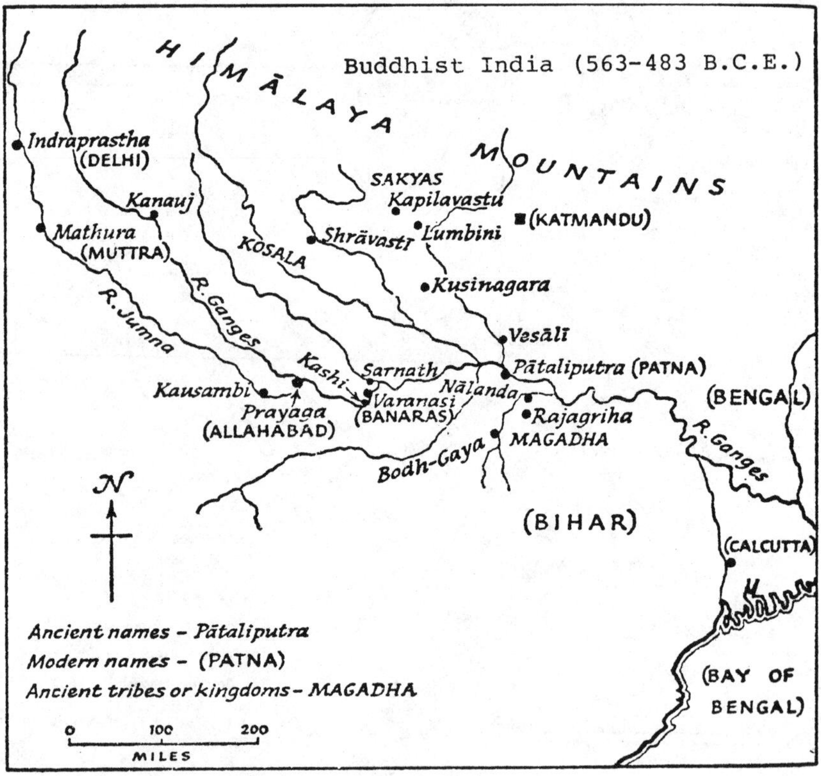
Buddhist India (563-483 B.C.E.)
HIMĀLAYA MOUNTAINS
Indraprastha
(DELHI)
Kanauj
Mathura
(MUTTRA)
SAKYAS
Kapilavastu
(KATMANDU)
Shrävastī
Lumbini
KOSALA
Kusinagara
R. Jumna
R. Ganges
Vesālī
Kashi
Sarnath
Pātaliputra (PATNA)
Kausambi
Nālanda
Varanasi
(BANARAS)
Prayaga
(ALLAHABAD)
Rajagriha
MAGADHA
(BENGAL)
R. Ganges
Bodh-Gaya
N
(BIHAR)
(CALCUTTA)
Ancient names - Pātaliputra
Modern names - (PATNA)
Ancient tribes or kingdoms - MAGADHA
(BAY OF BENGAL)
0 100 200
MILES

Chapter Two: The Early Life[5]

The dates that scholars generally assign to Gautama's life are 563-483 B.C.E.[6] Thus we are recalling a past time that runs parallel to, and overlaps the lives of, several Greek metaphysical philosophers such as Thales of Miletus (he predicted an eclipse for 585 B.C.E.); Pythagoras of Croton (c. 582-500 B.C.E.); and Parmenides, Empedocles and Heraclitus, all of whom flourished in the early 5th century B.C.E. When Gautama was born, the Persian Empire under Cyrus the Great (555-529 B.C.E.) was being established, and when Gautama died that Empire had been all but crushed by Greek arms and Athenian sea power at Thermopylae and Salamis in 480 and then at Plataea and Mycale in 479 B.C.E. At the time of Gautama's birth, the period of Indian history that is called "the Age of the *Upaniṣads*" was in triumphal ascendency, and in China Confucius and Lao Tzu were probably in their mothers' wombs.

All across the civilized and ancient world it was a time for new thoughts and new ideas. For just as the pre-Socratic Greek philosophers signalled an end to "the Age of Legends" of Homer and Hesiod, and just as the thought of Confucius and Lao Tzu was to supercede the age of animism, cult magic and superstition of the ancient Chinese religions, so also did the *Upaniṣads* signal the end of the age of the *Vedas* and the *Brāhmaṇas*: In each case the older age of ritual and sacrifice was being challenged by a new era of radical thought and speculation.

It was into this Indian Renaissance that Gautama (a name implying that he was a descendent of the brahmin sage, Gotama), Siddhārtha ("he whose aim is accomplished"), Śākyamuni ("Sage of the tribe of the Śākyas"), later to be called "the Buddha" ("the awakened one"), was born. Gautama was a kṣatriya "prince." His father, King Śuddhodana, a rāja or clan ruler of Kapilavastu, a city in the foothills of the Himālayas in Northeastern India, raised his son with fear and trembling. For it had been prophesied that the young man would grow up to be either a great King, who would conquer and rule the entire earth, or he would retire from the world of arms and politics and become the Savior of mankind. Śuddhodana, unable to accept the latter contingency, surrounded the prince with every possible luxury and pleasure-proving distraction; he even selected a bride for him when the youth was 16. By intentionally keeping all pains and sufferings away from the growing and maturing youth, Śuddhodana held him a psychological prisoner to pleasure within the confines of the palace grounds. And so the years passed, and it appeared that Gautama's future was safe, predictable and secure.

1. The Four Signs

But then, when Gautama was 29 years of age, events took a momentous and sudden turn. A charioteer named "Channa," who had strict orders from King Śuddhodana to keep his son's eyes free from the evils and sufferings of the world, was driving the prince about the grounds of the palace one day when Gautama suddenly saw a man, feeble and battered by age, sitting by the side of the road. Inquiring of Channa as to what this thing was, the driver of the chariot, contrary to his own orders from the King, informed Gautama that the dreadful sight was that of a man suffering from the miseries of old age, the condition to which all humans are, he added, inevitably and fatefully drawn. Disturbed and profoundly shaken by his first encounter with suffering, Gautama returned to the palace to brood upon what he had seen.

One might well ask why this initial experience of suffering from the first of four momentous journeys he was to take into the new and the terrifying, i.e. into the mythical and the liberating, proved to be so provocative, so overwhelming an experience, for the innocent young ruler? It is revealing of Gautama's character that this first bite of the fruit of the knowledge of good and evil did not send him, terrified and cowering, to some hidden recess where an angry God could neither see him nor punish him. The loss of his innocence, as well as the eventual collapse of the utopia that had sheltered him from that loss, proved to be the occasions at which Gautama began to develop and mature. It is no doubt true that the encounter with evil can destroy and demoralize, or that it can produce fear and loathing ending in the annihilation of the innocent experiencer. But it can also strengthen and enlighten the experiencer, and cause him or her to grow in measured pace with that experience.

Within the world's mythology one of the symbolic functions of Satan or the Devil is to bring man out of the darkness of innocence and ignorance into the light of knowledge, manhood and womanhood. That is the reason that Lucifer, whose name in Latin means "He who brings the light", functions as he does, viz., to prick and cajole, to tempt and persuade, to drive and push man from ignorance, sloth and innocence into knowledge, maturity and liberation. The role played by the teacher is often similar to the role played by Satan and Lucifer. The teacher brings the youth out of the garden of innocence and into the world of knowledge, from a nursery world of things as they ought to be into a colder world of things as they are, from a world of make-believes into a world of actuals.

The charioteer, Channa, in our story is, of course, the teacher, the tempter, the Lucifer of Gautama's life; the sheltered princely palace represents the garden of innocence; and the state of innocence turns out in the end to be identical with the state of wickedness, which might seem like a paradoxical turn of ordinary events. But that is precisely what the myths of awakening-from-innocence in the world's religions seem in fact to imply: That the state of primal innocence is wicked, that the subsequent condition of knowledge and suffering is better because it is man's natural lot, and that the sin of disobedience to God or King Śuddhodana is a necessary and priceless sin, if one is to reach the ultimate goal of eventual liberation and freedom.

For our purposes, a more significant interest lies in Gautama's immediate reaction to that first experience of suffering caused by the sight of old age. For Gautama could have been so horrified at what he saw that he might have fallen cowering to the floor of the chariot, asking to be taken home, vowing never to leave the palace again. And this is one quite universal reaction not only to old age but to pain and suffering in general, i.e. to be so overwhelmed that one is reduced to a quivering, quaking blob by the encounter. Evil, i.e. suffering, can devour and destroy, turning human lives into unendurable and unending nightmares.

Or Gautama could have been so horrified at what he saw that he might have immediately sought solace for his fright through the violent distractions and the pleasureable soporifics afforded by the sheltered life in the palace. In contemporary terms we might say that instead of being crushed and rendered neurotic or melancholic by one's own first encounter with real pain and suffering, one could turn to the kinds of dormitives and distractions which the 20th century produces so skillfully and energetically: Drugs, booze, T.V., and the horrendous thrills and excitements that define our society so well. All these artful devisings and devices seem guaranteed to make one forget by promising to banish forever the remembered evils of the world that prove to be so tormenting and destructive.

Or Gautama could have reacted by actually enjoying in some sadistic fashion the suffering that he witnessed that first day outside the palace. He might have relished the torment he saw and he might have felt exhilarated and titilated by it, coming back again and again to revel in the sight of the misery and anguish of the old and decrepit man. This third possible response to the first encounter with suffering is either an attempt to hold suffering away from oneself by continuously observing it in others, thereby hoping that as long as it is in others it can never exist in oneself; or it is the response of the psychopathic or sociopathic personality, i.e. the personality that is wholly unable to put itself into the place of the tormented other, in this case the old and feeble man observed by Gautama. For the normal viewer, i.e. the non-psychopathic or non-sadistic personality, the sympathetic response would be to see oneself in the place of the tormented other, the aged and decrepit man, and to be moved to pity by realizing that there someday go I.

Or Gautama could have reacted to the scene by the side of the road by displaying an indifference to the whole matter. That is to say, in place of being overwhelmed and immobilized by the sight, or in place of being depressed and sickened by it, or in place of being excited and titilated by it, Gautama might have looked at the sight, asked about it, and then ignored it.

But from the account that we're given by the Buddhist tradition, Gautama eschews all of these four possible responses. He rejects the two extremes of being overwhelmed and of being underwhelmed by the experience: He is not annihilated by the sight of the aged man nor is he indifferent to it. Instead, he ponders the event, thinks more on it, worries about its meaning and significance, and takes a path between these extremes, a taking that will turn Buddhism into the doctrine to be known ever after as "the middle way."

The middle way that Gautama takes brings him out of the palace in the same chariot with the same charioteer the next day. On this second day of Gautama's maturing, and contrary again to the standing orders of his father, he encounters a sick man lying by the road, his body tortured with pain. He once more inquires of Channa what it is that causes this man to appear in this state and to suffer in this way. The charioteer responds by saying, as with the condition of the aged man the previous day, that it is the nature and fate of man to endure the pains of sickness of the body as well as to grow old and feeble. Disturbed once more by what he has seen, he is taken back to the palace to ponder the suffering brought about by the inevitable human condition of sickness.

Undaunted, Gautama is out again on the following day for another ride into his estates and parks. On this third day he sees a dead man being carried to a funeral. He asks Channa what this figure is and his charioteer tells him it is a corpse, the body of a man who has ended his days, as we all shall, sooner or later. Once again they return to the palace where Gautama ponders once more the suffering, pain and death that he has met.

On the fourth and final day of these journeys into the unknown world of ubiquitous and inevitable human misery Gautama and his charioteer observe a man in a yellow robe, appearing tranquil and peaceful, his face alight with some inner joy. On inquiring as to the meaning of this fourth sign, Channa tells his master that the man is a religious wanderer, a solitary monk, begging for his food. Upon discovering that the mendicant had conquered the pain and suffering of old age, sickness and death, Gautama may have made up his mind then and there to overcome these sorrows, himself, and by a similar route. Brooding on his experience he returns once more to the palace and to the protective shelter of his family and station.

His father, discovering what has occurred, is deeply disturbed by the events of the past several days. He increases the guards that have been set over his son. Gautama's wife now presents him with an infant son. The young prince displays his mood by naming the boy "Rāhula" which means "a chain." Thus bound and fettered to his princely existence, he waits to put into practice the conclusions to his thoughtful meditations on all that he has seen and felt.

Several questions and problems emerge in connection with what the Buddhists have come to call "the myth of the four signs", problems that might cause us some intellectual uneasiness and this is as good a time as any to bring them out.

2. Questions and Problems

First, how is it possible for anyone to live 29 years, as young Gautama apparently had, without ever experiencing some kind of suffering or pain? Taken literally, the story of the four signs, which depends on the ignorance of suffering, just doesn't ring true. Surely living conditions must have been such, however exaggerated the story of Gautama's upbringing may be, that stomachache, headache, dysentery, itch, flu and all the rest would have been either in him or around him.

Second, there is an element of the comic or the bizarre, if one tries to imagine what it would be like to raise a child in antiseptic, painless, sorrowless environment of the kind that the legend would have us believe the young prince was raised in. One would have to indulge in popping some pills after the manner of Aldous Huxley's citizens in *Brave New World* , or engage in some even more ludicrous avoidance activities to allay the experience of pain, if one were to be consistently and forever in a blessed state of analgesia.[7] But, someone might suggest, this is a myth, not a mere story or legend. And the myth is speaking symbolically and not descriptively. The myth of the four signs,like the myth of the birth of the future Buddha, is designed for pondering and meditation, and its truth and its meaning lie in the metaphysical states or conditions that such ponderings and meditations lead to. Taken literally the story is ludicrous; taken mythically the story may harbor truth and meaning.

But we are plagued, nonetheless, by several of the things which the myth says, and it is not always wise to squelch serious questions, even about a myth, by saying, You shouldn't ask questions like that, or,

Your questions are based on a literal interpretation of the story, and so on.

So, third, let's go behind the myth and return to a close literal examination of the whole affair. Let's suppose that Gautama had been born and raised 'midst effeteful ease and pleasure. Suppose that he had never known pain, sorrow and suffering, had never experienced stomachache, hangnail, or scraped knee. Suppose, further, that he really made those journeys beyond the luxurious and insulating security that his father had caused to be thrown up around him. And suppose, finally, that he saw the three signs of old age, sickness and death. Our question now is: Would the pain, the sorrow and the suffering that he supposedly experienced have meant anything to him without some kind of previous knowledge of pain?

Suppose that I've never had a pain experience nor been witness to anyone else's pain experience. Then suppose that I suddenly encounter you, all doubled up and groaning. I'd probably ask you, What are you doing? instead of asking you, What's wrong? And suppose that you answer, Can't you see, I'm in pain. The dialogue might then proceed by my trying to guess what the word "pain" means with your supplying all kinds of synonyms to my perplexing question. The end of the dialogue would probably involve your attempting to give a definition of "pain" by giving me a direct experience of pain: Here, you idiot (you say), this is pain (and you crack me across the head).

This kind of definition of a word is said to be an *ostensive definition* and it is used whenever any sort of pointing, together with an immediate experience of what is pointed at, is needed in order to define a word. An entire class of terms is defined ostensively and this class of terms deals with words that name experiences related to external and internal sensations. Examples of words naming external sensations are "green", "sweet", "smooth", "harsh (sound)" and "stench", where each word is related to one or the other of the five senses, viz., sight, taste, touch, hearing and smell, respectively. Thus to someone who doesn't know what the word "green" means I need only point to the color of the grass and say, That's green, in order to demonstrate to him the meaning of "green." Examples of words naming internal sensations are "stomach gurgle", "heart beat", "muscle twinge" and "pain." And to someone who doesn't know what the word "pain" means it would be necessary for that person to have the direct experience of pain in association with the word "pain" in order to understand the meaning of the word.

Return now to our analysis of the four signs together with our supposition regarding Gautama's ignorance of pain, sorrow and suffering. Would the experience of the pain of old age, the first of the four signs, have meant anything at all to him? Never having experienced pain, himself, could what he saw be called (as it was) a "dreadful sight"? "Dreadful" in what sense? It's just a man, a different looking man to be sure, sitting by the road. Where's the dread in that? Could Gautama have become "disturbed and profoundly shaken"? Why should he? And if it was "his first encounter with suffering and pain" then how on earth would he know it?

Thus a first encounter with pain is quite unlike a first encounter with the color green. It all depends on whose pain is being referred to. On the one hand, if the pain is the old man's lying by the road then pointing to the distorted features and saying "pain" is no different from pointing to the grass around him and saying "green." On the other hand, if the pain is to be yours then it is necessary to crack you across the face and tell you that what you're feeling is pain. In other words, though "pain" is defined ostensively in both cases, seeing pain, an external sensation, is a lot different than feeling pain, an internal sensation.

Without conscious selection and labeling through ostensive definition certain words dealing with external (green) and internal (pain) sensations would never be defined, and certain sensations that might have occurred would never become identified. If the feeling of pain was there but the word for it was not, or if the word for pain was there but the feeling it described was not, then it would be impossible for Gautama to have experienced, known, or understood the pain. "First encounters" with pain or with any other sensation are strange encounters, indeed.

If someone were to object, once again, that it is only because we have subjected the myth to a literal analysis that we have gotten the kind of problem that we have and that we ought to reserve literal analyses for things other than myths, then we might respond as follows: First, the suggestion is well taken in one respect. No matter how outrageous the myth may appear to modern sensibilities one can always say, Well, so much the worse for modern sensibilities. A myth can stand on its own quite apart from internal literal contradictions and fussy-minded inconsistencies. The myth is a focus for meditation, and Aristotelean rules of logic simply don't apply; if the myth works then that's enough; to try to apply logical analysis to the myth is to become stuck at the literal level of interpretation; it is to fail to reach the metaphorical level of meaning altogether, and it is at that latter level alone that we ought to analyze myth.

But, second, nobody, and particularly a Buddhist who interprets his mythology at both the literal and the metaphysical levels of meaning, wants to admit to the presence of a logical inconsistency or an unanswerable epistemological conundrum in his mythology. One need only recall the pugnacious efforts of many Christian fundamentalists to rescue *Genesis* and the *Old Testament* from similar accusations in the early part of the 20th century. Inconsistencies and conundrums, whether in logic or epistemology, can be sticky, messy affairs and no one likes to have his myths gummed-up with either.

Third, and finally, one can take seriously the critique of pain, and the problems that it led to, and look for some ways out of the inconsistencies or conundrums. I mention now three of the more obvious solutions: One, Gautama was previously acquainted with pain; he knew more about it than the myth tells us. And the myth doesn't tell us more about his previous knowledge of pain because that's not its purpose, i.e., its purpose is not to give a psychoanalytical account of Gautama's previous acquaintance with pain; its purpose is to set out the mythology that will call forth metaphysical change in all who hear and meditate upon the myth. Two, Gautama received some form of extra-sensory insight at the time that the three signs were presented to him. And in Aśvaghoṣa's account this is, indeed, what is hinted at as we are told that Gautama reacted to Channa's explanation of old age like a bull when a bolt of lightning crashes near him.[8] Thus Gautama saw the aged man and suddenly he knew and understood, immediately and intuitively, what "pain" both meant and was. Three, Gautama did not totally and completely understand the pain to which he was witness at the time he saw the three signs of suffering. What Gautama did was to discover the experience of pain in later meditation on his new experiences and this discovery finally drove him into the mendicant's life. I leave the reader to ponder the puzzles and these obvious solutions, further, and to seek a way out in a more leisurely fashion.

3. The Great Renunciation

At the age of 29, disturbed by the meaning of the four signs and sickened by the life of pleasure and sensuality at his father's palace, and shaken by the birth of his son, Rahula, Gautama resolved to renounce that royal life and to seek other ways to the happiness that that existence could not give him. Late at night, with a word to no one, he traveled forth alone into the unknown world. In the Buddhist literature this momentous leaving is referred to as "the Great Renunciation." Gautama moved from the state of life of the householder, i.e. what later came to be called the "gṛhastha āśrama"[9], with all of its material and psychological comforts, and he became a renunciate of the world.

The Great Renunciation is justifiably celebrated in the Buddhist tradition in myth, paintings, sculpture, poetry, drama and legend. After this "great going forth" Gautama never returns to the life of a prince destined to rule the world; he is committed to the life of the renunciate, and from this moment onwards his life is changed and altered forever.

But it is a strange renunciation in a way. For Gautama's leaving of his family is stealthy and abrupt, secretive and hurried. He leaves shortly after the birth of his son and long before his family has ceased to be dependent on him. The commitments made to his wife and child are summarily terminated, and his seemingly cavalier attitude towards his princely vocation and to those dependent on him, e.g., his father, the community, the tribal government and the clan, is certainly unworthy of a future Savior of mankind. So it would seem that the Great Renunciation is not so great after all and that, if our conjectures are true, we must suppose that it bodes ill as a moral foundation on which to rest the future of one of the world's great religions. What Gautama seemed to be engaging in, if we take the Buddhist texts literally, is what has come to be called "premature revulsion"[10], i.e. an unwarranted leaping ahead into stages of life, here from householder to mendicant, into which one is not entitled to leap.

But perhaps we're being unfair in our conjectures regarding the Great Renunciation, and for three reasons. First, to repeat a familiar point, one ought not to take the story of Gautama's life literally; to do so is, once again, to mix myth with history. To focus on the historical renunciation together with its moral implications is to miss the mythic point: The great symbolic leave-taking that all human beings must undergo if they are to set out on the path to liberation and permanent happiness. But this objection to our conjectures regarding the Great Renunciation still leaves the literal interpretation open to moral censure, and surely no one, particularly the Buddhists, want their mythology put into such a morally vulnerable position. Even after resorting to a plea for a strictly mythic interpretation there would still be that literal interpretation with its gnawing moral implications; and as long as the former is given the latter must somehow or other be accounted for, i.e. the mythic or symbolic meaning of the Great Renunciation cannot be separated from the literal and moral interpretations of the Great Renunciation without running certain philosophicaland religious risks.

Second, even if we accept the historical or literal interpretation, the putative premature revulsion can easily be explained, an apologist for Gautama's Great Renunciation might say. For the times and dates might be so scrambled and the events turned around in such a way that the charge of "premature" renouncing of family and princely vocation simply doesn't apply. Thus it is quite possible that Gautama married earlier and that his child was older than the texts indicate, and that a longer period had passed between the time of his birth and the Renunciation. We simply don't know what the real order of the historical events was, so why make a big deal out of anything based on that ignorance? but this objection to our conjectures regarding the Great Renunciation won't do either, for it is precisely what people have come to believe about those events, rather than those events "as they really happened", that is most important here. And what people have come to believe, and what they take to be the order of historical events, is this: That a prince married a girl when he was about 16, that at the age of 29 he had a child by her and that late one night, shortly after the birth of that child, he secretly and stealthily left her and the child. That's the story the tradition gives and the tradition is stuck with it.[11]

Third, even if we accept the historical tradition as it is described above, one very important thing that has been left out is the state of Gautama's mind in the period leading up to the Great Renunciation. For if we could fully appreciate that state during the period between seeing the four signs (old age, sickness, death and the mendicant), his subsequent fatherhood and the final renunciation of it all, then the accusation of premature revulsion would have to be rejected. Gautama is no Indian Gauguin.[12] Psychologically, Gautama can be seen as a man who was intensely shocked by his first encounter with evil.

The tradition does not tell us about the brooding and the questioning that must surely have gone on in his mind during this period. And it is that brooding and the questioning about the suffering that he witnessed that led naturally and inevitably to the Renunciation rather than to the continuation of the householder's life. The wife and child are Gautama's responsibility, true enough, but only in a purely formal sense; for they will be cared for by Gautama's father. There are no real responsibilities, therefore. The householder's life had probably been psychologically abandoned months before the Renunciation. Those who see it differently are reading too many 20th century urban social issues into Gautama's situation: Desertion of wife and child, child support and non-support, Aid to Dependent Children, welfare mothers, food stamps, poverty families, and all the rest. Seen in the context of Gautama's state of mind at the time of the Renunciation and seen against the background of the prince's family, Gautama's revulsion was not premature nor harmful to that family. Thus the reply by the apologist.

But a gnawing doubt might still remain with the 20th century reader, urban social issues to the contrary notwithstanding. Whether Gautama was a romantic Indian Gauguin and whether he was, therefore, guilty of a moral error towards his family and against his varṇa or vocation or class by premature revulsion depends on the events subsequent to the Great

Renunciation as much as it does on those events that preceded it.

For if after leaving his family and the life of pleasure and decadent frivolity in the palace, Gautama were to sally forth to some kind of Parisian Benares, there to indulge in fermented palm juice and the local dancing girls, then the mask of moral purity covering the Great Renunciation would necessarily be ripped away. And if that happened then Gautama would clearly be guilty of premature revulsion and the moral foundations of Buddhism would be soft and sandy, indeed.

If, on the other hand, after the Great Renunciation, Gautama were to move to the forest solitudes for meditation or to don the robes of the mendicant sannyāsi and travel the roads of the Northern hills seeking only enlightenment and nothing else, then there would be no premature revulsion at all, and the foundations of Buddhism would seem to be built on hard rock, indeed. But Gautama does neither of these things; he neither heads for the local flesh pots nor does he hie off to the forest or to the solitary life of the wandering mendicant. Instead, at the age of 29 and until his enlightenment at 35, he falls in with various troups of traveling teachers, yogis, renunciates and philosophers, and spends the intervening six years in a philosophic and ascetic quest for liberation. So the charge of premature revulsion must be left open until we have examined his later life and the people with whom he spent it.

Chapter Three: The Philosophic Environment of the 6th Century B.C.E.

When Guatama Siddhartha Śākyamuni stepped out of the world of sheltered and secured pleasures, into what kind of world did he enter? More particularly, what was his relation to that world? i.e., was he a pleasure-seeker looking for erotic stimulations and titillations? or was he a renunciate seeking solitude and silence? or was he a student seeking knowledge and undertanding? The world that he entered was, as we shall see, a philosophic world, and he entered it, having abjured the world of pleasures and having renounced the world of the householder, as a student (brahmacārin) seeking knowledge and release from the suffering that he had so suddenly and terribly discovered.

The philosophic world that Gautama chose to enter was a world dominated, very likely, by the proto-Hindu tradition. I say "proto-Hindu" for in the 6th century B.C.E. Hinduism as a religion had not yet completely evolved. What Gautama's contemporaries actually accepted or rejected of that evolving religion is largely hypothetical. But several conjectures can be made rather safely, if we stay within the bounds and standards that have been set by the historical Hindu tradition.

In what follows I shall begin with a reconstruction of the proto-Hindu environment of the 6th century B.C.E. and conclude with an examination of several of the contemporary non-Hindu or heterodox philosophers of that same period, teachers with whom Gautama sought instruction. My purpose in effecting this reconstruction is to try to put ourselves into Gautama's own time in order to see what he might have seen, and feel what he might have felt, and, possibly, understand what he might have understood about the world in which he entered. To this end, knowing something about Gautama's philosophic and religious environment as well as having an acquaintance with several of Gautama's contemporaries in that environment are both essential to understanding Gautama's world.

1. The Āryans

When the Āryan ("noble") warriors came rumbling down into the Punjab of northwestern India in the middle of the 2nd millennium B.C.E.(about 1500 B.C.E.) they brought with them more than chariots, bows and arrows, spears and some rather novel military arts. What they brought, and what has survived even that outstanding martial heritage, is the Vedic religion complete with its priestly (brahmin) tradition, its oral texts, its rituals and way of life committed to, and guided by, that religion. Vedism or "brahminism", as it came to be called, dominated the life of the Āryan tribesman for nearly 1000 years after its arrival in the subcontinent of India.

With the occupation of the lands of the Punjab and of the Indus River Valley both Āryanism, i.e. the social and political milieu of the Āryans, and Vedism, i.e. the Āryan religion, gradually spread eastward over the centuries to the Ganges River Valley and into Gautama's own region. Its survival as a religion consisted, as often as not, in a series of syncretic compromises with the indigenous native religions and with the social and political practices encountered in the non-Āryan subcontinent. These compromises can be documented by comparing the older religious compositions (the older *Vedas* from about 1200 B.C.E) with the more recent compositions (the *Brāhmaṇas* from about 900 B.C.E.) with the most recent compositions (the oldest *Upaniṣads* from about 800 B.C.E.).

One such encounter may have been with the Harappāns, the aboriginal inhabitants of the Indus River Valley. The Harappāns, so-called by archeologists after one of their principal cities in the Indus Valley, viz., Harappā, possessed a culture that was in many respects superior to the culture of the Āryans. Thus while the Āryans were a nomadic, cattle-tending, martial tribe dependent on the meandering whims of climate and generalship for their physical survival, the Harappāns were an agrarian and sessile people who lived in rather splendid, well-planned, bricked cities. These cities, one of the wonders of the ancient world, contained technologically advanced grain storage facilities, centralized city governments remarkable for their sagacity, philanthropy and durability (Harappān cities and civilization flourished with a far-flung trading empire from about 2500 to about 1700 B.C.E.), police forces, nighttime street lighting systems and fastidious water and sewer systems and public baths that existed centuries before their nearest Western counterparts.

While the Āryans have left us few examples of their culture, save for their orally transmitted, sacred mythological and religious compositions called "Vedas", the Harappāns have left us a written language (as yet untranslated), bronze and stone sculptures of a simple beauty and grace that could rival anything that the Greeks and Romans would later produce, together with a monumental architecture whose magnificent dimensions archeology has only recently begun to reveal.[13]

But to grant them their proper due, the Āryans have given us religious compositions whose contents have now become part of a common spiritual heritage for all those who can understand Sanskrit or its translations. This heritage embraces the numerous Gods and Goddesses of sky and earth, moral concepts proclaiming a belief in universal order and cosmic lawfulness, notions of an afterlife that include a heaven and a hell, poems and hymns of incomparable beauty and passion, and rites and rituals that bear witness to a sophisticated mythology and religious symbolism.

The Harappāns and other non-Āryan inhabitants of India have added to that spiritual heritage many beliefs and practices of their own. Over the centuries this syncretising of indigenous non-Āryan elements with Vedism has led to the religion we now call "Hinduism." These non-Vedic additions to Hinduism include such elements as the cult of the Mother Goddess or Great Goddess, animal worship, phallism, the cults of trees and waters, village deities, demons, ghosts and spirits; in addition, there are several other non-Āryan concepts which will directly affect the later development of Buddhism, concepts such as meditational yoga, devotional or bhakti yoga, mokṣa, nirvāṇa or liberation, and, probably, saṁsāra or rebirth. Hinduism evolved then, from a syncretism or amalgamation of Āryan and non-Āryan elements.

But the syncretism was not carried out without a series of upheavals and radical changes in the Vedic religion. The accommodations within Vedism that eventually led to Hinduism occurred sometime between 1000 B.C.E. and 200 B.C.E., for by the latter date the essentials of Hinduism, as we know them today, were more or less complete. We have very little evidence regarding the attitude of the brahmins or conservative priests to the changes and reforms that swept through

Vedism. But it is not too wide of the truth to say that these changes were probably fought and resented by the brahmins who did not wish to anger the gods or their Āryan ancestors by any kind of additions and changes to the older and traditional rites of the religious sacrifice.

All of this talk about reform and change is more than mere conjecture, however: Vedism did accept the changes that led to Hinduism. But side by side with those accretions to the older brahminism there developed a more general non-brahmin or non-Vedic spirit of religious and philosophic revolt and rebellion against the brahmins and Vedism. This spirit gave rise to concepts and philosophies and religions that either could not be incorporated, or would not be incorporated, into evolving Hinduism.

The 6th century B.C.E. was the century that best exemplified the spirit of this revolt and rebellion. From within the turmoil of that period there came at least two other major Indian religions, viz., Jainism and Buddhism, that were to rival later Hinduism; in addition, from this same period there came two major Indian philosophies that were also to rival later Hindu philosophy, viz., the philosophy of the Ājīvakas or nihilists and the philosophy of the Lokāyatas or materialists. The 6th century B.C.E. in India was a renaissance, the first of many for the subcontinent, as it gave birth to new ideas, ideologies, religions, systems of salvation and liberation, orthodox and heterodox philosophies, revolutionaries, revolutions, Saviors and reformers. We shall be examining this renaissance in some detail in what follows.

We can best begin our discussion of Gautama's later life by looking first at the thought of developing Hinduism through the compositions of the Āryan *Vedas*, the *Brāhmaṇical* commentaries on them, and the syncretic *Upaniṣads*. We shall then turn to an examination of the non-brahminic teachers with whom the wandering and searching Gautama studied; and we shall look, finally, at the anti-brahminic philosophers with whom he debated. By seeing what Gautama might have rejected in the *Vedas* and in the *Upaniṣads* and in the philosophies of his contemporaries, we will be in a better position to understand what Gautama accepted and why he accepted it.

2. The Vedas

The Age of the *Vedas* (1500-800 B.C.E.) is followed by the Age of the *Upaniṣads* (800-200 B.C.E.); Gautama can, in a very legitimate sense, be said to be a product of the latter Age. We have no precise evidence to support the view that Gautama was consciously in revolt against either the philosophy of the *Vedas* or that of the *Upaniṣads* when he came to develop his own doctrines. The reason for this lack of evidence is two-fold: First, there are no surviving written documents about early Buddhism from the time of Gautama's life (563-483 B.C.E.). What was composed and what has survived came several hundred years after his death and it came, in turn, from an oral tradition that had not been concerned with Gautama's relations to early Hinduism, i.e. the Hinduism of the *Vedas* and *Upaniṣads*.

Second, when the written texts of Buddhism were finally compiled their authors could probably see little or no advantage to inserting references to earlier materials from a tradition which was already a religious and philosophic rival to Buddhism. Hence, we have no way of knowing whether in those early years the 29 year old Gautama was consciously reacting against the sacred texts and traditions of developing Hinduism.

But, whether mentioned or not, early Hinduism provides a background for Gautama's philosophic development since it forms part of what must have surely been the cultural milieu for any Indian living in the Ganges River Valley in the 6th century B.C.E. Further, Vedic and Upaniṣadic thought stand in such stark contrast to the philosophy of Gautama's teachers, as we shall see presently, and to Gautama's own mature philosophy, that an account of that thought cannot be neglected without risk of failing to understand either those teachers or that mature philosophy. So with the previous reasons in mind and to avoid the philosophic risk mentioned, let us look briefly at the essential thoughts of the *Vedas* and the *Upaniṣads*. We shall discover that much of Gautama's own later philosophy, whether consciously intended or not, can be seen as an interesting blending of Upaniṣadic doctrine and the rather peculiar philosophies of his teachers and contemporaries.[14]

The *Vedas* are a collection of poetical, mythological and liturgical compositions that record the cultural beliefs of the Āryan ṛṣis, or seers, and prists who remembered and used them. Since we are concerned only with the religious and philosophical beliefs of the Āryans, let me speak about the most philosophical of their four *Vedas*, the *Ṛg Veda*, characterizing it in a rather summary fashion.

The heart of Vedism lay in the ritual sacrifice. The Vedic sacrifice was an elaborately managed affair wherein, depending on the sacrificial rite being practiced, some four to sixteen or more priests officiated at the ceremony with the aim of securing the Gods' attention and presence so that certain requests or petitions could be made to them. These requests were for such ordinary things as sons, cattle, land, wealth, success in battle, rain, forgiveness of sins, both known and unknown, and so on. In return the Gods received something from the priests. e.g., praise and songs pleasing to divine ears, or they received soma, the intoxicating, heady concoction pressed out, offered and drunk during the sacrifice, or they received meat from the hundreds of cattle said to have been sacrificed for the Gods during certain of these ceremonies.

In addition the priests sought for their patrons a long and happy life in this world and a secure rebirth in the world that followed.

Finally, the Vedic sacrifice properly conducted assured the continued and orderly workings of the cosmos wherein the things of the universe maintained their natural and lawful places in that universe. The pragmatic belief that guided and lay behind the ritual sacrifice was a kind of *quid pro quo*, i.e. we feed you (the Gods) and you feed us (the people). This belief stands behind Vedic ritual to this day for, even with the growth of Vedism into Hinduism, the Vedic sacrifice is still celebrated throughout modern India and for the same reasons that it was celebrated 3000 years ago.

As we pass from the *Vedas* to the post-*Vedas* period the nature of the sacrifice changed and in three dramatic ways: First, the priests came to believe that certain sacred verses or holy words, called "brahman" in Sanskrit, uttered in the sacrifice could be used to entice or invite the gods to the sacrifice; second, and later, it was discovered that these uttered verses could force the Gods to attend; third, at some time after the *Vedas* has been composed, it was discovered and then recorded in the sacred *Brāhmaṇas* that merely uttering the sacred verses could compel the Gods to surrender their power to the priests; and it was this divine power that the priests had sought all along: Ritual sacrifice had now turned into ritual magic.

That is to say, it was believed that there was a power, now also called "brahman", in the uttered verses, themselves, which alone and by itself was sufficient to secure whatever it was that the sacrificial ritual had been seeking. It was now possible to simply dispense with the Gods altogether once one knew the sacred word (brahman), for that word was the power (brahman) that the sacrificer sought: Ritual magic had finally turned into ritual atheism.

With these changes the power and prestige of the priests grew, and a new concept, brahman, made its way into the post-*Veda* vocabulary. Franklin Edgerton has said of this evolution:

> The spoken word has a mysterious, supernatural power; it contained within itself the essence of the thing denoted. To "know the *name*" of anything was to control the thing. The *word* means wisdom, knowledge; and knowledge...was (magic) power. So *brahman*, the "holy word", soon came to mean the mystic power inherent in the holy word.[15]

But it will remain for the *Upaniṣads* to turn this earlier *Brāhmaṇa* concept of power into a metaphysical principle of tremendous universal significance for Hinduism.

The *Vedas* commonly and penultimately espouse a kind of polytheism, their ultimate ritual atheism to the contrary notwithstanding; the following are the most well-known of the Āryan deities: Indra, the God of the thunderstorm and battles and the deity to whom most of the 1028 hymns of the *Ṛg Veda* are dedicated; Agni, the God of fire, second only to Indra in importance in Vedism since he was present, as fire, at most of the public, as well as the private, household, rituals; Sūrya, the sun God; Uṣas, Goddess of the dawn; Pṛthivī, the earth Goddess; Dyaus, the sky God; Apas, God of waters; Viṣṇu, the God who measured out the earth and now upholds and maintains it; Varuṇa, the Savior-like God of justice and the deity to whom prayers and sacrifice for the forgiveness of sins and transgressions may be addressed; and Soma, the God who presided over the soma sacrifice and who was identified with the inebriating libation offered during that sacrifice, to mention only a few of the dozens of Gods and Goddesses spoken of in the *Ṛg Veda*.

3. The Upaniṣads

Turning to the *Upaniṣads*, they are, among many other things, technically speaking, philosophical discussions about the *Vedas*. They come as appended commentaries to the *Vedas* and they are regarded as the end (*anta*) of the *Vedas*, or the *Vedānta*. But because of their late addition to the Vedic corpus (800-200 B.C.E.) they can be treated separately, and they generally are. For the *Upaniṣads* are not only postcedent to the *Vedas* but they offer a new and rather revolutionary philosophic outlook on the world. They not only speak deprecatingly at times of the *Vedas*, themselves, but they offer a fairly consistent vision of man and the universe that is not present in the *Vedas*.

But the *Upaniṣads* are neither as revolutionary nor as consistent as many Hindus would like to believe. These philosophic commentaries on the *Vedas* carry over much that is Vedic, and much that relates to the thought of the philosophical period that fell between the *Vedas* and the *Upaniṣads*, the so-called period of the *Āraṇyaka* (forest) texts and the period of the *Brāhmaṇa* (priestly) texts (about 900-800 B.C.E.). The *Upaniṣads* include much that undoubtedly comes from the Harappān and the pre-Āryan indigenous traditions of India. But the one theme that interests us and that will be a starting point for later Buddhist thought is the revolutionary change brought about by the *Upaniṣads*, a change that seems patently inconsistent with the earlier thought of the *Vedas*. This revolution in Indian thought can be summarized by reference to seven essential concepts, basic to the *Upaniṣads* and to later Hinduism, viz., saṁsāra, Brahman, Ātman, māyā, jñāna yoga, mokṣa and, finally, the law of karma.

Religions, like philosphies, are problem-solving disciplines. Religions are established and they survive as disciplines or institutions because they answer so-called "religious questions", questions that relate to religious problems that affect human beings; consequently, religious problems, questions and solutions differ from economic and political problems, questions and solutions. I mention these facts about religion because we tend to forget that religions are socially useful inventions. They are, after all, human responses to certain human needs. When those human needs are removed, religions die or they change or they become fossilized and unresponsive.

This attempt to see religions as social institutions meeting human needs should not make religions any the less awesome or sacred, however. The awesome and the sacred are important adjuncts to religions and prove to be necessary elements in the structuring of most religions. Many theologians feel that without these transcendental, metaphysical elements, e.g., a God or the Gods, a soul, a heaven and a hell, and so on, certain human needs could never be properly met.

But if religion is a social institution designed to meet certain human needs, we might profitably ask, What need is being met? and What is the nature of the meeting? More explicitly, if religions solve human problems then what's the problem and what's the solution for the religion of the *Upaniṣads* that makes it different from the religion of the *Vedas*? This question brings us to our first essentially Upaniṣadic concept, viz., saṁsāra.

The word "saṁsāra" literally means "a flowing together" and in the Upaniṣadic period, 800-200 B.C.E., it comes to mean two things: First, it means "rebirth" in another life or existence, and, second, it also means "this world", i.e. the world of life, death and suffering, i.e. the anxiety-producing world of the four signs that triggered Gautama's renunciation. In the *Upaniṣads*, however, it is the former meaning which concerns us, i.e. saṁsāra is rebirth, i.e. reincarnation or transmigration.

The principal problem for Upaniṣadic man in this world or the next is saṁsāra and, to revert to our previous discussion, saṁsāra is the problem that the religion of the *Upaniṣads* was designed to solve.

Saṁsāra in the *Upaniṣads* involves the rebirth of a continuous self into body after body, or into existence after existence, until something is done to stop the rebirthing. This self is variously interpreted by commentators on the *Upaniṣads* and the discussion about the nature of the self forms the focal point for the highly original philosophy of the *Upaniṣads*. To examine that focal point we turn next to the second and third key Upaniṣadic concepts, viz., Brahman and Ātman.

What the *Upaniṣads* have done, in effect, is to take the concept of brahman from the post-*Veda* compositions such as the *Brāhmaṇas*,and by skillful interpretation turn it into one of the central concepts of Hinduism. "Brahman" in the *Vedas* had meant "sacred formula" or "sacred word" for achieving the Gods' help and power; now, following the *Brāhmaṇas* Brahman becomes identified with that very Power, Itself. And since to have knowledge is to have control, it was believed that whoever knows Brahman also controls or possesses the holy Power.

But, the Upaniṣadic ṛṣis must have reasoned, since knowledge is always subjective and personal, then the Brahman that is knowable must also be as subjective and intimate to man as that knowledge by which Brahman is known. Hence, Brahman comes to be identified with the true Subject, the Self or Ātman. Thus by another identification man's true Self or Ātman is really the holy Power of the universe, i.e. Brahman. Man in his ignorance is oblivious of this identity between Ātman and Brahman and as long as he is ignorant he is subject to saṁsāra, i.e. to continuous, unending and painful rebirth, in existence after existence.

Saṁsāra, thereby, comes to be identified with this world of birth and death, the second of the meanings of "saṁsāra" mentioned previously, since it is rebirth, the first meaning of "saṁsāra", that brings the self, the ego or personal self, as well as the Self, the Ātman, back into this world. However, it is the sufferings of the self or ego and not of the Self or Ātman (Atman cannot and does not "feel" so It cannot suffer), that makes life in the world unbearable.

To undertand the Indian, i.e. Hindu and Buddhist, attitude towards saṁsāra, interpreted now as both rebirth as well as suffering, involves recognizing life in the raw, replete with all the heart-aches and thousand natural shocks that flesh is heir to: Desires, needs and wants that never are satisfied or assuaged, the terrors of life filled with loathesome horrors, madness-producing ills and diseases, the deaths of loved ones and friends, the fear of demons, gods, ghosts, goblins, the unseen and unknown ghouls and monsters that waylay, maim and dismember the minds and bodies of man, the sickness, old age and death that Gautama saw and never forgot.

The *Upaniṣads* are propounding an essentially non-dualistic metaphysics that argues that Brahman (i.e. Ātman, another name for the same reality) alone is real. Brahman is ultimately real because It possesses the three essential properties that any entity must have in order to be called "real", i.e. It is eternal (uncreated and unending), It is independent of all other entities which in turn are dependent on It, and It is unchanging. A curious consequence of the non-dualistic, or perhaps monistic, nature of Brahman reality is that Upaniṣadic metaphysics tends to end in atheism. It is a metaphysical atheism that says that since impersonal Brahman alone is real then the personal Gods cannot be real. Just as the *Vedas* previously ended in ritual atheism, and the *Upaniṣads* now end in metaphysical atheism, so also Hīnayāna Buddhism will later end in an atheism, viz., a theoretical atheism. In each case, the metaphysics of the system dictates the nature of the religious object and in each case atheism is the logical result.

But with this metaphysical monism a problem emerges which we might call "the dilemma of monism" and this will bring us to our fourth Upaniṣadic concept. Essentially the dilemma of monism comes to this: If Brahman (Ātman) alone is real then what's the metaphysical, the reality, status of my body, my mind, this table and let's say, a cricket named "Sam"? The metaphysical monist must hold either that those four things are unreal (which seems absurd) or that those four things are real (which also seems absurd), and there's no third alternative. That is to say, the metaphysical monist is either hung up on the first horn of the dilemma of monism by having to admit that nothing in the world is real and everything is unreal except Brahman (Ātman), which is as uncommonsensical a view as one could ever tangle with; or he's hung up on the second horn of the dilemma of monism by having to admit that everything in the world, including Sam, is Brahman (Ātman), a pan-Brahmanism that seems uncommonsensical. The *Upaniṣads* bravely accept the first horn of the dilemma and they are courageously followed in their choice by certain Mahāyāna Buddhists, as we shall see, who will elaborate and expand the entire metaphysical position.

The problem that the *Upaniṣads* then face is one of having to explain the metaphysical status of the space-time and experiencable world, i.e. the existing world that certainly seems to include Sam and me. Which brings us to our fourth Upaniṣadic concept introduced to explain the relation between Brahman and this phenomenal world, viz., the concept of māyā.

"Māyā" means "magical power", and it is, first, the power by which Brahman both reveals the creation and, at the same time, conceals Itself from the creatures and beings of that creation. Māyā is, second, the concealing product of that power, i.e. māyā is the creation, itself. In other words, māyā is both the power and the product of Brahman's creative activity.

In order to further clarify the relationship between Brahman and māyā, the *Upaniṣads* distinguish two aspects of Brahman. In the oldest *Upaniṣad*, the *Bṛhadāraṇyaka* (about 800 B.C.E.), a distinction is made between formed (mūrta) and formless (amūrta) Brahman:

> Truly, there are two aspects of Brahman, the formed and the formless, the mortal and the immortal, the moving and the unmoving, the existent and that which is beyond existence.[16]

The formless, immortal, unmoving and supra-existent Brahman, furthermore, is said to be *neti, neti, 'not* this and *not* that', i.e. It is beyond description and beyond predication, a reality about which one must be silent. This apparent dualism of Brahman is further extended in the *Muṇḍaka Upaniṣad*, a work from the early Buddhist period of the late 6th century B.C.E., with a devastating commentary on the four *Vedas*:

> There are two kinds of knowledge as the knowers of Brahman are said to declare: a higher [parā] and a lower [aparā].
>
> Of these, the lower is the Ṛg Veda, the Yajur Veda, the Sāma Veda, the Atharva Veda.... Now, the higher is that by which the Imperishable is apprehended.

So much for devastating comments. But aside from an interesting rejection of the *Vedas* as sources for higher knowledge, the *Upaniṣads* and the later Hindu tradition will draw two important conclusions from these brief passages: First, Brahman is actually a metaphysical entity with two aspects, a higher and a lower, an imperishable and a perishable, a formless and a formed, an indescribable and a describable. Higher Brahman is imperishable, beyond creation and beyond description, while lower Brahman is the world of māyā, the created universe, the universe of Gods, Heavens, Hells, the world of men, demons, animals, plants and rocks.

Second, while both higher and lower Brahman can be known, the way of true knowledge does not lie in knowing lower Brahman, the existing world described by the *Vedas* and the brahmins. That world, along with the *Vedas* and the way of lower knowledge and sacrifice, is rejected in favor of the second way, the way of true knowledge, i.e. jñāna yoga.

The *Muṇḍaka* continues:

> That which is invisible, ungraspable, without family, without class [avarṇa], without sight or hearing is It, without hand or foot, eternal, all-pervading, omnipresent, exceeding subtle: That is the Imperishable which the wise see as the womb of all being.

And concludes:

> As a spider secretes and then draws back [its web], as herbs grow from the earth, as the hairs of the head and body grow from a living person, so from the Imperishable arises the entire universe.[17]

The *Upaniṣads* conclude from all this that higher Brahman creates with Its māyā (power) a māyā world (product), an appearance or illusion, and lower Brahman is that māyā world. Which brings us now to our fifth key Upaniṣadic concept, viz. jñāna yoga.

The *Upaniṣads*, in seeking a solution to the problem of saṁsāra, reject both the way of sacrifices and rituals of the earlier *Vedas* as well as the way of pleasure and the titillating distractions exemplified in Gautama's early life. Instead, the *Upaniṣads* adopt a new and revolutionary way called "the yoga of true knowledge" or "jñāna yoga."

The revolutionary discovery made by the Upaniṣadic ṛṣis was that, first, ignorance (avidyā) of reality could be overcome through jñāna yoga, the way of intuitive or mystical knowledge; second, that one could come to have knowledge of the ultimate identity of immanent Ātman and transcendent Brahman; and, third, that by this knowledge saṁsāra could be conquered once and for all. What one comes to know through this first of many yogas that Hinduism will introduce into the world is that the Self (Ātman) is not different from the holy Power (Brahman) of the universe. Which brings us then to the sixth key concept of the *Upaniṣads*, viz., mokṣa.

"Mokṣa" means "release" or "liberation" in Sanskrit and it is the goal or end of yoga, viz., the ending of, or release from, avidyā (ignorance) and saṁsāra. Jñāna Yoga reveals that Brahman is the true Self; it reveals that bondage in saṁsāra was caused by ignorance of the true Self together with the false belief that māyā, this world, was real; and with that revelation saṁsāra, i.e. rebirth and suffering, comes to an end.

That end has been variously treated by the Upaniṣadic commentators who claim either that mokṣa constitutes mystical absorbtion of the Self back into Brahman, or that mokṣa is a liberation from pain into heavenly bliss. These two interpretations will be reflected below in our presentation of the two major philosophies of Buddhism: Hīnayāna and Mahāyāna.[18] We turn next to the seventh, and final, key concept introduced in the *Upaniṣads*, the law of karma.

Very briefly, the Indians of the Upaniṣadic period believed that the universe was a just place in which to live. Being a just place meant, of course, that everyone got what was coming to him in that universe, viz., rewards for the good, and punishments for the evil, that was done, together with the appropriate results for the rituals and sacrifices performed. This view was actually taken over from the *Vedas* which also held that the universe was a just place and that it was guaranteed to be just by virtue of the Vedic principle of Ṛta, i.e. the principle of universal justice and order. Ṛta functioned as a kind of moral and physical law of gravity such that when people or rocks or sacrifices got out of order or out of their proper place, Ṛta saw to it that they were brought back into line or order again, i.e. the person would be punished, the rock would be lowered, the sacrifice would not yield the expected result.

The *Upaniṣads* incorporated the moral side of the principle of Ṛta, or order, into their law of karma. The law of karma was merely a principle of moral causation that guaranteed that justice would always be done, i.e. everyone would get his due, one's efforts in the sacrifice or in yoga would be effective in solving religious, as well as moral, problems.

This law of karma is stated most eloquently in the *Bṛhadāraṇyaka Upaniṣad* when it says:

> Just as one acts, just as one conducts oneself, just so does one become. The one who does good becomes good. The one who does evil becomes evil. One becomes virtuous by virtuous action, one becomes bad by bad action.[19]

And the law of karma is, finally, conjoined with the concept of saṁsāra ("rebirth") to warrant that if justice is not done in this life then it will surely be done in the next. Thus the second oldest *Upaniṣad* that we have, the *Chāndogya Upaniṣad* (about 750 B.C.E.) states:

> Those whose conduct here has been good, they will enter a good womb in the next life, the womb of a *brahmin*, a *kṣatriya*, or a *vaiśya*. But those whose conduct here was been evil, they will enter an evil womb, the womb of a dog or a pig or an outcaste caṇḍāla.[20]

The law of karma has a long and honorable history in both Hinduism and Buddhism and we shall have occasion to return to it below.[21]

The essential doctrines of Hinduism are now practically complete. It will take one other later work, the *Bhagavad Gītā* (composed about 400-200 B.C.E.), to complete the religion of Hinduism, but the *Gītā* is not a text that we will be pursuing here since it falls outside the period of Gautama's early life.[22]

For the present, however, we can say that several of the chief elements of the Hindu religion have been identified: The central *problem* was saṁsāra, a problem grounded in the law of karma. Further, the *cause* of that problem was improper conduct resulting from ignorance of the true nature of Self or Ātman and mistaking māyā, i.e. the appearance of Brahman, for that real Self (Ātman). The way to the solution of that problem has also been identified: That *way* was jñāna yoga, the way of knowledge, in which the identity of transcedent Brahman and immanent Ātman is mystically and suddenly revealed. Finally, the solution to the problem has also been noted: That *solution* was moşka, the ultimate liberation from all sorrow and suffering. So much for this very brief Hindu (Vedic and Upanişadic) background to Buddhism.[23]

Conclusion

We have examined the Hindu background to Buddhism through a description of seven central Hindu concepts. Of these seven concepts Buddhism, in general, will use four, viz., saṁsāra, the doctrine of rebirth; the law of karma, the principle that guarantees moral justice; māyā, the ever-changing space-time world; and finally, mokṣa or, as the Buddhists prefer to call it, "nirvāṇa", freedom or liberation from saṁsāra. But while Buddhism, in general, will employ these four concepts, early Buddhism will reject the other three central concepts of Hinduism, viz., Brahman, the holy Power in the universe; Ātman, the ultimately real Self or immanent Brahman; and, finally, having rejected Brahman and Ātman, early Buddhism must reject jñāna yoga as we have defined it previously, i.e. as the way of knowledge of the identity between Self and Brahman. It is the rejection of these concepts that will turn early Buddhism into a revolutionary philosophy and religion.

The reforms that the *Upaniṣads* brought to Hinduism were radical and revolutionary enough, to be sure; and the dissatisfaction with Vedism that has led to these reforms is further evidenced in this same historical period that saw further philosophical and religious turmoil outside the so-called "orthodox" or Vedic and even Upaniṣadic, circles. Reform, change, evolution and revolution were in the air and the best proof of this lay in the fact that neither before nor after in the history of Indian thought have so many doctrines clashed and struggled over the hearts and minds of man with quite the same fervor and intensity as in the 6th century B.C.E. in India.

In order to undertand Gautama's philosophic environment better, therefore, we turn next to an examination of several "heterodox" or non-Vedic, non-Upaniṣadic philosophies and religions that were alive and well in India during this renaissance. The heterodox doctrines I want to look at are those that are represented first by the teachers of Gautama, and second by the so-called "Six Heretics" and their allies, all of whom were contemporaries of Gautama.

4. Gautama's Contemporaries

According to the Pali text, the *Mahā-Parinibbāna-Sutta*, Gautama was 29 years old at the time of his renunciation. This would mean, if we can accept 563 B.C.E. as the date of his birth, that the Great Renunciation took place in about 534 B.C.E. The question before us now is simply, What kind of philosophic world was it into which Gautama was plunged in 534 B.C.E.? We have seen what the proto-Hindu world of the *Vedas* and the *Upaniṣads* may have been like, and now we must attempt to reconstruct what the philosophic world and the world of the heterodox philosophers may have been like.

This reconstruction can be divided into two parts: First, we shall examine the philosophic doctrines of Gautama's two teachers, gurus with whom he studied in the very early years following the Renunciation and about whom he speaks in two texts composed, long after his death, from the remembered accounts of his disciplines; second, we shall examine the philosophic doctrines of the so-called "six heretics" who were also contemporaries of Gautama. The story of the six heretics forms part of the later history of Buddha's life coming during the time of his ministry and some years after his enlightenment at 35 years of age in 528 B.C.E.

a. Two Teachers: Āḷāra Kālāma and Uddaka Rāmaputta

The Introduction to the famous Buddhist text, *Jātaka*, recounts Gautama's meeting with two teachers, both disciples of a certain Rāma, a sage he never meets. He desires instruction from these two teachers in the art of meditation. The first teacher, Āḷāra Kālāma, invites him to join his band of disciples and endeavors to teach Gautama, promising him that he will achieve success quite soon if Gautama will only obey his instructions. Gautama tells us that he quickly memorized what Āḷāra told him and that he understood it completely. Gautama then, rather brazenly, asks his first teacher up to what level of understanding he, Āḷāra, had advanced. Āḷāra tells him that he has progressed up to the stage of nothingness. Gautama then practices the meditational art that he has been taught until he too arrives at the same level of understanding as that of his teacher.

On telling Āḷāra that he has caught up to him in meditational realization, Āḷāra, on perceiving that this is, indeed, the case, invites Gautama to join him as an equal in directing the other disciples. Gautama says, in recounting the incident,

> Thus...did Āḷāra Kālāma, my teacher, take me, his pupil, and make me every whit the equal of himself, and honor me with very great honor. And it occurred to me...:
>
> "This doctrine does not lead to aversion, absence of passion, cessation, quiescence, knowledge, supreme wisdom, and Nirvana, but only as far as the realm of nothingness.
>
> ...and being averse to that doctrine I departed on my journey."[25]

Now what does all this mean? and What's the point of the turning away? We can suppose that Āḷāra, the disciple of Rāma, has been practicing meditation, a technique and doctrine that he learned from his teacher, and that he had reached a very advanced state; indeed, the stage of the realization of nothingness.[26] But this realization of nothingness is rejected by Gautama because it does not bring the peace and tranquility that he seeks. Deep meditation, we know now, does produce such states described by such predicates as "nothingness" or "emptiness"; and we know that while one is in such stages of samādhi, or trance, there is indeed a kind of "peace", a kind of "tranquility."

But nothingness-peace is wholly negative, i.e. it purchases peace merely because there is no pain and no suffering and no consciousness while in that state; in fact there's no anything in that state except total absence of everything, including positive peace and positive tranquility. And one can't live in a state of nothingness for long; its biologically impossible unless one is hooked up to mechanical life support systems. When one leaves the trance state one is back in the waking world. We must suppose that Gautama rejected the philosophy of nothingness, for he discovered that when he returned to the waking world, the old fears and anxieties also returned. If they had not returned, he would not have rejected Āḷāra's teachings; he would have been in the state of nirvāṇa, awake and at peace. But he does reject them, so he was not in a state of peace and tranquility.

The story of the first teacher also tells us something else. For the first time we're told what Gautama is searching for, viz., nirvāṇa, which is not merely a condition of nothingness, a negative state of absence of pain. Nirvāṇa has a positive side, a condition of release *from* suffering, to be sure, but a condition of release *to* something, viz., conscious peace and tranquility.

Gautama now turns his way to Uddaka Rāmaputta, his second teacher and the son and disciple of the sage Rāma. He makes the same request to Uddaka and is accepted by him as a disciple. Much the same result follows this discipleship and Gautama quickly arrives at the stage of deep meditation that Master Rāma, himself, had achieved, viz., the stage of neither consciousness nor non-consciousness. Uddaka tells him that that is as far as Master Rāma's doctrine went and he invites Gautama to stay and become his teacher, for we are led to believe that Uddaka, himself, had not attained to this stage of neither consciousness nor non-consciousness. Gautama rejects the offer and turns his steps elsewhere.

The point is the same point made above in discussing Gautama's encounter with Āḷāra: The stage of neither consciousness nor non-consciousness does not produce the positive state of nirvāṇa that Gautama seeks.

What has Gautama obtained from his two gurus? Has it all been in vain, a great waste of time? Have these first experiences as a disciple, as a student, rendered the whole occasion of the Great Renunciation nugatory and useless? I would suggest that the experiences led to three important things: First, we can suppose that Gautama learned the art of meditation, an art that became the foundation of both his later philosophy and Buddhism. Meditation as a technique is, in fact, the *sine qua non* of nearly all "Eastern philosophy" and it is the single most important doctrine and technique that distinguishes Eastern from Western philosophy.

Second, Gautama now knows what he's looking for; or better, he knows what he's not looking for. He knows that the nirvāṇa he seeks is not a condition of nothingness, nor a state that transcends the negative and the positive. He tells us, quite simply, that he seeks a doctrine and a practice that leads to "aversion, absence of passion, cessation, peace, knowledge, supreme wisdom and nirvāṇa." Until he has reached that he knows that his quest is incomplete.

Third, and finally, he has learned that he is more or less on his own. He has learned that the teachings of the sage Rāma and Rāma's two disciples, his teachers, are defective because they are limited. No one alive can teach him the way to peace and tranquility. He must go alone or not at all. And therein lies the uniqueness of Gautama's entire message in a sense. No one can save you, no one can push you over the brink of those final stages into nirvāṇa, not even the Buddha can push you. Each person must carry himself - there is aid and advice up to a point, but beyond that everyone is on his own.

Tradition tells us that Gautama next fell in with a group of five ascetics with whom he practiced for six years the most severe austerities possible in an endeavor to achieve his long sought goal. He disciplined his body, living on a starvation diet, eating the juice of beans, pulse and chick peas "as much as my hollowed hand would hold," until he could clutch his spine through the emanciated skin of his abdomen. And thus he practiced meditation, disciplining his breath, until he almost killed himself by this ascetic path. Saved finally from near death, he renounced the ascetic way to enlightenment. His five ascetic companions, disgusted with Gautama's faint-heartedness, promptly renounced him.

Gautama realized that the way to peace is not found along the path of pleasures (recall the life of pleasure in his father's house) nor is it found along the path of ascetic mortification of the body. Another way, a middle way, between these two extremes must be found and that way will form the subject of the later life of Gautama.

We turn next to the second reconstruction of Gautama's philosophic environment, an environment that includes the six heretics of Gautama the Buddha's later ministery.

b. Six Heretics

The story of the so-called "six heretics" comes from a time later in the history of Gautama's life, six years after he had achieved enlightenment, i.e. six years after he had become the Buddha, "the Awakened One."[27] However, the ideas expressed by these six philosophers are representative of the 6th century, itself. As Debiprasad Chattopadhyaya has said of the six philosophers we are going to examine, "These were the philosophies of frustration and futility. ...these were the major prophets of the Buddha's times."[28] Therefore, for the sake of the philosophic reconstruction of Gautama's times our brief investigation is warranted.[29]

According to the Pāli account in the *Dīgha-Nikāya*, King Ajātasattu of Rājagaha was seated one full moon day surrounded by his ministers. King Ajātasattu asks his ministers which ascetic, or priest, shall they call upon that night to bring peace to their hearts. Six of the King's ministers come forward and describe in turn the philosophies of the six men who are the subjects of our investigation. Each one is said to be "the head of an Order, of a following (of disciples), the teacher of a school, well known and of repute as a sophist, revered by the people, a man of experience, who has long been a recluse [a samaṇa, i.e. an ascetic or monk or mendicant] old and well stricken in years."[30] Thus our six subjects are not without reputation and some honor in the country.

But the King after questioning his ministers about the six turns aside each of the names together with their respective philosophies. Then his physician and confidant, Jīvaka, suggests to him the name of the Buddha, the Blessed One. Upon advice from this physician the King goes to the outskirts of Rājagaha where the Buddha was then living in Jīvaka's mango-grove. The King meets with the Buddha who then asks the King with whom else he has spoken. On mentioning the six philosophers he has just heard about, the King is then asked by the Buddha to recount for him their philosophies. King Ajātasattu obliges and gives a summary of the philosophies of the six heretics.

The King then puts to the Buddha the same question he had already put, through his six ministers, to the six heretics: "Can you, Sir, declare to me what are the immediate results, visible in this world for all to see, of the life of an ascetic (samaṇa)?" In other words, the question was something like this: Why should I follow your way of teaching? or Can you guarantee that I will be happy in this life, if I adopt your teachings? The King is looking for the immediate, positive and practical cash-value results of the philosophies that these men profess. With this question before us let us turn to a brief summary and discussion of the philosophies of the six heretics. I will mention each one in turn, giving his name in Pāli, together with the philosophy that he represents and teaches as stated in the Pāli and/or the Tibetan texts, and then, continuing with our theme of philosophic history, conclude by pointing out some obvious problems that each philosophy seems to entail.

1) Pūraṇa Kassapa: An Akiriya Materialist. Pūraṇa Kassapa was a metaphysical materialist who held that the law of karma was ineffective and inoperative, i.e. there is no guilt and no merit for there is no causal and metaphysical principle that guarantees that all right actions will be rewarded and that all wrong actions will be punished. Consistent with this, Kassapa also denied the principle of saṁsāra, or rebirth, as well. When this life is over, he held, the body and mind, being composed of the four elements, water, air, fire and earth, return to the separate elements of which they are merely compounds.

This philosophy of a-kiriya (non-action, i.e. the law of karma produces no action) materialism raises some purely technical problems, and I mention two: First, the problem of mind: If all that exists is merely a compounding of the four elements, it is difficult to see how mind and intelligence can have any place in such a system. But then if akiriya materialism is an intelligently planned and defendable philosophy, and Kassapa apparently thought that it was, and if intelligent men accept it, and his numerous disciples apparently did, then this would seem to necessitate making a place in that philosophy for a non-material mind together with its non-material thoughts. And yet Kassapa's rather strict materialism seems not to have made such a place nor dealt with this problem. That a solution of sorts can be found I have no doubt, and the Cārvāka materialists of ancient India, along with their Atomist and Epicurean counterparts in ancient Greece and Rome, did precisely that. But from what we know of Kassapa's philosophy, the problem of mind seems not to have occurred to him.

Second, the problem of moral incompleteness: If there is no punishment for any crime, nor any reward for any good action and, therefore, no guiding and no sanctioning moral principles for conduct, i.e. no principles with teeth in them, then Kassapa's akarmic moral philosophy, as ordinarily understood, is simply inadequate. Later materialists will introduce ethical hedonism and a full-blown doctrine of pleasure to guide and sanction human actions, i.e. an action is right, these later materialists will say, if it leads to pleasure, and wrong if it leads to pain. But Kassapa fails to note the moral impracticality of his akiriyavāda (non-action view), and fails to note, as a result, the inadequacy of his moral philosophy.

2) Makkhalin Gosāla: An Ājīvaka. Makkhalin Gosāla was an ājīvaka, a materialist, atheist and fatalist, who earned his livelihood, much as the Greek sophists did a century or so later, by teaching his doctrines for money or for room and board. As a fatalist he argued that all human effort is ineffective in determining the goals and ends of life, and that man is powerless to change his life in any way. Like Kassapa, Gosāla argued that the law of karma is inoperative but, since everything is predestined, man cannot be held responsible for his actions. While the power of destiny (niyati) is all-powerful, Gosāla does not indicate who or what controls that destiny, nor

whether it is directed to good ends or not. Unlike Kassapa, Gosāla believed that there was rebirth, though it was limited; but since it is all predestined, anyway, there is nothing man can do to shorten or lengthen his rebirths. Further, he mentions six pre-destined rebirth states, viz., as gods, demons, men, animals, ghosts and as beings in hell. Finally, he believed that man wanders in pain until his alloted births in these states are used up, just as when a ball of string is cast out it will unravel so far and then no farther.

This philosophy of fatalism raises one serious problem already familiar to us from above, viz., the problem of moral incompleteness: If there is nothing that I can do to alter events in my own life and in the world around me, i.e. if I am propelled through life just like a ball of unraveling string, then obviously the moral life, as ordinarily understood, is impossible. Therefore, fatalism, like akiriyavāda, is impractical as a philosophy of life.

3) Ajita Kesakambali: An Ucchedavādin. Ajita Kesakambali, a materialist like Kassapa and a fatalist like Gosāla, denied the law of karma and the possibility of the survival of the individual after death: He espouses the view (vāda) of uccheda (cutting off) or annihilation. From the few fragments that remain about his philosophy we don't know if he would have been able to answer the problems mentioned previously or not. However, he does expand the list of the four traditional material elements to make a total of seven, viz., the usual four, earth, water, fire, wind, to which he now adds pleasure, misery and soul, or life. These seven elements are "real", i.e. uncreated and indestructible. The Tibetan text gives this list of seven, commenting, curiously enough, that with respect to life no one can kill or be killed or realize or experience killing. But the Pāli text indicates that he also held that there is no life after death, i.e. he advocated annihilationism; nor are there, it concludes, any other worlds in which life could survive. The two texts are apparently contradictory for on the Tibetan account, death, the ending of life, would clearly be impossible, and yet the Pāli text plainly introduces the possibility of death. We shouldn't, however, necessarily attribute this apparent contradiction to Kesakambali's own philosophy.

Kesakambali's ucchedavāda with its materialism and fatalism has problems but they differ from the problems previously mentioned as a consequence of the curious introduction, in the Tibetan text, at least, of pleasure and soul, or life, as real entities; for if life and pleasure are really real, and if they can never be annihilated, then Kesakambali's ucchedavāda is, indeed, inconsistent, for people do die. The same text also states that Kesakambali held that all laws, rules and vows are useless in changing or altering the fixedness of earthly misery and happiness. Thus, it would appear that the problem of moral incompleteness returns to plague Kesakambali's fatalist philosophy, as well.

4) Pakudha Kaccāyana: A Materialist. This philosopher was a metaphysical materialist much like Kesakambali. In fact the Pāli text attributes to him the same doctrine of the seven eternal elements. He, too, argues that killing is impossible, saying that in so-called "killing" a sword only penetrates into the spaces between the seven elementary substances. Whether death is possible he does not say, but if life is eternal we would have to suppose, once again, that death is an impossibility. The Tibetan text attributes a curious sort of multi-valued logic to him, stating that he argued that there both is and is not another world beyond this one and that there is both another world and not another world, and, finally, that there neither is nor is there not another world.

This philosophy would be subject to the same criticisms and problems mentioned previously since nothing different has really been introduced to alter the force of those objections.

5) Sañjaya Belaṭṭhiputta: An Agnostic. This philosopher like his fellow "heretics" denied the existence of the law of karma and concluded, therefore, that all things are lawful. Whether one kills, chops or maims people, or makes salutary gifts or offerings to them, it is all the same and there is neither sin nor merit in the act. Regarding the existence of another world, of life after death and the like, he refused to commit himself, saying that he neither affirmed nor denied it, sounding very much like the agnostic that he apparently was.

This philosophy would also be subject to the problem of moral incompleteness mentioned previously and for similar reasons.

But now matters take a dramatically different turn as we take up the sixth and final philosopher whose views found acceptance in the 6th century B.C.E.

6) Nigaṇṭha Nataputta (Mahāvīra): Jainism. This philosopher was the reputed founder of the religion of Jainism, a religion which is contemporaneous with Buddhism and, like the latter, has continued in existence into the 20th century. Mahāvīra argued that future punishment for sins can be prevented by atonement for past wicked deeds and by obeying the moral law. The law of karma, in other words, is operative and efficacious for man. He also argued that all that happens to a person is simply the result of his previous karma or actions. Mahāvīra's philosophy stands in stark contrast to the previous philosophies. By including both mind and moral principles for guiding actions in his philosophy he avoids both the problem of mind and the problem of moral incompleteness attributed to our previous philosophies.

Jainism is very close, philosophically, to Buddhism and it will emerge as a rival to Buddhism in the centuries that follow, competing for the hearts and minds of Indians up to the present day. Therefore, until we know what Buddhism is like it would be presumptuous for us at this stage to criticize Jainism since any criticism of one could apply in many respects to the other. It is enough to say that both claim to offer paths to ultimate peace and contentment in this world, claims that the other five heretical philosophies could not make.

This completes our very brief catalogue of the philosophers and philosophies that were alive and well in Gautama's environment in the 6th centry B.C.E. Several of them are fragmentary to be sure, and it is moot as to how aware the pre-enlightenment Gautama might have been of these several doctrines, including even the *Vedas* and the *Upaniṣads*. But regarding whatever was philosophically abroad and alive and well during that formative stage of his studentship we can at least say this: He rejected all of them; he struck out in his own direction in order to find the goal that would lead once and forever to the cessation of suffering and to peace and tranquility.

c. Conclusion

Having rejected the philosophy of his two teachers, and having turned his back on the traditional and orthodox teachings of the *Vedas* and *Upaniṣads*, and having spurned the various other available heterodox sects and philosphies of hedonism, materialism, fatalism, annhilationism, agnosticism and Jainism, Gautama resolved to seek his enlightenment alone and unaided. Strictly speaking this is, of course, an exaggeration: No man can escape his past, i.e. the experiences that make up that past. His studentship had been well-served and his teachers gave him more, both in a positive aswell as in a negative sense, than appears at first glance. He had discovered, after all, that meditation is the way to enlightenment and for this he needed the experience with his two teachers. He also discovered that neither the way of pleasure nor the way of asceticism are the ways to the goal he sought. He had armed himself well with those previous experiences in that philosophic environment. What happened next is the inevitable outcome of those rejections, experiences and discoveries.

We turn consequently to Gautama's enlightenment and its aftermath.

Chapter Four: The Later Life

1. Enlightenment and Afterwards: Pristine Buddhism

Rejected by his five ascetic companions because of his refusal to live by their self-mortifying discipline, Gautama journied alone to Gaya in modern Bihar.[31] There, under a Bo or Bodhi tree ("the tree of wisdom") he seated himself resolving not to rise until he had achieved the nirvāṇa that he had sought for so long. During the great night that followed he experienced the four states of meditational trance. In the first watch (evening) of that memorable night he experienced his own previous existences. In the second watch (mid-night) he experienced the death and rebirth of all living beings. In the third watch (late night) he destroyed the impurities in his own nature, kāma (sensual desire), bhava (desire for existence), dṛṣṭi (false views), and avidyā (ignorance), and experienced the four noble truths and pratītyasamutpāda (the principle of dependent origination). Finally, with the coming of dawn, Gautama saw into the fundamental nature of all things, he saw things as they really are (yathābhutam); it was then that he became totally and completely awakened. Thus, in the year 528 B.C.E., Gautama Siddhartha Śakyamuni became the Arhat, 'the worthy one', the Tathāgata, 'the thus-become', the Buddha, 'the awakened one'.

Rather than dwell on what the experience of nirvāṇa must have been like for him, for such dwellings would be highly conjectural and the language describing it would be necessarily imprecise and metaphorical, let's turn instead to determining what were the fruits and results of that "experience." The question we wish to raise is a question about what occurred as a result of Buddha's discovery of the peace and tranquility for which he had searched, viz., What did the Buddha do and say after nirvāṇa? The answer to this question brings us to the high point of Buddhist literature and philosophy and to the first sermon Buddha preached after his enlightenment.

Following his nirvāṇa we are told that Buddha sat blissfully for forty-nine days enjoying the peacefulness of emancipation and pondering the two great truths which he had discovered during that blissful meditation, viz., the four noble truths and the doctrine of pratītyasamutpāda. Buddha then journied to Benares and to the Deer Park in order to seek out his five former ascetic companions who then accepted him as the Enlightened One. He then delivered the first sermon of his ministery called "Setting in motion the wheel of the law."[32] The substance of that first sermon together with the doctrine of dependent origination constitute the subjects of the present chapter, and these two doctrines form what has been called "pristine Buddhism", i.e. the Buddha's original and essential teaching.

a. The Four Noble Truths

The Buddha is said to have summarized his teachings in one sentence: I teach but one thing: Suffering and the release from suffering.[33] Ultimately the matter is far more complicated than that, but penultimately that is precisely what Buddha's doctrine comes to. And the four noble truths which he preached at Benares are merely an extension of that one thing, compactly summarized above. The first three noble truths are about the essential nature of suffering; and the last noble truth is about how to be released from it. And yet upon the foundation of these four truths an enormous corpus of theological and philosophical literature has been erected, and dozens of separate sects, schisms and individual interpretations have sprung from them, underscoring both their singular complexity and their extraordinary influence.

Let me now state the four noble truths that the tradition says were enunciated by the Buddha in the Deer Park at Benares, and then offer a critical comment upon each one. We turn to the first noble truth:

> 1. Now this, O monks, is the noble truth of suffering: birth is suffering, old age is suffering, sickness is suffering, death is suffering, sorrow, lamentation, dejection, and despair are suffering. Contact with unpleasant things is suffering, not getting what one wishes is suffering. In short the five *khandas* [groups or heaps of entities constituting forms, sensations, wantings, impressions and consciousness] of grasping are suffering.[34]

Buddha is mindful here of the three signs of suffering or anguish, i.e. duḥkha (Pāli dukkha), viz., sickness, old age and death which, in his earlier career some six years previously, had set him off on his long search for peace and tranquility.

It seems fair to ask, following such a pessimistic catalogue, Is that the way life really is? Or is the middle way on which Buddha has established his philosophy a rather one-sided way at that? It would be unfair to characterize what Buddha says as a pessimistic doctrine, really, for he does not say that life is always suffering or painful. The catalogue of sorrows or pains that he lays before us does, indeed, consist of painful elements. But all of life is not characterized by these elements nor does the passage quoted above admit that it is. To believe that life is always painful would be pessimistic in the extreme.

Finally, to argue that life is always painful would be just plain false, if not pure non-sense, and for several reasons: First, without some pleasure, or the absence of pain, in some form or other, the identification of pain would be psychologically impossible. Moments of pain are recognized only because there are moments when there is no pain. To argue otherwise would be to fly in the face of common sense.

Second, right at this moment are you feeling any pain? I suspect that you are not, but pause and check. Doesn't this prove then that life is not always painful? And even if you have a tummyache or headache you know they won't last.

Third, it would seem to be logically impossible for the word "pain" to have any meaning as a comparative adjective unless there was a concept with which to compare it, viz., non-pain. That is to say, it would be logically impossible to have a meaningful concept, pain, unless there was another meaningful concept, non-pain.

Fourth, suppose that all life did consist only of pain states. But then there would have to be degrees or levels of pain-intensity in order for the concept of pain to have any meaning. Otherwise in a non-degreed state of constant undifferentiated pain the comparative adjective "pain" would be meaningless as shown above. So, suppose that degrees of pain were experienced from high intensity to lowest intensity;

but then those of lowest intensity would probably be denominated "non-pain", in order for the high intensity pains to have any meaning at all. If, however, there were no pains of low intensity, and if constant high intensity pain were continuously experienced, then we would be dealing with a whole society of exceptionally sick persons. But a society in which everyone was in constant high pain would be impossible, as we have seen above. In other words, we don't deny that there are people who may be in constant pain, but that is the exception not the rule of life and society.

Fifth, and finally, the very fact of nirvāṇa as a condition beyond all pain means that, to the Buddhist, life is not ultimately painful; hence, life cannot be characterized as always "painful." To argue otherwise would make non-sense of this ultimate optimism of Buddhism.

Buddha seems to have uttered a commonplace, therefore, for what the first noble truth says, in effect, is something that we all know, viz., that there are certain aspects of life that are painful. And who is going to be driven or enticed into searching for nirvāṇa after being told that?

But the first truth is not a commonplace, if it is either spoken by one who has experienced exceptional suffering himself, or if it is spoken to persons who are now experiencing exceptional suffering. Thus while life is not always characterized by suffering, some persons have found so much suffering that the commonplace of the first noble truth becomes, for them, filled with significance. For it is the recognition of exceptional suffering in oneself or others that leads to the religious search, or, at times, to a social, political and psychiatric search.

Faced with exceptional, extraordinary suffering, people turn to any number of means for escaping from it; Buddha sought release in "religious conversion" or metaphysical transformation; today, many people confronted with exeptional suffering in themselves turn to psychoanalysis, drugs, religious and aesthetic distractions, and the like. And many people confronted with exceptional suffering in others turn to political and social conversion, to politics, social reform, philanthropy, and the like.

Recall that it had been prophesied at Gautama's birth that he was to become either a Buddha or a great universal monarch. One might speculate that had Gautama's initial discovery of suffering not been existentially grounded in his own being, if he had been able to transcend the egocentric thrust of the three signs, he might have become that great world monarch that his father had hoped he would become. And instead of renouncing the world in order to find peace and tranquility for himself, he might instead have become a physician (at the sign of sickness), a geriatric social worker (at the sign of old age) or a laconic wit noted for his ironical quips and homilies (at the sign of death). But Gautama chose the option of the way of the religious seeker because the pain he saw was, we must suppose, his pain and not the pain of the sick man, the old man and the dead man.

The religious search was initiated by pain. Without the recognition of pain there would be no religions.[35] Nothing diminishes the human commitment to churches, synagogues and temples more quickly than good times and prosperity: Religion is the barometer of societal and personal pain. And when man does learn to cope with the pain that exists by instituting social reform or employing drugs and psychoanalysis, then religion declines. Buddha has simply pointed to the axiomatic truth from which all religions spring: Suffering exists. We turn next to the second noble truth.

> 2. Now this, O monks, is the noble truth of the cause of suffering: that craving which leads to rebirth, combined with pleasure and lust, finding pleasure here and there, namely, the craving for passion, the craving for existence, the craving for non-existence.[36]

Buddha, whether aware of it or not, here follows the Upaniṣadic teaching that craving or desire, tṛṣṇa (Pāli taṇhā), is the cause of suffering. And this is no commonplace utterance but a tremendously important discovery. The cause of suffering is existentially grounded in the individual; suffering is not the result of metaphysical evil, like original sin, resulting from some ancestral Fall, as suggested by many Christians; nor is it simply due to actions performed by the individual in society and against God, as detailed in the Hebrew *Decalogue* and

Pentateuch by Moses; nor it is one economic class in society exploiting another, as pointed out by the Marxists. In fact, original sin, individual sin and societal sin can all be neatly subsumed under that cause that all three sins have in common, viz., they are all expressions of craving, desire, lust, thirsting and wanting, i.e. they all follow logically from tṛṣṇa.

Paradoxically, suffering lies in wanting what you can't get, and suffering also lies in wanting what you can get. The former is easy to see, the latter is not, but both seem to be important truths. When I get what I want then I worry and feel pain wondering if I can keep it. I want the 'A' on the test, the love of a friend,the summer job, the prize for being best, the inheritance from my rich aunt, and so on. If I don't get them, I'm pained and disconsolate. If I get them, then I worry about the 'A' on the next test, keeping the friend's love, the next job, the next prize, another aunt.

The nature of the mind seems to be characterized by wants; it moves restlessly from one obtainable or unobtainable object to another. You no sooner pass from one desire than another appears to take its place. Man is the anxious animal because he's the only desiring animal, living fretfully and forever in a future of anticipated wants. Satisfaction of the wants doesn't stop them; it only fuels them and feeds them. Frustration doesn't stop them; hope springs eternal, but with hope the fearful round of desiring continues. Buddha has wisely pointed to the cause of pain and suffering by calling attention to this one essential element of the suffering human mind: Desire exists. We turn next to the third noble truth.

> 3. Now this, O monks, is the noble truth of the cessation of suffering: the cessation without a remainder of that craving, abandonment, forsaking, release, non-attachment.[37]

Buddha would have been a negligent religious guide, indeed, if he had identified both the existence of suffering and its cause, desire, but had said nothing about the fact that pain can be stopped.

In a way this is a curious "truth." It seems only half finished, for the listener wants to ask immediately, Okay, how? What's the way? But the answer to that question is found in the fourth noble truth, below. The third noble truth doesn't seem as noble as the other three, particularly because it leaves one hanging, waiting for some second eschatological shoe to fall.

Furthermore, the third noble truth is out of chronological and, even, logical, order with the fourth noble truth that describes the way to stop suffering. For how could Buddha know that the third is true unless he knew that the fourth was true? After one sees the way and follows it (the fourth noble truth) only then would one know that the possibility of stoppage (the third noble truth) was an actuality and worthy of being included as a noble truth. Why is it included at all? Why not have three noble truths, viz., there is suffering, its cause is desire, and there is a way to stopping desire and with it all suffering. That's neat, elegant and tidy. So what's the point of introducing this third noble truth that simply says cessation or ending of desire is possible?

I would suggest that it's mentioned in the order that it is in order to underscore, to stress, the fact of stoppage. The fourth noble truth, as we shall see, repeats the stoppage motif in order to reinforce this most significant truth of Buddha's meditations: You're suffering but there can be a complete and total ending of that suffering. This deliverance, or salvation, motif is essential to any religion: "Come to me ye that labor and are heavy laden and I will give you peace."[38] Without such a promise, without such a possibility of the stoppage of suffering, religions would be empty and useless, indeed. Buddha, in citing this third truth and in placing it where he does, emphasizes the promise and the optimism of the Buddhist way: Suffering can be permanently stopped. We turn, finally, to the fourth noble truth.

> 4. Now this, O monks, is the noble truth of the way that leads to the cessation of suffering: this is the noble eightfold Path, namely, right views, right intentions, right speech, right action, right livelihood, right effort, right mindfulness, right concentration.[39]

Buddha ends his first sermon at Benares with this description of the way to the cessation of pain and suffering. It must appear as both simple and disappointing at first glance. We might have expected something more complicated, something more esoteric and mystical, than this list appears to offer. But the simplicity and the disappointment are assuaged when one realizes that there is a great deal that is practical and common sensical packed into each one of these "rights." For the listener is told that there is something that he or she can do, must do, and is able to do, *right now*, in order to overcome desire and thereby destroy pain and suffering.

In the *Majjhima-Nikāya* each of the elements of "the noble eightfold path", as the way came to be called, is elaborated still further:

> Right views is to know suffering, the origin of suffering, the cessation of suffering, and the path that leads to the cessation of suffering.
>
> Right intentions are the intentions to renounce the world and to do no hurt or harm.
>
> Right speech is to abstain from lies and slander, from reviling, and from gossip.
>
> Right acts [actions] are to abstain from taking life,from stealing, and from lechery.
>
> Right vocation [livelihood] is that by which the disciple of the Noble One supports himself, to the exclusion of wrong modes of livelihood.
>
> Right endeavor [effort] is when...[one] brings his will to bear..., struggles and strives with all his heart, to stop bad and wrong qualities which have not yet arisen from ever arising, to renounce those which already have arisen, to foster good qualities which have not yet arisen, and, finally, to establish ...multiple, ...and perfect those good qualities which are already there.
>
> Right mindfulness is when realizing what the body is - what feelings are - what the heart

is - and what the mental states are - ..[one] dwells ardent, alert, and mindful, in freedom from the wants and discontents attendant on any of these things.

Right concentration is when, emptied of lusts and emptied of wrong dispositions, ...[one] develops, and dwells in, the first ecstasy with all its zest and satisfaction, a state bred of aloofness and not divorced from observation and reflection. By laying to rest observation and reflection, he develops and dwells in inward serenity, in the focusing of heart, in the zest and satisfaction of the second ecstasy, which is divorced from observation and reflection and is bred of concentration - passing thence to the third and fourth ecstasies.[40]

The eight "rights" are easily divisible into three quite distinct categories. The first category we might label "the internal path"; it compries the first two rights, viz., right views about the nature of suffering, and right intentions not to increase the suffering in the world. The internal path is concerned with mental activities in relation to the world of suffering where those mental activities can be seen as propaedeutics, or necessary preliminaries, to action or inaction in that world: As your mind is, so are your actions.

The second category we might label "the external path"; it comprises the next three rights, viz., right speech in relation to others in the world, right acts towards others in the world, and right livelihood or vocation while living in the world. The external path is concerned with the actions that one performs and that directly concern other human beings and not merely oneself. Consequently, Buddhists respect truth, life and property, they refrain from soldierly occupations and other businesses that involve killing in any form, e.g., the occupations of herdsman, tanner, leather worker, butcher and the like.

The third and final category of the paths we might label "the meditation path"; it comprises the last three rights, viz., right endeavor to control the qualities of the mind through yoga, right mindfulness achieved again through meditational yoga in which one rises above the wants, lusts, and desires of the body and mind, and finally, right concentration, the deepest stage of yogic meditation or penetration where one advances by further levels to the highest stage of realization, viz., nirvāṇa. Yoga meditation is then the *sine qua non* of the noble eightfold path and it is the cornerstone not only of Buddhism but of all the major nonmaterialistic and nonfatalistic philosophies of India.

Let me direct several critical questions to the doctrine espoused in the noble eightfold path before we move on to examine the second element of pristine or original Buddhism, the doctrine of pratītyasamutpāda. First, is the noble eightfold path practiceable and, if so, by whom? Buddha undoubtedly intended the path for monks, for those who had retired from the world of activities (note the admonition under "right intentions") to lead a celibate and monastic life.[41] One of the problems for later Buddhism will be to adapt this monastic list of "rights" to the increasing number of householders and laymen interested in practicing or following the Buddhist life. Indeed, a major distinction between the older Hīnayāna Buddhism and the later Mahāyāna Buddhism will lie in the answer that each gives to the question, Who can practice the eightfold path? Hīnayāna emerges as the champion of monastic Buddhism, while Mayāhāna emerges as the champion of both lay and monastic Buddhism. The question of the practice, and by whom, of the noble eightfold path is, therefore, central in the development and evolution of Buddhism.

In discussing the relation between ethics, which is composed essentially of the internal path and the external path, and religion, which is composed essentially of the meditation path, certain other questions and difficulties are bound to arise. If one is to keep ethics and religion separate and distinct, one might simply lay down some very common-sensical distinctions. These distinctions are important in order that one not confuse ethics with religion and come to believe that when, for example, one is engaged in moral ativities, one is also being religious: After all, moral behavior does not produce nirvāṇa. That is to say, moral behavior is not a sufficient condition for enlightenment in either Buddhism or Hinduism; but moral behavior seems to be a necessary condition, a propaedeutic, for enlightenment. If so, then one can't reach enlightenment by moral behavior alone; but one can't reach enlightenment without it.

The following distinctions ought to be kept in mind:

Ethics is concerned with man and the world and the rules which guide man's actions in that world; *religion*, on the other hand, is ideally concerned with transcendental or metaphysical states or conditions which may have no relation *per se* to the world and man's actions in the world. Most religious sects combine ethics and religion; recall the Decalogue or Ten Commandments of Judaism and Christianity, where, in reality, only the first four are religious commandments while the other six relate to actons in the world; but the two sets are, nonetheless, logically separable.

If Buddha had promulgated only the first five of the noble eightfold truths into a noble fivefold path, Buddhism would be an ethical discipline; similarly, if Buddha had promulgated only the last three of the noble eightfold truths into a noble threefold path, Buddhism would be a singularly religious discipline. As enunciated the religious discipline of such a noble threefold path could only be practiced by a monastic order since those three truths make no provision for activity in the world.[42] It may well be that such a religious life or any religious life, for that matter, is meant only for those who have abandoned the world. On this interpretation, religion emerges as an aristocratic activity, meant for the few and not the many, and abandonment of the world, along with all moral concern for the world, becomes one of its defining characteristics.

Second, how does one go about fulfilling the mental norms of the internal path (right views and right intentions)? How, in other words, do I gain the insight into suffering and its nature, and set my mind firmly against harming and injuring others? One would expect that such insight and mental discipline could only come about through meditation, for this is precisely how, we are told, Buddha, himself, gained that insight and discipline. But if this is true, then aren't we mixing the internal path with the meditation path? Probably so, but this need not be a horrendous problem for the Buddhists. Some applications of meditation, they might say, enable us to perform moral actions while other applications of meditation lead to ecstatic transcendental states and nirvāṇa.

I raise the question merely to dispel misunderstanding that all meditation must of necessity lead to religious goals. Meditational yoga can prepare one for all aspects of life, as Indian yogis have been at some pains to point out for centuries. Yoga can lead to supernormal powers, displays of magic and feats of physiological prowess; but it can also prepare the mind for actions in the world, baking cakes, taking exams, studying, as well as for transcendental states beyond the world.

Third, what does one do in cases of conflict among the three ethical norms established in the external paths (right speech, right acts, and right livelihood)? What take precedence when the ethical norms conflict? Suppose that by telling a lie I can save someone's life, or that by killing an animal I can prevent several people from starving to death? or that by stealing a handful of rice I can save my own life? What ought I to do?

Or, with respect to the paths, suppose that I have a religious duty to meditate as the meditational path enjoins but that by doing so someone else will be harmed or made to suffer? What should I do? What takes precedence, the external path or the meditational path? In other words, when ethical norms and/or paths conflict, what takes precedence? Which duty comes first? My ethical duty to help suffering mankind or my religious duty to reach nirvāṇa?

On the conflict among ethical norms, Buddhism offers no practical insight whatsoever, and the problem remains a puzzle. On the conflict between paths, as we shall see, Buddhism will divide, with the Hīnayāna school of Buddhism tending to stress, or apearing to lean toward the primacy of religious duty, and the Mahāyāna school of Buddhism stressing either the primacy of ethical duty or its inseparability from religious duty.[43]

We turn finally to the second of the elements which form part of the Buddha's original insights into the nature of human suffering and its cessation, the doctrine of dependent origination.

b. Pratītyasamutpāda[44]

The doctrine of dependent origination or pratītyasamutpāda (Pāli Paṭiccasamuppāda) has been called the single greatest discovery made by the Buddha before or during the forty-nine days he spent in meditation following his enlightenment. Be that as it may, it is an important concept whose significance cannot be too strongly stressed.

Essentially the doctrine states that there is a chain of causes together with their effects that bind the self or some-self-or-other to repeated births in the world. I say "the self or some-self-or-other" for, as we shall see later, there are at least two interpretations regarding the nature of that self or self-like entity. This chain of causes and their effects are made up of twelve links, or nidānas, beginning with the link labeled "ignorance" and ending with the link composed of old age, death, suffering, and despair, which then leads, in turn, back to ignorance which is the ultimate cause of rebirth, i.e., ignorance of the four noble truths and the noble eightfold path. Briefly summarized the twelve causal links and the chain that they forge are:

Table II. Pratītyasamutpāda and the Twelve Causal Links

1. Ignorance of the four noble truths causes (or is the condition for or which leads to) karma (action) and the desire to live again.

2. Karma causes consciousness and life, the first characteristics of a newly formed human embryo.

3. Consciousness causes name and form, the mental and physical self, in the developing embryo.

4. Name and form cause the six organs of sense and the desire to use these organs (eyes, ears, nose, touch, taste, and manas, or mind, which is the organ of internal perception).

5. The six organs of sense cause contact with objects and the desire to seek out objects in the infant of two to three years of age.

6. Contact causes sensation or feelings of pleasure and pain in the child of four to ten years of age.

7. Sensation causes craving or coveting in the youth of eleven to fifteen years of age.

8. Craving causes attachment, the active seeking of sense objects, in the young adult.

9. Attachment causes the desire for existence and continued life wherein the seeds of karma are sown all over again.

10. Existence causes birth in the future as the desire for continued life extends beyond this existence into the next life.

11. Birth causes old age, death, suffering and despair, one's entire life in a future existence.

12. Old age, death, suffering and despair cause ignorance which, again, is the real cause of rebirth, and we are back where we began at the first link of the chain.

It might be helpful to see the entire round of birth and death as a wheel made up of the causal links with arrows to represent the causal connections between the parts of the wheel. Let the arrows also be interpreted as the desire which causally leads to the next state or link on the wheel, for it is desire which moves the "self" from one state to the next:

Table III. Pratītyasamutpāda Seen as the Wheel of Dependent Origination[45]

	→ 1. Ignorance →
12. Old Age, Death, Suffering & Despair	2. Karma
↑	↓
11. Birth	3. Consciousness
↑	↓
10. Existence	4. Name and Form
↑	↓
9. Attachment	5. Six Organs of Sense
↑	↓
8. Craving	6. Contact
← 7. Sensation ←	

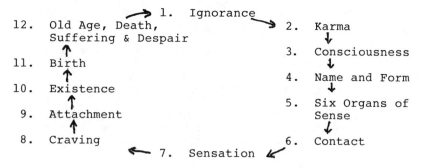

Each link in the chain, each part of the wheel, is dependent on what precedes it such that on one arising the next will arise from it. In this way, as Buddha says, the entire aggregation of misery arises. But what Buddha also discovered was that the chain could be broken, the wheel of birth and death sundered, by finding the weakest link and destroying it; and the weakest link was the link of ignorance. Buddha states, beginning with the cessation of ignorance:

> But on the complete fading out and cessation of ignorance ceases karma.
> On the cessation of karma ceases consciousness.
> On the cessation of consciousness cease name and form.
> On the cessation of name and form cease the six organs of sense.
> On the cessation of the six organs of sense ceases contact.
> On the cessation of contact ceases sensation.
> On the cessation of senstion ceases craving.
> On the cessation of craving ceases attachment.
> On the cessation of attachment ceases existence.
> On the cessation of existence ceases birth.
> On the cessation of birth cease old age, death, suffering and despair.[46]

Several observations might be in order, now, regarding the doctrine of dependent origination. First, the doctrine is a metaphysical principle of causation operating in the same fashion as the Upaniṣadic law of karma. Being a metaphysical principle the doctrine is not an empirical law established by empirical, i.e., sensory, observation. Newton's law of gravity, on the other hand, is an empirical law; it is confirmed by sensory observation and it is, consequently, contingently true, i.e., true until further notice. And that notice was given by Albert Einstein's theory of relativity which showed the limitations of Newton's law for the world of quantum physics. But the doctrine of dependent origination, like all metaphysical laws, is not dependent on empirical confirmation for its truth though it may receive empirical instantiation, i.e., its workings may be and are, the Buddhists contend, instanced or exemplified in the world.

Placed beyond the realm of scientific, empirical testing and public, sensory investigation one might well ask of this doctrine of pratītyasamutpāda, But how do you know that the doctrine of dependent origination is true? Buddhist philosophers might well respond that the meaning of truth being expressed by the doctrine is not that of the correspondence theory of truth in which statements must correspond to the world's facts or states of affairs, if they are to be called "true." Rather, we have here truth established by an original intuitive insight of the Buddha which is then sanctified by the Buddhist tradition. The usefulness of the tradition's believing the doctrine to be true further serves to ground the doctrine in what we previously called "the mythic theory of truth", i.e. accepting or believing the doctrine of dependent origination leads ultimately to the best possible results within the tradition, viz., nirvāṇa.

But it is the doctrine's original discovery by the enlightened, i.e., all-knowing, Buddha, through intuitive insight, that carries the greatest force in answering the question that we raised. For it is his discovery, the Buddhists would say, and the condition under which he discovered it, enlightenment, that led to its initial acceptance by the tradition. Its usefulness as a metaphysical principle to explain bondage and the cessation of bondage is secondary, but by no means insignificant. Thus in establishing the truth of pratītyasamutpāda its intuitive grounding probably takes precedence over its pragmatic grounding.

Second, one might well ask, How important is it to accept the doctrine? i.e., Must one believe it in order to achieve enlightenment? The answer is an unqualified 'No.' Buddhism is not a religion of dogmas the believing of which is a necessary condition for nirvāṇa.[47] The doctrine of dependent origination is a metaphysical explanation that leads to an understanding of bondage, its cause and the way to its cessation. But there are other explanations, as well, and we've seen them operating in the four noble truths, previously. The doctrine of pratītyasamutpāda could even be termed "a useful fiction"[48] to underscore its position in the Buddhist philosophy as both unnecessary, i.e., you don't have to believe it or accept it in order to achieve liberation, and as a useful interpretation, i.e., you ought to see it as a convenient metaphysical model to explain liberation.

One might even dismiss the doctrine as mere intellectual insight since the commitment to it does not necessarily lead to liberation. But the danger here is that one might then tend to undervalue the insight *per se* and dismiss it as so much metaphysical nonsense. The Buddhists don't regard it as nonsense, arguing instead that meditation on the doctrine of pratītyasamutpāda can, in and of itself, lead to enlightenment. Thus while believing that the doctrine is not a necessary condition for enlightenment, meditation upon it, and insight into its metaphysical meaning, can be a sufficient condition for liberation.

Third, the doctrine is pervaded by one central concept that lies at the heart of both Buddhist and Hindu theories of bondage, and that concept is desire. Desire is the fuel that energizes the growth and development of the embryo, that brings it into existence to begin with, that leads to adolescence, adulthood, old age and death. It is this ceaseless striving and thirsting that brings about future bodies in order that desire may continue its workings. Only with the cessation of desire is the weary round of birth and death, of sorrow and despair, finally brought to a halt. One might well ask, If Buddha has brought desire to a stop in himself then how could he continue living for another forty-five years, and How could he, during those years, preach, establish retreats, monasteries, nunneries, and an entire Church? for surely he must have been motivated by desires of all kinds, including that of saving suffering mankind. And didn't he go on eating and sleeping and aren't they the results of desire, too?

Buddha answers the question by using the analogy of the potter's wheel, i.e. the wheel on which the potter "throws" his pots. This wheel is driven by a treadle which is operated by the potter's foot. As the potter pushes or turns his foot the wheel turns and the products of his labor are turned on the wheel. The foot of the potter, Buddha says, is like desire, driving the wheel of birth and death. Removing the foot from the treadle is like nirvāṇa; desire ceases but the wheel continues to turn, carried round by its own momentum. In the same way the enlightened man or woman is no longer driven by desire, but the momentum of past and present karmic forces continues to turn his or her life even though there is no desire left to give new momentum or new force to those turnings. Actions are carried out, preaching, eating and sleeping are done, even though there are no longer any new desires to initiate the actions.

The interesting thing about the analogy of the potter's wheel is that it draws attention to a class of actions that are neither good nor bad; they are karmically neutral for they are neither motivated by desire nor do they lead to karmic consequences that must be paid for or rewarded in another existence. Is this consistent with the law of karma and the doctrine of dependent origination? The answer, of course, is Yes, it is. During the 5th and 4th century B.C.E. the same idea was being promulgated in the Hindu text of the *Bhagavad Gītā*. The doctrine of karma yoga in that text had argued quite forcefully that it was possible to escape the effects of one's actions by a yoga technique called 'karma yoga.' The situation is described in what has been called 'the dilemma of action.'

> If one does good acts, this produces good results. If one does evil acts, this produces bad results [thus the law of karma]. Good acts and bad acts will produce these good or bad results either in this life or a later one [the doctrine of saṁsāra guarantees this]. Therefore, the ultimate effect of all acts,good or bad, is bondage to future good or bad results - future necessary rewards or punishments. Therefore, no matter what one does, one is in bondage.[49]

Is there any escape from the dilemma of action? for it surely looks like a case of 'you're damned if you do and you're damned if you don't.'

The *Bhagavad Gītā* introduces the doctrine of karma yoga at this point and slips between the horns of the dilemma. The *Gītā* says that there is a third class of actions which are neither good nor evil; therefore, they produce no consequences for which there must be either reward or punishment. And these are the actions produced under karma yoga: The yogi learns to act without desire for, or attachment to, the consequences of his action. The Hindus use karma yoga as a technique for liberation, but the character of those actions produced by karma yoga is precisely the same as the character of those actions produced by the enlightened man in Buddhism. The Buddha, like the karma yogi, continues to act but because desire is absent the actions produce no karmic consequences.

Fourth, and finally, if the chain of links can be broken at any point why choose the link of ignorance as the weakest? The answer to this question lies in the nature of bondage in Buddhism, a topic that will be with us through much of the remainder of this book. Briefly put, later Buddhism comes to adopt the thesis that there really is no bondage; that is to say, bondage is the consequence of a delusion, a false belief, that we are in bondage and that "it" holds us in saṁsāra. This false belief is, of course, a kind of ignorance, hence the easy identification of bondage with ignorance.

Enlightenment is the realization that there is no "it" that holds us, that there is no bondage, and there never was any bondage: You're bound because you believe you're bound; you're free when you know that you're not bound. Hence, again, the easy identification of bondage with ignorance and enlightenment with knowledge. But this is a later philosophic interpretation.[50]

In the early tradition when Buddha speaks about bondage, he is not so clear. For Buddha, bondage is suffering and suffering is everything in this sentient world: Life is bondage, death is bondage, pleasure is bondage, pain is bondage, the world of all opposites, heat and cold, light and dark, good and bad, right and wrong, are all bondage. And the cause of all this bondage is desire, hence desire is bondage.

In fact, anything or any process that is not immediately relatable to enlightenment and the knowledge that leads to it is bondage for Buddha.

There is, of course, a horrendous mixing of bondage as a thing and bondage as a process, here, that often give the impression that for Buddha bondage is something substantial and nearly permanent. This identification of bondage with some sort of substance will be replaced in the development of later Buddhism with the realization that bondage is as evanescent and unreal as the world, māyā, itself.

For the historical period that we are examining in early Buddhism, however, we can say that bondage according to Buddha is essentially identified with ignorance, i.e. the failure to understand the four noble truths. And that is why the weakest link, i.e. the most directly attackable link in the chain of dependent origination for Buddha is the first link, ignorance. We will return to this discussion of bondage when we come to examine the later schools of Buddhist thought.

Conclusion

In summary, the essential doctrines that may be safely traced to the original teachings of the Buddha are two in number: The four noble truths together with the noble eightfold path, and the doctrine of dependent origination. It will remain for the later traditions, both Hīnayāna and Mahāyāna, to draw out the implications of this pristine beginning, systematize it, put their conclusions into the mouth of the historical Buddha, and establish their orthodox codes and philosophies. In suggesting that pristine Buddhism, i.e. the original teachings of the historical Buddha, can be reduced (or expanded) to these two doctrines we might seem to be too conservative. I think not. The two doctrines set forth above constitute the core of nearly all of the later multifarious Buddhist schools and religions, for these two doctrines are about all that they are in agreement on together with certain basic beliefs about Buddha's life. Hence, if this central agreement is conservative then so are we. We turn next to a brief examination of the latter days of the Buddha and his death.

2. The Death of the Buddha

Following the first sermon in Benares, where the four noble truths were preached, Buddha set about gathering converts to the new doctrine. The tradition tells us that at first a few, and then hundreds, and finally thousands, flocked to his religion's standard as he preached and traveled (up to 20 miles a day!) throughout northeastern India, to the cities of Rājagṛha, Sravasti, the capital of Kosala, Pāṭaliputra or Patna, Vaiśālī and Kuśināra and elsewhere for the remaining forty-five years of his life.

Beginning with his five ascetic associates, other disciples soon joined him, including one Yasa, the son of a wealthy guildmaster of Benares. The tradition says that Yasa left his riches behind in disgust, sought out the Buddha in the Deer Park at Benares and after hearing the Four Truths from him became the sixth disciple of the new movement. Buddha accepted a meal at Yasa's house and soon Yasa's mother and former wife became members of the lay or secular Order.[51] Then four of Yasa's companions entered the Order as monks, and soon fifty other men of Benares became arhats (Pāli arahants) or enlightened monks of the Order. As monks they engaged in a ceremony of shaving their head, wearing yellow robes, and reciting the vows three times, promising to take refuge or have faith in the Buddha, the Doctrine or Dharma that he preached, and the Order, or Saṅgha, of monks. The number of adherents eventually grew to such a number, we are told, that Buddha ceased to direct the ceremony personally and left its performance to the monks, themselves.[52]

After three months of seclusion because of the rainy season,[53] Buddha went to the town of Uruvela making converts along the way. One event that the later tradition relates is worth mentioning. Buddha came across a group of thirty young men having a picnic with their wives. One of them, who was without a wife, had brought a prostitute with him and she had stolen everyone's valuables and fled. All were looking for her when they came upon Buddha and asked him if he had seen the woman:

> "What do you think, young men," Buddha replied, "which is better for you to go in search of a woman, or to go in search of yourselves?" "It is better, Lord, for us to go in search of ourselves."[54]

With that Buddha preached to, converted and ordained them.

The later tradition also tells us that at Uruvelā Buddha converted a master named Kassapa together with his five hundred disciples, along with his brothers, Nadī and Gayā, and their five hundred disciples, by preaching to them the famous Fire Sermon.[55]

With nearly a thousand monks, Buddha now went on to Rājagṛha where he converted King Bimbisāra who donated a parcel of land known as the Bamboo grove to the Order of monks. Finally, at Rājagṛha Buddha converted two of his most famous disciples, Sāriputta (Pāli) and Moggallāna (Pāli).

Grumblings were heard from the people of Magadha, the kingdom in which he was making these early conversions, and it is not surprising. The people complained that Buddha was bringing about childlessness and widowhood by dissolving the families of the young men he converted. The new converts were expected, after all, to leave their homes, parents, wives and children, much as the young Gautama, himself, had done originally, and to join the celibate, womanless Order. This abandonment could produce economic hardship on the abandoned families, one can well imagine, for Buddha's disciples were not all wealthy as Buddha, himself, had been.

Why did young men abandon the world and their families? what was the attraction? What drove them to it? Undoubtedly the charismatic personality of Buddha had very much to do with the conversions to monkhood. These conversions were not merely "decisions for Buddha" after the manner of evangelical tent meetings so familiar in the West, today. The young men didn't merely resolve to devote their lives to the new ideal, sign a pledge, sign a hymn and then return to their former lives (although the lay conversions of householders may have been something like this, to be sure). The monkish conversions required total abandonment of their previous lives, positions, duties and responsibilities. The personality of Buddha must have been overwhelming, indeed, to effect such a change, for the conversions were, if we can believe the tradition, true "turnings around" in the most radical sense. And so complete were they that backsliding is hardly mentioned.

The attraction, then, may have lain in the charismatic nature of the live Buddha, himself, an attraction, exaggerations to the contrary notwithstanding, that must find few parallels in the West. But the attraction of early Buddhism lay not only in the founder but in his message, as well. For even after Buddha's death the religion flourished, indicating that there was something in the message that could attract and bring conversions, alone and by itself. What was the appeal of Buddha's message?

The early conversions appear to fall into two classifications: First, wealthy and independent youths and, second, men who were already monkish converts to another order.[56] And there is no reason to suppose that either group would turn to Buddhism to escape poverty and economic despair. Hence the appeal is not economic security. Nor could the appeal lie in any sort of social or intellectual security; social companionship was something already present within the two groups mentioned, and there is not eough intellectual content in the early sermons alone to lead us to believe that that was where the appeal of the message lay. But if the appeal of Buddha's message was not economic, social or intellectual what was it?

The attraction of early Buddhism probably lay with two things: The promise in the message of liberation from suffering and despair, together with the physical presence of the man who had achieved that liberation. Buddha's charisma was in part the result of that liberation. Recall that before his nirvāṇa, while he attracted no disciples, his two early teachers, Āḷāra and Uddaka, had seen something in him, one offering to become his partner and the other his disciple. But he had also been rejected by his five ascetic companions; they were converted, but only after his enlightenment. These companions had accepted him after hearing his message and witnessing what it had done to him: Gautama, now the Buddha, was the living proof of the efficacy of the Way. But many persons could still hold out against both his personality and the message of the Way, and the grumblings of the people of Magadha province are apparent proof of this fact.

Following his conversions in Rājagṛha, Buddha went back to Kapilavastu, his former home, to see his father. All the women at the palace did obeisance to him except his wife, who refused. One can read whatever one wishes into her initial reluctance. She requested that her former husband come to her first. He complied with her wish and she then showed honor to him. The later tradition [57] indicates that she tried to win him back to her by adorning herself and sending him a love potion. The story tells us that Buddha gave the potion to his son, Rāhula, who on drinking it became devoted to his father and followed after him.

Another version says that she remained faithful to her husband and that, when she heard that he had put on the yellow robes of the ascetic monk, she then did likewise.

Buddha converted his father, Śuddhodana, and converted and ordained his half-brother Nanda on the occasion of the latter's marriage. It was this half-brother who became one of the leaders of the Order on Buddha's death. Another famous conversion was that of the beloved disciple Ānanda, a cousin, who would also play a significant role in the development of the later Order.

In the fifth year after his enlightenment, i.e. sometime around 523 B.C.E., Buddha's aunt and step-mother, Mahāpajāpatī (Pāli), came to Buddha with a most unusual request. She asked that women be allowed to enter the Order as nuns. Three times Buddha refused her request. Disconsolate, Mahāpajāpatī cut off her hair and with other women of the Śākya clan followed after him, barefooted, over the rough and dusty Indian roads. She appealed to Ānanda to plead her cause with her step-son, and Ānanda, too, is thrice turned down. Ānanda then makes a final appeal, asking Buddha, Is a woman, who has left her home and taken up the life of a houseless wanderer while living under the rules of the Order, not capable of realizing the fruit either of entering the stream, or of the Once-returner or of the Non-returner, or Arhatship? the four stages of Buddhist discipleship culminating in liberation. Buddha answers that they are. Ānanda then reminds Buddha of the debt that he owes to his aunt, who had nursed him lovingly after the death of his mother, and had become his own step-mother after marrying his father. Buddha finally relents and allows her to enter the Order of nuns provided that she adheres to eight strict rules for nuns. These eight rules, in effect, bind the nun in obedience and reverence to all monks who shall be her superiors in every manner and situation. Mahāpajāpatī agrees to abide by these eight draconian regulations and, as the first nun, she is accepted into the Order. With prophetic forebodings Buddha says to Ānanda:

> If, Ānanda, women had not retired from the household life to the houseless one, under the Doctrine and Discipline announced by the Tathāgata [he who has "gone to Being", i.e. Buddha], religion, Ānanda, would long

> endure; a thousand years would the Good Doctrine abide. But since, Ānanda, women have now retired from household life to the houseless one, under the Doctrine and Discipline announced by the Tathāgata, not long, Ānanda, will religion endure....

How long will it endure with women now admitted to the Order? Buddha continues:

> ...but five hundred years, Ānanda, will the Good Doctrine abide.

Buddha concludes with three reasons for his reluctance to allow women to become nuns. I mention two:

> Just as, Ānanda, those families which consist of many women and few men are easily overcome by burglars, in exactly the same way, Ānanda, when women retire from household life to the houseless one, under a doctrine and discipline, that religion does not long endure.

And finishes,

> Just as, Ānanda, when the disease called rust falls upon a flourishing field of sugar-cane, that field of sugar-cane does not long endure....[58]

There is another legend, a powerful story, from the period of Buddha's forty-five years of preaching that is worthy of mention as well. Kisā Gotamī's beloved son had died when he was just a toddler. In her anguish she carried the body of the dead child to Buddha hoping for a miracle, for the tradition attributes many miraculous powers to Buddha, e.g. walking on water, flying through the air, knowing events before they happen, reading the hearts and minds of men, as well as raising the dead. Perhaps it was this reputation that brought her, sorrowing and in despair, to him. Buddha tells her that she was wise in coming to him for medicine, and promises to help her. He tells her to return to the city and to seek for a mustard seed from a house in which no one has died. Full of hope for her innocent, dead babe she goes to the city enquiring from door to door for the mustard seed from a house that cannot be found. Realizing her own folly and the wisdom that Buddha has shown her, that death touches everyone, she returns to Buddha. The sorrowing mother takes up the body of her child and carries him to a cemetery. Gently laying her son down for the last time and holding his tiny hand she says, "My little son, I thought that death had come to you alone; but it is not so; it happens to all people." She leaves him there, returns to Buddha and asks him for help in her despair. And Buddha says to her,

> Him whose mind is set upon the love of children and cattle, upon him as on a sleeping village comes a flood,
> Even so comes death and seizes him.[59]

It is during this period of his wanderings that Buddha encounters the six heretics that we mentioned previously.

In the twentieth year of his preaching he chooses Ānanda as his bowl-bearer and heir-apparent leader of the Order. Converting kings, princes, and commoners, the wealthy and the poor, he travels about the northeastern parts of the subcontinent firmly establishing his reputation and the Order.

One day, towards the end of his long ministry, Buddha became dangerously ill. Ānanda becomes concerned because Buddha has made no official provision for the continuation of the Order. He enquires of Buddha what he has determined for the Order. Buddha, now in his eightieth and final year, replies rather sharply, we may suppose, saying, in effect, what more would you have from me? I have told you everything that there is to be told. And then adds,

> What does the Order expect from me? I have taught the Doctrine without making any inner and outer [differentation], and herein the Tathāgata has not the closed fist of a teacher with regard to doctrines.... But the Tathāgata does not think, 'I will lead the Order', or 'The Order looks up to me.' Why then should the Tathāgata determine something about the Order?

Buddha concludes with the famous 'Be ye lights unto yourselves' commandment:

> Therefore, Ānanda, dwell as having refuges [or "being islands"; in Sanskrit *dvīpa* means both "island" and "refuge"; *pace* John Donne who said "no man is an island unto himself"] in yourselves, resorts in yourselves and not elsewhere, as having refuges in the Doctrine [Dharma], resorts in the Doctrine and not elsewhere.[60]

That Buddha wished not to be revered as a God and that he desired not to fix attention on the Order as an institution seems clear from these remarks. The only source for enlightenment for future Buddhists is to be in the Doctrine, in the Dharma, that he has preached, i.e. in essentially, but not exclusively, the four noble truths and pratītyasamutpāda, and what each man and woman will make of this Doctrine within himself; that, he seems to be saying, is where the real strength and power of Buddhism must rest.

In rejecting theism and institutional or sectarian religion together with his own canonization as Saint or Savior of the new Order, Buddha is making a radical change in the nature of religion. The repercussions of these penultimate remarks before his death will be strongly felt in the later development of the Order and will lead directly to the schisms and heresies that will beset the Order in that later evolution: For where anything goes, everything goes.

A few days later, Buddha went to the village of Bhaṇḍagāma where he preached on the four things that destroy rebirth, viz., morality, concentration, insight and enlightenment. Perhaps acceding to Ānanda's request, he established in the village of Bhoganagara, shortly thereafter, four criteria for determining what is to be called "canonical," i.e. what is to be authoritative, and what is not, in the doctrine and discipline of the Order. The aim of the four criteria is obviously to set limits on what is to be orthodox and what is to be heterodox (so that not anything goes, after all), as far as the Order is concerned, prior to anything being formally established or even written down.

Recall that we are still in the period of the oral transmission of Buddhism. In other words, we are talking of events recalled several hundred years after they were supposed to have happened, since the texts, themselves, were not committed to writing until the reign of Vaṭṭagāmanī in Ceylon (29-17 B.C.E.).[61] It will remain for the several Buddhist Councils later to determine what is orthodox and what is heterodox, and that will be established with these criteria in mind.

The four criteria for admitting materials into the official doctrine or canon are: First, whatever a monk has heard directly from the Buddha and is then found to be in the Dharma (Pāli dhamma, a complex concept with many meanings), the doctrine or law, particularly the moral rules laid down in the noble eightfold path, or in the sayings, Sūtras (Pāli suttas), of the Buddha, or in the *Vinaya*, the discipline of rules for the Order of monks and nuns. Second, whatever a monk has heard from a gathering of the Order at a certain time and place. Third, whatever a monk has heard from a number of the elders or theras. And, fourth and finally, whatever a monk has heard from a single elder or thera. Presumably, in instances of conflict regarding who remembers what, the first criterion is to take precedence over the second, the second over the third, and the third over the fourth. And, human memory being what it is, and human islands, refuges, lights and interpretations being what they are in the absence of the Buddha, himself, the stage is now perfectly set, once again, for future schisms and schools, orthodoxies and heterodoxies. Buddha's prophecy of there being but five hundred years for the stable maintenance of the Order seems to be short by nearly three hundred years.

Buddha left Bhoganagara moving to Pāvā where he stopped at the mango grove of a blacksmith named Cunda. The latter provided a meal of sūkaramaddava which means "the soft food of a pig." Whether this means "the soft food that pigs eat" or "the soft part of the pig's flesh" is uncertain, i.e. whether Buddha ate mushrooms or pork is not clear.

He was taken ill with gushing blood and violent pains, but he controlled his mortal illness and set off with Ānanda for Kusinārā. On the way he rested and spoke further about the Doctrine. He indicated that there were four places worthy to be visited by monks: The place where the Buddha was born; where he attained enlightenment; where he first turned the wheel of the law; and where he attained parinirvāṇa, or complete nirvāṇa, i.e. where he died. Thus the way is prepared for the raising of future stupas (relic-chambers for Buddha's bones) and temples at these holy places.[62]

Now dying, Buddha spoke to the sorrowing Ānanda,

> The Doctrine and Discipline, Ānanda, which I have taught and enjoined upon you, is to be your teacher when I am gone.

And then addressing all the monks gathered at the sacred spot at Kusinārā he spoke to them for the last time:

> And now, O monks, I take my leave of you; all the constituents of being are transitory; work out your salvation with diligence.[63]

And then, surrounded by his sorrowing disciples, Gautama Siddhārtha Śākyamuni, he who was called 'the Buddha', died.

We turn next to the development of Buddhist thought following the death of the founder, as that thought evolved and changed through the history of four of the great Buddhist Councils.

II. THE PHILOSOPHIC HISTORY OF BUDDHISM

Chapter One: The Four Buddhist Councils[64]

Following the death of Buddha in 483 B.C.E. an event occurred which compelled the survivors in the Order and Buddha's immediate disciples to call for a general meeting. An old monk named Subhadda (Sanskrit Subhadra), on learning of the death of the Master is said to have commented, "Enough friends! Do not grieve or lament. We are at last freed from the Great Ascetic. We have been troubled long enough by being told, 'This is fitting for you, this is not.' Now we shall be able to do all that pleases us, and that which does not please us we shall no longer be forced to do."[65] Kassapa (Sanskrit Kāśyapa), the senior monk of the Order, was shocked by the comment of Subhadda, and hastened to call a general meeting of some five hundred monks of the Order, a meeting that has come to be called 'the First Buddhist Council.'

Subhadda's remarks that the monks should cease grieving since they were now freed from the Great Ascetic and his rule-bound orders, and that it was now, more or less, every monk for himself, can mean two things, both of which will have effects on the later history of Buddhist thought. In the first place, he might have meant that Buddha and his rules were a barrier to realization. It's good that he's gone. Startling as this interpretation might appear it will have an important place in later Buddhist thought, particularly in Zen Buddhism. For, after all, if Buddha, as he lay dying, did tell Ānanda to tell the monks to be refuges or islands unto themselves and to seek their own salvation with diligence then even Buddha, himself, would or could be a barrier or distraction to that diligence and, therefore, he ought to be expunged. It may be that this is the insight that Subhadda had, and it may well be that this is what caused him to cry out with some relief, as we are led to believe, at the death of the Great Barrier. Zen Buddhists will say things just as strong and just as gleefully, e.g. that Buddha is dirt and filth, Buddha is manure, and the like, in order to shake devotees loose from their attachments to the Buddha; hence, this first interpretation of Subhadda's remarks, while arcane and perhaps rather sophisticated for early Buddhism, may not be too wide of the mark.

In the second place, Subhadda might have meant that the lawful authority of the Order was now gone so do what you will, it doesn't matter. This is probably the interpretation that Kassapa gave to Subhadda's comments: If Authority is dead then all things are lawful. So the First Buddhist Council was convened.

The older scholarly tradition had established that there were some fifteen Buddhist Councils of which only eight were significant (five in India, three in Ceylon, or Śri Laṅka). Modern scholarship now believes that there was another Council in India, held sometime between the second and third Councils. We are going to assume that there was such a "second" Second Buddhist Council and treat it in its proper place, below. Thus there are now believed to have been sixteen Buddhist Councils of which nine were significant. The first four of these nine were significant for it was at them that the three piṭakas, or baskets, containing the doctrines and rules and philosophy of the Order began to be recited and collected. Let me take these four Councils in their supposed historical order and discuss, quite briefly, the philosophical significance of each one.

1. The First Buddhist Council (at Rājagṛha, the capital of Magadha, in 483 B.C.E.)

We have seen that the First Buddhist Council at Rājagṛha (Pāli Rājagha) was very likely called because of the common fear that with the Master gone, laxity and general ignorance about the purpose of the Order might cause Buddha's message, and with it the Order, to deteriorate or die. It is at this time that early Buddhism, while emphasizing the need for personal effort towards enlightenment, rejects the notion that Buddhism is to be a purely personal religion, as Subhadda's remarks indicated, wherein it is every monk for himself.

Hereafter, for Pāli Buddhism or Southern Buddhism or Hīnayāna Buddhism or Theravāda Buddhism (the four terms have been used interchangeably) the Order of monks becomes the focal point for all earnest strivings after enlightenment. The First Buddhist Council affirmed this belief that the proper locus for enlightenment is the monastic Order, and that without that Order, i.e. the Saṅgha, the community of monks, enlightenment is impossible. It is this peculiar insistence, that Buddhism is henceforth to be a monastic religion and that enlightenment is impossible outside the Order, i.e. impossible for householders and the Buddhist lay or secular community, that will eventually lead to a revolt and then a reformation within Buddhism, with the establishment of Sanskrit Buddhism, or Northern Buddhism, or Mahāyāna Buddhism, or Indian Buddhism (the four terms have been used interchangeably).

Some five hundred monks met, the later Vinaya, or rules of the Order, indicate, to try to find new ways of preventing the decay of the Order and the destruction and loss of Buddha's teaching. They met, in other words, to lay out the teachings of Buddha, in virtue of believing which one could be said to be a follower of the Dharma, the Buddhist tradition. The three remaining councils that we shall discuss will meet for similar reasons, to reaffirm the Dharma but also to allay heresies, for where Dharma goes, heresies are sure to follow; and combatting heresies was to become one of the chief concerns of the three later Councils.

The method that the Council of Five Hundred chose for establishing orthodoxy was very simple. According to the tradition, Kassapa called upon the two monks who were closest to Buddha, and who must have had phenomenal memories, to recite what they could remember that Buddha had said about the two chief matters of concern to the Order. First, he asked Upāli to recite what Buddha had said about the Vinaya, the rules of the Order pertaining to monks, the rules by which the novices become monks, i.e. the rules of monastic discipline.

Second, Kassapa asked Ānanda, who had been Buddha's favorite disciple, to recite what Buddha had said about the Dharma, i.e. the doctrines and moral precepts that were to be included in the Sūtras, i.e. the homiletic sayings and stories of the Buddha. Immediately prior to this request, Ānanda had been harshly admonished by the Council for committing several faults. This admonishment, the first of its kind, will set a dangerous precedent for future fault-finding, heresy-hunting councils.[66] After all, who gave them the power to scold anyone? We are told that Ānanda, probably bristling from the Council's unprecedented scoldings, recited the five *Nikāyas* ("collections") or Agamas ("traditions"). Further, Ānanda stated that Buddha had agreed to abolish all lesser and minor percepts, but because no one knew what precisely these were, the Council decided to accept all of the Buddha's pronouncements regarding the Order. Ānanda begins his recitation and the tradition has it that henceforth all the orthodox sūtras will begin in the same fashion, viz., *evaṃ mayā śrutam ekasmin samaye*, i.e. "thus have I (Ānanda) heard at one time...." Let's look at the Vinaya first and then turn to the Sūtras afterwards.

The Vinaya, part of which may actually have been recited by Upāli at Rajagṛha, can be briefly summarized by referring to examples of the rules that came out of the later tradition since all direct evidence of the first recitation, if there was such a first recitation, at Rājagṛha is now lost.

First, permanent expulsion from the Saṅgha,[67] or monastic community, would result from disobeying such rules as:

1. Sexual intercourse is prohibited.
2. Stealing is prohibited.
3. Killing a human being and suicide are prohibited.
4. Claiming to know the higher knowledge or complete knowledge when one does not know, and lying about it later, are forbidden.

In addition, there are other rules whose violation carries less stringent consequences than expulsion from the Saṅgha. These are rules involving touching a woman (don't do it), the proper construction or building of a monk's cell (keep it plain and simple), prohibitions against causing problems within the Order, disobedience, rules regarding the begging for food, rules directing public confession, before the Saṅgha, of one's sins, rules for dress and robes, what property may be owned by a monk, the use of money (don't touch gold or silver), association with nuns (don't touch them, either), the drinking of intoxicants (don't), travel to distant places, sleeping and meditation times, general rules of behavior in daily life, and the correct procedures for bringing charges against monks who violate these rules.

Finally, here is one such rule along with a story which comes from the *Cullavagga* of the later *Vinaya-Piṭaka*. A monk had been bitten by a snake and had died. The other monks tell Buddha of the death and Buddha says it was the monk's own fault, "For if, O monks, that monk had suffused the four royal families of the snakes with his friendliness, that monk would not have been killed by the bite of the snake." Buddha then orders them to chant the following verses in order to infuse the families of snakes and of all creatures with their own compassion and love:

> Creatures without feet have my love,
> And likewise those that have two feet,
> And those that have four feet I love,
> And those, too, that have many feet.
>
> May those without feet harm me not,
> And those with two feet cause no hurt;
> May those with four feet harm me not,
> Nor those who many feet possess.
>
> Let creatures all, all things that live,
> All being of whatever kind,
> See nothing that will abode them ill!
> May naught of evil come to them!

And Buddha then concludes with this counsel:

> Infinite is the Buddha, infinite the Dharma, infinite the Order. Finite are creeping things: snakes, scorpions, centipedes, spiders, lizards and mice! I have now made my protection, and sung my song of defence [of them].[68]

We will meet with the Vinaya rules, again, when we come to the Second Buddhist Council, below.

The Sūtras containing the Dharma, some of which may have been recited by Ānanda at Rajagṛha, can be briefly summarized by calling attention to the later *Sūtra-Piṭaka* and its five *Nikāyas*.[69] The *Nikāyas* contain, among other things, the stories andlegends told by and about the Buddha that illustrate the moral doctrines and creeds of early Buddhism. How much of this, if any of it, was actually recited by Ānanda at Rajagṛha is moot, to be sure, and what we draw on here, from a list made up by the great philosopher and exegete, Buddhaghoṣa, in the fifth century C.E., merely gives an impression of what the later Sūtra literature became for Hīnayāna Buddhism.

a. The *Dīgha-Nikāya* ("Collection of Long Sermons")

The moralities propounded in the 900 pages of the modern *Dīgha-Nikāya* consist of a pseudo-historical account of Buddha's life and the lives of the Buddhas that preceded him (yes, Gautama was not the only Buddha!), all with a moral tale to tell, filled with injunctions and prohibitions regarding actions in the world. The work contains discourses on such diverse topics as the advantage of being a Buddhist monk, on the four occupational classes, or varṇas, on animal sacrifice, on the nature of a true brahmin, on the self, or soul, which Buddha refuses to discuss since such topics do not lead to enlightenment, on Buddha's disapproval of miracles, on the four noble truths, on the perfect teacher, and on the proper conduct of monks and laymen.

Here, for example, is the Buddha speaking in this *Nikāya* on the pragmatic test of the true doctrine:

> Thus I have heard at some time...."Of whatever teachings you can assure yourself that they conduce to dispassion, and not to passions; to detachment and not to bondage; to decrease of worldly gains, and not to their increase; to frugality and not to covetousness; to content and not to discontent; to solitude and not to company; to energy and not to sluggishness; to delight in good and not to delight in evil, of such teachings you may with certainty affirm: This is the Norm. This is the Discipline. This is the Master's Message."[70]

b. The *Majjhima-Nikāya* ("Collection of Medium Length Sermons")

The *Majjhima-Nikāya* with over 1000 pages consists of discussion and discourses on such diverse topics as the terrors of the forest and how to live there, on things that a monk may wish for, on how to remove false views, on suicide (it's wrong if one only wants a new body, but not wrong if it brings one to nirvāṇa), on austerities and asceticism, on Jainism, on meditation by breath practices, on not getting angry even though you are being sawed limb by limb, on heaven and hell, on eating meat (okay, but only if it was not prepared especially for the monk), on karma, on the conversion of a notorious robber, on varṇa, again, and on the presence of differing mental and physical qualities due to past karma.

Here, for example, is a *Majjhima-Nikāya* vision of hell:

> To begin with, the wardens of hell subject the sinner to the fivefold trussing. They drive red-hot iron stakes first through one hand, then through the other, then through his two feet and then his chest. After that they carry him along to be trimmed with hatchets. Then, head downward, they trim him with razors. Then they harness him to a chariot, and make him pull it to and fro across a fiery expanse blazing with fire. Then those wardens make him climb up and down a huge mountain of red-hot embers, all afire, aflame, and ablaze. Next...[but why go on?].[71]

c. The *Saṁyutta-Nikāya* ("Collection of Grouped Sermons")

The *Saṁyutta-Nikāya* with over 1700 pages contains discourses on such topics as the twelve links in the chain of dependent origination, the five skandhas (Pāli Khandas), "heaps of elements," and the noble eightfold path.

Here, for example, is a dialogue with a delightful riddle to illustrate a significant point in the Dharma:

> Have you a little hut? Have you a nest?
> Have you a little line stretched out?
> Are you free from ties?
>
> "No, no hut is mine, nor any nest,
> Nor is a line stretched out. Yes, I am
> free from ties."
>
> What do I mean when I speak to
> you of 'hut'
> And 'nest', and 'line stretched out,' and 'ties'?
>
> "You mean *mother* when you say 'hut'
> And *wife* when you speak of 'nest',

And *children* when you say 'line stretched out',
And *men's desires* when you speak of 'ties'".

Oh, well are you for whom no hut waits.
And well are you who has no nest at night.
And well are you who has no line stretched out,
And happy are you freed from all ties.[72]

d. The *Aṅguttara-Nikāya* ("Collection of Sermons on Ascending Order Enumerations")

The *Aṅguttara-Nikāya* with over 1800 pages contains discourses on lists of such topics as things which are one in number, e.g. the one sound, the one sight, the one smell, etc., that occupies the thoughts of men and women; then the things which are two in number, and so on, up to things which are eleven in number, e.g. the eleven bad and good qualities of a herdsman and a monk. Here, for example, Buddha speaks on the enumeration of three's and offers the following warning:

> Three things, O monks, act secretly and not openly. Which three? Womenfolk, O monks, act secretly and not openly. The incantations of the Brahmans act in secret and not openly. False doctrine acts in secret and not openly. These, O monks, are the three things which act secretly and not openly.[73]

Buddhist monks, like the priests of many other religions, have, once again, little good to say of women.

e. The *Khuddaka-Nikāya* ("Collection of Minor Sermons")

The *Khuddaka-Nikāya* is a *pot-pourri* of some fifteen works, including many shorter compositions, all gathered together in this *Nikāya*. It contains materials as diverse as the triple refuges universally recited by all Buddhst monks, i.e. 'I take refuge in the Buddha, the Doctrine (Dharma) and the Order (Saṅgha)', the ten questions for novices, poems on making offerings to ghosts, and on friendship, further legends of the Buddha's life, an analysis of concepts like knowledge and heresy, the *Dhammapada* ("path of dharma"), the *Theragāthā* and *Therīgāthā* ("Hymns of the Elder Monks and Nuns"), treatises on meditation and breath control, and thirty-five stories from the *Jātaka*, or stories about Buddha's previous births.

Here, for example, is the famous story of the blind men and the elephant: It seems that some ascetics and brahmins had been quarreling furiously over the questions, Whether the world is eternal or not?, finite?, or infinite?, and Whether the body and soul are separate or not?, and Whether the soul survives death or not? The monks report the story to Buddha who then relates the following parable:

> There was once a King, who had all those who had been born blind, brought together. When they were all assembled, the King commanded an elephant to be shown to them. An elephant was brought, and they made some feel his head, others his ear, others his tusk, others his trunk, etc., and the last one the elephant's tail. Then the King asked them: "How does an elephant look?" Then those who had touched the elephant's head, said: "An elephant is like a pot"; those who had touched the ear, said: "An elephant is like a winnowing basket"; those who had touched the tusk, declared: "An elephant is like a plough-share"; those who had touched the trunk, said: "An elephant is like the pole of a plough"; and those who had felt the tail, maintained: "An elephant is like a broom." A great tumult now arose. Each one maintained: "An elephant is like this, and not otherwise; he is not like that, he is like this," until at last they came to blows, at which the King was mightily amused.

Buddha then concludes the parable by likening the tumult in the King's palace (one wonders to what other wierd and grim amusements this King was also committed) to the tumult raised by the ascetics and learned brahmins,

> each of whom has only seen a portion of the truth, and who then maintain: "Thus is truth and not otherwise; truth is not thus, but thus."[74]

The five *Nikāyas* are a mixed bag to be sure, but in it the Sūtra literature regarding the proper conduct and beliefs of a Buddhist are to be found.''

Another, a third, group of texts that comprises the final part of the later Orthodox canon was not recited at the First Buddhist Council, a recitation that probably included only portions of the Vinaya and the Sūtra literature. This third group of texts is referred to as the *Abhidharma* (Pāli Abhidhamma) literature and it constitutes the philosophical commentaries and metaphysical paraphernalia of early Buddhism. Together with the Vinaya and the Sūtra, the Abhidharma will form the third basket of the so-called *Tripiṭaka* (Pāli Tipiṭaka), "three baskets", into which the rules of the order, the rules for moral conduct, and the philosophical commentaries, i.e. the Vinaya, Sūtras and Abhidharma, respectively, were believed to have been placed. Most Buddhologists are now agreed that the Abhidharma literature probably did not exist as a separate piṭaka until the time of the Third Buddhist Council in 247 B.C.E. The completed Tripiṭaka therefore, did not exist until at least that Third Buddhist Council. We shall reserve comment on the Abhidharma and the Tripiṭaka, itself, until we reach the Third Buddhist Council.

The Vinaya and the Sūtras having been publicly recited and committed to memory (!), and the orthodoxy of the new religion having been located and identified in a new set of codified dogmas (what else?), the First Buddhist Council disbanded. They resolved, however, that in one hundred years they would convene another, a second, Buddhist Council to consider anew the state of the Order and the problems with which it would most surely have met (from other admonishable Ānandas?) in the intervening century.

2. The Second Buddhist Council (at Vaiśālī in 383 B.C.E.)

Tradition says that the Second Buddhist Council at Vaiśālī (Pāli Vesālī) in 383 B.C.E. came about in this way: A certain aged monk, and one of Buddha's earliest disciples (he would now have to be over 165 years of age), named Yaśa was traveling about in the village of Vaiśāli when he discovered other monks in that town engaged in some rather peculiar non-Buddhist activities. Contrary to the Vinaya rules of the Order he found these monks permitting the following ten objectionable practices:

1. To keep salt in a horn (thus enabling them to travel away from the monastery

or to flavor their food in a luxurious manner).

2. To eat food after noon (thus allowing them to spend afternoons in the town begging in place of at the monastery).

3. To return to the village and eat even though one had already eaten at the monastery.

4. To hold more than one fortnightly meeting for monks in the same district.

5. To conduct monastic business even when the assembly was incomplete.

6. To follow a bad practice merely because it was done by one's tutor or teacher.

7. To drink unchurned milk, that was between the state of milk and curd, after one had finished eating.

8. To drink wine before it had fermented (thus running the risk that it *had* fermented).

9. To sit on an improperly sized rug (thus adding to one's worldly comforts).

10. To use gold and silver (thus tempting one to accumulate wealth).[75]

What particularly angered Yasa and drove him into admonishing these monks, however, was neither the luxurious cells, the fermented palm juice, nor all the other indiscretions, but the fact that the Vaiśālī monks were accepting contributions of gold and silver from the laity: When he admonished them, they told him they could do as they pleased (shades of Subhadda!). The issue was that of authority and discipline over laxity and liberality.

Yasa called a Council of seven hundred monks at Vaiśālī and the obstreperous monks were disciplined.

Another account then tells how the admonished monks refused the censure of the elders, or Theras, (Sanskrit sthaviras), of the Order, how they then broke away, and with ten thousand liberal or radical monks formed their own great council, or Mahāsaṅgha. But if such a revolt did occur, and it would be the first instance of a recognized heresy and schism within Buddhism as well as the first attempt at a reformation of the older, conservative, Theravāda (the views or doctrines of the elders), it probably took place some 37 years after the Second Buddhist Council. We turn next to this second Second Buddhist Council and the heretical school of the Mahāsaṅghika.

3. The "Second" Second Buddhst Council (at Pāṭaliputra in 346 B.C.E.)

Many modern scholars now believe that there was a second Buddhist Council at Pāṭaliputra (Pāli Pātaliputta) in 346 B.C.E. under King Mahāpadma Nanda. At this Council the problems that had been unresolved since the ending of the "first" Second Buddhist Council were confronted, once again.[76] These were problems not only of discipline and monkish laxity but they were also problems of philosophy and belief, of dogma and interpretation, of explanation and explication of what the Buddha had said, and more importantly, of what the Buddha had meant by what he had said.

With the emergence of the first heretical school, viz., the Mahāsaṅghika (Pāli Mahāsangiti), we find a practice being employed that is to become common in the development of some seventeen other philosophic schools by the time of the second Second Buddhist Council in 346 B.C.E. This practice will enable these schools to claim orthodoxy despite the cries of "heterodoxy" and "heretic" from the older and more conservative school of the Theras. This practice we might label "the implication-intention game" and it works like this: If you are in a position of real Authority, because you are Buddha, let's say, and you tell me that I must live in a retreat or monastery during the rainy (monsoon) season, then I know that you believe that it is right for me to live in a retreat or monastery during the rainy season. Now, by implication, I also know that to live in a retreat or monastery is tantamount to staying in one place; therefore, even though you didn't say it, I know, by implication, that you intended or meant that I should also stay in one place in the rainy season. By implication, I also know, from what you told me, that you intended or meant that I should do a lot of other things as well, e.g. eat nutritious food, dress comfortably, stay under shelter, get along with other sheltered retreatees or monks, and so on.

The form of the implication-intention game is this: If one is told to do A, and if A entails or implies B, C and D, then one is also being told to do B, C, and D. It seems innocent enough; but the schisms within early Hīnayāna Buddhism, and within later Mahāyāna Buddhism, as well, will make some rather fantastic declarations, or so orthodox Hīnayāna Buddhism will claim, with respect to B, C and D; and it is there that the problems for later Buddhism will develop.

The first of the schismatics to play the implication-intention game were probably the Mahāsaṅghikas, and they probably played it publicly at the second Second Buddhist Council in about 346 B.C.E.

The *Dīpavaṁsa*, the fourth century C.E. text from which much of our knowledge of the Mahāsaṅghika monks comes, tells us that some seventeen other heretical schools arose at about this same time. The Theras suddenly had their hands full of schisms and schismatics. It is believed that the obstreperous Mahāsaṅghika continued in existence in India after the Council and that it probably admitted the laity into its meetings, a practice that the Theras had not permitted. If this is true then it is the first indication that we have of Buddhism losing its strict monastic exclusiveness as a consequence of being now opened to householders. In fact, as we shall see, the survival of Buddhism in India, brief as it was compared to the rest of Asia, can be traced precisely to this practice of reforming and liberalizing the rules regarding who may and who may not be a follower of the Dharma.

It is probably true that many of the other seventeen heretical schools that were to develop within Buddhism owe their very existence to these rather brave but schismatic monks at Pāṭaliputra and to the Mahāsaṅghika that they founded.

What may have happened was something like this. The conservative Theras had put forward the concept of the arhat, the perfected Buddhist saint, the Tathāgata, i.e. the one who has become or gone to pure being or suchness (tatha). And the pure being to which each arhat or Tathāgata has gone is, of course, enlightenment. The arhats are, therefore, like the enlightened One, himself, i.e. they are like the Buddha.

One of the great leaders of the Mahāsaṅghikas took issue with this theory. His name may have been Mahādeva and he probably has the honor of being the first heretic in Buddhist, if not Indian, history. Mahādeva claimed that arhats fell short of the divine magnificence which many of the Theras had attributed to them, and they fell short in five (curious) ways):

1. Arhats could have seminal emission in their sleep.

2. Therefore, demons still haunted their dreams.

3. Arhats are still subject to doubts.

4. Arhats are ignorant of many things.

5. Arhats owe their enlightenment to the guidance of others.

Because the arhats are subject to these temptations and imperfections they are not like the Buddha in any way. Two consequences of Mahādeva's reasoning were that the arhat was lowered in esteem while the Buddha was raised.[77]

The Mahāsaṅghika as a school seems to have held six heretical beliefs and all may have developed from Mahādeva's initial attack on the concept of the arhat: First, they held, as Mahādeva argued, that the arhat is not perfect. Second, and as a corollary to this, they held that Buddha was not merely an ordinary man, as the Theras maintained, who had achieved an extraordinary insight into the cause and cure of the world's suffering. Rather, they held that the historical Gautama Buddha was a special kind of person, an extraordinary, superhuman being, created and sent into this world by an eternal, perfect and infinite Buddha, a pure transcendental Being. Third, they held that during the long period before he became enlightened, during those aeons before his last birth (yes, the Buddha had existed in many former lives!), the historical Buddha was a bodhisattva, a Buddha-to-be. As a boddhisattva he was reborn into places of suffering in order to help beings trapped in those places.

These three heresies, viz., the rejection of the arhat, the elevation of the historical and the transcendental Buddha, and the development of the Boddhisattva doctrine, will form the foundation for the later Mahāyāna belief in the Bodhisattva, the Savior who puts off his own nirvāṇa until he has saved, through his teachings and compassion, all suffering mankind.[78]

Fourth, the Mahāsaṅghikas held, contrary to the Theras, once again, that the way to end suffering was not by mere moral conduct coupled with meditation, but that enlightenment was to be achieved through wisdom, through pure intuitive insight, not unlike the jñāna yoga of the *Upaniṣads*. And, since such wisdom could be achieved outside the monastic community, this heresy threatened the very existence and perpetuation of the traditional Saṅgha.

Fifth, the Mahāsaṅghikas held, as the *Upaniṣads* had before them, that worldly things and this world, itself, are unreal, and that talk and beliefs about them, in fact all conceptual knowledge, can only lead to misconceptions and perversions. Attention came to be focused then on that which transcends the world. This epistemological scepticism with respect to knowledge, and this metaphysical transcendentalism with respect to reality, led them to a conviction that only the transcendent, and what can be called "emptiness", is real. These Mahāsaṅghika convictions will have an important influence on later Mahāyāna philosophy, particularly on that school of Mahāyāna called "Mādhyamika."

Sixth, and finally, they held that the mind of the newly born was not determined or restricted by karma (Pāli kamma) inherited from a previous life as the Theras had held. Rather, they held that the mind of the newborn was free of the taint of old karma. This latter heresy was doomed to be short-lived, for the Mahāyāna school that developed out of both the heresies of the Mahāsaṅghika and the other later schisms, and which managed to survive them all, appears to have been in agreement with the Theras on the matter of inherited karma; however, Mahāyāna will develop some interesting twists centering around the nature of the self, ātman (Pāli attan), as we shall see.[79]

The second Second Buddhist Council thus presents us with the first major division in Buddhist thought. The roots of the two later major Buddhist religions, Hīnayāna Buddhism and Mahāyāna Buddhism, are found here in 346 B.C.E. as the orthodox doctrine of the Theras and the heterodox Mahāsaṅghika, respectively. A reforming and liberalizing trend had set in which was to continue in India with a philosophic vengeance as Vedism, and then Hinduism, continued to influence and be influenced by Buddhism.

4. <u>The Third Buddhist Council (at Pāṭaliputra, the modern Patna, about 247 B.C.E.)</u>

The Third Buddhist Council, again at Pataliputra, was called into being in about 247 B.C.E. by the ecumenically-minded Buddhist Emperor Aśoka (304-232 B.C.E.). Dates become fairly reliable now and the chronicles say that Aśoka became emperor 218 years after Buddha's death. He was the grandson of the founder of the Mauryan dynasty in India, the very remarkable Candragupta (Pāli Candagutta) 322-298 B.C.E., who, we know, had made a treaty in 304 B.C.E. with Seleucus Nicator, one of the generals of Alexander the Great. According to the Buddhist sources, Aśoka, like St. Paul after him, had been a notorious sinner, filled with greed and a lust for power. When Aśoka's father, the Emporer Bindusāra (298-273 B.C.E.) died, Aśoka killed his own one hundred brothers and took the throne. Four years later, in 269 B.C.E., he was made emperor.

Not only do we have fairly reliable dates from this time forward but, thanks to the engraved edicts of Aśoka on stone pillars and rocks, many of the official pronouncements of the great emperor in Māgadhī, a Prākrit, Sanskritized vernacular, language in which Buddha, himself, probably taught, can still be seen throughout India. The first written records of Buddhism, therefore, can be dated from this reign of the third and last of the Mauryan emperors.

Before converting to Buddhism, and long before issuing his memorable edicts, Aśoka conquered and united India under his Mauryan banner. Many thousands were slain in this endeavor, we are told, and it looked as if an era of blood and bronze was about to be established. But then a curious thing happened: Eight years after assuming the emperorship Aśoka became a Buddhist. He forsook the sword, repented of his slaughter and instituted a reign of peace and order for everyone; a period of tolerance for all religions and practically all doctrines was inaugerated, and under the compassionate guidance of this first Indian philosopher king Buddhism flourished and spread.

Here, from the 13th rock inscription (about 258 B.C.E.) and in Aśoka's own words, is an apt description of what he had become:

> When the King of Gracious Mien and Beloved of the Gods [Aśoka], had been consecrated eight years Kalinga [a district along the east central coast, which meant that all of India, save the very southern tip of the penninsula, by this time was now under his Mauryan control] was conquered. 150,000 people were thence taken captive, 100,000 were killed and many more died.

But then came Aśoka's conversion:

> Just after the taking of Kalinga the Beloved of the Gods began to follow Righteousness, to love Righteousness, to give instruction in Righteousness. When an unconquered country is conquered, people are killed, they die, or are made captive. That the Beloved of the Gods finds very pitiful and grievous....

He then states what the consequences of his new found "Righteousness" (Dharma) will be for the people he rules and, also, what its limitations are:

> Today, if a hundredth or a thousandth part of those who suffered in Kalinga were to be killed, to die, or to be taken captive, it would be very grievous to the Beloved of the Gods. If anyone does him wrong it will be forgiven as far as it can be forgiven. The Beloved of the Gods even reasons with the forest tribes [a particularly savage and dangerous lot] in his empire, and seeks to reform them.

And now for the limitations:

> But the Beloved of the Gods is not only compassionate, he is also powerful, and he tells them to repent, lest they be slain. For the Beloved of the God desires safety [in particular, for merchants and traders, we may suppose, who had to travel through those forests and along the two major land highways in India], self-control, justice and happiness for all beings.

He then concludes with what might be taken to be the heart of this Buddhist message on statecraft:

> The Beloved of the Gods considers that the greatest of all victories is the victory of Righteousness, and that [victory] the Beloved of the Gods has already won, here and on all his borders...[80]

Aśoka's aim was to bring peace and order to his realm through humanitarian and religious means, i.e. through righteousness. He declared that all men were his children; he instituted reforms in the administration of the kingdom and in the courts of law; advocated ahiṁsā (harmlessness to all creatures); outlawed animal and blood sacrifices in Patna (which would not have pleased the brahmins who still practiced blood pūjā); established a law forbidding the slaughter of endangered species of animals in the kingdom; undertook pilgrimages to sacred Buddhist sites in lieu of hunting expeditions; and promoted vegetarianism throughout the country.[81]

The Order had prospered, the *Mahāvaṁsa* tells us, and many heretics had moved in with the monks. Aśoka in collaboration with a Thera leader named Tissa Moggaliputta (Pāli) assembled all the monks of the world, we are told rather hyperbolically, and put to each of them one question: What did Buddha teach? All those who gave the wrong answer were expelled from the monasteries. Aśoka, it seems, was not above a little intolerance, himself, when it came to his own Buddhism.

A second major heresy was discovered. It, too, was to have a spectacular influence, along with the Mahāsaṅghika, on later Mahāyāna Buddhism. This second heresy came from a group called the "Sammitīyas" who raised an issue that was to divide Buddhism on the nature of the self (ātman). What the Sammitīyas proposed is merely a hint of the general dissatisfaction that may have obtained with the orthodox Thera doctrine of the self. This orthodox view was that there was no real self at all, that it was a fiction, an illusion and, therefore, a barrier to enlightenment. The problems raised by such a view are notorious in the history of Western, as well as Eastern, thought and we shall deal with them shortly.[82]

The Sammitīyas sought to mollify the dissatisfaction with the Thera view by proposing the concept of the pudgala (Pāli puggala). The pudgala, or person, theory maintained that the individual self was not non-existent. Rather, pudgalavāda, the view (vāda) about the person, maintained that the pudgala lasted, the same and unchanged, throughout all of an individual's lives, disintegrating only upon the nirvāṇa of the individual. Well, this was creeping Hinduism, to say the least. It was not orthodox Thera doctrine, it was not the right answer to Aśoka's question, it was not what Buddha had taught, and so it had to be suppressed. And suppressed it was. Pudgalavāda and the Sammitīyas passed swiftly out of Indian history. But the Sammitīyas will have their revenge: Pudgalavāda will re-emerge, substantially enlarged, in the doctrines of later Mahāyāna Buddhism.

A second important event of the Third Buddhist Council was probably the establishment of the Abhidharma doctrine as the third of the three baskets of texts, or compositions, of early Buddhism: Together with the Vinaya and the Sūtras, the Tripiṭaka, the three baskets of doctrine, was nearing completion. The Abhidharma constitutes the psychological, metaphysical and general philosophical commentaries of Buddhism. The Abhidharma piṭaka of the Theras, or Hīnayāna Buddhists, consists of seven works dealing with such diverse subjects as the enumeration of human mental elements and processes, descriptions of the nature of individuals (pudgalas), discussions and refutation of other schools, a treatise on psychology, and a work on the relations, such as causality, between things in some twenty categories. The discussions in the Abhidharma are involved, complex and extremely technical, but they form the foundation for the highly advanced philosophical discussions and analyses of later Hīnayāna Buddhism.[83]

Here, for example, is a set of questions found in the Pāli *Kathāvatthu*, one of the seven books of the *Abhidharma*, compiled by Tissa Moggaliputta, supposedly at the time of the Third Buddhist Council. Try to answer all of the questions, yourself, and see if you are a closet heretic. The orthodox Thera answer to all of them, I might advise you, is 'No':

> Is there such a thing as a person (an individual soul) which can be regarded as a real or absolute substance? Does everything exist? Are there two kinds of cessation (of suffering)? Do the pupils of Buddha share in his superhuman powers? Can a householder be an Arhat? Can an Arhat lose his Arhathood as a result of karma? Is virtuous behavior unconscious? Can a person who has arrived at the right view (i.e. the true faith) intentionally commit a murder? Is it correct to say that the Buddha lived in the world of human beings? Were the excrements and urine of the sublime Buddha more fragrant than all other fragrant things? Can animals be reborn among the gods?[84]

By the time of the Third Council, then, some eighteen different schools of Buddhism, including the Sammitīyas and the Mahāsaṅghikas had evolved, each carrying on active disputes with the others. One of these schools, the Sarvāstivāda, was strongly influenced by the Abhidharma literature and will be discussed in the chapter on Hīnayāna Buddhism which follows.

5. Conclusion

The four Buddhist Councils have provided us with some insight into the dogmas and the heresies of developing Buddhist thought. The Tripiṭaka of the Theras, i.e. the three baskets of the Vinaya, the Sūtras and the Abhidharma, while not yet complete, is present in bold outline. It will later be committed to writing in Ceylon, though subsequent accretions will extend and expand this basic Pāli Scripture until its final compilation by the Great Buddhaghoṣa, again in Ceylon, in the 5th Century C.E. But the Mahāsaṅghika and Sammitīya heresies show that not everyone was happy with this basic literature.

The stage is now set for the emergence of the Mahāyāna, or Northern, Buddhist doctrine as a reforming and revolutionary alternative to the orthodox Thera, or Hīnayāna, Buddhist doctrine. We turn next to a philosophic discussion of these two great Buddhist doctrines and to an examination of the four major schools of thought which they fostered.

Chapter Two: Anitya and Some Problems

By the time of the second Second Buddhist Council in 346 B.C.E., Buddhism had split into two great factions, viz., the Mahāsaṅghika, which was to have a powerful impact on Northern, or Mahāyāna Buddhism; and the faction of the Theras, the Sthaviravāda (Pāli Theravāda), which was eventually to become Southern, or Hīnayāna, Buddhism. By the time of the third Buddhist Council in 247 B.C.E., the Theras, as we have been calling the Sthaviravādins, had splintered once again into three different groups, viz., the Vātsiputrīyas, or Sammitīyas, with their pudgala, or person, theory; the Sarvāstivāda, or realist, school; and the Vibhajyavāda, or analytic, school.[85] After another hundred years, i.e. in about 150 B.C.E., the Vibhajyavāda will divide yet again into two schools, viz., the Mahīśāsaka school and the Theravāda school. Thus the Theravāda faction, which existed in 346 B.C.E., is the distant ancestor of the Theravāda school which survived the splits, splinterings and schisms of developing and evolving Southern, or Hīnayāna, Buddhism.

But out of all these factions and their progeny, it is this surviving Theravāda school of 150 B.C.E. which is going to concern us in our philosophic history of Buddhism, for it is this Theravāda school which survives today throughout South and South-east Asia.

The following diagram might help to summarize what we've said thus far:[86]

Table IV The Development of Hīnayāna Buddhism

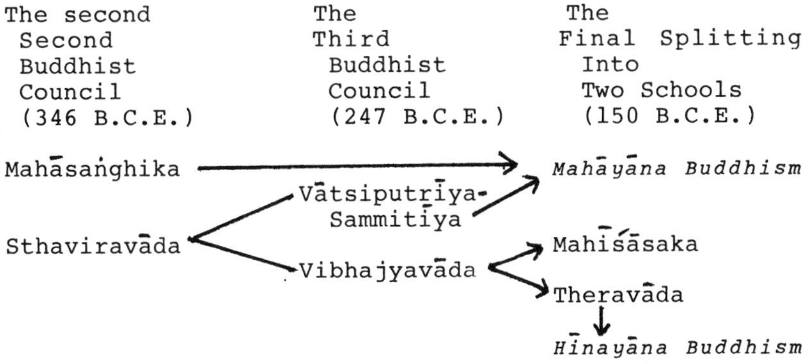

As Southern Buddhism evolved through these factions, groups and schools it carried with it a set of dogmas, or fundamental precepts, that were to define the character and the limits of that evolution.[87] Before we move to an examination of the ten general tendencies of the Hīnayāna school of Buddhism, I want to examine one of the most important dogmas of Buddhism, a dogma that can be said to be responsible, in a sense, for all of the ten propensities of Hīnayāna, viz., the dogma of anitya.

It will be the task of later Mahāyāna to attempt to temper and alter the overwhelming impact of this dogma. That attempt constitutes the later philosophic history of Northern Buddhism in India as we shall see in our examination of *its* ten general tendencies. This dogma is then a central concept of Buddhism, for in playing the intention-implication game Hīnayāna drew out the full implications of this dogma; and in playing the same game the Mahāyāna attempted to avoid those implications. We turn, then, to a brief examination of this central concept of Buddhism.

1. The Dogma of Anitya

The dogma of anitya (Pāli anicca) makes its appearance early in the history of Buddhist thought where we find it stated by Buddha in the *Aṅguttara-Nikāya*:

> Whether Buddhas arise, O monks, or whether Buddhas do not arise, it remains a fact and the fixed and necessary constitution of being,
> that all its constituents are transitory [anitya].[88]

Anitya means "not eternal , transient , or perishable." In addition, the word has the sense of something being unusual, irregular, casual, unsteady and uncertain. But its primary sense for the Buddhists is that of ceaselessly flowing and changing. Buddha says:

> Impermanent, alas! are all compound things. Their nature is to rise and fall. When they have risen they cease.[89]

The dogma of anitya is simply this: All existence is characterized by ceaseless change.

Two western philosophers of the ancient world seem to have been saying things remarkably similar to what the Buddha had enunciated. Heraclitus of Ephesus (535-475 B.C.E.) is said to have held that the world and all existence is like a flowing river, i.e. forever changing. According to Plato of Athens (427-347 B.C.E.):

> Heraclitus somewhere says that all things are in process and nothing stays still, and likening existing things to the stream of a river, he says, that you could not step twice into the same river.[90]

And Aristotle (384-322 B.C.E.), commenting on the Heraclitean philosophies of his own period, says,

> And some say not that some existing things are moving, and not others, but that all things are in motion all the time, but that this escapes our perception.[91]

Thus, according to this view, changes are occurring continuously even though we can't or don't perceive them. The image that Heraclitus and his imitators wished to evoke was that of an ever-flowing river.[92]

But one of Heraclitus' own later followers, Cratylus, went the master one better and in doing so may have come closer to what Buddha, himself, was talking about in the *Nikāyas* when he spoke of anitya. Cratylus, a contemporary of Plato's, is reported to have said that you could not step even *once* into the same river,[93] i.e. nothing remains the same moment to moment. In fact, on this extreme Heracliteanism of Cratylus, the concept of sameness is seen to be empty of meaning: If everything changes then nothing can ever be the same as anything, not even itself.

One doesn't have to search Buddhist and Greek texts to see the truth and force of this dogma as applied to the world. Look around you. See the trees and grass grow and die, the days turn into night, the seasons wax and wane, the years, decades and centuries roll inexorably past. Look at your hands that are holding this book. Dermatologists tell us that all the lovely colored flesh that you see is really dead epithelial cells, pushed up from the growing dermal layer of the skin that lies beneath them. These dead cells are scraped, washed and sloughed off as the growing tissues live and die. Your body is a colony of such cells, a microcosm of the changing, flowing universe, never the same from moment to moment, in its orderly processes of creation, maintenance and destruction, producing life, growth and death.

Furthermore, things that seem permanent really only seem that way. Look at this book. If we were to place it on a table and take a motion picture of it at the rate of one frame per year for the next thousand years, and then show a movie of those one thousand frames, what we'd see would be a gradual disintegration of the seemingly permanent book as it oxidized and sulfurized its way into decay and eventual dust. All this should surprise no one. The Buddhists have simply taken a rather ordinary, common-sense property of objects in the space-time world and by calling philosophical attention to that property's universality they have made it an essential dogma of their doctrines.

The Buddhists, as we shall see, have gone further with the implications of the dogma than either the Greek natural philosophers or many of us would care to go. First, from the dogma of anitya it follows logically that there can be no Gods, i.e. no ultimately real, permanent and unchanging, divine beings; in this the Buddhists seem to be in agreement with the Upaniṣadic philosophers who placed their Gods, as we have seen, in the realm of lower Brahman, the realm of māyā. Hīnayāna Buddhism will admit to the existence of gods and demi-gods, but it cannot, and remain consistent, admit to the existence of Gods. Thus one of the implications of anitya is atheism.

Second, if the dogma of anitya is accepted then from it one can generate the doctrine of universal suffering or anguish, duḥkha, which, as we have seen, lies at the heart of all Buddhist doctrine. Recall the three signs of suffering witnessed by Gautama in his early life, viz., sickness, old age and death. It was the impermanence of the body that led to these three states of pain and it was the search for a way to permanent peace and tranquility that finally drove Buddha to leave his household life and set out on the path to that permanence. Buddha says to his disciples:

> What [monks], is the Noble Truth of suffering? - *Birth* is a suffering; *decay* is a suffering; *death* is a suffering; grief and

> lamentation, pain, misery and tribulation are sufferings; it is a suffering not to get what is desired; - in brief all the factors of the fivefold grip on existence are suffering.
>
> Birth is, for living creatures of each several class, the being born or produced, the issue, the arising or the re-arising, the appearance of the saṁskāras ["impressions" or "dispositions"], the growth of faculties.
>
> Decay, for living creatures of each several class, is the decay and decaying, loss of teeth, grey hair, wrinkles, a dwindling term of life, [the loss of] faculties.
>
> Death, for living creatures of each several class, is the passage and passing hence, the dissolution, disappearance, dying, death, decease, the dissolution of the saṁskāras, the discarding of the dead body.[94]

Thus another of the implications of anitya is duḥkha.[95]

Third, the existence of anitya manifested as duḥkha drives one to seek an escape from it in the bliss of nirvāṇa. Buddha summarizes the reasons for this setting out on the path to escape the effects of anitya mentioned, in part, above:

> Impermanent, alas! are all compound things. Their nature is to rise and fall. When they have risen they cease. The bringing of them to an end is bliss.[96]

Hence, the knowledge of the fact of anitya drives one into seeking its dissolution in the bliss and serenity of nirvāṇa. Thus a third implication of anitya is the search for nirvāṇa.

A fourth implication of the concept of anitya involves the notion of tṛṣṇa (Pāli tanha), which forms part of the Hīnayāna tradition and later Buddhism, as well. *Tṛṣṇa* means "thirsting or lusting or desire." Tṛṣṇa results from being caught in anitya for, when faced with continuous change and mounting duḥkha and anxiety, one desires to cling to whatever one already possesses. In other words, anitya is a cause of tṛṣṇa, for desire has its origin in the attempt to find things, as well as states or conditions, that are, once and for all, safe and secure from change. Thus a fourth implication of anitya is tṛṣṇa.

Fifth and finally, the concept of anitya leads to the doctrine of anātman, the doctrine, as held by Hīnayāna, that the self is unreal or impermanent. For if everything is in perpetual flux then it follows that there can be no abiding or permanent self. Thus a fifth implication of anitya is anātman.

In conclusion we might say, then, that anitya is, indeed, one of the central and, apparently, common-sensical concepts in Hīnayāna Buddhism. Mahāyāna will accept it also, but it will not accept all of the implications to which that concept seems inexorably to lead. Those implications, as we have seen, are bound up with five concepts, viz., atheism (there are no real Gods), duḥkha (anguish is the chief characteristic of this bodily life), nirvāṇa (liberation is what one is driven to search for by the realization of the fact of anitya), tṛṣṇa (desire is manifested by the presence of anitya), and anātman (there is no real self).

Adopting these concepts and making them part of one's philosophy, as the Hīnayāna Buddhists have done, leads to problems, however. In our philosophic history of Hīnayāna, below, we shall re-examine these concepts together with the problems and puzzles that they generate. But, for the moment, let's consider several problems connected with anitya, itself. Let's look at what we might now conveniently call "the problems of anitya".

2. The Problems of Anitya

I mention three problems: First, on the microcosmic, or subatomic, level, there is nothing common-sensical at all about the interpretation of change given by Buddha, Heraclitus and Cratylus. On this level, if things that supposedly change escape our perceptions, as the atomic parts of this rather permanent stone pot or that very stable gold ring apparently do, then how do we know that they change at all? Without instruments common sense can't go beyond the commonly sensed to the microcosmic level; but the Heracliteans tell us that even those things we can't sense are in constant change. How does common sense know this?

Second, on the macrocosmic, or physical object, level, if one is to recognize change then there must be some things that either don't change or that change at a different rate. In other words, the concept of change is relative and makes sense only against a background of either the unchanging or the differently changing. But on either interpretation there are problems: On the one hand, neither the Heracliteans nor the Buddha can admit that change (anitya) can be understood against a background of the unchanging (nitya), for the existence of the latter is denied by both; on the other hand, if they admit that macrocosmic change can be understood against a background of the differently changing, against a sort of continuum of change, then this would seem to run counter to the descriptions given by Plato and Aristotle of the Heracliteans and by the *Nikāyas* of the Buddha. In other words, to admit to a continuum of change that included the slowly changing (as well as the wildly changing) would be inconsistent with the obviously exaggerated Heraclitean and *Nikāya* interpretations of change that says, 'all things are in process and nothing stays still', and 'all things are in motion all the time', and 'all compound things are impermanent': Heraclitean and Buddhist interpretations of change cannot support, and are inconsistent with, the slowly changing. But this needs further explanation and we'll return to the argument and the continuum of change, in a moment.

Meanwhile, on either the microcosmic level or the macrocosmic level, it would appear that the Heraclitean and Buddhist interpretations of change are either unsupported by observation or they are gross exaggerations of what is observed.

Perhaps what Buddha and Heraclitus meant was that everything is *subject* to change - not that everything is changing right now but that in time everything will change, i.e. everything is change*able*. In this case the radical change espoused by Cratylus is replaced by a more moderate and common sense notion that says simply that while that stone pot and this gold ring are not undergoing change right now, we all know from inference based on past experience that eventually they will change, dissolve, alter their form and wear or dust away. But, again, this move to save the appearances won't help for this is not what the Buddha and anitya are saying. Anitya claims that all existence is characterized right now by change. Later Buddhism, expanding on this notion in its *Abhidharma* philosophy with a doctrine of dharmas, or momentarily existing points of energy, will draw itself even closer to the same kind of extreme Heracliteanism espoused by Cratylus.[97]

In order to save the Buddhist dogma of anitya might we not turn to a compromise between these positions that would both admit common sense and at the same time be fair to the Buddhist interpretation of change? Let's construct, again, a continuum of change that has the wildly changing at one end of the continuum (call it "the Cratylus end") and the previously rejected unchanging at the other (call it "the Ātman end" after the Upaniṣadic concept of that name). Both the Cratylus end and the Ātman end are to be avoided as interpretations of Buddhist anitya; the former because it violates common sense and the latter because it violates the Buddhist sense of the *Nikāyas*. Somewhere in the middle, between these extremes, then, might there not lie the Buddhist common sense interpretation of anitya?

I think there is much appeal to this continuum of change. By avoiding the Ātman end, the Buddhist can save the dogma of anitya from heterodoxy. By avoiding the Cratylus end, the Buddhist can save common sense by admitting that while things change there is a difference in the rate of change, thereby avoiding the false claim that river waters change at the same rate as stone and gold. But to admit rates of change is, once again, to admit the possibility of the slowly changing and to admit the slowly changing is to come dangerously close to the Ātman end of the continuum and heterodoxy: For some change is so slow as to be not only imperceptible but, for all practical purposes, unchanging, e.g., the rates of change in Brahmā, Viṣṇu and Śiva, or the rates of change in Bodhisattvas or the Buddhas. In other words, there is a point on the continuum near the Ātman end, where Ātman and those very slowly changing (those apparently and practically unchanging) entities meet. But here's the difficulty: It's at this junction of the Ātman end with those very slowly changing entities that the temptation exists to slide back into nitya, e.g., back into Ātman. And later Buddhism, as we shall see, did precisely that; it slid back into that unchanging world of nitya which the dogma of anitya had enjoined it to avoid.[98] Thus the continuum of anitya will not solve the two problems of anitya, for the continuum gives or gets back the very things that the dogma of anitya sought to avoid, viz., nitya, Ātman and heterodoxy.

Third, and finally, there is a most telling criticism given by Plato of Athens against all metaphysical theories of flux. In his dialogue *Sophist*, Plato sets out to criticize the doctrines of two of his predecessors, Parmenides (5th century B.C.E.) and Heraclitus.

On the one hand, Parmenides had characterized the metaphysically real as pure being, i.e. as eternal, uncreated, unending, occupying a totally filled space, or plenum, and permitting no motion and no change since motion and change were both signs of the unreal. Plato rejects this vision of reality as pure being because it excludes all change or becoming. For, Plato reasoned, if there is no becoming then there could be no becoming known. In other words, if reality is pure being then knowledge (*becoming* known) would be impossible.

Heraclitus, on the other hand, had characterized existence as pure becoming, i.e. as perpetual flux and change. Plato similarly rejects this notion of reality as pure becoming because it excludes being. For, Plato reasoned, again, if there is no being then there could be no final state of knowledge. In other words, if reality is becoming then knowledge (*being* known) would, once again, be impossible. For Plato, knowledge is the foundation of philosophy and of life, and knowledge demands both being and becoming. Plato adopts, in other words, a Greek middle way between being and becoming, and solves the above dilemma of knowledge by holding that both are essential to knowledge, philosophy and life.[99]

Buddha, similarly, is said to be the founder of a middle way, as we have seen. But, and this is crucial, his beginning point is different from Plato's. He begins with the alternatives of being and non-being, rather than, as in Plato's case, with the alternatives of being and becoming. Hence Buddha's ending point will also be different, i.e. he ends by accepting only becoming, rather than, as Plato did, both being and becoming. What Buddha did was to reject both the practical and the theoretical extremes of being and non-being; "practical" because he was seeking a way of life that lay beyond the hedonistic titillations of his early life at his father's palace, on the one hand, and the extreme asceticism of his five life-mortifying companions, on the other; "theoretical" because he was seeking a way of thought that avoided the metaphysical eternalism of both the materialists and Upaniṣadic Hinduism, on the one hand, and the metaphysical nihilism of the Ājīvikas and the fatalists with their pessimistic views of life and the world, on the other. The middle way for Buddha led to the path of becoming and anitya, and by implication it also led to atheism, duḥkha, tṛṣṇa, anātman and, finally, nirvāṇa. So it would seem that there are middle ways (for Plato) and there are middle ways (for Buddha). And it all depends on where one begins.

That third problem of anitya is simply this: If anitya is true then how is nirvāṇa possible? The problem can be generated by turning the epistemological tables on Buddha and asking Plato's question of him: How can there be knowledge, which for Plato was the final objective of metaphysical struggle and dialectic, if there is no being as well as becoming? More particularly, since the final objective for Buddha is nirvāṇa, i.e. the ending of anitya, we might ask: How can there be nirvāṇa unless there is being (the final blissful condition) and becoming (the condition of anitya by and through which the condition of being is attained)?

If everything were only anitya, the final goal of being would be impossible, just as knowledge was impossible for Plato if the Heraclitean view of "reality" was the only state of the world. And this claim for the universal pervasiveness of anitya generates what we have called "the third problem of anitya": In other words, anitya cannot be as pervasive as the Buddhists claim or else nirvāṇa would be impossible.

The four later schools of Hīnayāna and Mahāyāna Buddhism will attempt to solve the three problems of anitya. The Hīnayāna schools will try to show that the problems of the macro- and microcosmic world, knowledge and nirvāṇa can be treated by the theory of dharmas; and the Mahāyāna schools will try to show that these problems can be treated only by rejecting or reinterpreting such a theory. Thus one of the

Mahāyāna schools, the Mādhyamika, will attempt to solve the third of the problems of anitya, the problem of nirvāṇa, by claiming, rather paradoxically, it must seem, that "nirvāṇa is saṁsāra", i.e. that there is no difference between being and becoming, i.e. that the final state of being, release and liberation, exists right here and now in the round of birth and death that constitutes saṁsāra. Buddha, it would appear, is not able to arrive at that position, and a good deal of philosophic waters must flow before even the Mādhyamika can come to their curious but happy conclusion.

Chapter Three: Hīnayāna Buddhism

We turn now to an examination of Hīnayāna Buddhism. By "Hīnayāna Buddhism" I mean the orthodox Buddhism that has its roots in India from the time of the First Buddhist Council until some time in the first century B.C.E. Hīnayāna thus includes the three major schools of Southern Buddhism, viz., the Sarvāstivāda, the Sautrāntika and the Theravāda. The latter school, writing in Pāli, survives in South Asia to this day.

In order to break the monotony of always saying "Hīnayāna", I shall on occasion say "Southern Buddhism" or "Pāli Buddhism", though these epithets are, strictly speaking, at times inappropriate descriptions of all of Hīnayāna Buddhism; inappropriate, for example, for the Hīnayāna Sarvāstivādins who wrote in Sanskrit and lived in Kaśmīr, or for the Hīnayāna Pāli text *Milindapañha* which was composed in Northern India.[100]

In what follows, I want to look at tendencies or general characteristics of this evolving and developing religion and philosophy under ten separate headings. This division into ten categories will allow an easy comparison with Mahāyāna Buddhism, the chief rival of Hīnayāna, when we turn to it in the next chapter. Below I shall state and briefly discuss the properties that elucidate each of these tendencies, and then, in keeping with our intention to present a philosophic history of Buddhism,[101] point out a problem or problems that each doctrine seems to entail. In several cases I shall suggest some attempts that might be made to dissolve or solve the problems mentioned. I must warn the reader, again, that the ten characteristics indicated below are, in most cases, tendencies, i.e. they are propensities or inclinations, of Southern Buddhism rather than necessary and sufficient conditions for being a Hīnayāna Buddhist. I hope that this caveat together with the language of tendencies will become clearer as we proceed.

1. Naturalism

Hīnayāna Buddhism *tends* to be a naturalistic religion. By this I mean that Hīnayāna eschews as essential to enlightenment the kind of supernatural paraphernalia that is found in both Hinduism and, later, in Mahāyāna Buddhism. For this religion, therefore, there are no essential beliefs in the Gods or God, no essential beliefs in a Creator or divine Supervisor of the world, nor in a Last Judgment; nor are there any divine decrees or dispensations, in the form of sacred scriptures or prophecies, made to recalcitrant or contrite sinners, that are *essential* to reaching liberation. In theory (i.e. cognitively), but perhaps not in practice (i.e. affectively), there is no system of yajña (sacrifice), no organized religious ritual centering around a divine figure or His or Her symbolic representations such as statues, sacred icons or the usual adorable debris exemplified by venerable bones, fingernails, ashes and pieces of true cross that call for extravagant worship and aweful reverence.[102] The Hīnayāna is able to reject as inessential and unnecessary other kinds of supernatural accoutrements such as divine grace and the forgiveness of sins, miracles, and similar theurgical sleights-of-hand. And Hīnayāna is not above resorting to a little ridicule at times to drive home their naturalistic and anti-supernaturalistic point. In the *Therīgāthā* we find:

> If water baptism can free one of evil karma
> then the fishes, tortoises, frogs, etc.
> should go straight to heaven.[103]

In the place of all of these otherworldly or extraworldly practices and transcendental products, they have set the purely natural and the worldly at the center of their religion. Like pristine Buddhism before it, Hīnayāna Buddhism preaches but one thing: Suffering and the release from suffering. The suffering is grounded in the psychophysical nature of man, and the release from suffering is found in the same place; it is found in the daily life and practices of the monastic community. There is no need to posit supra-physical entities like a soul or self which is anything other than physical and natural.

Further, there is no need to posit a heaven or a hell since such positings do not relate to the purely naturalistic character of man's sufferings. The entire concept of heaven entails the most selfish of motives for a monk's striving. The Buddha says:

> If wandering ascetics, O monks, members of another sect, were to say to you, 'Sirs, is it in order to be reborn in the world of the gods that the monk Gotama leads a holy life?' would ye not, O monks, if that

> question were put to you, be distressed at, ashamed of, and loathe the idea?'[104]

By rejecting heaven as the goal of man, Buddha places stress on the present, mundane and unselfish moral life of man, a life dedicated to, among other things, good works towards others rather than the gaining of heaven for oneself. Buddha continues:

> So it appears, O monks, that ye are distressed at, ashamed of, and loathe the idea of life in heaven, heavenly beauty, heavenly happiness, heavenly glory; that ye are distressed at, ashamed of, and loathe the idea of heavenly power.[105]

Thus the rejection of the supernatural. Buddha concludes:

> But much more, O monks, should ye be distressed at, ashamed of, and loathe doing evil with the body; be distressed at, ashamed of, and loathe doing evil with the voice; be distressed at, ashamed of, and loathe doing evil with the mind.[106]

The supernatural, in other words, is rejected as a way to enlightenment, peace and tranquility in order to concentrate on the moral and the compassionate life of natural man in this natural world. That rejection will form the topic of our second characteristic of Southern Buddhism, but before turning to it let's examine a problem that emerges with respect to this stress on naturalism in Hīnayāna.

1'. The Problem of Naturalism

The naturalism of Hīnayāna tends, *prima facie*, to reject the supernatural. And yet Pāli Buddhism is not loath to talk about heaven and talk about it in such a way that we are led to believe, quite correctly, that there really is a heaven (or heavens) which does (or do), indeed, transcend this world. The problem of naturalism is simply this, then, that while speaking overtly of a naturalism, Hīnayāna nonetheless speaks covertly of heaven and heavens: How is it possible to do both? and isn't this inconsistent?

The answer that Buddha gives is that there are heavens (and Gods, too, as we shall see in our discussion of atheism, below) but that the heavens are not metaphysically ultimate. In fact, they are interpreted as merely higher, but not the highest, states of the natural condition. Notice the naturalistic, i.e. phenomenalistic, or psychological, talk of "life in heaven", "heavenly beauty", "heavenly happiness", "heavenly glory and power", in the previous quotations. These are states of psychological enjoyment but they are merely temporary: They are as naturalistic and transcient and as mundane as the human condition, itself. In other words, the problem of naturalism is no problem at all, for the apparently inconsistent talk about a non-natural heaven is just that: Only *apparently* inconsistent. Heaven is as natural as the world, and one ought not to be taken in by the lip service paid to such seemingly supernatural places or conditions. More on this same subject will follow with our discussion of atheism and the Gods.

2. Atheism

Hīnayāna Buddhism tends to be, and many argue that it is, an atheistic religion. This atheism follows hard upon the naturalistic character of the religion. Neither Buddha nor the arhats are Gods or supernatural beings. They are, or were, men and women like you and me. They differ from us, however, in being enlightened, and possessing the several distinct characteristics of enlightened beings. If there are Gods, and the *Nikāyas* refer to the Hindu Gods on many occasions, then they are merely beings who are neither omnipotent nor omniscient. They are simply Devas, "shining ones", human-like inhabitants from inconsequential worlds.

But to say this empties the concept of God of all of its traditional meaning. That traditional meaning generally connotes a supernatural, transcendent and divine being, possessing various powers to hear prayers, spoken or silent, work miracles, create and demolish worlds, forgive sins, and by pure fiat deliver Its, His or Her worshippers to eternal states or conditions of blessedness. Hīnayāna, theoretically, will have none of this.[107]

Here are two Hīnayāna arguments, incomplete as they stand, which aggressively set out to prove that God does not exist. The arguments come from the *Jātaka*, the stories of the previous lives of the

Buddha. The first we might denominate "the Designer Argument." The Buddha-to-be of the *Jātaka* states:

> If God designs the life of the entire world - the glory and the misery, the good and evil acts - then man is but an instrument of his will and God (alone) is responsible.[108]

The completed Designer Argument would probably look like this:

1. If God exists (as the all-knowing Designer) then man is not free.

2. But man is free (common sense tells us so).

3. Therefore, God does not exist.

The second atheist argument we might label "the Good God Argument":

> If Brahmā is lord of the whole world and creator of the multitude of beings then why has he ordained misfortune in the world without making the whole world happy, or for what purpose has he made the world full of injustice, deceit, falsehood, and conceit; or the lord of beings is evil in that he ordained injustice when there could have been justice.[109]

There are probably two arguments buried in the Good God Argument, and one of them looks like this, a version of the familiar theological problem of evil:

1. If God exists (as an all-good and all-powerful being) then there should be happiness and justice.

2. But there is unhappiness and injustice (common sense tells us so).

3. Therefore, God does not exist.

From these two arguments we can conclude that Hīnayāna is an atheistic religion. However, a problem emerges with respect to this atheism, a problem that parallels the problem of naturalism dealt with previously.

2. The Problem of Atheism

The atheism of Hīnayāna appears *prima facie* to reject the Gods. And yet there is from time to time a great deal of God-talk within the religion's canonical, or authoritative, texts that must give us pause. If Buddha rejects the Gods, the problem of atheism points out, then why is there so much talk about the Gods? Unblushingly, Buddha is made to say:

> In former times, O monks, Sakka, the leader of the Gods, was admonishing the Gods of the Suite of the Thirty-three [the chief Gods], and on that occasion pronounced the following stanza....[110]

And there follows a pronouncement from Sakka about how great He is because He keeps all the fast days and the vows. If there are no Gods then what are Sakka and his thirty-three cohorts doing in the *Nikāya* text fasting and keeping vows?

What they're doing there is found in the answer that Buddha gives to the problem of atheism. The Gods are there to be used by Buddha to point out that the arhats and saints are superior to the Gods in every respect. These are not "Gods" at all, but gods, beings serving time in heaven for past good deeds, and not necessarily *their own* past good deeds, either, as we shall see when we discuss anātman and rebirth, below.

If heaven is a purely naturalistic extension of the world, as we argued previously, then the gods are purely naturalistic extensions of humans. Buddha says of Sakka:

> Because Sakka, the leader of the Gods, O monks, is not released from birth, old age, death, sorrow, lamentation, misery, grief, and despair; in short he is not released from misery.[111]

Sakka, as it turns out, is a rather inferior extension of man, for Sakka must eventually be reborn as man, a human being, if he is to attain enlightenment.

Buddha concludes by contrasting the condition of the monks to Sakka's condition:

> But that monk, O monks, who is a saint, who

> has lost all depravity, who has led the holy life, who has done what it behooved him to do, who has laid aside the burden, who has achieved the supreme good, who has destroyed every fetter that binds him to existence, who is released by perfect knowledge, such a monk, O monks, ... is released from misery.[112]

These "Gods", to reiterate, are not Gods but "gods"; consequently, the problem of atheism with respect to these gods is answered. That is to say, the question of "atheism" is ambiguous: For Hīnayāna is atheistic with respect to the Gods, but it is theistic with respect to the gods. Therefore, theoretical atheism with respect to the Gods tends to dominate Hīnayāna Buddhism, just as ritual atheism dominated Vedism, and metaphysical atheism dominated Upaniṣadic Hinduism.

At the center of this religion, with its naturalism and atheism, stands, not heaven or the Gods, then, but man, and it is to the subject of man that we now turn for the third characteristic tendency of Hīnayāna.

3. Anthropocentrism

Hīnayāna Buddhism tends to be a human- or man-centered religion. It is man-centered because it is suffering-centered and liberation-centered, and only man, as we have said, is capable of both suffering *and* liberation.

The ages-long controversy between man-centered philosophies and God-centered philosophies can be nicely illustrated by a story about Harvard College from the year 1905. In that year Harvard had constructed a new building off the Yard called "Emerson Hall." It was to house the Department of Philosophy, then one of the most prestigious such Departments in the world. The Board of Overseers of Harvard College and its president, Charles William Eliot, thought that it would be fitting if a motto or epigraph epitomizing philosophy could be carved in the frieze that ran along the front and top of the new building. It requested that the Department of Philosophy suggest such a motto.

The Department deliberated and brought forth what they considered a quotation worthy of the discipline, the Department and the College. The quotation they chose was taken from Protagoras, the great sophist philosopher of 5th century B.C.E. Greece, and it was his justifiably famous claim, "Man is the measure of all things." They forwarded their choice to the Board and, the story goes, it was promptly rejected by President Eliot.

Instead the Board chose their own motto of what they believed ought to epitomize the philosophic enterprise. The quotation they chose comes from the book of Psalms in the *Old Testament* and it was, "What is man that Thou art mindful of him."[113] Today, if you journey to Harvard and peep beneath the lush ivy covering the frieze on the front of Emerson Hall, you would see there, still, the words of the psalmist and President Eliot, carved in eternal stone.

The legend about Emerson Hall's motto illustrates very clearly two views about philosophy and two views about life. Let's call the first, illustrated by the quotation from Protagoras, the anthropocentric view; and let's call the second, illustrated by the quotation from the *Bible*, the theocentric view. It is, of course, the former, the anthropocentric view, which lies at the heart of Hīnayāna religion; and it is the latter, the theocentric view, which, with a few alterations in the interpretation of *theos*, lies at the heart of Mahāyāna religion.

To begin with, Gautama, the future Buddha, was the measure of all things for the Hīnayāna Buddhists. Gautama, the man, had discovered the cause of suffering and this man had found a way to stop that suffering. Gautama, the man, had found a way to peace and tranquility for other human beings. That way involved no supernatural or theistic elements. It lay wholly within the power of every person to follow that way and become what Gautama subsequently became.

Thus the center of the religion is man, suffering man, knowing man, self-conquering man. It is, as the Buddha has said, a rare and wonderful thing to be born a man, for to gain a birth as man is hard, indeed. Recall Aśoka's concern for the people of his kingdom in the 13th rock inscription. And here is the Pāli *Dhammapada* on the subject of man:

> If one man conquer in battle a thousand times a thousand men, and if another conquer himself, he is the greatest of conquerors.
>
> One's own self conquered is better than all other people; not even a god, a divine Gandharva not evil Māra, nor Brahmā could change into defeat the victory of a man who has vanquished himself, and always lives under restraint.

The author continues:

> If a man for a hundred years sacrifice month by month with a thousand sacrifices, and if he but for one moment pay homage to a man whose soul is grounded in true knowledge, better is that homage than a sacrifice for a hundred years.

And concludes:

> If a man for a hundred years worship Lord Agni in the forest, and if he but for one moment pay homage to a man whose soul is grounded in true knowledge, better is that homage than sacrifice for a hundred years.[114]

Ultimately, it is left to each person to measure Buddha's words. The measuring can only be done by each person, alone and, ultimately, unaided: "Ānanda", Buddha cries out during his final days on earth, "be a lamp unto yourself, be a refuge unto yourself; seek not any outside help in this matter."[115] However, a puzzle with the anthropocentric view emerges and we shall deal with it next.

3. The Problem of Anthropocentrism

The anthropocentrism of Hīnayāna can be interpreted in two quite distinct ways. Who is this man that stands at the center of the anthropocentric view? If it is me and me alone, as Southern Buddhism seems to hold, then we have an egocentric view of man and religion; if it is other persons and not me then we have an altruistic view of man and religion. The former view would appear to put a Buddhist ethics of compassion and love for others into some jeopardy; while the latter would appear to put a religion of self-enlightenment and personal salvation into some jeopardy. Who do I serve? Myself first (the egocentric view) or others first (the altruistic view)?

The egocentric view is often attributed to Hīnayāna by the Mahāyāna; in fact, it is the principal reason that the Mahāyāna have hung the unflattering appellation "hīnayāna", or "little vehicle", i.e. "the narrow, selfish way", onto the Southern Buddhist tradition. And many texts on Buddhism still refer to modern Theravāda Buddhism as "the Hīnayāna Buddhist religion", an epithet which 20th century Theravādins strongly resent (how would you like to belong to the "little vehicle"?).

The reason for the attribution and reference is not difficult to discover: The Hīnayāna arhat seeks, the critics say, his own salvation first and foremost, while the Mahāyāna seeks to put off his own salvation until as many as possible, all humanity if necessary, have or has been saved by his insights; only then does the Mahāyāna Buddhist, i.e. the so-called "bodhisattva", as this universal Savior is called, enter into nirvāṇa, having carried all mankind with him or her in the mahāyāna, "the great vehicle."

We shall return shortly to this difference between the arhat ideal and the Bodhisattva ideal of Hīnayāna and the Mahāyāna Buddhism, respectively. But for now we are still stuck with the problem of anthropocentrism, viz., the claim that Hīnayāna is egocentric in nature and not likely to produce the kind of sympathetic and compassionate arhat that Buddhist ethics (or any ethics) would seem to demand. For how, one might well ask, can a person who is thinking of saving only himself possibly be moral?

The problem of anthropocentrism may rest on a simple confusion between a religious goal, i.e. metaphysical self-transformation, and a moral goal, i.e. the production of good karma for the sake of a happier and more peaceful existence in this life and for the sake of a better birth in the next. If this distinction is kept in mind then the Hīnayāna might answer the problem by claiming that what the arhat, or the potential arhat, does morally could constitute an altruistic ethics, and that what the arhat does religiously could constitute an egoistic religion, and the two are quite separate. Only when one mixes the moral and the religious ends and means with one another is the problem of anthropocentrism generated.

On this view, the moral life is merely a propaedeutic, a necessary condition, for enlightenment, i.e. being good is one prerequisite to nirvāṇa, but it is not a sufficient condition for enlightenment, i.e. being good will not alone and by itself lead to nirvāṇa, as we have seen.

The noble eightfold path provides ethical rules but it also advocates meditation which is the essence of the way, or yoga, to nirvāṇa. One might say, in conclusion, that meditation is easier if one's moral house is in order rather than in disorder. Hence, egocentric ethics involving moral duties to oneself (recall the rules of the Saṅgha), as well as the altruistic ethics involving moral duties to others (recall the first five injunctions of the noble eightfold path), are both necessary ethical preliminaries for the would-be arhat.

Here is an example of that altruistic ethics. It is the very moving story from the Vinaya of Buddha's moral injunction to tend the sick:

> Now at that time a certain brother was suffering from dysentery and lay where he had fallen down in his own excrements... [The Buddha with Ānanda comes to that brother's lodging]. Now the Exalted One saw that brother lying where he had fallen in his own excrements, and seeing him he went towards him, came to him and said:
>
> 'Brother, what ails you?'
> 'I have dysentery, Lord.'
> 'But is there anyone taking care of you, brother?
> 'No, Lord.'
> 'Why is it, brother, that the brethren do not take care of you?'
> 'I am useless to the brethren, Lord; therefore the brethren do not care for me.'
> Then the Exalted One said to the venerable Ānanda: 'Go you, Ānanda, and fetch water. We will wash this brother.'
> 'Yes, Lord,' replied the venerable Ānanda to the Exalted One...[And the water is fetched and poured and they wash the brother and lay him on a bed. The Buddha leaves and calls the Order of Brethren together]
> 'Brethren, is there in such and such a

> lodging a brother who is sick?'
> 'There is, Lord.'
> 'And what ails that brother?'
> 'Lord, that brother has dysentery.'
> 'But, brethren, is there anyone taking care of him?'
> 'No, Lord.'
> 'Why not? Why do not the brethren take care of him?'
> 'That brother is useless to the brethren, Lord. That is why the brethren do not take care of him.'
> 'Brethren, you have no mother and no father to take care of you. If you will not take care of each other, who else, I ask, will do so? Brethren, he who would wait on me, let him wait on the sick.'[116]

There need be no problem of anthropocentrism, therefore, because Pāli Buddhism advocates an altruistic ethics as a preliminary to its egocentric religion.

We turn next to the personification of that egocentric religion in the ideal of the arhat.

4. The Arhat Ideal

Hīnayāna Buddhism upholds the ideal of the arhat. He is, as his name connotes, the one who has "slain the foe (desire)", or the one who is "worthy." The name also denotes those who have achieved the final goal of enlightenment. In the arhat all wrong views, all becoming, all ignorance and all desire have gone forever. This perfected one is aptly described as follows:

> He exerted himself, he strove and struggled, and thus he realized that this circle of 'Birth-and-Death', with its 'Five Constituents' (Skandhas) is in constant flux. He rejected all the conditions of existence which are brought about by a compound of conditions, since it is their nature to decay and crumble away, to change and to be destroyed. He abandoned all the 'defilements' and won Arhatship. ...Gold and a clod of earth were the same to him. The sky and the palm of his hand were the same to him... He became averse to worldly gain

and honor, and he became worthy of being honoured, saluted and revered by the Devas (gods), including Indra, Vishnu and Krishna.[117]

Arhatship, however, lies at the end of a series of stages leading to perfection. One doesn't leap from ignorance to enlightenment in one blink; instead there is a continuum composed of four stages in the Hīnayāna path to liberation (the Mahāyāna, in defending the Bodhisattva ideal, will complicate this continuum by adding several additional stages of its own). The four stages consist of, first, the stage of the stream-enterer, srotāpatti (Pāli sotāpatti), represented by the novice monk who joins the Saṅgha and leads a holy life. By eradicating the three false beliefs, viz., belief in one's self as eternal, belief in skepticism, and the belief in superstitious rites, one becomes a stream-enterer and advances toward the second stage.

Second, the once-returner stage, sakṛdāgāmin (Pāli sakadāgāmi), represented by the monk who will return only one more time in his next life at which time he will receive enlightenment and arhatship. By eradicating the sins of lust, hatred and delusion in this life, one becomes a once-returner and advances toward the third stage.

Third, the non-returner stage, anāgāmin (Pāli anāgāmi), represented by the monk who will never be born again into this world. By eradicating all intellectual and emotional impurities one becomes a non-returner and advances toward the fourth stage.

Fourth, the arhat is one who is fully enlightened; he is one who has 'laid down the burden of desire.' Buddha asks, " And what, brethren, is "the laying down of the burden?" and then replies to his own question:

> It is the utter passionless ceasing of craving, the giving up of craving, the renouncing of, the release from, the absence of longing for this craving. That, brethren, is called "the laying down of the burden."[118]

The arhat stage becomes the idealized goal of all Southern Buddhists.

In response to this idealization the question arose, How does the arhat differ from the Buddha? The question opens the way for proclaiming either that there is no difference, as early Hīnayāna seems to have taught, or that Buddha is a very special kind of arhat, even a divine Being, a God in the Hindu or Christian sense of that term. Hīnayāna will later argue that arhats are destined for Buddhahood and that Buddha was a very special kind of arhat, but not a God, to be sure, and yet not a mere arhat either. The Pāli texts thus come to specify certain characteristics of the Buddha that are not characteristics of the arhat; after all, Buddha alone found the way, and then passed on to others his knowledge of it, and this took special talents, indeed.

But the predominant view in Southern Buddhism remains that Buddha was a man and that all men and women are destined for arhatship and Buddhahood, however one cares to distinguish the two. With this admission, that Buddha was really a special kind of arhat, the way was then opened, as the Mahāyāna discovered, for the glorification of, together with the subsequent divinization of, the historical Buddha. However, a problem emerges with respect to the arhat ideal and we shall deal with it next.

4. The Problem of the Arhat Ideal

The arhat ideal of Hīnayāna is a strange ideal, to be sure. The description of the desireless arhat is not unlike the Hindu ideal of the jīvanmukta, one who is liberated while still alive. The Hindu jīvanmukta is nicely described in the *Bhagavad Gītā*, and what the *Gītā* says about the jīvanmukta is not unlike what the Pāli texts seem to be saying about the arhat; and if there is a problem with the jīvanmukta then there is also a problem with the arhat. Here's a description of the jīvanmukta from the *Bhagavad Gītā*:

> He who bears no ill-will to any being, who is friendly and merciful, who is without selfishness and egoism, indifferent to pain and pleasure, patient;
>
> He who does not make sorrow for the world, and whom the world, in turn, does not make sorrowful, who is freed from the anxiety of joy, intolerance and fear....

> He who...abides in the Ātman, who values a lump of earth, a stone and a piece of gold equally, who is the same to the loved and the unloved, who is steadfast, and to whom both blame and praise of himself are equal.
>
> He who is the same in honor and dishonor, and the same to friend and enemy, and who has abandoned the starting of all actions....[119]

A nice person; maybe someone you'd want for a friend. But there is more, and here is where the problem arises:

> He who wants nothing, ...unconcerned and untroubled, who has renounced all undertakings....
>
> He who is neither rejoiceful nor depressed, neither grieves nor desires, renouncing both good and evil....
>
> He who takes praise and blame indifferently, who is restrained in speech, contented with whatever happens....[120]

And now we might begin to wonder just what kind of human being, or what kind of ideal, we have. If the jīvanmukta has crossed over the stream of desire, if he is a being who wants nothing, who has renounced all startings of actions, who has renounced both good and evil, and who is content with whatever happens, then just what kind of human being is he? Isn't the jīvanmukta merely a withdrawn and passive blob? And, if he is, then so is the arhat. Therefore, isn't the idealization of the arhat an idealization of inert quietism, if not pathological introversion? If this is the ideal and the goal of Southern Buddhism then who needs it?

The problem of the arhat ideal comes down to appraising the life of an individual in whom the flame of desire has been extinguished. To meet the problem of the arhat ideal two defenses might be offered. First, the Hīnayāna might say that it is not true that all desires have been extinguished in the arhat, but rather that all lusts and karma-producing cravings have been extinguished, and that is all. This first defense goes on to state that absolute quietism does not result from such extinguishing but only a relative quietism such that all egomaniacal drives that previously resulted from lust must have been stopped. And the contentment with whatever happens is a tranquility and peacefulness that comes from such stoppage. No actions are produced or initiated that have ego lustings and desire as their cause. That does not necessarily mean that one doesn't eat food, eliminate wastes or put on clothes. Rather, these actions are no longer actions directed by or driven by unrequited lust and desire. "Desire" remains, but it is a desire for the needs, the true needs, not the artificial, pretentious and unreasonable needs, of the body. Consequently, the arhat ideal is not an idealization of pathologial passivity and quietism. Thus the first defense.

Second, the Hīnayāna might say that it is true that all desires have been extinguished such that even the beneficial "desires", present in the first defense, are absent. But the body goes on working and acting, nonetheless. Recall Buddha's use of the simile of the potter's wheel to make this same point. A potter turns his wheel with his foot in order to throw his pots. When he takes his foot off the wheel, the wheel turns for a while by sheer momentum from the original foot-force applied to it. Nirvāṇa is like the removing of the foot-force from the wheel of life. But uncompensated karma, the karma that remains to be rewarded or punished, keeps the body moving, keeps the agent acting, even though, strictly speaking, there is no longer any desiring agent or actor or ego there to do the initiating. The momentum of this remaining karma keeps the actions going as if directed by will and desire, but in reality that is only an appearance. There is nobody there because desire has been totally extinguished. But, and this is the point, actions continue. The arhat is not an inert mass, a passive blob.

We will return to the subjects of desire and nirvāṇa shortly; for the moment I leave the reader to mull over these two defenses as solutions to the problem of the arhat.

We turn next to the fifth characteristic of Hīnayāna Buddhism, its practicality.

5. Pragmatism

Hīnayāna Buddhism, and here it stands in complete agreement with Mahāyāna Buddhism, tends to believe in the inherent practicality, or utility, of the Buddhist insight in relation to suffering, its cause and its stoppage. Buddhism is empirically pragmatic in the sense that all Buddhists believe that the usefulness and, therefore, the truth of the doctrines can be tested and effectively confirmed or verified right now, right here, in one's own lifetime.

The pragmatic approach is best exemplified by a story taken from the *Majjhima-Nikāya*. Buddha has been asked a number of speculative questions by a disciple, Māluṅkyāputta, about whether the world is eternal or not, whether the world is finite or infinite, whether the soul and body are identical or not, and whether the arhats exist after death or not. Buddha refuses to answer any of the questions and in the context of this refusal he resorts to the following analogy:

> It is as if, Māluṅkyāputta, a man who had been wounded by an arrow thickly smeared with poison, and his friends and companions, his relatives and kinsfolk, were to procure for him a physician or surgeon; and the sick man were to say, 'I will not have this arrow taken out until I have learnt whether the man who wounded me belonged to the warrior caste, or to the Brahman caste, or to the agricultural caste, or to the menial caste.'
>
> Or again he were to say, 'I will not have this arrow taken out until I have learnt the name of the man who wounded me, to what clan he belongs... whether the man was tall, short, or of middle height... was black, or dusky, or of yellow skin... whether the bow string which wounded me was made from swallow-wort, or bamboo, or sinew, or from milkweed... whether the shaft which wounded me was a kaccha or a ropima... whether... it was feathered from the wings of a vulture, or of a heron, of a falcon, or of a peacock...[121]

Buddha goes on to explain that in the same way that this wounded and dying man will not be cured by answering the questions that he poses, in the same way the religious life does not depend on answers to the theoretical and philosophical questions posed by Mālunkyāputta. Buddha explains that he, himself, has not dealt with those questions and for a very practical reason:

> Because Mālunkyāputta, this profits not, nor has to do with the fundamentals of religion, or tends to aversion, absence of passion, cessation, quiescence, the supernatural faculties, supreme wisdom, and Nirvāṇa; therefore have I not elucidated it.[122]

Finally, Buddha explains why he has dealt with the questions and topics that he has, viz., because such elucidations profit a man:

> Misery, Mālunkyāputta, have I elucidated; the orgin of misery have I elucidated; the cessation of misery have I elucidated; and the path leading to the cessation of misery have I elucidated.

Buddha has just mentioned, of course, the four noble truths, and he has claimed that they are all that he has ever taught. He continues,

> And why, Mālunkyāputta, have I elucidated this? Because Mālunkyāputta, this does profit, [it] has to do with the fundamentals of religion, and tends [to produce or lead to] aversion, absence of passion, cessation, quiescence, knowledge, supreme wisdom, and Nirvāṇa; therefore I have elucidated it.[123]

In other words, the doctrine that is taught, the four noble truths, is taught because it profits, it works, it leads to beneficial results for the practicer.

Buddhism is practical in a double sense, then, for it recommends practical action *now* for stopping suffering, and it also allows each devotee to test out the recommended practical action for himself. As the mythic theory of truth would put it: If the practical advice works, if it produces the useful result of nirvāṇa, then the Buddhist techniques are true or right or good. Since Buddhism does lead to nirvāṇa, the argument concludes, Buddhism is practical and useful and, therefore, true.[124] However, a problem emerges with respect to pragmatism and we turn to it next.

5. The Problem of Pragmatism

Buddhist pragmatism as a way of deriving (or identifying) truth from (or with) practicality, runs into the same problem that any pragmatic theory of truth encounters. Thus it might be extremely useful for me to believe the most outrageous things imaginable, e.g. that Gautama Buddha was a lady, that Hindus are inferior, that God does not hear the prayers of heretics, that this book is beautifully written, and so on. Now any theory that leads to absurdities, and the above all seem patently absurd, must be absurd.

The pragmatist, it would seem, must be extremely wary in conjoining usefulness with truth lest he fall into absurdity. For it turns out, as a little consideration will plainly show, that the dimensions of truth are far wider than the unidimensional theory of pragmatism might lead us to believe.

Further, the pragmatic theory says that B (the doctrine of Buddhism) is true if and only if believing or accepting B leads to fruitful, useful or practical consequences for the believer. But if there are many B's, and we have at least two, Hīnayāna and Mahāyāna, then according to the above stipulative definition both B's must be true. But each B, as we shall see, contradicts the other B in several places with respect to the doctrine. So, on the pragmatic theory of truth, both a doctrine and its contradictory are true, and that conclusion is also patently absurd.

Still further, suppose I try B or use B or believe B and I never achieve nirvāṇa, or peace and tranquility. Does that make B false? Suppose I am a stream-enterer or a once-returner. Then we know that in this life I'll not reach nirvāṇa. Therefore, B will not be useful to me in this life, at least as far as reaching nirvāṇa in this life is concerned. Are we then to conclude that B is false in this life but that it may be true in another life? That conclusion also seems plainly absurd.

Finally, if there is no cash-value, no practical nirvāṇic pay-off in this life, but I feel a bit more tranquil and peaceful believing B than I did before I believed B, then is B a *bit more* true for me than it was previously. To end up, as we must, speaking of degrees of truth in relation to Buddhism must seem an absurdity and a travesty not only to Buddhism but to our common sense views of truth, as well. The problem of pragmatism, then, would seem to entail several puzzles that stand in need of theoretic solutions, if one cares to pause in one's arrow-pulling or elephant-examining long enough to take them up. I leave this task, once again, to the reader's ingenuity.

We turn now to the sixth characteristic of Hīnayāna Buddhism and to a discussion of nirvāṇa as the goal of religious endeavors.

6. Nirvāṇa

Hīnayāna Buddhism believes in the reality and possibility of nirvāṇa (Pāli nibbāna) a highly interesting, but also extremely complicated, concept, as we shall see. From a phenomenological, i.e. from a personal and experiential, point of view nirvāṇa stands within the framework of the philosophies of utopia, i.e. it denotes a utopia and it connotes a utopian condition. "Utopia" is a Greek word that in one of its meanings (*ou-topos*, "no place") connotes a state or condition that does not (yet) exist; in another of its meanings (*eu-topos*, "best place") it connotes a state or condition of the highest and finest order. Nirvāṇa, in the history of Buddhism, has come to mean both of these states or conditions, i.e. a best place that is (as yet) no place. Now what does this mean?

Utopias have always fascinated man and one has only to look at the utopian literature in both the West and the East in order to realize the intensity and the depth of his fascination. Utopian literature arises during times of great political, social, economic and religious turmoil. The utopianist, the utopian dreamer or sage, envisions a happier state for man and then transmits this vision to others. This vision may be that of an ideal political state in which case we have a political utopia as in Plato's great vision called *Republic*. Or the transmitted vision may be that of an ideal economically based state as in Karl Marx's great vision of the proletarian or communist utopia. Or the vision may be of a religious utopia as in St. John's vision of heaven in the book of *Revelation* in the *Bible*.

All of these examples of utopias are grounded, however, in three necessary conditions; that is to say, in order to have a utopia of whatever variety, i.e. political, economic or religious, three conditions, it would seem, would have to be present: First, a time of suffering or trouble must above all be present. If one is already living in a cultural paradise, there is no need to desire anything to supercede it. It is the time of suffering that pushes one into hoping for and then envisioning something better, i.e. a utopia.

Second, a way out of that trouble must be envisioned, and that way out must be better, in some sense, than the condition one is now in. A sufferer who merely envisioned more suffering and produced an imagined culture embodying more of the same suffering (think on Dante's *Inferno*) could not be said to have produced a utopia. Only a promised way out, with obvious reasons demonstrating why it is a better way out, could be considered a utopia (think on Dante's *Paradiso*).

Third, and finally, the way out of the suffering, i.e. the utopia, must be an "ideal" in two senses of that word: On the one hand, the utopia must be the best conceivable, it must really solve the problem of suffering; and, on the other, it must be an idea only, it cannot exist physically, i.e. it cannot exist in this world. The second meaning of "ideal" is extremely important here, for it serves to underscore the purely imaginary, theoretical and intellectual, status of the utopia and points out that if utopias became actualized in space and time, if any ever could, they would cease to be utopias. If Plato's political state, or Marx's economic state, or St. John's heavenly state were ever actualized, they would cease to be utopias: A Utopia is a *best* place that is *no* place.

The Buddhist concept of nirvāṇa satisfies all three of these necessary conditions for a utopia. One has merely to look to the four noble truths in order to find the first two necessary conditions, viz., suffering and a way out of the suffering. The third condition, the idealness of the utopia, is not stated there but comes out of the later literature of Buddhism. A discussion of that later literature will serve to get us into the topic of the present section, nirvāṇa.

There are two kinds of utopias, ideal states or conditions, of which one might speak: Internal utopias and external utopias. Internal utopias are characterized by the absence of suffering and are brought about by changes within the individual sufferer. Psychoanalysis and most of the world's religions have internal utopias as their goal. External utopias are characterized by the absence of suffering and are brought about by changes external to the individual sufferer. The political and economic systems of Plato and the Marxists have external utopias as their goal.

The difference between internal and external utopias is more a matter of a stress on the means to internal states or external states than it is a matter of the internal states or the external states, themselves. After all, suffering itself is an internal condition, and since both internal as well as external utopias aim to end this suffering, both are intent on producing certain kinds of internal states. Internal utopias hope to achieve this end by changing the individual first; while external utopias hope to achieve this end by changing society first. Since all utopian schemes ultimately come down to the production of internal states, this kind of utopia will be our chief concern. That is to say, in place of looking at Buddhist (Aśokan) political states, or at the Saṅgha, itself, as a microcosm of an external utopia, we shall concentrate on internal utopias, for this is where nirvāṇa lies.

Internal utopians have as their motto, "You are the cause of suffering; hence, if you want to end that suffering then you must change yourself." The original Buddhism set forth by Buddha would seem to have argued in this way, and Hīnayāna and modern Theravāda Buddhism follow this original doctrine quite closely. Though Buddha does not seem to have specifically stressed nirvāṇa as the goal, in fact, we don't know if he even used the word at all, the concept, i.e. the idea but not necessarily the word, seems to have been directly intended by him in his earliest sermons.

Mahāyāna Buddhism, on the other hand, while it regards nirvāṇa as the ultimate goal, is content, as we shall see, to play down this ultimate goal in favor of more penultimate goals, viz., one's future life as a Bodhisattva and/or a future existence in heaven.

We have already seen that Buddha rejected a negative internal utopia as a viable solution to the problem of suffering. For Buddha, liberation without peace and tranquility was not the goal he pursued. He seems to have held that such a negative goal was attainable, however. One could experience an absence of suffering but feel no peace or tranquility, i.e. feel nothing at all but merely an absence of all feeling. Dreamless sleep, as the *Upaniṣads* have pointed out, would be such a state, as was the state of nothingness of Āḷāra Kalama: And those states are rejected as the goal by at least one *Upaniṣad* and by the Buddha.

In the Hindu *Chāndogya Upaniṣad*, the God Indra comes to Lord Prajāpati for instruction on the true nature of reality and how to find it, i.e. on how to reach mokṣa, the Upaniṣadic utopia. Prajāpati teaches that reality is to be found through three stages of descent: The first stage is waking consciousness; the second stage is dreaming consciousness; and the third stage is the wholly negative stage of dreamless sleep. Indra experiences and then rejects each of the three, in turn, as unacceptable utopias. In a panic, he cries out against the third: If dreamless sleep is to be identified with the true Self then I would be "like one who has gone to annihilation. I see nothing enjoyable in this."[125]

"Nothing enjoyable," indeed, where there is no person to do the enjoying and where the object of the search is void and empty. The utopia of this *Upaniṣad* would seem to end in nothingness.

But Prajāpati then instructs Indra further and carries Indra, the *Chāndogya* and Hinduism out of what threatened to become philosophic nihilism. In a fourth stage, the Self is shown to be capable of experiencing enjoyment, i.e. bliss or ānanda.[126] Therefore, since the essence of Self is enjoyment, the final stage of mokṣa will be a state that manifests that essence: The utopia of mokṣa is enjoyment, just as, later, nirvāṇa is enjoyment, viz., the manifestation of peace and tranquility, at least to the Buddha.

But Hīnayāna Buddhism would seem to have rejected both the Upaniṣadic characterization of enlightenment and Buddha's characterization of it, as well. The Upaniṣadic characterization would be rejected because for Hīnayāna, as we shall see, there is no self or person to experience anything; and the Buddha's notion of enlightenment would have to be rejected because where there is no self there could never be an enjoyer of peace and tranquility.

There has been much squabbling over the centuries within Buddhism and among Buddhologists over the interpretation of nirvāṇa. The squabbling centers precisely around the question of the essential nature of nirvāṇa as either positive or negative, as personal bliss or self-annihilation. Guy Welbon in his *The Buddhist Nirvāṇa and Its Western Interpreters* has catalogued the contrary and contradictory views taken with respect to nirvāṇa, views held by such eminent Indologists as H.T. Colebrooke, Eugene Burnouf, Jules Barthelemy Saint Hilare, F. Max Müller, T.W. Rhys Davids, Th. Stcherbatsky, Arthur Berriedale Keith and Louis de La Vallée Poussin. What the various negative and positive interpretations give us, Welbon observes, is really a measure of each scholar's own insight into Buddhism:

> ...their evaluations, never based exclusively on philosophical and historico-critical considerations, in every instance reflect the individual scholar's own personal commitment, his *sitz im leben*, and his understanding of the essence of Buddhism.

Welbon concludes:

> The response to the question of nirvāṇa's meaning is at the same time an answer more or less complete to all questions about Buddhism.[127]

I would only remark that if Welbon is correct then nirvāṇa can legitimately be seen as both a positive as well as a negative concept, and that it is an important touchstone by which to judge the interpreters' own attitudes towards Buddhism in general.

Several Buddhists take exception to the characterization of nirvāṇa as either negative or positive. Thus a contemporary Theravāda bhikkhu (monk), the Venerable Walpola Rahula, writes:

> Because Nirvāṇa is thus expressed in negative terms, there are many who have got

> a wrong notion that it is negative, and expresses self-annihilation. Nirvāṇa is definitely no annihilation of self, because there is no self to annihilate. If at all, it is the annihilation of the illusion, of the false idea of self.

Perhaps that's all true, but illusions *qua* illusions are held just as fanatically as veridical interpretations of the world. And any removal of such hard illusions must be seen as negative despite what Rahula goes on to say:

> It is incorrect to say that Nirvāṇa is negative or positive. The idea of 'negative' and 'positive' are relative, and are within the realm of duality. These terms cannot be applied to Nirvāṇa, Absolute Truth, which is beyond duality and relativity.[128]

'Beyond' or not, people will, Buddhists among them, in their more communicative moments, continue to speak about the unspeakable. All that philosophy can do is to make sure that the talk, the bickering and the squabbling included, is as consistent and meaningful as possible. I take it that this is precisely what Rahula, himself, is bent upon in his own writings, beyondness, duality and relativity, and upper case initial letters to the contrary notwithstanding.

But, however Buddha's early attitude towards nirvāṇa may have gone, Hīnayāna Buddhism does, indeed, seem to stress negative nirvāṇa to the exclusion of positive nirvāṇa; and this negative interpretation of nirvāṇa follows quite consistently from the atheism and the anātman doctrines of Hīnayāna.

"Nirvāṇa" means literally "blown-out." The analogy most frequently employed is that of the blowing out of the flame of a candle, thereby making it impossible for other candles or fires to be started from this flame. The flame is the flame of desire which, once extinguished, can never rise again. In the famous Pāli text called "the Fire Sermon" Buddha tells his disciples:

> Everything, brethren, is on fire.... The eye...is on fire, visible objects are on fire, the faculty of the eye [for perceiving] is on fire, [impressions

> received by] the eye are on fire, and also the sensation, whether pleasant or unpleasant or both...is on fire. With what is it on fire? With the fire of passion, of hate, of illusion, is it on fire, with birth, old age, death, grief, lamentation, suffering, sorrow, and despair.

Buddha repeats this same scenario for the ear, the nose, the tongue and the body in general, together with the mind and pleasure and pain from the inner sense: All are afire. The way out of the fire is through indifference or aversion:

> The wise and noble disciple, brethren, perceiving this, is indifferent to the eyes, indifferent to visible objects. Indifferent to the faculty of the eye, indifferent to sensation, whether pleasant or unpleasant or both, which arises from the sense of sight.

And so on for indifference to the ear, nose and the other organs previously mentioned. Buddha concludes,

> And being indifferent he becomes free from passion, by absence of passion is he liberated, and when he is liberated the knowledge 'I am liberated' arises. Rebirth is destroyed, a religious life is lived, duty is done, and he knows there is nothing more for him in this state.[129]

There is no mention of the peace and tranquility that Buddha, himself, had previously sought in his early life. The utopia that this Pāli text does describe, however, lies in blowing out, once and forever, all of the flames of desire.

Hīnayāna tends to be chiefly and primarily concerned with interpreting nirvāṇa in negative terms, and we will have to wait until we reach Mahāyāna Buddhism to meet directly with positive nirvāṇa. However, as you might guess, a problem emerges with respect to nirvāṇa and we turn to it next.

6'. The Problem of Nirvāṇa

Nirvāṇa as conceived by the Southern Buddhists is a curious utopia, to be sure. But in speaking about nirvāṇa as a utopia or a goal or a result or as the effect of a cause, the Buddhists warn us to be wary. They themselves try to be extremely careful on this matter, pointing out that nirvāṇa is "unconditioned" and cannot, therefore, be the effect of any cause. If it were "conditioned," i.e. produced or brought into existence by prior efforts or causes or conditions, then, given the fact of anitya, nirvāṇa, like any other effect, or caused thing, could come to an end. In other words, unless the Buddhists can protect nirvāṇa in some way, e.g., by calling it "unconditioned," enlightened arhats could pop into and out of nirvāṇa just as one pops into and out of bed.

The Venerable Walpola Rahula writes, again:

> It is incorrect to think that Nirvāṇa is the natural result of the extinction of craving. Nirvāṇa is not the result of anything. If it would be a result, then it would be an effect produced by a cause. It would be *saṁkhata* 'produced' and 'conditioned.' Nirvāṇa is neither cause nor effect. It is beyond cause and effect.

Rahula continues by drawing an analogy with truth:

> Truth is not a result nor an effect. It is not produced like a mystic, spiritual, mental state, such as *dhayāna* or *samādhi*. TRUTH IS. NIRVĀṆA IS. The only thing you can do is to see it, to realize it. There is a path leading to the realization of Nirvāṇa. But Nirvāṇa is not the result of this path.[130]

This is orthodox Theravāda (modern Hīnayāna) doctrine, but I find the defense quibbling and obfuscating. "Quibbling" because it flies in the face even of Buddhist common sense where paths that lead to things, if followed, get you to those things; and that's all one wants to claim about nirvāṇa, viz., it's what happens after following a certain path. Rahula concludes:

> You may get to the mountain along a path, but the mountain is not the result, nor an effect of the path. You may see a light, but the light is not the result of your eyesight.[131]

I find this "obfuscating" because the analogy is misleading and the point is hopelessly lost. If one gets to the mountain along a path then the mountain-experience one subsequently gets is the result of following the path. What more could one want? Finally, the light is not the result of my eyesight, and it's surely misleading to assume that this is what anyone ever wanted to prove in the first place: All that is needed is to state that my seeing or experiencing the light is the result of my eyesight conjoined with light and several other necessary conditions being present and experienced under so-called "standard conditions".

But the problem of nirvāṇa centers not around the question "What is it?" so much as around the question, "Who needs it?" or better yet, "Who wants it?" Recall the story mentioned previously about Lord Prajāpati and his pupil, the young Vedic God, Indra. What panicked Indra was the realization that the penultimate stage of the Self was annihilation and nothingness. So to save Indra's panicked mind from this result, i.e. that the Self is nothing, Prajāpati tosses him a sop: The Self, Prajāpati says, is capable of feeling enjoyment when it resides thoroughly and completely in Itself.

But the Hīnayāna Buddhists, as we have seen, have rejected the Ātman and Its enjoyments, and they have heroically accepted the logical result of the No-thing-ness of the Self. And therein lies the problem of nirvāṇa: Who wants a philosophy that leads to self- or Self-annihilation? The Mahāyāna, as we shall see, revolt against this Suicidal metaphysics, but the Hīnayāna are stuck with it: Who, indeed, wants a religion that purchases the annulment of suffering at the price of their very selfhood? Well, the answer is, the Hīnayāna Buddhists do!

Could suffering ever be so great that suicide, or Suicide, in the metaphysical sense, is the only way out? But the question is wrongly stated, the Hīnayāna would say, for it begs the very point at issue. That point is that you can't lose something or kill something that was never there to begin with. You can't annihilate what you never had.

The problem of nirvāṇa from this practical point of view is no problem, therefore. But it might still remain a theoretical problem, for who wants to accept a religion that will try to take away and destroy my self? Like Indra, we don't wish the self to die, ever, and if Hīnayāna argues, however theoretically, that it was never there to begin with, then so much the worse for Hīnayāna.

This brings us back, once again, to the question about the purpose of religions, a path we have trod previously. It remains a fact that many millions of Buddhists have found this interpretation of nirvāṇa appealing, and perhaps their number and their enthusiasm for Southern Buddhism to this day is a sufficient answer to one aspect of the problem of nirvāṇa.

This conclusion brings us quite aptly to the seventh characteristic or tendency of Hīnayāna Buddhism, a discussion of meditation as the way to nirvāṇa.

7. Meditation

Hīnayāna Buddhism, following the doctrine of the noble eightfold path, generally believes that the way to nirvāṇa lies in the practice of meditation. It may seem superfluous to mention meditation as a characteristic of Hīnayāna since, as we have pointed out previously, the noble eightfold path has meditation as a part of that path and that path is accepted by both Hīnayāna and Mahāyāna. The reason for mentioning meditation, again, is merely to emphasize a significant difference in stress or tendencies that will become apparent between the two divisions of Buddhism. In order to call attention to this significant difference and its implications we treat meditation here as a distinct characteristic of Pāli Buddhism.

Concentration of the mind leads to four stages of meditation, or dhyāna (Pāli jhāna), where concentration is simply "intentness of meritorious thoughts." The *Aṅguttara-Nikāya* describes these levels or stages of dhyāna when Buddha says:

> Whenever, O monks, a monk, having isolated himself from sensual pleasures, having isolated himself from demeritorious traits, and still exercising reasoning, still exercising reflection, enters upon the first [meditation], which is produced by isolation

> and characterized by joy and happiness; when, through the subsidence of reasoning and reflection, and still retaining joy and happiness, he enters upon the second [meditation] which is an interior tranquilization and intentness of thoughts and is produced by concentration....

Having dealt with isolation and concentration Buddha goes on to the third and fourth levels of meditation:

> ...when through the paling of joy, indifferent, contemplative, conscious, and in the experience of bodily happiness...he enters upon the third [meditation]; when, through the abandonment of happiness, through the abandonment of misery, through the disappearance of all antecedent gladness and grief, he enters upon the fourth [meditation], which has neither misery nor happiness, but is contemplation as refined by indifference, this, O monks, is called the discipline in elevated concentration.[132]

Three points can be noted from this presentation of the four stages of meditation: First, as Buddha has said, "And moreover, O monks, I have taught the gradual cessation of karma."[133] In other words, these meditations do in fact form stages to the final release from all karma, from the threefold fires of lust, hatred and infatuation, from rebirth, and from the stream that constitutes individual existence; and this final release is, of course, nirvāṇa. This doctrine of gradual release, nirvāṇa by evolution (gradual change) rather than by revolution (rapid change) forms, indeed, the cornerstone of traditional Buddhism.

Second, these stages that lead gradually to nirvāṇa are characterized by certain recognizable, empirical signs whereby one can determine not only what stage one happens to be in now but also what stage one can anticipate next. The doctrine of the stages of meditation forms thereby a kind of psychological road map to guide the priests or monks on their metaphysical journey to nirvāṇa. For if one recognizes a certain internal joy and happiness then one knows that one is in the first stage; if one recognizes internal tranquility and intentness of thought then one knows that one is in the second stage; and, presumably, if one recognizes the paling and dissolution of joy and happiness, and if one then subsequently experiences, if it can be called that, neither misery nor happiness then one knows that one has reached the third and fourth stages, respectively.

I suggest that these recognitions of signs at these stages might be empirical for each stage could issue in behavior of a publicly observable sort. In other words, it is quite compatible with both the Hindu and the Buddhist traditions that metaphysical changes be accompanied by empirically observable behavior. The monk who is being liberated while living, or who has been liberated while living, could, theoretically, be singled out and identified as such.[134]

Third, and finally, the practice of the four stages of meditation must be carried out in isolation and an isolation that could even entail suicide (the ultimate isolation). The latter is beautifully illustrated by the story of Godhika the Elder as told by Buddhaghoṣa:

> This venerable man, while dwelling at Black Rock on the slopes of Isigili, being vigilant, austere, and strenuous, attained release for his mind in ecstatic meditation, and then, through the power of a disease which beset him, the trance [the meditation stage] was broken up.

Thus begins a curious tale of a monk's inability to maintain or reach nirvāṇa because of the intrusion of some unspecified disease.

After this first failure Godhika tries again and again to reach and then maintain that final stage but each time the disease interrupts the trance of the final release. Just before the seventh trial he resolves to enter once more into ecstatic meditation, reach the trance stage and then commit suicide before he can backslide for the seventh time:

> At the seventh time, he thought, "Six times has my trance been broken up, and doubtful is the fate of those who fail in trance. This time I will resort to the knife."

So taking up a razor he lies down on a couch, prepared to cut his windpipe. Reaching the appropriate stage of meditation he uses the knife and is successful. Buddha, commenting on the above story, speaks these words:

Thus, verily, the valiant act,
Nor think to hanker after life!
Lo! Godhika uproots desire,
And, dying, has Nirvāṇa gained.[135]

The story of Godhika the Elder is curious, primarily because it appears to condone suicide; and yet suicide is expressly forbidden by the Dharma. But, suicides apart, the story illustrates the attitude towards life that the seeker of nirvāṇa must be prepared to adopt: He must be willing to give up not only the desire for life, but life itself, in order to achieve his purpose; and that purpose, like the means to it, is, as we stated above, the ultimate isolation.

However, a problem emerges with respect to the isolation needed for meditation, and it is a problem that challenged the popularity and appeal of Hīnayāna Buddhism. We turn next to that problem.

7. The Problem of Meditation

The problem of meditation relates to the necessity for isolation in the practice of meditation. If meditation is the key to nirvāṇa, and if isolation from the world and ordinary life is necessary to meditation, then it follows that the place for meditation must be relatively isolated from the world and ordinary life, as well. This necessitates, then, either a solitary, or anchorite, existence in forests or caves for monkish aspirants, or else it demands a monastic life where the solitude of forest or caves can be duplicated. And this is probably one of the reasons for the development of the Saṅgha where aspirants, novices and adepts could practice meditation in isolation from the world and ordinary life.[136] Cave and forest proved to be generally unsatisfactory for nirvāṇa candidates, largely because the isolation could only be temporary and the need for food, alone, would sooner or later drive the candidate out of rocky retreat or leafy bower.

The monastery proved to be a happier solution for the monk but it also led to a problem. Hīnayāna

Buddhists appear to have adopted the attitude that nirvāṇa was only possible within a monastic community, and yet that community could not be too demanding on his time so as to deny the isolation necessary for meditation. A balance was struck, of course, between duties to and for the community, and the need for meditational isolation for candidates within it.

But in stressing that the only way to nirvāṇa lay within that balanced Saṅgha, the problem that we are investigating arose. For, if the only way to salvation lay in monastic life with monastic isolation then Southern Buddhism emerges as a monastic religion. And this is apparently what happened. Southern Buddhism, was, for the most part, isolated, spiritually and temperamentally, not geographically, from the lay society that was not part of that community. The life of the householder that was led by the overwhelming majority of the people was not the life that could guarantee nirvāṇa, because meditation outside the Saṅgha was impractical. Lay, i.e. non-monastic, Buddhism was, therefore, practically impossible under Hīnayāna Buddhism. Buddhism was meant only for those persons who had given up the life in the world and resorted to a Saṅgha.[137] And this is what we are calling "the problem of meditation."

To be sure, the monastery and the nunnery depended in great part on the financial, material and psychological support of the lay community. Without that support Buddhism would not last long in India nor in any other country for that matter. But the exclusive way of meditation to the goal of nirvāṇa led to a division between the monastic community and the lay community and it proved to be a difficult gap to bridge. With the introduction of alternative ways to enlightenment other than meditation within the Saṅgha that bridge was finally built but it would take Mahāyāna Buddhism to do the constructing. This concludes the problem of meditation and the apparently untoward conclusion for Hīnayāna Buddhism to which it led.

We turn next to a discussion of Anātman and the Hīnayāna denial of the self.

8. Anātmavāda

Hīnayāna Buddhism denies the reality of both the Self (Ātman) as an unchanging substance and the self (ātman) as an enduring personality; and this double denial is referred to as the view, or doctrine (vāda), of non-self, or anātman (Pāli anatta), i.e. anātmavāda. This denial of a Self or self follows logically from the anitya, or flux, doctrine discussed previously. The Hīnayāna must have reasoned that if everything is in flux then nothing remains the same from moment to moment; and if nothing remains the same from moment to moment then neither the Self of the *Upaniṣads* nor a self as an enduring ego or person through time can be real. Therefore the Self or self is non-existent and the anātman doctrine must be true.

In the *Aṅguttara-Nikāya* we find three fundamental dogmas of Buddhism being boldly propounded by a preaching Buddha, viz., the dogma of anitya, and the dogma of duḥkha which we have touched on briefly, above, and, third, the dogma of anātman. The order is significant, with the dogma of anitya coming first, for if anitya is true then the other two dogmas must necessarily be true:

> Whether Buddhas arise, O monks, or whether Buddhas do not arise, it remains a fact and the fixed and necessary constitution of being, that all its constituents are transitory. This fact a Buddha discovers and masters, and when he has discovered and mastered it, he announces, teaches, publishes, proclaims, discloses, minutely explains, and makes it clear, that *all the constituents of being are transitory*.
>
> Whether Buddhas arise, O monks, or whether Buddhas do not arise, it remains a fact and the fixed and necessary constitution of being, that all its constituents are misery. This fact a Buddha discovers and masters, and when he has discovered and mastered it, he announces, teaches, publishes, proclaims, discloses, minutely explains, and makes it clear, that *all the constituents of being are misery*.
>
> Whether Buddhas arise, O monks, or whether Buddhas do not arise, it remains a fact that the fixed and necessary constitution of being, that all its elements are lacking in a self. This fact a Buddha discovers and masters, and when he has discovered and

mastered it, he announces, teaches, publishes, proclaims, discloses, minutely explains, and makes it clear, that *all the elements of being are lacking in a self.*[138]

For the Southern Buddhists the dogma of anātman refers not only to a psychological self's impermanence, but to the impermanence and unreality of *any* substantial entity, including the self. The following subtle argument from the *Saṁyutta-Nikāya* brings out the wider application of the anātman doctrine.

Here, Buddha is, once again, preaching on the non-existence of the self, or any "real" entity that could be taken for a self, to his former five ascetic companions who had deserted him shortly before his enlightenment and who now return to him at Benares:

> And the Blessed One spoke to the five monks: The body (rūpa), monks, is *not* the *self* [i.e. it is not a real, permanent, imperishable substance standing behind phenomena]. If the body, monks, were the self, the body would not be subject to disease.... But since the body, monks, is not the self [a real entity], therefore the body is subject to disease....

In other words, if the body were a real or permanent entity then it would not be subject to pain and disease which are constituents of the unreal, the perishable and the changing.

The argument continues (in Pāli) as a dialogue as Buddha discusses the four other candidates for reality:

> Sensation or feeling (vedanā), monks, is not the self..., perception (saññā) is not the self..., the psycho-physical predispositions (sankhāras) are not the self..., consciousness (viññaṇa) is not the self.
>
> Now what do you think, monks; is the body permanent or perishable?
> It is perishable, Lord.
> And that which is perishable, does that cause pain or joy?
> It causes pain, Lord.
> And that which is perishable, painful,

subject to change, is it possible to regard that in this way? This is mine, this am I, this is myself?
That is impossible, Lord.
(Here follows the same argument with respect to sensation or feeling, perception, the predispositions, and consciousness as occurred above with respect to the body).[139]

Again, all five of the arguments have the form: If anything is real (permanent, unchanging, imperishable) then it is not subject to disease and would not cause pain. But the body, sensation, perception, the predispositions, and consciousness are all subject to disease and they do all cause pain. Therefore, the body, sensation, perception, etc., are not real, i.e. the body, etc., are not the self.

The metaphysical defense of anātman is grounded not only in the Sūtras, as above, but in two later Hīnayāna traditions, viz. the *Abhidharma* texts and the Sarvāstivāda school of philosophy, about which we shall have more to say shortly. It is from Sarvāstivāda and the *Abhidharma* texts that Hīnayāna borrowed much of the terminology that gave philosophical expression to its basic anātman view.

Briefly, later Sarvāstivāda will state that the phenomenal or experiencable world is composed of some seventy-five basic kinds of elemental moments called "dharmas." These dharmas, or moments of energy, exist in complete accord with the anitya doctrine by being in a constant state of change, themselves; but, even as they change, they can be organized into relatively stable patterns that, as patterns, would appear not to change. In our ignorance we believe, therefore, that physical objects, for example, do not change, though subsequently enlightened by wisdom we realize the truth of anitya and the fact that inexorable change is the central reality of all existence.

For example, this book is made up of several of the dharmas, viz., earth, air, water; the pattern they have assumed, the shape of the book, might lead us into believing that the book is permanent, unchanging and real. But closer examination of the object over several years can show us that we are wrong, e.g. the ink fades, the pages wither, the cover oxidizes and decays.

Modern quantum physics parallels this doctrine of dharmas with its own belief in micro-particles and waves, those transitory configurations of the space-time continuum that compose the subatomic universe of physical objects. Modern physics, like the metaphysical doctrine of anitya, instills humility by reminding us that our uncritical and simple views of the world are not always the way the world really is.

What the Hīnayāna calls "self" is, in one sense, a lot like this book. The sets, or aggregates, of dharmas that compose the "self" are called "bundles", "heaps", or *skandhas* (Pāli khandas). These skandhas, or sets, exist only momentarily and then cause new sets to come into existence as the earlier skandhas pass away. So in reality there is, and can be, no such entity as a self; there are only the five skandhas.

The word "self" is used, however, whenever the five skandhas are present. The five are: first, body, i.e. sense organs and the physical body of which they are parts; second, sensations, i.e. mental and physical stimulations that come about through contact with sense objects and thought objects; third, perceptions, i.e. judgments or interpretations that we make about what the senses, internal and external, have grasped which allow us to say, for example, "this hand is brown"; fourth, psychophysical predispositions and forces called "saṁskāras" (Pāli sankhāras), i.e. conscious and unconscious manifestations of will: *Conscious* willing would include such processes as desire, memory, attention, faith, courage, laziness, excitement, and the like; and unconscious willing would include a mysterious force called "prāpti", the force that holds the skandhas, in particular, and the dharmas, in general, into temporal, and seemingly permanent, patterns. Prāpti is a force about which we shall have more to say, shortly; unconscious willing also includes the life force and decay, and three curious forces that give meaning to syllables, words and sentences; the fifth and final skandha is consciousness, itself.[140]

For the Hinayana, then, what we take to be a self would seem to be merely a set of processes, giving rise, in turn, according to both the anitya doctrine and the doctrine of pratītyasamutpada, to other sets of processes, all in an orderly causal series.

For example, let's take the saṁskāra of desire and construct a causal chain of desires such that desire d_1 gives rise to desire d_2 which then gives rise to desire d_3, and so on, where the subscripts are meant to differentiate the desires and also to indicate a relation of later than to earlier than in a causal temporal series. These desires become arranged in a recognizable continuum or pattern called a "saṁtāna" and the saṁtāna is held together by the force of prāpti.

Such saṁskāra patterns of desire along with the other four skandha patterns (body, sensation, perception, and consciousness) are the only things of which the so-called "self" could be composed. For, let me ask you, is there, could there be, anything else to which you can point, in your own experience, of which the self could be made? Try to find it. Look into your mind right now; can you discover anything there other than sets of particular momentary thoughts, perceptions or desires? Is there anything else besides these, such as a person, or an ego, or an I, or a self or observer? over and beyond those particular dharmic and skandhic phenomena? Consider the following statement:

> For my part, when I enter most intimately into what I call *myself*, I always stumble on some particular perception or other, of heat or cold, light or shade, love or hatred, pain or pleasure. I never catch *myself* at any time without a perception, and never can observe any thing but the perception. When my perceptions are remov'd for any time, as by sound sleep; so long am I insensible of myself, and may truly be said not to exist.[141]

The author of that very Hīnayāna sentiment is David Hume (1711-1776), an empiricist and phenomenalist philosopher of the British Enlightenment. For Hume, as for the Hīnayāna, the self is a fiction, an artifice, Hume says, of memories held together by the force of imagination. And, though the terminology is different from the Hīnayāna, Hume's meaning and intent are the same. There is no self.

B.F. Skinner, a contemporary Western behaviorist and psychologist, says some things about the self that, again, might help us to grasp the Hīnayāna insight a bit more securely. Recalling Western notions of a permanent and substantial self, Skinner observes:

> It is often said that a science of behavior studies the human organism but neglects the person or self. What it neglects is a vestige of animism, a doctrine which in its crudest form held that the body was moved by one or more indwelling spirits. When the resulting behavior was disruptive, the spirit was probably a devil; when it was creative, it was a guiding genius or muse. Traces of the doctrine survive when we speak of a *personality*, of an ego in ego psychology, of an *I* who says he knows what he is going to do and uses his body to do it, or of the role a person plays as a person in a drama, wearing his body as a costume.[142]

The behavioral analysis of "person" or "personality" leads to the abolition of this modern devil or genius, the homunculus in mufti, an illusion created out of our ignorance. The behaviorist, like the Buddhist, seeks the exposure of this illusion, its exorcism and abolition:

> What is being abolished [say the defenders of this person or self] is autonomous man, the homunculus, the possessing demon, the man defended by the literature of freedom and dignity. His abolition has long been overdue... He has been constructed from our ignorance.

The purpose of the dispossession is made clear by Skinner when he says, again, sounding, in part, very much like a Hīnayāna Buddhist:

> Only by dispossessing him can we turn to the real causes of human behavior. Only then can we turn from the inferred to the observed, from the miraculous to the natural, from the inaccessible to the manipulable [controllable].[143]

In the West, the concept of the self has evolved from the staunch belief in an indwelling demon or spirit, to a ghost in a machine, a notion attacked by Hume and ridiculed by Skinner, and finally, to a fiction for Hume and a behaving organism for Skinner.[144]

Three interesting implications would seem to follow from the doctrine of anātman, all of which have strong influences on both the philosophy and religion of Hīnayāna. First, a kind of Buddhist nominalism (term-ism or word-ism) results from anātamavāda. According to the Buddhist nominalist, the word "book" is a handy and useful convention that we use when certain "constituent parts are present"; but, and this is the point, the word "book" does not name or point to those parts, i.e. it does not "refer", i.e. it has no reference to any permanent thing, neither an abstract, general thing nor a permanent, particular thing. How could it point to anything when, according to anātmavāda, as well as anityavāda, there is nothing that is permanent enough to get named?

The word "self", furthermore, is another conventional term that neither names nor refers to any class of entities nor to any substantial entity; how can it when there is no self, no reality or thing or entity that is a self? Thus the doctrine of anātman in Hīnayāna Buddhism leads from a view that seems to identify "self" with a process, a saṁtāna, to a view that seems to say that general terms like "self" do not name or refer or point to real existents, but are mere empty vocal sounds. The Hīnayāna will have problems in trying to decide which version of the "self", the saṁtāna, process "self" or the nominalistic "self", they wish to retain.

Listen to this interesting nominalistic dialogue between a Buddhist monk, Nāgasena, and a certain 2nd Century B.C.E. Greek King of India, Menander (Pāli Milinda) from the non-Canonical work *Milindapañha*. Nāgasena has just told the King that his name, Nāgasena, is a mere word, "a way of counting, a term, an appelation, a convenient designation", which does not point or refer to any thing, real or tangible, for "there is no ego to be found here." The King is intrigued by this conclusion and takes up the argument:

> Bhante [Venerable] Nāgasena, if there is no self to be found, who is it, then, furnishes you priests with the priestly requisites - robes, food, bedding...?

A good question from a king who is footing the bill for the monkish life of Nāgasena and his friends. Milinda continues:

> ...who is it that makes use of the same? who is it keeps the precepts? who is it applies himself to meditation? who is it realizes the Paths, the Fruits, and Nirvāṇa?

A good question for those monks who have set out on the monkish path. If there is no identifiable self or ego, how can there be merit, reward and punishment, or an ethics, or a rebirth of a self into another body? The King questions Nāgasena further endeavoring to find out just who or what the good monk is, and Nāgasena answers him like a good Buddhist nominalist:

> Pray, bhante, is the hair of the head Nāgasena?
> Nay, verily, your majesty [Nāgasena answers].
> ...Are nails... teeth... skin... bones... kidneys... blood...brain of the head Nāgasnea?
> Nay, verily, your majesty.
> Is now, bhante, form... sensation... perception... the predispositions... consciousness Nagasena? [The King has just mentioned the five skandhas, or aggregates, that compose all individuals.]
> Nay, verily, your majesty.

The King asks if Nāgasena is the united collection or combination of all of these particulars; and the monk replies that he is not. Then the King asks if it is something besides, or over and above, these thingsthat is Nagasena; and again the monk replies in the negative. Then, in exasperation, the King concludes that there is no Nāgasena.

The venerable monk then asks the King how he had traveled when he came to meet with him. "By chariot", the King replies. And now it's Nāgasena's turn to play inquisitor:

> Pray, your majesty, is the pole the chariot?
> Nay, verily, Nāgasena.
> Is the axle the chariot?
> Nay, verily, Nāgasena.

And so on for the wheels, the body, the yoke and the other particular elements of the chariot; and to all of these separately named parts the King denies that any one of them is the word "chariot." Similarly, the King denies that the word "chariot" is the united collection of these particulars, and he denies that it is something over and above the particulars. The word "chariot," Nāgasena asserts, is a "mere empty sound." It does not refer or point to or name any thing at all. The King is persuaded by this form of extreme nominalism and says,

> Bhante Nāgasena...the word "chariot" is but a way of counting, [a] term, appellation, convenient "designation" [that does not designate]....

To which Nāgasena responds,

> Thoroughly well, your majesty, do you understand a chariot. In exactly the same way, your majesty, in respect of me, "Nāgasena" is but a way of counting, [a] term, appellation, convenient "designation", mere "name" for the hair of my head, hair of my body... brain of the head, form, sensation, perception, the predispositions and consciousness [the five skandhas]. But in the absolute sense there is no self here to be found.[145]

The "self" is a mere sound that we make up and use whenever certain particulars are present, but, and this is the point, the sound does not name or point to those particulars. Quoting a nun, Sister Vajira, when she was face to face with Lord Buddha, Nāgasena concludes:

> Where all constituent parts are present, the word 'a chariot' is [used]. So likewise where the skandhas are, the term a 'being' commonly is used.[146]

Thus since compounds or collections, like self, are non-existent, words cannot refer to them meaningfully.

A second implication follows hard upon anātmavāda and the Buddhist nominalism of Hīnayāna, and this is the apparent commitment to a philosophic empiricism within Hīnayāna. This empiricism, the view that there is nothing in the mind that was not first in the senses, follows, in part, the naturalism, humanism, atheism and pragmatism of Hīnayāna; but it is also connected in an interesting way to the anātman doctrine: I know that there is no self because I never see (external sense) nor intuit (internal sense) a self. If I do not experience, either externally or internally, a self then I have no grounds for arguing that there is a self. I do not; so there isn't.

This empiricist view is mitigated, in part, by Hīnayāna's insistence that I can know the dharmas, those metaphysical energy-moments, which I cannot sense, by a kind of transcendent wisdom, a special trans-sensory way of knowledge open only to the arhats who have achieved enlightenment. This mitigated empiricism may be inconsistent with the naturalism of Hīnayāna, but such inconsistencies do not seem to have bothered the Pāli Buddhists.

A third and final implication follows from the doctrine of anātman, with its attendant Hīnayāna nominalism and mitigated empiricism, and this is the apparent acceptance of a view similar to what is called "behaviorism" by modern psychologists like B.F. Skinner. The Hīnayāna can be called "behaviorists" in so far as they hold that the "self" is to be identified with empirically observable behavior, and that any inference to any entity behind, or as a cause of, that behavior is unwarranted. Consistent with their nominalism, once again, "self" is merely a word that convention has chosen to use in the presence of certain behaviors or skandha patterns. Or, to put it another way, there is no self, there is only behavior, i.e. the processes and flowing movements of the skandhas.

Buddhist monks practice a curious kind of phenomenalistic reductionism on language or sentences that contain self-words. This reductionist exercise is not unlike certain phenomenalist attempts in the West to reduce physical object terms and language, like "elephant" and "I see an elephant", to sense data terms and utterances, like "large grey sense datum with hard white tusk-like sense data, and long grey rope-likeness sense data, are here and now." The aim of the Western phenomenalist reductionism was to get rid of physical object language entirely and replace it with a language about which one could be absolutely certain, viz., sense data language.[147]

For the Buddhists the point was to get rid of self language by reducing it to dharma or skandha language, thereby reducing the self to pure but empty phenomena, thereby, once the self had been shown to be empty and non-existent, reaching the inner truth of anātmavāda, viz., nirvāṇa. Thus all talk about 'I', 'mine', 'me', 'my', 'soul', 'individual' and 'self' vanishes in the process of reducing such talk to pure experience, pure phenomena, somewhat after the manner of the Western phenomenalists, above.

For example, "I am angry" becomes "feelings of anger, here and now" in which there is no person who is angry, who is to be blamed, or made to feel guilty, or who is to be punished for his anger, and all the rest. "My soul is depressed" becomes "depression feelings, here and now"; "I hate you" becomes "feelings of hatred are here in this place and are now directed towards experiences of such and such sense data ("you")." This linguistic depersonalization through phenomenalistic reductionism thus replaces the self with behavior which can be empirically experienced: The self disappears and one comes to see that it was never really there to begin with.[148] Buddhist phenomenalism, Buddhist empiricism, Buddhist behaviorism and Buddhist linguistic reductionism are all logically bound up in Buddhist anātmavāda, and all conspire to bring about nirvāṇa.

However, several problems arise with respect to the anātman doctrine and we turn to them next.

8. The Problems of Anātmavāda

The first problem of anātmavāda is this: While the Hīnayāna theoretically deny the reality of self, they secretly smuggle a self, a pudgala, or person, back into their philosophy. In other words, their theoretical denial of self cannot be upheld if one looks carefully at their metaphysics. The Hīnayāna self is not at all what David Hume or B.F. Skinner called a "self", but, rather, the Hīnayāna "self", despite all the protesting to the contrary, is a relatively substantial and fairly permanent entity, after all.

Recall the metaphysics of the Hīnayāna-Abhidharma-Sarvāstivāda psychology. We have a series of causally related skandhas, and let's use the saṁskāra of desire, once again, as an example of these skandhas. Desires, d_1, d_2, and d_3, are arranged in a series held together by a mysterious force, prāpti, to form a pattern, a saṁtāna. This pattern of desires allows me to speak, nominalistically to be sure, of "my desires." This patterned series with my earlier and later desires differs from your patterned series of desires, we must assume, or there would be no way of distinguishing you (still nominalistically speaking) from me. Thus $d'_1 \rightarrow d'_2 \rightarrow d'_3$ is me while $d''_1 \rightarrow d''_2 \rightarrow d''_3$, let's say, is you, where the arrows indicate causal connections and the single prime and double prime signs allow the individuating distinctions to be made; for without the latter signs the entire notion of "individual", i.e. separate and distinct patterns with causally related desires, would be lost - and the Hīnayāna would certainly not wish that indistinguishing eventuality on their metaphysics.

Further as d_1 decays and gives rise to d_2, a trace of d_1 remains, we are told. It is these traces of previously existing desires, for example, that make both memory and recollections of past desires possible. Finally, the mysterious force of prāpti, which holds the saṁtāna of these saṁskāras together and that makes this saṁtāna my saṁtāna and not yours, is a *real* force. If it were not real, in some sense, then it could not be effective in making the differentiation between my desires and your desires.

But, I would suggest, this metaphysical psychology is all that we need to establish the reality of a self. What more could one ask for in such a psychology than to have an individuating principle, the saṁtāna of patterned desires, together with a force that keeps the pattern in existence as traces capable of being recollected through memory? And recall that desire is only one such saṁskāra out of numerous others capable of being saṁtāna-ized and prāpti-ized in order to make a distinctly individualized self: The Hīnayāna doctrine of self as a process comes perilously close to the Pudgalavāda doctrine of self as a person.

The Hīnayāna differ from David Hume on this matter because Hume, as we saw, regards the self as a fictional product of the imagination: Memory, he says, dredges up past recollections while the imagination passes down the patterns of recollected memories, binds them together, and dubs the resultant fiction a "self."[149] Prāpti, on the other hand, as a saṁskāra, is a *real* and significant force for the Hīnayāna and bears little resemblance to Hume's imagination. The result for Hīnayāna Buddhism would seem to be a *real* self, founded on a metaphysics that produces anything but a nominalistic fiction. Thus one of the problems of anātman for the Pāli Buddhists.

Second, it might be argued that if there is no self then ethics can make no sense and if ethics makes no sense then moral common sense is irreparably violated. In other words, if there is no self, identical through time, then how can anyone be held responsible for the things that they do? How can anyone be rewarded or punished for their deeds, if there is no self doing, and responsible for, those deeds. D.T. Suzuki has put the same moral objection to the dogma of anātman when he says:

> Without self there will be no individual. Without the idea of responsibility morality ceases to exist...human community becomes impossible. We must in some way have a self.[150]

If there is no self then not only is ethics in serious trouble but such doctrines as the law of karma and the principle of saṁsāra or rebirth, both of which *seem* to depend on an identifiable self through time, would appear to be in serious trouble, as well.[151] The dogma of anātman leads to unsupportable consequences and it does irreparable harm to basic Buddhist doctrines, therefore it must be false.

A third problem for the dogma of anātman, aside from the moral and doctrinal difficulties mentioned above, comes from the fact that, Hume and Skinner to the contrary notwithstanding, the self is obviously and intuitively present for all to see. Recall that Hume offered an intuitive argument against the existence of the self, inviting the reader, in effect, to look within and note the emptiness. But the critic of anātaman could respond: I've looked within and I've found my self!

In a manner remarkably similar to the *cogito* arguments, the "I think therefore I am" arguments, of Aurelius Augustine and René Descartes, the advaita Vedānta philosopher, Śaṁkarācārya (693-725 A.D.), argues in his great commentary on the *Brahmasūtras*:

> We reply that Brahman is known. Brahman, which is all-knowing and endowed with all powers whose essential nature is eternal, pure intelligence and freedom, exists.

Then Śaṁkara identifies this Brahman with the Self of which, he claims, we are all conscious:

> In addition, the existence of Brahman is known from the fact of It being the Self of everyone; for everyone is conscious that his Self exists and never thinks, "I do not exist." If everyone did not recognize the existence of his Self then everyone would think, "*I* do not exist."[152]

There are really two arguments advanced by Śaṁkara in the above paragraph. The first is a positive argument based on direct, intuitive awareness of the Self wherein, as Śaṁkara has previously said, "The Self is not beyond apprehending, because It is well known in the world as an immediately recognized [intuited] entity."[153] But what kind of self, or which self, is it that Śaṁkara has intuited? Is it self or Self? i.e. is it jīva (ego) or Ātman Brahan)? Eliot Deutsch comments on the ambiguity of Śaṁkara's discovery:

> The argument is not without its difficulties. A subtle and unsupported transition is made between Ātman and the *jīva* (the individual conscious being) so that the argument does not so much prove the Ātman as it does the *jīva* - the *jīva*, which has the kind of self-consciousness described in, and presupposed by, the argument, and not the Ātman, which is pure consciousness.[154]

A similar confusion and transition is found in the early Buddhist tradition with respect to ātman and the dogma of anātman. We shall return to this confusion shortly when we discuss the continuum of self.

The second argument from the *Brahmasūtrabhāṣya* quoted above is a "negative" argument and it rests on the first:

1. If everyone did not recognize the existence of Self then everyone would think, "I do not exist."

2. But no one thinks "I do not exist" (quite the contrary).

3. Therefore, everyone recognizes the existence of the Self.[155]

This second argument is interesting for several reasons: To begin with, it acknowledges a common sense connection between intuition ("recognition") and language, i.e. between reality and the way we speak: The way we speak reflects our beliefs, and those beliefs are grounded, for the most part, in common sense attitudes towards the world.

Further, the second argument is predicated on the common and defensible assumption that language can reveal the way the world is: The fact that we speak a certain way can indicate, not merely a belief, but a truth about existence and about the world.

Finally, the second argument is negative in the sense that it is stated as a counterfactual conditional in the first premise. Śaṁkara does not rest the argument on what we might call a "negative intuition." Negative intuitions are notoriously problematic; for example, merely because anyone or everyone failed to directly and immediately recognize something-or-other does not mean that something-or-other doesn't exist. Thus it was a negative intuition that failed to uncover a self for Hume and it is obvious that such failed uncoverings don't prove anything. On the other hand, positive intuitions succeeded in uncovering a self for Śaṁkara and it is precisely on such positive grounds that the common sense intuitionist does and ought to proceed.

But what was it then that Śaṁkara's positive intuition discovered that Buddhist intuition failed to discover? Śaṁkara says it was "ātman"; but the word, as Deutsch indicates, is plainly ambiguous for it can mean either "self or jīva" ("living soul") or it can mean "Self or Pure Consciousness." Since neither Sanskrit nor Pāli has capital letters, the ambiguity becomes all the more secure in the classical texts.

What Śaṁkara thought he'd discovered is precisely one of the things that the Buddhists believed they had denied by the dogma of anātman, viz., the eternal, unchanging Self. But if Deutsch is correct in his interpretation of Śaṁkara's intuition, what Śaṁkara really discovered was self or jīva; and the denial of this changing self is more problematic for a Buddhism which pretends to be grounded in common sense. In other words, the dogma of anātman, grounded in common sense and empiricism, was not meant to deny both self and Self; but the strict interpretation of the dogma led to the denial of both self and Self and this confusion has been maintained. Meanwhile, the less strict and common sense interpretation that would have saved self has been rendered nugatory by tradition.

But where does this leave us then? Imagine, once again, a continuum with an unchanging "Self or Pure Consciousness" at one end and both "no Self and no self" at the other. The first Self refers to Śaṁkara's Vedāntic Self and it is rejected by the Buddhists on the grounds that it contradicts the dogma of anitya, and that it's foolish and violates common sense.[156] The second, a conjunction of no Self and no self, refers to the strict interpretation of anātman by the early Buddhists and Hume and Skinner. On the basis of our previous discussion it is also to be rejected by common sense. Both extremes are to be rejected. Buddhist common sense tells us that the truth of the interpretation of the dogma of anātman must lie elsewhere, and it must lie at some midpoint between the extremes. If what we have said about intuition earlier is the case then it is at that mid-point that there must exist a changing self.

This purely psychological entity is known, perhaps, by Śaṁkaran intuition; it is justified by common sense and the need for self-identity through time; and it is a self that makes responsibility, ethics, the law of karma and rebirth acceptable to the plain man. On this continuum interpretation, the early Buddhists were wrong and Śaṁkara was right about self: There is a self, apprehended by immediate and direct intuition. But on this same continuum interpretation, the early Buddhists were right and Śaṁkara was wrong about Self: There is no Self apprehended by intuition. In other words, if what we have suggested is correct, the Buddhists may legitimately support a dogma of anĀtman but not a dogma of anātman.

The conclusion for the critic, once again, is that the dogma of anātman is both morally and common sensically impractical and that it represents an extreme and indefensible position. The dogma of anātman simply overstates the case for non-self and in doing so it seems patently false.

We turn next to the ninth characteristic of Hīnayāna Buddhism, a characteristic closely allied with the anātman doctrine, viz., rebirth and the Hīnayāna doctrine of reincarnation.

9. Rebirth (A Reincarnation)

Hīnayāna, because of its denial of the reality of a Self, tends to accept the kind of rebirth that we shall call "reincarnation." The problem that Hīnayāna faced was essentially that of making a theory of saṁsāra (rebirth) consistent with their own doctrine of anātman. The solution to that problem was both ingenious and simple. It can best be explained by returning to the doctrine of anitya and applying that doctrine to a physical object, for example, a lighted candle.

According to anityavāda the candle and the candle flame are never the same from moment to moment. In this sense, the candle is like the human body, a set or collection of orderly changing dharmas. But because the change is orderly we are inclined to say that the candle, like the human body, is the "same" from moment to moment. The macroscopic appearance fools us. But both physics and the doctrine of anitya are standing by to correct our naive realistic view of candles and bodies.

If we were to take the lighted candle and, in a darkened room, whirl it around in a wide arc, and if it were whirled fast enough in this arc, we would see a wheel of light that would appear both solid and real. When we turn on the lights in that room, however, we see the wheel for what it really is: An illusion of solidity made up of the momentary positions in the arc of the moving lighted candle. Turning on the lights illuminates the illusion just as physics and the doctrine of anitya illuminate the appearance of all "solid and real", "permanent and unchanging", physical objects.

The Buddhists liken the flame of the candle to the self. Just as this flame, flickering, leaping and jumping about, is not the same flame from moment to moment, and you can see that, so also the self is not the same from moment to moment, and the anitya and anātman doctrines point this out. The flame with its semi-orderly momentary dharmas is likened to the self with its saṁskāras, saṁtānas and prāptic forces. But because of the semi-orderly manner in which the flame burns, and because we don't whoof it out and relight the candle, and because of the continuity that this flame exhibits in association with this candle, and because we wish to distinguish it from that other candle flame over there, we can say, in a common sense, but naive, way, that this flame is still *this* flame, i.e. it is the *same* flame from moment to moment.[157]

But now suppose that I pass this flame over to another unlighted candle, and as I light the second candle, the first flame goes out. Is it still the same flame? In an ordinary and naive sense it is, perhaps. I haven't relit the flame, it just exists on a different candle. The continuity of momentary dharmic flames has been maintained, though in a new locus. And I can still distinguish this flame from another candle flame over there. As a result there is this naive sense in which it is the same flame, i.e. the same flame on a different candle. (If the first candle flame had not gone out in the transfer, would the second candle flame still be the same as the first?) But this naive view of sameness is not only naive, it is wrong, the Hīnayāna would say.

The Hīnayāna borrow the analogy of the transferred flame to explain their doctrine of rebirth. Just as the flame continues to burn even as it is transferred to the second candle and simultaneously goes out in the first candle, so at the death of this body my saṁtāna (pattern) of saṁskāras (psycho-physical forces) continues as an orderly series of burning desires in a new body. But no thing, i.e. nothing substantial, nothing unchanging or permanent, is transferred from one body to another: This doctrine of rebirth is not, therefore, the Hindu doctrine of *transmigration* in which some Thing, Self or Ātman, unchanging and the same through time, is transferred from one body to another; it is, rather, *reincarnation*, where an insubstantial pattern of dharmic saṁskāras is merely continued in a new space-time locus.

Here is the *Milindapañha*, once again, as King Milinda continues his questioning of the able monk, Nāgasena:

> Bhante Nāgasena, does rebirth take place without anything transmigrating [passing over]?
> Yes, your majesty. Rebirth takes place without anything transmigrating.
> How, bhante Nāgasena, does rebirth take place without anything transmigrating? Give an illustration.
> Suppose, your majesty, a man were to light a light from another light; pray, would the one light have passed over [transmigrated] to the other light?
> Nay, verily, bhante.
> In exactly the same way, your majesty, does rebirth take place without anything transmigrating.

Apparently impressed, Milinda asks for another example:

> Do you remember, your majesty, having learnt, when you were a boy, some verse or other from your professor of poetry?
> Yes, bhante.
> Pray, your majesty, did the verse pass over [transmigrate] to you, from your teacher?
> Nay, verily, bhante.
> In exactly the same way, your majesty, does rebirth take place without anything transmigrating.
> You are an able man, bhante Nāgasena.[158]

Able man, indeed! As with all analogies that attempt to explain metaphysical truths we are in the realm of symbols, images and metaphors. Taken descriptively or empirically the analogies with flames and professors of poetry break down. A modern materialistic physics of heat and sound gives an entirely different explanation of what gets transferred when flames are lighted from other flames and when ears hear words from teachers. If we were to take the analogies descriptively we would be in the realm of transmigrating physical entities, heat and sound. But analogies in the realm of metaphysics invite a philosophical suspension of belief in the descriptive mode of language. The metaphysical analogy, like the myth, points beyond the literal and the material, and in pointing beyond it attempts to suggest a likeness and similarity between the metaphysical and the material, not an identity between the symbolic and the literal or the metaphysical and the material.[159]

An earlier non-Canonical text, i.e. earlier than the *Milindapañha*, from the *Visuddhi-Magga* makes the same point but without the picturesque metaphysical analogies of the *Milinda*:

> For when, in any existence, one arrives at the gate of death...then consciousness residing in that last refuge, the heart, continues to exist by virtue of karma, otherwise called the predispositions.[160]

This consciousness, which is bound to the saṁtāna of the former, as well as the present, chain of saṁskāras, then, out of ignorance, desires continuation in another body:

> Now while the consciousness still subsists, inasmuch as desire and ignorance have not been abandoned and the evil of the object is hidden by that ignorance, desire inclines the consciousness to the object [the new body]; and the karma that sprang up along with the consciousness impels it toward the object.[161]

There follows a delightful metaphysical analogy to illustrate the rebirth that then occurs:

> This consciousness being in its series thus inclined toward the object by desire, and impelled toward it by karma, like a man who swings himself over a ditch by means of a rope hanging from a tree on the hither bank, quits its first resting-place and continues to subsist in dependence on objects of sense and other things, and either does or does not light on another resting-place created by karma.[162]

The analogy uses the symbol of a swinging man to make a point that veers suspiciously close to a theory of transmigration. But, as the concluding passage states, it is reincarnation that is meant all along:

> Here the former consciousness, from its passing out of existence, is called passing away, and the latter, from its being reborn

> into a new existence, is called rebirth. But it is to be understood that this latter consciousness did not come to the present existence from the previous one, and also that it is only to causes contained in the old existence - namely, to karma called the predispositions, to inclination, an object, etc. - that its present appearance is due.[163]

Thus the problem raised by the attempt to integrate the theory of saṁsāra with the new doctrine of anātman is solved by the Hīnayāna with the theory of reincarnation.

However, several problems emerge, as you might imagine, not the least of which is the problem of personal identity, i.e. the problem of sameness of the person through time with respect to the rebirth doctrine. We turn to that problem next.

9. The Problem of Reincarnation

The problem of reincarnation that we shall explore is "the problem of personal identity" as it is called in the Western philosophical tradition. Essentially the problem revolves around two questions: How do I know that I am the same person today that I was yesterday? and In what does this sameness reside? In the West, the problem receives its first and most careful consideration in the *Essay Concerning Human Understanding* (1690) by the English philosopher John Locke (1632-1704). Locke had two very practical reasons for wishing to answer the questions posed above. One reason was religious and the second was legal.

The practical religious reason that set John Locke upon his quest was rooted in this question: If, after I die, I am brought before the great Judge in the hereafter, how can I be justly rewarded or punished for my deeds in this life if there is no identifiable person, through time, who can be held responsible for those deeds? Therefore, there must be a sameness of person, a personal identity, that enables me to answer this question, else the religious life would make no sense.

The practical legal reason that set Locke upon his quest was rooted in a second and similar question:

If I have committed a crime, and if I am brought before the courts, how can I be charged with that crime, if there is no identifiable person who can be held responsible for that crime? Therefore, there must be a sameness of person, a personal identity, that enables us to meet this question, else the legal and moral life would make no sense.

The question uppermost in answering these questions and in solving the problem of personal identity was, for Locke, above all else, a question of justice in the religious and moral life of man. If there is nothing that remains the same in self from one moment to the next then in a very practical sense I am not the same person today that I was yesterday. And if I'm not the same person today that I was yesterday then how can you judge, convict and punish me, either in the next life or in this one, for a crime that I didn't commit?; this would make a mockery of justice, indeed.

Locke's way out of the problem was to have personal identity depend on personal consciousness:

> For it being the same consciousness that makes a man be himself to himself, personal identity depends on that only.[164]

And this consciousness for Locke, as for Hume several decades later, was essentially "memory":

> ...and as far as this consciousness can be extended backwards to any past action or thought, so far reaches the identity of that person.[165]

But Locke's way out runs up hard against certain problems such as forgetting and amnesia; for once the latter two possibilities are admitted into one's philosophy of psychology, Locke's solution to the problem of personal identity, like Hume's later, fails.

The Hīnayāna Buddhists have adopted a much more radical way out of the problem of personal identity than either Locke or the Lockeans ever imagined. To begin with there is no self, and that's an end to that! But that's precisely one of the reasons why we probably feel that a genuine problem about justice is present. So the Abhidharma-influenced Hīnayāna say something like this: The karma and the saṁtāna (pattern) of the saṁskāras of desire and consciousness that I have inherited in this life are not mine, for I didn't produce them in a previous life (How could I? I didn't exist), someone else did. And the karma and saṁtānic saṁskāras that remain when I die are passed on in reincarnation to someone else.

Hence, I suffer with someone else's karma in this life; and someone else suffers with my karma in the next life: But where's the justice in that? For if by "justice" we mean, more or less, the state or condition where everyone gets their due or what they deserve, i.e. everyone gets what's coming to them, then obviously I got what wasn't coming to me, and I'm going to give someone else what's not coming to them. So much for the "justice" of reincarnation and the problem of rebirth.

The Hīnayāna have an obvious way out of this problem, of course. Once the concept of the unchanging personal self is challenged and rejected as absurd, the concept and question of personal justice also disappears. What Hīnayāna has erected in the place of the Lockean concepts of personal self and personal justice is the concept of an impersonal self where "self" is a mere term, following our previous discussion of nominalism, used whenever there is or happens to be present a changing pattern, or saṁtāna, of particular saṁskāras held together by the glue of prāpti. There is no thing or entity to which "self" refers; it's a fiction, a handy and useful one to be sure, but merely a fiction.

But two questions then arise: Have the Hīnayāna solved the problem of identity? and answered the question of justice? Or have they merely avoided both, leaving us with no solution and no answer? I leave the reader to mull, again, at leisure.

We turn next to the tenth and final characteristic of Hīnayāna Buddhism, viz., the tendency towards a philosophy of realism. In this final section we shall attempt a reconstruction of the philosophic history of the two major schools of Hīnayāna Buddhism, viz., Sarvāstivāda, direct realism, and Sautrāntika, indirect realism.

10. The Philosophies of Realism

Hīnayāna Buddhism tends to be realistic in its metaphysical philosophy and in what follows I want to explain what this means and illustrate that tendency by examining two schools closely linked to Hīnayāna Buddhism.[166]

a. An Excursion Into Metaphysics

To get clear on what philosophical realism entails take the following example. Consider the book that you are now reading. It has certain properties which you experience through sensation and which you then judge to be the properties of this book. Thus you sense the color of the page and the print, you sense the smoothness of the page and the roughness of the cover. If you smelled the page you could detect its odor, and if you struck the book with your fist it would emit a sound, and, I dare say, if you put your tongue on it you could pick up the taste of the paper and the print, as well. Following each sensation certain predicates or names are assigned to those sensed properties. We form judgments like, "The color is black and white," "The texture is smooth," "The odor is ink-y," and so on. Thus sensations lead to perceptual judgments wherein we assign predicates to those sensed properties.

But now come the philosophic questions: Where are those properties that you sense? What is their location? Where do they exist? Are they in the book or on the surface of the book? Or are they in your mind and not in or on the book at all? More particularly, where are the black and white properties? Out there in the space-time, page and book, world of physical objects? Or in your mind, or in some mind or other?

The *realist*, as we shall see, wants to claim that the properties of the book, as well as the book, are out there in the world, and independent of mind, for all to see and experience.

The *idealist*, as we shall see when we come to Mahāyāna Buddhism, wants to claim, on the other hand, that the properties of the book, as well as the book itself, are not out there at all. They are, instead, in here, in the mind, and dependent on the mind or on some Mind or other.

The argument between the *perceptual realist*, who believes that physical objects and their properties are public and objective and mind-independent, and the *perceptual idealist*, who believes that physical objects and their properties are private and subjective and mind-dependent, is a continuing argument among philosophers in both the West and the East. So it is not at all surprising to find the Buddhists, too, like their Hindu and Western philosophic brethren, taking opposing views on the same issue.

But perceptual realism and perceptual idealism stand on metaphysical foundations that are as different as the two views of perception that spring from them. Let's locate these two views of perception within the several systems of metaphysics available to us by doing two things, viz., getting clear on what "real" means, and then looking at some classifications of the real.

First, metaphysics is the field of philosophy that attempts, *inter alia*, to determine what kinds of things are ultimately real. Traditionally, "real" things have been taken to be ultimate entities which are said to possess the following three properties: They are *unchanging*, i.e. they are unalterable in their essential nature; they are *independent*, i.e. they are not dependent on some other entity for their existence or their essential nature; and they are *eternal*, i.e. they have no beginning (they are not created) and they have no ending (they cannot be destroyed).

But Hīnayāna Buddhism along with modern physics would seem to have taken exception to this traditional conception of the real, and both seem to offer "reals" or "ultimates" that are not real in the above sense at all. For, in one very good sense, neither the dharmas of the Hīnayāna nor the microparticles, i.e. the electrons or quarks (which possess 1/3 to 2/3 of the electric charge of the electron) of the physicist, seem to satisfy the traditional definition of the "real" offered above. Thus individual dharmas and quarks, the ultimates out of which everything else comes, are constantly changing; they are causally created by, and therefore dependent upon, other dharmas and quarks; and they are, as individual moments of energy or force, certainly not eternal.

And yet, in another equally good sense, these dharmas and quarks do satisfy the traditional definition of "the real", and they do it very nicely, indeed. For as a class, group or set of ultimate entities, though not as individuals, dharmas and quarks *never change* their nature; and they are *independent* from other entities and things, all of which are dependent on them; and they are *eternal*, i.e. they have always and forever will exist. They are, in this class or group sense, as real as the more traditional individual candidates for the "real", e.g., God, Brahman and the Absolute.

Second, having admitted dharmas and quarks as classes to the realm of the real, let's see what kinds of classifications are available to metaphysicians who ponder the nature of the real. I list the three major metaphysical positions, the first of which has five subdivisions:

1) Metaphysical realism holds that there are ultimately real entities which, building on our previous discussion, either as individual ultimates (like God or Brahman) or as a class of ultimates (like dharmas or quarks) are said to be unchanging, independent and eternal. Metaphysical realism, in turn, is subdivided into five possible subdivisions:

a) Metaphysical materialism is the view that only matter or body, e.g. earth, air, fire and water and quarks, is, or are, ultimately real. Thus Pūraṇa Kassapa, Makkhalin Gosāla, Ajita Kesakambali, and Pakuda Kaccāyana, together with the ancient Greek and Roman atomists and Epicureans, along with most modern physicists, would probably belong to the class of metaphysical materialists.

b) Metaphysical idealism is the view that only mind and/or ideas is, or are, ultimately real, where mind is both the cause and container of the ideas. The Yogācāra Mahāyāna Buddhists probably belong here, along with one phase of Bishop George Berkeley's (1685-1753) Western idealist-phenomenalist metaphysics wherein Berkeley seems to admit that there are many minds and many ideas. Another phase of Berkeley's philosophy appears to argue that God's Mind alone is the only reality. Thus Berkelian phase-one subjective idealism spills over into Berkelian phase-two objective idealism. (But see metaphysical theism, below.) George Berkeley avoids *metaphysical solipsism*, the view that only my mind and my ideas are real, by his move to absolute idealism or metaphysical theism.

c) Metaphysical body-mind dualism is the view that combines metaphysical materialism with metaphysical idealism to claim that body and mind are both ultimately real. Hīnayāna Buddhists who maintain that the dharmas represent two kinds of reality, viz., a materialism as well as an idealism, would belong to the class of metaphysical body-mind dualists. The Sāṁkhya followers of the great Kapila (7th century B.C.E.), at least on the prakṛti, or material nature, side of their metaphysics, might be considered metaphysical body-mind dualists though they might be more comfortable with the classification of "metaphysical puruṣa (spirit)-prakṛti (body-mind) dualists." Rene Descartes (1596-1650), the great French polymath, is sometimes thought to be a mind-body dualist in this sense, though mind and body are not *ultimately* real, for him, both having been created by Spiritual substance, viz., God.

d) Metaphysical theism is the view that only a personal God (or spirit) or Gods (or spirits) is, or are, ultimately real. Certain Hindu Upaniṣadic seers who, as theists, maintain that Brahman is describable and ultimately real, or that Viṣṇu and Śiva exist as personal deities, as well as those theists, like Rene Descartes, who also maintain that God is a loving and fatherly Being Who is ultimately real, would belong to the class of metaphysical theists. Bishop George Berkeley's God may belong here, as well.

e) Metaphysical absolutism is the view that an ultimate reality exists but that it is neither material, mental nor Godly or spiritual, but beyond all description and empty of all properties. The Yogācāra Buddhists who claim that vijñaptimatra, pure Consciousness, is ultimately real, as well as the Mādhyamaka Mahāyāna Buddhists who hold that śūnyatā, emptiness, is the sole reality, together with certain other Upaniṣadic seers, once again, who hold that highest and propertyless Brahman is the only reality, would all be classified as metaphysical absolutists.

Thus the five divisions of metaphysical realism. There are two remaining major classifications of metaphysical philosophies:

2) Metaphysical nihilism holds that there are no ultimately real entities. The position of metaphysical nihilism, like the position of philosophical nihilism, is difficult to state, maintain and defend, and whether anyone has ever held it consistently is moot.

3) Metaphysical agnosticism holds that no one yet knows if there are any ultimately real entities. The position is close to *metaphysical scepticism* which holds that no one *can* ever know if there are any ultimately real entities. The latter position is frequently attributed to modern logical empiricists and positivists like A.J. Ayer; and Bertrand Russell sometimes speaks this way. The former position, metaphysical agnosticism, has been attributed to the Greek and Roman Pyrrhonists and Skeptics (who weren't really sceptics), to David Hume, to the Mādhyamaka Buddhists and to the Buddha, himself.[167]

The metaphysical agnostics can be divided, in turn, into two camps, viz., the *optimistic metaphysical agnostics* who say that no one knows *as yet* if there are any ultimates (but hope springs eternal); and the *pessimistic metaphysical agnostics* who say that no one will *ever* know if there are any ultimates. The pessimists can be identified, as one can see, with the metaphysical sceptics.

We can see now that the foundation of both perceptual realism as well as perceptual idealism is *metaphysical realism* which holds that there are real, i.e. unchanging, independent and eternal, material or mental or spiritual entities in the world; but while sharing that foundation, the real entities that each accepts are obviously quite different. The perceptual realist generally argues that the mental can know the material, i.e. he's a metaphysical body-mind dualist; while the perceptual idealist argues that the mental can know only itself and its own ideas, i.e. he's a metaphysical idealist. Neither is a metaphysical nihilist nor a metaphysical agnostic.

In our discussion of the philosophies of realism we shall be concerned with two tendencies in Hīnayāna: First, with the tendency towards metaphysical realism in Hīnayāna Buddhism, particularly as that realism is expressed in the dualistic metaphysics of the body and mind dharmas; and second, with the tendency towards perceptual realism in Hīnayāna Buddhism, particularly as that realism is expressed in the way in which mind knows body, i.e. in the way in which the mind perceives the material world. But first a little historical background and a puzzle.

b. The Problem of Kṣaṇikavāda

Buddha left his followers with a disturbing philosophical problem, a problem with which all of the major schools of Buddhism had subsequently to deal. Buddha, as we have seen, probably taught the dogma of anityavāda, the view that everything is in a state of ceaseless flux; and he probably held the view that came to be called "kṣaṇikavāda" (from *kṣaṇa*, "moment" and *vāda*, "view"), the view that everything, meaning every dharma, lasts but a single moment, a view which seems to follow logically from anityavāda.[168] The disturbing philosophical problem is the problem of kṣaṇikavāda: If everything is constantly changing, and if everything lasts but an instant, but a moment, then how can anything cause or bring about anything else? The Buddha is said to have stated the problem of kṣaṇikavāda as follows:

> All forces [dharmas] are instantaneous. But how can a thing that has no duration nevertheless have the time to produce something?[169]

Thus the problem of kṣaṇikavāda gives rise to the problem of causation which will occupy not only Hīnayāna Buddhism, viz., the Sarvāstivāda and Sautrāntika schools, but it will haunt the two schools of Mahāyāna Buddhism with which we shall deal shortly, as well, viz., the Mādhyamaka school and the Yogācāra school.

Put in another way, the problem of kṣaṇikavāda says that if everything endures for only an instant or a moment (think of those dharmas) then those things which seem to last longer than a moment, or which depend on things that seem to last longer than a moment, would never exist. And there are at least three very important things which seem to last longer than a moment or which depend on things that seem to last longer than a moment, viz., the perception of physical objects, the presence of knowledge, and the reality of nirvāṇa. Consequently, the problem of kṣaṇikavāda leads, in turn, to three other philosophic puzzles, viz., the problem of perception, the problem of knowledge and a new problem of nirvāṇa.

Perception, knowledge and nirvāṇa all involve stopping or arresting the dharmic processes in some way in order that I can, for example, perceive this book, or have knowledge that what I perceive really is a book, or, ultimately for all Buddhists of whatever school, break the chain of pratītyasamutpāda, halt forever the dharmic and karmic processes of existence, and achieve liberation. But if kṣaṇikavāda is true then perception, knowledge and nirvāṇa would all seem to be impossible.

We begin our discussion of realism and its problems by looking at the chief school of Hīnayāna Buddhist realism, the Sarvāstivāda School, which was one of the first schools to turn its attention to the problem of kṣaṇikavāda.

c. The Sarvāstivāda School and Direct Realism

The Sarvāstivāda School of Hīnayāna Buddhism probably began in Kaśmīr during the reign of King Kaniṣka, sometime in the first century C.E. Some 500 monks were convened, we are told, in what has been called "the fourth Buddhist Council." Tradition has it that the majority of these monks, whose origin is obscure, were Sarvāstivādins. The school they founded was to remain and prosper in India for over 1000 years.[170]

The canon of the Sarvāstivāda includes an original tripiṭaka of their own composed in Sanskrit, extant now only in fragments. However, the canon survives completely in a Chinese translation and, in parts, in Tibetan. Its value to us lies in its commentary on, and additions to, the *Abhidharma* tradition and its profound philosophic insights into the early Hīnayāna literature. The Sarvāstivāda represent, according to one Buddhologist, "...the chief exponents of 'Hīnayāna scholasticism'"; and their influence on later philosophers, like the late fourth century Yogācārin and one-time Sarvāstivādin, Vasubandhu, who wrote his *Abhidharmakośa* in response to their philosophy, has been singularly important.

The Sarvāstivāda espouse several important doctrines of which three seem sufficient for our purposes here: First, the doctrines of the dharmas; second, the doctrine of body-mind dualism; and, finally, the doctrine of direct perception, or direct realism.

1) The Doctrine of the Dharmas. The problem of kṣaṇikavāda arose in the first place because the points of energy or moments of force, called "dharmas,"[171] seemed to be involved in a causal chain such that as one dharma arose it immediately vanished, but in vanishing it immediately gave rise to, and was replaced by, another dharma which in turn also lasted but an instant and gave rise in turn to another dharma, and so on and on: This is Heracleitean-becoming with a vengeance, for the doctrine of pratītyasamutpāda held that the process never ceases, not even with death.

As their name, *sarva*, "everything," *asti*, "exists," implies the Sarvāstivāda held that there are entities, dharmas, which in their ultimate nature exist in all the three periods of time, viz., past, present and future. The Sarvāstivāda believed, furthermore, that there were 75 different kinds of these basic "elements" of existence which composed external objects as well as thoughts and perceptions. They believed, further, that 72 of these 75 dharmas were formed into five sets, or skandhas, that included body (rūpa) or matter; sensation (vedanā); perception (saṁjñā); fourth, the mental constituents and residues (saṁskāras) which are primarily conscious and unconscious willings but which includes prāpti, that very curious force that we have seen keeps certain streams of dharmas together; and a fifth and final skandha of consciousness (vijñāna).

The chains of causal forces formed by the above 72 dharmas are said to be "saṁskṛta", forceful or full of forces, because they produce karmic residues (saṁskāras) transmitted from one life to the next, and which continue to produce karmic effects into the future. The self, as we've already seen, is just such a chain, or saṁtāna, of momentary saṁskṛtas, or forces, held together by prāpti. But if this self-chain were the whole metaphysical story for these Buddhists then stopping the flow of existence and breaking the chain would be impossible and nirvāṇa would never be achieved.

The Sarvāstivāda may have reasoned in this fashion: If the 72 saṁskṛta dharmas, and kṣaṇikavāda, and anityavāda were the whole story then nirvāṇa would be impossible. But, to continue their hypothetical reasoning, nirvāṇa is possible (the Buddha said so and experience teaches that it is so). Therefore, the 72 saṁskṛta dharmas and kṣaṇikavāda and anityavāda are not the whole story, i.e. there must be modifications of kṣaṇikavāda, anityavāda and the normal saṁskṛta dharmas. There were, indeed, four modifications perpetrated by the Sarvāstivāda and each led to the commission of a metaphysical howler with vast implications for the entire system of dharmas.

The Sarvāstivāda introduced four theses: First, they believed that there must be something substantial and unchanging (svabhava) underlying the dharmas, themselves; second, they argued that something in the dharmas, themselves, was relatively permanent through time; third, they came to hold that several new dharmas, not yet introduced, viz., prajñā and nirvāṇa, were special and didn't behave like the other normal dharmas; fourth, they stated that one of the normal dharmas, viz., prāpti, had a still more special property. These are the four modifications directed at kṣaṇikavāda, anityavāda and the saṁskṛta dharmas that led to the metaphysical howlers mentioned above. Let's have a look at these four theses along with the metaphysical howlers that they induced.

First, they believed that some permanent substance must underly the dharmas. David J. Kalupahana has put this first modification nicely:

> It is true that the Sarvāstivādins denied the substantiality of the individual (*pudgala*). But compelled by the need to explain the problem of continuity resulting from the acceptance of discrete momentary *dharmas*, they came to believe in an underlying substratum (*svabhāva, dravya*) considered to be eternal (*sarvadā asti*).[172]

This is, at best, creeping metaphysical materialism or, at worst, closet metaphysical absolutism.

Second, they argued that the dharmas in their moments (think of a moment as the blinking of an eye) of existence are static and frozen. For, the dharmas in those moments when they do exist can be said to endure through three periods of time, viz., the past, the present and the future: They are therefore permanent during these moments as momentarily unchanging moments. Thus with respect to the adoption of this theory of static or unchanging moments, sthitikṣaṇa, as well as with the adoption of an eternal subtratum, svabhāva, the Sarvāstivāda would appear to be in violation of the dogmas of kṣaṇikavāda and anityavāda, as well as pratītyasamutpāda and the expressed beliefs of the Buddha.

Third, Sarvāstivāda now hustled into their metaphysical system of dharmas three asaṁskṛta, or non-forceful, dharmas which they held left no karmic residues or dharmic effects. The first, and the only one of these three non-caused and non-causing dharmas that matches its description, was ākāśa, space, a totally inert and inactive container or place of the normal dharmas; the second non-forceful dharma was prajñā, intuitive wisdom; and the third was nirvāṇa, itself. Here we lower our eyes and blush with shame for the impetuous recklessness displayed by the Sarvāstivāda in introducing prajñā and nirvāṇa in this manner. For it is obvious that these two asaṁskṛta, abnormal, dharmas are, first of all, patently inconsistent with kṣaṇikavāda and the 72 normal dharmas (these two aren't even "dharmas", they're more like "states"); and that they are, second of all, mere expediencies trotted out to solve the problem of nirvāṇa. We blush and pass on to the fourth modification of the dharma system that led to a metaphysical howler of even grander proportions.

All blushings and howlers aside for the moment, with the introduction of the asaṁskṛta dharmas of prajñā and nirvāṇa, the Sarvāstivāda would now seem to be in a good theoretical position to claim that one of the problems of kṣaṇikavāda, viz., our problem of nirvāṇa, was solved. But one difficulty remained: How does one get that one asaṁskṛta dharma of nirvāṇa to stick into the ever-changing series or pattern of saṁskṛta, normal, dharmas that make up my 'self'? i.e. What keeps nirvāṇa in my saṁtāna? The answer lay in the fourth and last of our four modifications introduced by Sarvāstivāda to temper the force of kṣaṇikavāda, viz., the modification wrought by prāpti.

Prāpti is a saṁskṛta dharma and a kind of gluey power or force that has the ability to hold the other traces of dharmas into their saṁtānas, or patterns. This metaphysical mucilage enables elephants and books, the observed physical world, as well as selves and individuals, the mental observers, to stick together long enough to observe and be observed.

Edward Conze, a long-time prāpti-watcher, has said of this sticky dharma that makes nirvāṇa, and even perception and knowledge, possible:

> In order that any dharma can be inserted into a series of dharmas, or a 'personal series' (saṅtāna, a polite word for the 'individual') [for example, in order that prajñā, nirvāṇa, perception or ordinary knowledge be inserted into, and then stay in, my saṁtāna of dharmas], one must assume a separate dharma called 'possession' [prāpti].... When one 'obtains' salvation, when one 'adheres to', 'achieves' or 'realizes' enlightenment or Nirvāṇa, the Nirvāṇa would in a sense be linked permanently to this continuity, at least until that ceases altogether.[173]

So our new problem of nirvāṇa would appear to be solved: Nirvāṇa can be permanently achieved in the midst of momentariness and change. But at a metaphysical and logical price; for the use to which prāpti was put, viz., saving nirvāṇa and ultimately, as we shall see, saving perception and knowledge to boot, is blushingly, shamefully inconsistent with kṣanikavāda and anityavāda. Prāpti is a conceptual blunder of monumental proportions, and we're not finished with it or its implications yet. This ends our discussion of the dharma system, the four modifications advocated by the Sarvāstivāda, and the four curious blunders to which those modifications led.

Before moving on to the second of the doctrines introduced by Sarvāstivāda, the following table might help the reader to see in a moment the entire Sarvāstivāda system of dharmas.

The list is helpful, if you happen to be a Sarvāstivāda, because it tells you what to beware of (the saṁskṛta dharmas), and what to aim for (the asaṁskṛta dharmas, two of them, anyway); the list says, 'Don't store up your treasure where moths, rust and saṁskṛta dharmas doth corrupt.'

The lists of dharmas differ from one school to another in early Budhism, even among the Hīnayāna, themselves. Indeed, the Theravāda school of Hīnayāna, which compiled a theory of moments under Buddhaghoṣa in the early 5th century, C.E., rejected large parts of the following list.

Table V The 75 Dharmas of the Sarvāstivāda School

Saṁskṛta Dharmas (72) (conditioned processes)	Total Number of Dharmas	Explanation of the Dharmas
1. rūpa (body, matter)	11	5 sense organs 5 objects of sensation 1 unmanifested action
2. vedanā (sensation)	1	
3. samjñā (perception of judgment)	1	Dharmas that are conscious 44 (doubt, desire, memory, etc.) & unconscious 14 (anitya, prāpti, life force, etc.)
4. saṁskāras (mental) constituents)	58	
5. vijñāna (consciousness)	1	
Subtotal	72 dharmas	
Asaṁskṛta Dharmas (3) (unconditioned states)		
1. prajñā (intuitive wisdom)	1	While attachment to the saṁskṛta dharmas, above, lead to bondage and pain, the asaṁskṛta dharmas produce no karma and do not, therefore, lead to bondage.
2. nirvāṇa (liberation)	1	
3. akaśa (space)	1	
Subtotal	3 dharmas	
Grand Total	75 dharmas	

The Theravāda counted only 51 dharmas; and they held, furthermore, that nirvāṇa alone is asaṁskṛta, i.e. nirvāṇa alone is not caused and it produces no traces. Further, the Theravāda held that monks have the greatest chance for reaching nirvāṇa. They also believed, unlike the Sarvāstivāda, that the past and the future do not exist, and that the arhats are perfect in all respects. Finally, these Theravāda hedged on the non-soul, anātman, doctrine, arguing only that a Self could "not be found," while their rivals, the Sarvāstivāda, had denied the existence of such a Self outright. But on many other issues both schools seem to have been in fairly close agreement.[174] We turn next to the second of the doctrines introduced by Sarvāstivāda, viz., the metaphysical body-mind dualism that underlies the Sarvāstivāda solution to the problem of perception.

2) <u>The Doctrine of Body-Mind Dualism</u>. Both the Theravāda and Sarvāstivāda schools of the Hīnayāna *Abhidharma* adopt a dualistic view of the world, with mind (citta) moments, on the one hand, and matter (rūpa) moments, on the other, forming the metaphysical dharma components of that dualism. This common *Abhidharma* tradition states that all of the material and mental phenomena of the world have their origin in these two substances. David J. Kalupahana commenting on this dualism states:

> It [material substance] was the very basis of derived matter (*upādāya rūpa*); hence it was itself not derived (*no upādā*), [it] is irreducible. It was the *material substance*.

And similarly for mental substance:

> In the same way, the Abhidharmika [the philosophers of Sarvāstivāda and the Theravāda] analysis of psychic phenomena (*nāma*), into two types, mind (*citta*), and mental coefficients (*cetasika*), leads ultimately to a theory of mental substance.[175]

In attempting a philosophic history of Sarvāstivāda thought we might well ask what were the philosophic questions that led to the adoption of this dualistic metaphysical realism? I would suggest that one question was probably something like this: What is the origin of all the things that I experience? Or, perhaps, begging that question, but more to the metaphysical point: When I look at my experiences they seem quite naturally to fall into two quite distinct categories, viz., the physical and the mental. Now why is this? For, first, I have ideas that I get from a physical world out there, external to my mind and will and attentions; and second, I have ideas that I get from a mental world in here, an internal world, seemingly under the control of my will and subject to my attentions and consciousness. Now, why do my experiences seem to fall into these two categories and no others? i.e. into no more than two, and no fewer than two?

The answer that the Sarvāstivāda found to these questions lay in their metaphysical conclusion that that was simply the way the world had to be, i.e. the world must be constituted by a metaphysical dualism of body, on the one hand, and mind, on the other. In other words, the epistemological question, Why do I know only body and mind? leads to the metaphysical answer, Because that's all that there is.

But now two major problems enter. If we assume that mind and matter are both ultimately real, that neither one is reducible to the other, i.e. that body isn't really mind, as the metaphysical idealists say, and that mind isn't really body, as the metaphysical materialists say, nor are both reducible to some third substance like Brahman as the metaphysical Absolutists say, then how is it that one of these two can affect or causally influence the other? And if one of them can affect or causally influence the other, such that mind, for example, can come to know matter or body, then what is the nature of that knowledge?

Let me take the first question first. If our two substances, mind and body, are totally distinct, irreducible and eternal reals then how is it that the two can ever interact with or affect one another? For interaction would seem to be difficult if not impossible, so it is argued, between two such disperate, unlike and altogether different substances as mind and body. And yet body does affect mind, e.g., in perception where my sensing color causes me to perceive or to have an idea of color; and mind does affect body, e.g., in willing where my willing to move my arm causes me to move my arm. Now, how are these activities possible given the metaphysical separateness and distinctness of mind and body? This question constitutes what is technically called "the mind-body problem." We'll return to it, below, when we discuss the problem of interaction in Sautrāntika.

The second question, If mind can know body or matter or the physical world (the words are interchangeable) then what is the nature of that knowledge?, leads us into the second major problem with which our two Hīnayāna schools were concerned. This second question follows from the assumption that the mind-body problem and the problems of perception and knowledge have been solved in some fashion or other, and it is this: What is the nature of the knowledge that the mind has of body? In other words, when I perceive the world and claim to know the world, do I know it directly as it really is, or only indirectly and only as it appears to consciousness? These questions constitute what is technically called "the problems of direct and indirect perception", problems that we shall also be considering, below. This ends our discussion of metaphysical body-mind dualism. We turn next to the third and final doctrine introduced by Sarvāstivāda, viz., the doctrine of direct perception.

3) The Doctrine of Direct Perception or Direct Realism. Consider these questions, again. When mind knows the world (and the solution to the problems of perception and knowledge permit us to say this), then what is the nature of that knowledge? i.e. Do I know the world, directly, as it really is? Or do I know the world, indirectly, as it merely seems? If the world endures or holds still long enough for me to perceive it, and the Sarvāstivāda with their metaphysical dualism and their metaphysical glue of prāpti, and their belief in static moments, have argued that it does, then I ought to be able to perceive things the way they really are. My ideas of the world ought to be identical to the way the world really is. However, if the world is always changing, as the Sautrāntikas will maintain, then I am able to perceive things only indirectly and only in the way that they seem or appear.

The Sarvāstivāda hold that there are three necessary conditions for direct perception or direct knowledge of an object. They are, first, a seer or eye or sense organ which sees when the conditions are right, e.g. when the light is right, when the eye is not diseased, and so on; second, eye-consciousness, the knowledge that consciousness (vijñāna) has when the eye sees; and thirdly, the object that the eye sees and that the mind is conscious of:

> The object, the eye, the eye-consciousness,
> and the light, all manifest their power,

> i.e. become active and flash forth simultaneously. The object appears, the eye sees, and the eye-consciousness knows it. This is called the direct knowledge of an object.[175]

The Sarvāstivāda theory of direct perception, then, comes down to the following three points: First, the external world and mind are both "real", composed of permanent individual moments, i.e. momentarily unchanging dharmas, leading to a dualism of two real substances, mind and body; second, the external world of body is "real", in a secondary sense, in that it exists independently of mind, i.e. even if there were no minds that external world would still be there; third, that independent external world of "real" physical objects can be known directly by minds in the sense that what appears to mind is precisely and exactly what exists in the world, i.e. when eye-consciousness or mind perceives this black and white book being held by these brown hands then there really is a book and it really is black and white, and it really is held by hands that really are as brown out there in the world as they appear to be up here in the mind. But that this theory of direct perception is patently absurd and indefensible will be demonstrated below.

This ends our discussion of the three important doctrines of Sarvāstivāda, viz., first, the doctrine of the 75 dharmas, and especially the asaṁskṛta dharmas of prajñā and nirvāṇa, the two necessary ingredients for making nirvāṇa possible, and the saṁskṛta dharma of prāpti, the metaphysical glue that holds saṁtānas together and that makes nirvāṇa stick once it has been reached, and the theory of static moments of the dharmas, sthitikṣaṇa; second, the doctrine of metaphysical body-mind dualism, the doctrine of the two real substances underlying the dharmas; third, and finally, the doctrine of direct perception, or direct realism, which is made possible as a result of the presence of prāpti, sthitikṣaṇa and the body-mind dualism, all three of which then make both perception and knowledge possible, as well. In other words, despite some blushing inconsistencies, messy modifications and blundering howlers, in spite of it all, it would appear that Sarvāstivāda has solved the problem of kṣaṇikavāda, and along with it the problem of perception, the problem of knowledge and a new problem of nirvāṇa. But the price has been high. And just how high can be seen, in part, as we examine three problems of direct realism: The problem of sthitikṣaṇa, the problem of prāpti and the problem of direct perception.

c. The Problems of Direct Realism.

The three problems that we are about to present all seem to have one thing in common: They are all groping for something substantial, permanent and identical through time, in the face of a dogma, a world, a religion and philosophy that offer nothing but insubstantiality, impermanence and diversity through time. It is these gropings that lead to the three problems that follow.

1) The Problem of Sthitikṣaṇa. Sthitikṣaṇa refers to an "unchanging moment", a moment with a past, present and future, that we had previously defined, rather clumsily, as a "momentarily unchanging moment."[177] But the clumsiness of the expression is merely a sign of a problem inherent in this concept. So what's going on here, anyway?

The Sarvāstivāda must have been concerned about an argument like the following:

1. If kṣaṇikavāda is true then everything is momentary (by definition).

2. If everything is momentary then perception, knowledge and nirvāṇa are impossible (by implication).

3. But perception, knowledge and nirvana are possible (by common sense, the Canon and the Buddha).

4. Therefore, kṣaṇikavāda is not true (by valid deduction from 1, 2 and 3).

Well, one thing that's to be done is to tinker with kṣaṇa, i.e. those moments. Show that moments are a lot different than anyone thought they were. Show that they last longer than anyone thought that they would last. Show that each moment has a past, a present and a future and that, as a consequence, it endures during that time. Show, in other words, that moments are permanent. Show, in still other words, that moments are not moments. And therein lies the problem.

One is reminded, in a way, of the "problem of time" and the argument which demonstrates that time does not exist. That argument begins by dividing time into past, present and future. It then shows that neither the past nor the future exists, for one is gone and the other is not yet, and the present is merely a momentary and non-existent dividing line between these other two non-existent entities; hence the present doesn't exist either. Therefore, the argument concludes, time does not exist. Thus the problem of time.

The problem of time illustrated by this argument is attributed to the African theologian, St. Aurelius Augustine (354-430 C.E.), who discusses it in his *Confessions*.[178] The problem was "solved" by the American philosopher, William James, in a manner reminiscent of the Sarvāstivāda "solution" to the problem of kṣaṇikavāda. James introduced the notion of the "specious present", an arbitrarily long, present moment stretching several seconds into the past and several seconds into the future.[179] Thus a present moment, a rather long one, existed after all and the problem of time was "solved." In other words, the present wasn't a present, it was a specious present. Thus the specious moment solution to the problem of time.

The Sarvāstivāda have found themselves in a similar fix with kṣaṇa and have "solved" their problem in an audaciously similar fashion, i.e. by making the moment not a moment, i.e. by making it arbitrarily long by the simple device of stretching the moment into several moments. Thus an enduring moment exists, after all, it's just a bit in the past, a little bit in the present, and a little bit more in the future. In other words the moment isn't a moment, it's a specious kṣaṇa. Thus the sthitikṣaṇa solution to the problem of kṣaṇikavāda.

But it won't work. Philosophical problems aren't solved by introducing any old arbitrary concept, especially ones that fly in the face of either common sense or metaphysical tradition. Using specious anything to solve either the problem of time or the problem of kṣaṇikavāda is like trying to solve a philosophic problem by redefining the terms that were necessary to generate the problem to begin with. It is reminiscent of those notoriously putative solutions to the problem of the existence of God, "solved" by saying that God isn't God, but a necessary Being that must exist for if He didn't he wouldn't be God, e.g. as St. Anselm of Canterbury would say, God's essence involves His existence; or to the theological problem of evil (suffering) "solved" by saying, evil isn't evil but an illusion that doesn't really exist, e.g. as some Vedānists would say, evil (suffering) is māyā. These are "solutions" by way of the arbitrary alteration of the terminology of the original problems which leave us with new problems but with no new solutions to the old problems.

All of these putative solutions pretend to show that the terms of the original problem have been misconstrued, misunderstood or wrongly interpreted. James is telling us that the present moment is not a present moment but a specious present moment; St. Anselm is telling us that God is not God but a necessarily existing God; the Vedāntist is telling us that evil (suffering) is not really evil but a mere appearance of māyā. And now the Sarvāstivāda are telling us that a moment is not a moment but a sthitikṣaṇa. We blush and move on.

<u>2) The Problem of Prāpti</u>. The dharma of prāpti is a curious dharma to say the least. But it makes a kind of sense to talk about it as a metaphysical glue that holds saṁtānas together thereby giving back the common sense world that the Heracleitean kṣaṇikavāda had threatened to sunder. But one problem remains with prāpti: What is it that holds or links or connects prāpti to the dharmas that it's supposed to be gluing together? For consider: Suppose that I want to connect two dharmas together, either two desires one to another, or the dharma of nirvāṇa into the dharma of consciousness, or some such thing. I need three things (dharmas), i.e. two dharmas and one prāpti. Now, it's not as simple as it sounds, gluing those two dharmas together with prāpti. First, one dharma, $dharma_1$, has to have prāpti fixed to it, and then another dharma, $dharma_2$, has to have prāpti fixed into it, both in such a way that the two dharmas are kept separate yet connected. Consider the diagram:

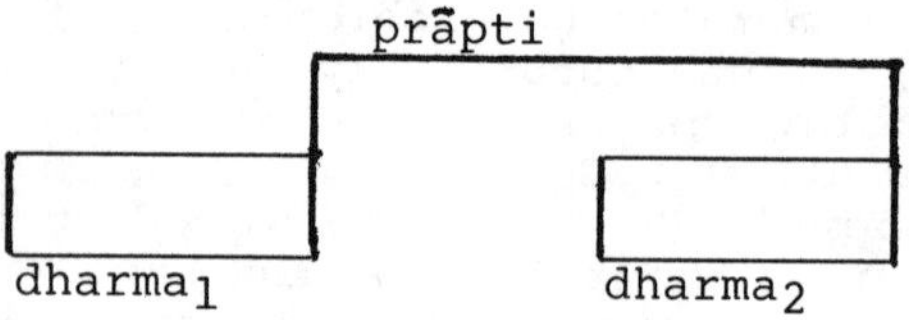

Now prāpti links, glues or sticks into dharma$_1$; but what holds it in that dharma? At the point of connection what connects the gluey point, or whatever it is that touches the dharma, on the left to dharma$_1$? And what links the gluey point, or whatever, on the right to dharma$_2$? Do we need another prāpti, prāpti$_2$, a sort of meta-prāpti, to link left hand gluey point to dharma$_1$? and another prāpti, prāpti$_3$, to link right hand gluey point to dharma$_2$? Consider the diagram?

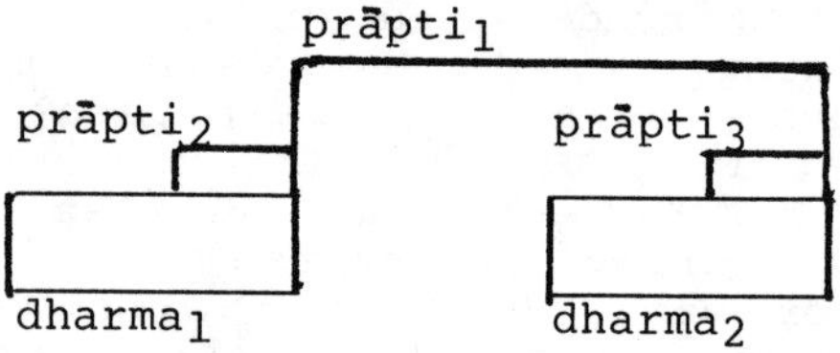

And so on *ad infinitum*, as we attempt to link not only dharmas to dharmas, the whole reason for the original silly introduction of prāpti, but prāpti$_1$ to dharma$_1$, then prāpti$_2$ to dharma$_1$, then prāpti$_4$ to prāpti$_2$ and dharma$_1$ and so on and on.[180] But if the use of links and connectors like prāpti leads to absurdities like infinite regresses then they must be themselves absurd.

As long as the Sarvāstivāda are handing out prāptis why not build the hooking and linking mechanism directly into the dharmas, themselves, and make them self-gluing, self-linking or self-sticking? That would be an elegant and parsimonious solution to the problem of prāpti; and it would certainly have avoided the regress, thereby saving everyone metaphysical embarrassment.

3) The Problem of Direct Perception. If the moments endure and if the glue holds then supposedly we're going to have perceptual knowledge. But one final problem remains, viz., the problem of direct perception. The critic claims that the direct realist is caught in an absurdity when the latter claims that he can have direct knowledge of an object. The theory

of direct realism states that what is perceived (and judged in the mind) is identical with what is out there in the world. There is, in other words, a relation of identity between what appears and what is. But that's absurd.

Consider this: Suppose that the eye senses, i.e. that it is visually stimulated by, a rope coiled up in the corner of the room. But suppose that, while the eye senses this rope, the mind perceives, i.e. it is conscious of, a snake so that it falsely judges, "This is a snake." This illusion, i.e. this mistaking what the senses sense, destroys the credibility of the theory of direct perception. For that theory said that what appears (to mind) is precisely what is (in the world). Hence, if illusions are possible, and common sense and our own experiences tell us that they are, then Sarvāstivāda's direct realism is a most naive theory of perception, if not a downright false theory of perception. For direct realism says, If I perceive a snake, when I see a rope, then there must really be a snake, and not a rope, out there in the world. So much for the problem of direct perception (direct realism).

Several repairs to the theory of direct realism were made by the second school immediately associated with Hīnayāna Buddhism. We turn to that school next with a brief examination of Sautrāntika.

d. The Sautrāntika School and Indirect Realism

The Sautrāntikas reject the Abhidharma philosophy of both the Theravāda Buddhists as well as the Sarvāstivāda Buddhists. They urge, instead, a return to the original discourses, to the Sūtra literature of the Pāli Canon; hence their name, which indicates how heavily they relied on the sūtrānta, i.e. the Sūtra doctrines. However, they do accept several doctrines that are not found in the Sūtras, most notably paramāṇuvāda, i.e. atomism, and kṣaṇikavāda, i.e. momentariness. Along with the latter, they also accept the Abhidharma doctrine of the dharmas, viz., that the world is in a constant and ceaseless state of flux, a macroscopic flux of wholes as well as a microscopic flux of dharmic parts of wholes.

Because of this flux, they argue, neither matter nor mind, whose dharmic parts are involved in perception, endure long enough to connect and coordinate one with the other in order to have direct perception:

> When the object (*rūpa*) and the eye exist, the visual consciousness is non-existent. When visual consciousness exists, the eye and the object are not existing. In the absence of their duration (*sthiti*) there is no possibility of the cognition of the object.[181]

As a consequence, all of my perceptions of an object must be indirect (apratyakṣa) perceptions for when the object exists then consciousness of it does not, and by the time consciousness of it exists then the object has fluxed away. This time lag between object and consciousness makes direct perception impossible; what is available to sensation is merely a representation of the now-vanished object. The existence of the material object must be inferred, therefore, from this representation. Hence the name for this theory, "the representative theory of perception" or "the theory of the inferability of the external object." But the time lag is not the whole story behind this story, as we shall see.

Notice that, on this theory, the snake-rope illusion mentioned previously can be neatly handled so that it ceases to be a problem, or at least it ceases to be the same problem that we met, above, with the Sarvāstivāda. For, suppose that I see a snake where there is really only a rope. In place of saying, as with the Sarvāstivāda, "There is a snake" (which is false), I am now committed to saying with the Sautrāntika theory of indirect perception, "There is something that resembles, or looks like, a snake" (which is true). The epistemological shift to indirect realism entails a linguistic shift from certainties and absolutes to tentativeness and probabilities. There is no longer an identity between what is (out there) and what appears (in here) but only a relation of likeness or resemblance. The Sautrāntikas have rescued perception from the clutches of naiveté and falsehood by altering the perceptual situation and the language employed to describe that situation.

The Sautrāntika theory of perception comes down to the following two points: First, permanence is illusory; neither mind nor matter are "real" in the permanent, dual-substance sense, held by Sarvāstivāda.

The orderly flux and regular change of the dharmas, however, gives the appearance of permanence, and it is that apparent permanence that forms the basis for cognition of the world. The Sautrāntikas vigorously rejected the Sarvāstivāda doctrine of substance (svabhāva) arguing that such a doctrine smuggled the notion of Ātman back into Buddhism. Momentary and transitory dharmas existing now, in the present, and not in the past or future, are all that exist. Consequently, for the Sautrāntikas, unlike the Sarvāstivāda, both past and future time are unreal.

Second, subject and object, mind and body, though distinct and real, are, nonetheless, related in such a way as to make cognition or knowledge of the world possible. And yet the relation is *not* one of causal interaction, as we shall see. In cognition, what becomes known is a representation that resembles the object being cognized. The object is known, then, by inference from what appears in consciousness and the latter is then "coordinated" with what exists in the objective world. Let's pursue this for a moment.

It might be asked, given these separate and distinct realities of body and mind, and given what appears to be a causal interaction between them, don't the Sautrāntikas run afoul of the same mind-body problem that proved to be such a puzzle for the Sarvāstivāda? The Saturāntikas attempt to avoid the problem by denying interaction completely and by some very sophisticated philosophic maneuvers which, even if unsuccessful, must be admired for their ingenuity.

In an imaginary dialogue composed by the great Vasubandhu, we witness a debate between a Sammitīya, or Vātsīputrīya, a philosopher who believes that the self or soul or pudgala was something more than a series of momentary events[182], and a Sautrāntika, committed to anātmavāda and to a dharmic phenomenalism of flashing and changing moments of forces. We find them here debating the existence of a real self and the relationship between the self (mind) and the world (body). Now, if the Sautrāntika admits either that the self is anything more than a series of connected momentary events of consciousness or that there is a causal interaction between self and world, he's going to be in philosophic trouble. There are at least three problems taken up by Vasubandhu in this dialogue, viz., the problems of memory, the self and cause, and

I shall label them as such as we pass through this classic debate.

1) <u>The Problem of Memory</u>.

Vātsīputrīya: If there is no self, who is it that remembers?

Sautrāntika: What is the meaning of the word "to remember"?

V: It means to grasp an object by memory.

S: Is this "grasping by memory" something different from memory?

V: It is an actor who acts through memory.

S: The agency by which memory is produced we have just explained [it consists of 1. attention directed toward an object; 2. an idea either similar or connected with it; 3. absence of pain, distraction, etc., i.e. the presence of the right conditions]. The cause productive of a recollection is a suitable state of mind (and nothing else)!

V: But when (in common life) we are using the expression "Caitra remembers" what does it mean?

S: In the current (of phenomena), which is designated by the name Caitra a recollection appears. We notice the fact and express it. It is no more!

V: But if there is no self, whose is the recollection (whom does it belong to?)?

S: What is here the meaning of the Genitive "whose"?

V: It denotes proprietorship.

S: Is it the same as when somebody enquires, of what objects who is the proprietor?

V: It is just as when we say "Caitra is the owner of a cow."

S: What does it mean to be the owner of a cow?

V: It means that it depends on him to employ her for milking or for driving purposes etc.

S: Now, I should like to know to what place must I dispatch my memory, since it is supposed that I am the master of it.

V: You must direct it toward the remembered object.

S: What for shall I direct my memory?
V: In order to remember.
S: Hallo! I must employ the very thing I already possess in order to get it! Indeed that is well spoken! Great is the merit (of such discoveries)!

The Sautrāntika reduces the Vātsīputrīya's position to an absurdity by showing that the latter has multiplied entities (try "remembering to remember a memory" for a start) beyond necessity. This is a deft application of Ockham's razor,[183] the principle of simplicity that says, *Don't* multiply entities beyond necessity, as the Sautrāntika slices off the Vātsīputrīya's self-as-Rememberer....

2) The Problem of Self, i.e. of "Action-Therefore-Actor":

Vātsīputrīya: There are others who argue as follows: (a self must exist), because wherever there is an activity it depends on an actor. Every action depends on an actor as, e.g., in the example "Devadatta walks" there is an action of walking which depends on Devadatta, the actor. To be conscious [to know] is likewise an action, hence the actor who cognizes [knows] must also exist.

Sautrāntika: It must be explained what this Devadatta is.

The Sautrāntika may be asking, "Is this Devadatta merely the subject of a sentence which stands in need of a verb?" in which case the problem of action-therefore-actor is simply a linguistic problem. Or is the matter more substantive, and is he saying that Devadatta is a self, again? The latter is the interpretation that the Vātsīputrīya now gives to "Devadatta":

V: It is a self.
S: That is begging the question.
V: It is what in common life we call a man.
S: This does not represent any unity whatsoever. It is a name given to such elements (of which man is composed). The elements [dharmas] are meant when we say "Devadatta walks." When we say that "consciousness knows", it is just the same. [A version of Buddhist nominalism

is offered here.][184]

V: And what is the meaning of the expression "Devadatta walks" (if there is no individuality whatsoever)?

S: It is an unbroken continuity of momentary forces (flashing into existence), which simple people believe to be a unity, and to which they give the name of Devadatta. Their belief that Devadatta moves is conditioned (by an analogy with their own experience, because) their own continuity of life consists in constantly moving from one place to another. But this movement is but a (series of new) productions in different places, just as the expression "fire moves", "sound spreads" have the meaning of continuities (of new productions in new places)....

The inference from action to actor is seen to be fallacious; it is the same with fire where we have plenty of action but, strictly speaking, no actor or agent or self who acts. The Sautrāntika, finally, is not above putting a little *ad hominem* touch to his attack by stating that only "simple people" could believe otherwise and agree with the Vātsīputrīya.

But now we come to the problem relating to perception, knowledge of the world, and the relationship between body and mind.

3) The Problem of Cause, i.e. Interaction:

Vātsīputrīya: But we read in Scripture "consciousness apprehends" [i.e. consciousness grasps the object of consciousness, so what is the relation between mind (subject), and body (object)?]. What is consciousness here meant to do?

What, indeed? The Sautrāntika in his answer must make it clear that there is no grasping or apprehending of the object by the subject - that way leads to interaction and the mind-body problem. Vasubandhu, here donning the robes of the Sautrantika, argues for a curious relation between mind and body called "coordination", *sādṛśya*. In doing so he sounds as if he were, first, espousing a Buddhist version of Spinozistic psycho-physical parallelism and, second, a version of what we can only refer to as "Sautrāntika coordinationism," a theory which tends to support even further the theory of indirect perception:

> *Sautrāntika*: Nothing at all! (It [consciousness] simply appears in coordination with its objective elements, like a result which is homogeneous with its cause). When a result appears in conformity with its own cause it is doing nothing at all, nevertheless we say that it *does* conform with it. Consciousness likewise appears in coordination with its objective elements. It is (properly speaking) *doing* nothing. Nevertheless we say that consciousness *does* know its object [though there is no "causal" connection between them wherein the object *makes* knowledge occur].
>
> *V*: What is meant by coordination (between consciousness and its objective element)? [What, indeed!]
>
> *S*: A conformity between them, the fact owing to which cognition, although caused (also) by the activity of the senses, is not something homogeneous with them. It is said to know the object and not the senses... And again the expression "consciousness apprehends" is not inadequate, inasmuch as here also a continuity of conscious moments is the cause of every cognition. ("Consciousness apprehends" means that the previous moment is the cause of the following one)....

But while body and senses are causally homogeneous, i.e. they are parts of the same causally related dharma-patterns of body, and while mind and consciousness are causally homogeneous, i.e. they are parts of the same causally related dharma-patterns of mind, it is not the case that these two dharma-patterns interact or are causally related, except in the sense of being "coordinated." It is important to realize that the Sautrāntika is claiming that the mind knows the external object and that it does not merely know its own sense organs nor its own ideas; the first suggestion is silly and the second constitutes idealism, and the Sautrāntikas are neither silly nor are they idealists.

The assumption underlying this entire discussion is that like acts on like, and since mind and body are unlike they can never interact. We have here further support for the Sautrāntika theory of indirect perception. In fact, in the end, the theory of coordination and the time lag theory that supports indirect perception are probably both saying the same thing about the relation between mind and body, viz., mind and body don't causally interact.

Vasubandhu concludes with two marvelous analogies that drive home the point of Sautrāntika causality:

> *S*: The actor here also denotes simply the cause, just as in the current expression "the bell resounds" (the bell is doing nothing, but every following moment of sound is produced by the previous one). (We can give) another (illustration): consciousness apprehends similarly to the way in which a light moves.
>
> *V*: And how does a light move?
>
> *S*: The light of a lamp is a common metaphorical designation for an uninterrupted production of a series of flashing flames. When this production changes its place, we say that the light has moved (but in reality other flames have appeared in another place). Similarly consciousness is a conventional name for a chain of conscious moments. When it changes its place (i.e. appears in coordination with another objective element) we say that it apprehends that object.[185]

So much for "interaction" and the mind-body problem.

Put in a slightly different way, there is causal intra-action among mind dharmas and body dharmas, but there is no causal interaction between mind and body. And because interaction does not occur, having been replaced by "coordination", the mind-body problem does not arise.

We are left to speculate, of course, as to just how much of a solution to the mind-body problem this theory of coordination actually offers. Perhaps the solution, or the theory, leaves us, or the Sautrāntikas, worse off than the Sarvāstivāda who were really stuck with the problem. Causal coordination in the form that Vasubandha presents it, must leave us wondering: If there is no interaction between mind and body, and if they are simply "coordinated" (like two wound-up clocks, one of which shows the time while the other chimes the hours, both in perfect alignment and accord) then why in the world do they *seem* to be causally interacting all the time? And if mind and body are "coordinated" what in the world does that mean? And what or who coordinates them? Is there room here or not for some kind of Leibnitzian pre-planned harmony? because mind and body seem to be coordinated in a most harmonious way.

As a way of giving the Sautrāntika the penultimate word on this problem of interaction, I invite the reader to consider the doctrine of indirect perception and the time lag theory which led to it. Doesn't the time lag theory tend to support the theory of mind-body coordination, both of which support the theory of indirect perception, by demonstrating that mind and body cannot possibly interact because of the lag of time between bodily sensation and mental perception? And if they cannot interact then isn't the theory of coordination a reasonable way out of the problem of interaction?

But the theory of coordination would seem to raise more questions and problems than it actually answers or solves. Perhaps we, along with the Sarvāstivāda, might be better off being stuck with the mind-body problem, after all.

In conclusion, we might just say that the Sautrāntikas believed that the phenomenal world, the world of external, momentarily existing dharmas, was composed of invisible units called "atoms", *paramāṇu*, which coalesce together to form impermanent physical objects. This theory of atoms together with the doctrines of indirect realism and indirect perception, and the theory of time lag between sensation and perception, and the theory of coordination all constitute the philosophic contribution of Sautrāntika to Buddhist thought.

However, there are also problems that metaphysical realism and the theory of indirect realism have that warrant further investigation. Again, we mention three such problems.

d. The Problems of Indirect Realism

1) The Problem of "Looks Like". Suppose that the eye senses the rope and suppose that the time lag enters so that mind perceives indirectly some object or other, whether the rope or the illusory snake. In each case it judges, "I see what looks like a rope" (true enough) or "I see what looks like a snake" (also true enough). What has this shift from the language of *is* to the language of *looks like* actually accomplished? It was claimed that the language of indirect perception saves us from the epistemological embarrassment of making false claims about illusory experiences. But so what? The Sautrāntika may find this epistemological face-saving useful in avoiding criticisms and cries of "falsehood" from his critics, but what has the move really accomplished as far as knowing the world is concerned? What one wants to know is, "Is that thing a snake or not" and not what it looks like. Looks-like snakes can bite just as mortally as real snakes, and therefore looks-like language, while it may protect an epistemologically cautious Sautrāntika from criticism, won't prevent one from getting bitten by a snake.

To show how vacuous the whole move to indirect realism actually is consider the logic of the language employed. There is a perfectly innocuous sense in which anything in the world is like any other thing in the world. The coiled rope in the corner, for example, is like an elephant (trunk and tail), like an oyster (flat and close to the ground), like the Taj Mahal (a physical object in space and time), and so on. Therefore, any statement of the form "x is like y", where 'x' and 'y' are variables standing for any named physical object whatsoever, is going to be logically true, i.e. necessarily true; and all similes have this curious property of being logically true. Therefore, if one is merely saving oneself from epistemological embarrassment by resorting to the linguistic move that we attributed to the Sautrāntikas why, then, let's resort away!

But such a move is vacuous, as I say, because in saving truth or in protecting truth in this way one is no closer to knowing the empirical world which is, after all, the very purpose of perception in the first place. We want to know whether it's a snake or a rope coiled over there in the corner, and not merely what it looks like, seems like or resembles. The

Sautrāntika's or anyone's theory of indirect perception would seem to be useless, therefore, in the practical cognition of the world.

2) The Problem of Verification. The Sautrāntika might respond, of course, that he could go over to the corner and check up on the object in order to determine whether it really does look like a snake (or a rope). Such a verification would lead to more and more "looks-like" statements; and with each one, he might argue, the original claim, "It looks like a snake (or rope)", would become more and more probable. At least he would know, he might conclude, whether to pick it up or call the zoo.

But look closely at this process of checking up. What's going on here? All that one is having are more and more indirect perceptions, more and more representations. I never see the rope directly, but only its representation: The rope might well be swiftly and miraculously replaced each time my perception is being formed (remember that vicious time lag between sensation and perception). In fact, all that I ever know is that representation, so how on earth can I check it with anything except other similar representations?

It now appears that I'm locked up in my own mind, staring at my mental representations, unable to break out at all to that rope (or that snake). Indirect realism would seem to lead, therefore, to a kind of subjective idealism that says that all one can ever know are the contents (representations) of one's own consciousness. And Sautrāntika realism seems doomed.

3) The Problem of Hallucinations. Finally, there is a problem common to all perceptual realists, whether they be direct realists, like the Sarvāstivāda, or indirect realists, like the Sautrāntikas. This is the problem of hallucinations. While an *illusion* is a case of misinterpretation of a sensation, e.g., mistaking a snake for a rope, an *hallucination* is a case of perceiving or judging where there is no prior associated sensation, whatsoever. Suppose I look in the corner of the room and perceive a snake but suppose on looking more closely I discover there is no snake there at all - and no rope either! Nothing! Then we say that I was having the hallucination of a snake, a situation where a purely

mental phenomenon is mistakenly "seen" and believed to be out there in the world.

Now the problem that the perceptual realist faces is that of trying to show that the sense experiences he has are really *sense* experiences. We have already seen that the Sautrāntika is unable to contact the world directly, for everything is conveniently "coordinated", and he is therefore unable to check up on his sense experiences in order to see that they really are *sense* experiences since all that he can examine are further mental representations of that experience. And since he cannot distinguish mental representations that are purely hallucinatory from mental representations that may be coordinated with objects that are sensed, the problem of hallucinations must remain a puzzle for him, indeed.

The Sarvāstivāda position is no better since the assumption on which he bases his entire theory of direct realism, i.e. the assumption that there is a physical object which he is experiencing directly whenever he has sense experiences, does not even allow him to distinguish hallucinatory experiences from true sense experiences. Recall the trouble that the Sarvāstivāda got into with illusions, and the curious conclusion that we came to, viz., that the Sarvāstivāda must admit that whatever appears must be what is really there.

The problems encountered by the metaphysical realist and the perceptual realist will have to wait for further treatment until we come to metaphysical and epistemological idealism.

The realist tendencies in the philosophy of Hīnayāna Buddhism gradually give way to the idealist tendencies of Mahāyāna Buddhism. I shall postpone summarizing the ten tendencies and characteristics of Hīnayāna Buddhism until we have completed our philosophic history of Mahāyāna Buddhism, and it is to the latter philosophy and religion that we shall now bend our efforts.[186]

Chapter Four: Mahāyāna Buddhism

The roots of Mahāyāna Buddhism can be found in both the second Second Buddhist Council in 346 B.C.E. and the Third Buddhist Council at Pāṭaliputra in 247 B.C.E. At these councils the heresies of the Mahāsaṅghikas and the Sammitīyas first made their appearance.[187] Both heresies exhibited a kind of "creeping eternalism", with the Sammitīyas plumping for a sort of eternal self and the Mahāsaṅghikas pushing for a sort of eternal Buddha. Recall that the Mahāsaṅghikas had contended that the Buddha was not an ordinary man but, rather, that he was superior to the common man, and a being with super-normal and extraordinary powers. As a super-human being the Buddha was worthy of special attention, consideration, respect and, ultimately, worship. It is in these early disputes about the true nature of the Buddha and the self that the seeds are sown for subsequent dissention, schism and, finally, Mahāyāna orthodoxy.

By the time of the Fourth Buddhist Council under the Emperor Kaniṣka in Kaśmīr in the 2nd century C.E., Mahāyāna had emerged as the most powerful new movement of Buddhist religion and philosophy of India. In subsequent centuries Mahāyāna spread northwards and eastwards to China, Tibet, Korea, Mongolia, Southeast Asia and Japan, geographical areas in which it still exists today.

During this period Mahāyāna appears to bear certain broad similarities to developing Hindu thought and many of those similarities seem to lie at the root of the subsequent disputes between Mahāyāna and Hīnayāna, including those earlier disputes over the nature of the Buddha and the self.[188] Many of those broad similarities result in what we have called "creeping eternalism", e.g. the slow erosion of the doctrine of anitya and its gradual replacement by more eternalist doctrines, such as the Mahāyāna doctrine of the holy Dharma[189] (i.e. the Buddhist Truth or Teaching); such as the emergence of the doctrine of the eternal Buddha[190] (Who came to be identified with the holy Dharma); such as the evolution of the doctrine of the eternal Buddhas and Bodhisattvas;[191] such as the doctrines of Ālayavijñāna and Vijñaptimātra,[192] (the storehouse of eternal Consciousness and Pure Consciousness, respectively, of the Yogācāra school); and such as, finally, the doctrine of śūnya or śūnyatā (the Void or eternal

Emptiness, respectively, of the Mādhyamika school). These are all instances of what look suspiciously like an eternal or ultimate "Reality" in Mahāyāna.[193] We are, of course, well ahead of our story in mentioning these other ultimate Reals of Mahāyāna but we shall deal with each of them separately in the discussion which follows.

We turn, consequently, to an examination of Mahāyāna Buddhism. As with Hīnayāna previously, I want to look at this religion and its philosophy under ten headings that will roughly parallel the ten tendencies or characteristics dealt with under Hīnayāna. I shall, once again, state and briefly discuss the properties that elucidate each of these tendencies, follow with a brief comparison of that property with its Hīnayāna counterpart, and then, in keeping with our intention to present a philosophic history of Buddhism, I shall point out a problem or problems that such a characterization entails together with an attempt, on several occasions, to dissolve or solve the problem or problems mentioned. Again, I must warn the reader that in many cases these characteristics are propensities or inclinations rather than absolute conditions of the new Buddhism.

1. Supernaturalism

Mahāyāna Buddhism tends to be a supernaturalistic religion. Mahāyāna emerges as a reaction against the relatively cold, passionless, monastic religion of the Hīnayāna, as we shall see. Mahāyāna redefines those persons that the Hīnayāna tradition called "Bodhisattvas", turning them into godlike and loving Saviors. It introduces methods and techniques for contacting these compassionate beings who, it was now believed, can aid man on the path to salvation. The chief thrust of Mahāyāna is religious reform, therefore, and the chief instruments of this reformation contain or entail supernatural or transcendental elements.

Mahāyāna philosophy tends to underplay the empirical, sense-oriented approach to knowledge and reality adopted by the Hīnayāna perceptual realists, and commits itself instead to the way of "mystical rationalism", i.e. to a non-empirical methodology involving prajñā, or intuitive wisdom. For example, Mahāyāna religion is committed to such transcendental, i.e. non-empirical, elements as divine grace and the forgiveness of sins and supernatural miracles and other divine slights-of-hand that can alter the empirical world and change the hard hearts of recalcitrant sinners. A greater significance is given to the supernatural worlds of the Gods, manifold Bodhisattvas and an infinite number of Buddhas, along with multifarious heavens and hells full of innumerable gods, demigods, demons and ghouls; add to this the belief in entities like transmigrating selves, which all come precariously close to similar concepts in the Hindu religion, and you have a full-blown Buddhist supernaturalism.

The chief source for this new religious thrust is the collection of Sanskrit texts called the *Prajñāpāramitā Sūtras*, "the perfection of wisdom," composed between 100 B.C.E. and 600 C.E. The *Prajñāpāramitā* literary corpus consists of some thirty-eight quite distinct books. Two of these books, from about 350 C.E., the *Diamond Sūtra (Vajracchedika-sūtra)* and the *Heart Sūtra (Hṛdaya-sūtra)*, have become classics in the history of Mahāyāna literature and they are singularly important basic religious texts in the Buddhism of China, Japan, Tibet and Mongolia, as we shall see.

All of the *Prajñāpāramitā Sūtras* are, of course, attributed to the Buddha and they employ bold, stylistic imitations of the earlier Pāli Sūtras. The new teachings begin, for example, with the familiar, "Thus have I (Ānanda) heard at one time," thereby giving an authenticity to these Sūtras that they would not otherwise possess. The authors of the *Sūtras* are playing, of course, the implication-intention game, composing, in effect, what Buddha intended to say from the implications gathered from what the tradition, or traditions, indicated he did say. Nowhere is this brought out more forcefully than at the beginning of the *Prajñāpāramitā Sūtra* where the rationale for the new literature is stated as "whatever is taught by a true disciple of the Buddha is in fact the word of the Buddha himself."[194] This is playing the intention-implication game with a new-found enthusiasm.

In the *Diamond Sūtra*, the Buddha speaks to a disciple named Subhuti, and ultimately leaves little doubt about the supernatural nature of what had come to be recognized as the new teaching. The dialogue between Subhuti and Buddha, or the Tathāgata, i.e.

that one who has come, or has gone, to nirvāṇa, here opens with a question:

> The Lord [asked]: 'What do you think, Subhuti, can the Tathāgata be seen by the possession of his marks?'[195]

A good question relating to the empirical recognition of real Buddhahood. But, for the *Diamond Sūtra*, the prajñā, or wisdom, that alone can signify the real mark or sign of a Buddha transcends the empirical and the sensory. Thus real Buddhahood is not related to the body of the physical Buddha with its empirical and sensory elements, but rather real Buddhahood is instead related to something that the Buddhists came to call the "dharma body" of the Buddha.

The dharma body represents, according to Edward Conze, "the absolute reality of Buddhahood"[196] and it is discovered not by the senses but by prajñā. The disciple, Subhuti, answers the previous question, as the dialogue continues:

> Subhuti replied: 'No, indeed, O Lord. And why? What has been taught by the Tathāgata as the possession of marks, that is truly a no-possession of no-marks.'[197]

The real knowledge of Buddha nature is empty of empirical content, and it is the discovery of that emptiness or void, śūnya, of the true Buddha nature that is to become the way to nirvāṇa. The phenomenal world, the self, and all that is taken by the ordinary person to be "real" are said now to be śūnya. When this emptiness, śūnyatā, is apprehended by the enlightened eye of prajñā, the organ of intuitive knowledge, then enlightenment (bodhi) or awakening occurs.

The Buddha counsels Subhuti further on the nature of this non-empirical, transcendental and intuitive way to enlightenment through prajñā when he says,

> Therefore then, Subhuti, the Bodhi-being, the great being, after he has got rid of all perceptions, should raise his thoughts to the utmost, right and perfect enlightenment. He should produce a thought which is unsupported by [emptied of] forms, sounds, smells, tastes, touchables, or mind-objects,

unsupported by dharma, unsupported by no-dharma, unsupported by anything. And why? All supports have actually no support.[198]

Fundamentally, all is emptiness, there is no thing to cling to or to grasp, to lean on or to stand on, for support. Realizing this by intuitive wisdom, one lets go, and in that letting go lies enlightenment.

We shall return to this philosophy of śūnya, which is the basis of Buddhahood and the central doctrine of the *Heart Sūtra* when we look to the philosophy of the Mādhyamika school of Mahāyāna Buddhism; and we shall also return to the doctrine of the Bodhisattva, a doctrine which is central in the *Diamond Sūtra,* when we characterize the Bodhisattva ideal of Mahāyāna Buddhism.

In conclusion, the form that the supernatural or the transcendental takes in Mahāyāna philosophy is something usually translated simply as "the Absolute", i.e. the unconditioned (asaṁskṛta), i.e. that which is unaffected by pratītyasamutpāda. In Mahāyāna religion this Absolute is expressed in a number of ways, as we have indicated above, as the Buddha (or Buddhas), and here as śūnya, and as the Bodhisattva (or Bodhisattvas), as we shall see shortly.

In this regard, David J. Kalupahana says of this essential difference between the early Buddhism of Hīnayāna and the Mahāyāna that sprang from the *Prajñāpāramitā* literature:

> Finally, it was pointed out that early Buddhism [Hīnayāna] does not contribute to a theory of absolutism [i.e. supernaturalism or transcendentalism]; it does not recognize a transcendental transempirical reality which is at the same time ineffable (*anirvacanīya*)... If what has been said here regarding the early doctrines is true, then the *Prajñāpāramitās* certainly represent a 'revolution' (*viparyāsa!*) in Buddhism. The revolution consists of the adoption of the transcendentalist standpoint, which is opposed to the empirical approach of early Buddhism.[199]

The details as well as the proof for this transcendentalist revolution must await our presentation below. But we have enough evidence at this stage to suggest a problem that Mahāyāna must face if it is to be a successful supernatural alternative to Hīnayāna, and we turn to that problem next.

1. The Problems of Supernaturalism

The supernaturalism of Mahāyāna presents the student of Buddhism with two quite distinct types of problems. The first problem is internal to Buddhism and the second is external. The internal problem of supernaturalism lies in the recognition that Mahāyāna transcendentalism is inconsistent with earlier Buddhism. It is a problem that is solved or dealt with by reinterpreting the earlier traditions in order to square those traditions with Mahāyāna. In this sense, the internal problem of transcendentalism is a problem of consistency peculiar to Buddhism and has no application beyond Buddhist thought. Exciting as it is, I don't wish to pursue that internal problem here.

The external problem of transcendentalism is a general philosophical problem rather than a particular Buddhism problem, and it is a problem in epistemology. The problem of supernaturalism is just this: How do I know that there is a reality that transcends the sensory realm? Let's pursue that.

"Knowledge" is generally taken by philosophers to mean "any justified true belief." In other words, to have knowledge three conditions must be met: First, what is claimed to be known must be *believed* by someone or other (one can't know something and not also believe it; and, please note, belief is not the same as knowledge); second, what is believed must be *true* (while one may believe the false, one cannot know the false); and, third, there must be some kind of *evidence* that turns the belief into knowledge (one can't know, that is *really* know, without some sort of justification).

The *empiricist*, who holds that the only acceptable evidence for justifying true beliefs must be from the senses, has, perhaps, the easiest time here simply because his position is so common-sensical and so readily defensible. The *rationalist*, however, who holds that some of our knowledge is non-sensory, or transcends sensory justification, is in a far less comfortable position: And Mahāyāna Buddhism espouses rationalism *par excellence*.

When the Mahāyāna claims to know that Bodhisattvas exist, or that nirvāṇa constitutes a transcendental state of being, or that heavens, hells, ghosts, demons, or that Buddhas exist, he is not making an empirical or sensory claim. He is maintaining that this knowledge has come to him through prajñā, a special non-sensory, intuitive or transcendental method or way of knowing. In the West, this transcendental way of knowing is sometimes referred to as "rational intuition", i.e. a special and superior insight into the true and necessary working of supernatural (trans-sensory, trans-material, trans-mental, trans-space-and-time) reality.

The problem of supernaturalism, then, comes down to this: How can prajñā, or rational intuition, be a justification for knowledge? The force of the problem, as the empiricist critic might see it, is twofold: First, prajñā, the empiricist might say, may be merely a strong feeling and not, therefore, a legitimate ground on which to rest knowledge claims, i.e. someone, in confusing a feeling with justification, has confused psychology with epistemology; and, second, prajñā may be a *way* of knowing but it cannot be a *justification* for knowledge, i.e. prajñā, itself, stands in need of justification. Thus the critic. Let me expand briefly on these two objections that spring from the problem of supernaturalism.

When we attempt to analyze the Mahāyāna Buddhist version of rational intuition what we discover are feelings of necessity and feelings of psychological certainty, feelings about which the rationalist claims he cannot be wrong. The certainty that he feels, e.g. that Buddha exists or that he, himself, exists, do not spring, the rationalist argues, from sensory observation of the world but from some kind of inner sense that cannot be confuted.

The empiricist critic, however, is quick to point out that the source of this certitude is merely a strong feeling about the knowledge claim, and feelings, whether strong or weak, are flimsy, superficial grounds on which to rest knowledge claims: Strong feelings, differ not at all from strong beliefs, and beliefs, no matter how strong, do not constitute knowledge.

To escape this criticism that reduces mystical intuitions to psychological feeling, the rationalist must claim that the reduction is falacious. Ordinarily this claim entails bringing in some other justification or source of evidence to shore up intuitionism. The rationalist may claim, for example, that the test for intuition as a valid means of knowledge lies in the happy or blessed life to which the intuition leads. But once he makes this appeal to extra-intuitional grounds, whether empirical or, as here, pragmatic, to buttress his intuitionism he falls prey to the second criticism mounted by the empiricist critic against the rationalist position.

Second, the rationalist's appeal to non-rational or extra-intuitional evidence to save rationalism or intuitionism from criticism leads the empiricist to claim that while intuitionism may be a way of knowing it cannot be a justification for knowledge. This conclusion follows from the fact that most intuitionists generally resort to empirical or pragmatic or psychological tests to justify their intuitionism.

For example, suppose that I "intuit" the whereabouts of a long-lost book. Suppose that I "see" in my intuitional state, clearly and distinctly, the lost book behind my refrigerator, and that I say, I know it's there and I know this with such certainty that I cannot be wrong. This is a common enough "intuition" and one need only recall similar revealing dreams and other special prognosticatory moments in one's own life where such certainties suddenly dawn in order to realize that the example is not implausible.

But now the question occurs, Is my intuition true? In order to discover whether my intuition is "true" I must go to the refrigerator, peer behind it and see what's there. In other words, the test or justification for my intuition is sensory, demonstrating that while intuition may be a way of arriving at knowledge it is not the ultimate test for knowledge, i.e. intuition cannot be a justification for a knowledge claim.

The same conclusion must follow, if the rationalist pragmatically claims that a life freed from sorrow is the best test for intuitively arrived-at wisdom. In other words, the ultimate ground for intuited knowledge lies, once again, beyond that intuition, itself, in psychological tranquility, in a detached state of mind freed from anxiety and suffering, and not in the intuition itself. Thus the critic.

The problem of supernaturalism, in the external sense in which we have been examining it, leads to two separate problems that the rationalist who makes knowledge claims based on prajñā must answer. The empiricist with his narrower and more hard-headed sensory approach to reality and the world denies that any knowledge, other than that based upon sense impressions, is possible. The rationalist, the Mahāyāna Buddhist in this case, argues strenuously that this narrow approach to knowledge won't do. He invites the empiricist to adopt the various techniques and yogas that he has adopted in order to see the inherent correctness and justifiability of his approach to extra-sensory, transcendental wisdom. Come, look through prajñā, he cries, and then we can talk. The empiricist claims either that prajñā reveals nothing, and that it cannot reveal anything that is not apprehendable by the senses in space and time; or, if he looks at all, he claims that what he sees can be easily reduced to, and accounted for, in empirical terms. And there the age-old battle between the rationalist and the empiricist is joined, and there it remains to this day.

To see what the squabble is all about we must examine the remaining nine elements of Mahāyāna Buddhism. The critic, whether Hīnayāna or empiricist, will have his chance from time to time in what follows to make his position clearer and to put the Mahāyāna defender on his best philosophical mettle. Therefore, we turn next to the theism of Mahāyāna and the new Buddhist attitude towards those transcendent Beings called "Gods, Bodhisattvas and Buddhas."[200]

2. Theism

Mahāyāna Buddhism in general, and despite many official protests to the contrary, tends to be a theistic religion. This theism is supported by the supernaturalism mentioned above and is most pronounced in Mahāyāna Buddhism's concepts of the Buddha, the Buddhas and the Bodhisattvas.

Sometime in the 3rd or 2nd century B.C.E. there seems to have begun a shift in concern from the

Hīnayāna question, "How can I reach heaven when this life is over?"[201] This concern with an afterlife and the ways of achieving it are indicative of Mahāyāna's early attempts to move away from what Sarvepalli Radhakrishnan has poetically referred to as the "cold, passionless metaphysics" of Hīnayāna to a religion wherein "the famishing soul and the thirsting fancy" could at last "derive nourishment from the suggestive symbolism of the prevailing religion."[202] That "prevailing religion" was, of course, developing Hinduism, and it may have been where "famished" Buddhist souls might have turned for the inspiration, cues and symbols that enabled them to fasten, finally, on the life and person of Buddha, himself, for their own religious inspiration and sustenance. If Hīnayāna was anthropocentric in its attempt to answer the problem of human suffering then Mahāyāna emerges as Buddhacentric, or Bodhisattvacentric, in its answer to that question, How can I be released from suffering? Since we will be examining the nature of both the Bodhisattva doctrine and the concept of the afterlife below, let me confine the discussion of theism here to this Buddhacentricity of developing Mahāyāna.

As early as the second Second Buddhist Council in 346 B.C.E. we can detect the first traces of Mahāyāna Buddhist elements relating to this theism. These traces are found, as we have already noted in our discussion of that Council, in the heretical doctrines of the Mahāsaṅghikas and the Sammitīyas wherein the former argued that Buddha was superhuman and not a mere man, and the latter argued that there is a substantive soul or person in human beings that endures through rebirths until liberation is reached. Both the Mahāsaṅghikas and the Sammītiyas, it would seem, were seeking something stable and permanent for their metaphysics, a permanence apparently denied them given the anityavāda of orthodox Hīnayāna Buddhism.

The story of the evolution of Gautama the Buddha and the other numerous Buddhas into objects of Buddhist devotion and worship will take us briefly into one of the most important of the *Prajñāpāramitā Sūtras* of the Mahāyāna movement, the *Saddharmapuṇḍarīka Sūtra*, "The Lotus of the good Law" or "Lotus Sūtra", wherein the arhat ideal of the Hīnayāna is condemned; wherein Hīnayāna doctrines in general are attacked as "partial, shallow, and selfish"; and wherein the supernaturalism and transcendence of the eternal Buddha is celebrated.[203]

Again, the aim would appear to be to find a permanent and ultimate religious foundation on which human religious aspirations can fasten and from which those aspirations can find legitimate expression.

In the *Saddharmapuṇḍarīka*, "...the Buddha has become an external being and an object of worship not differing in powers or qualities from the gods of the rival religions."[204] Here is a brief, but beautiful, passage from the *Saddharmapuṇḍarīka*, composed sometime in the 1st century C.E., that ilustrates the new status of the Buddha and the rising theism of Mahāyāna:

> Like a cloud,...which has risen above the world and, covering all, envelops the earth,
> Like this great cloud, filled with water and adorned with lightning, sounds its thunder and delights all beings,
> Like it (when) it releases a mighty mass of water (and), raining all around, refreshes this earth,
> Just so the Buddha rises in the world like a cloud and after he, the Lord of the World, has arisen, he reveals to (all) beings the Right conduct.
> And thus declares the great seer who is worshipped in the (whole) world including the gods:
> 'I am the Perfect One, the best of men, the victor, arisen in the world like a cloud.'
> I will refresh all beings whose members wither (and) who cling to the triple existence (in the three spheres of the world). Those who wither away in suffering I will lead to happiness; I will (fulfill) their wishes and give them peace (nirvṛti). Listen to me, you crowds of gods and men, draw closer to see me! I am the Perfect One, the exalted, the highest; I was born here into the world for the liberation (of all beings).[205]

The waters of salvation which the Buddha showers down are not absorbed by all men in the same way. The Buddha likens the classes of men to three kinds of plants, and in doing so identifies the individual differences and temperaments and stages of spiritual development among men. First, there are the small plants which corresponds to the arhats who must follow the Śrāvaka yāna, the vehicle of the hearers or pupils of the dharma and who, by following the scriptual teaching, will eventually reach nirvāṇa; second, the middling plants which correspond to men who follow the Pratyekabuddha yāna, the vehicle of the solitary hermit and who, through their solitary practices, ultimately reach nirvāṇa; third, there are the supreme plants, the best, which correspond to men who follow the Boddhisattva yāna, the vehicle of the greatest and strongest searchers who strive to achieve the state of the Buddha and thereby become Saviors of men and Gods. But, according to the *Sūtra*, there is really only one Dharma, one yāna, though, because of the differences in the spiritual capacities of men, there appear to be many:

> By means of one sole vehicle, to wit, the Buddha yāna, Śāriputra, do I teach the dharma; there is no second vehicle, nor a third.[206]

We have reached with the *Lotus Sūtra* what Mark Ehman has called, "the essence of popular Mahāyāna teaching, and...the final manifestation of true Buddhism."[207]

The Mahāyāna search for an end to suffering concludes, then, with the Buddha turned into God, a divine being who warranted as much attention, veneration and worship as the Hindu Śiva or Viṣṇu were to receive. However, as might be expected, problems emerge with the theism of Mahāyāna and we turn next to examine two such problems.

2. The Problems of Theism

In the Pāli text of the *Jātaka*, those stories of the Buddha's previous births, there are two passages which we have touched on before that constitute a critique of theism and have further application here.[208] Both passages said, in effect, that if one believes in God, or if one turns the Buddha into God, then there are two problems with which one must contend, for belief in God leads to these problems, viz., the theological problem of free will and the theologial problem of evil. Further, these problems, it is argued, are insuperable, i.e. unsolvable, problems, and any belief that leads to insuperable problems ought to be given up. Therefore, the argument concludes, theism is false, i.e one ought not to believe that God, or the Buddha, exists.

The logical form of the argument is generally called *modus tollendo tollens* by Western logicians wherein denying the consequent (the "then" part) of a conditional (if...then___) statement leads validly to the denial of the antecedent (the "if" part) of the same conditional statement. Put more elegantly the general anti-theist argument would look like this:

1. If theism were true then it would not lead to insuperable problems.

2. But theism does lead to insuperable problems, e.g. the theological problem of free will and the theological problem of evil.

3. Therefore, theism is false.

Let me make two comments about the two premises: First, the first premise seems plausible, i.e. it seems to make some practical sense to hold that any belief or doctrine, whether theism or atheism or deism or what-have-you, that leads to puzzles, difficulties or problems, is worth reconsidering before one becomes too closely attached to the belief or doctrine. Second, the second premise needs to be shown to be true, i.e. the theological problem of free will and the theological problem of evil must be shown to be insuperable and theism must be shown to lead to them. But if both of these premises of the argument are true then, since the argument is already valid, we can conclude that this Buddhist antitheism argument is sound, i.e. it is a valid argument with true premises. We have then to deal with this second premise and the two problems of theism.

Let me take each of the problems of theism separately, quote the appropriate passage, once again, from the *Jākata* that states the argument, and then comment briefly on each of the arguments.

a. The Theological Problem of Free Will

The *Jākata* states the theological problem of free will as follows:

> If God designs the life of the entire world - the glory and the misery, the good and the evil acts - man is but an instrument of his will and God (alone) is responsible.[209]

Stated more elegantly in the *modus tollendo tollens* logical form which the *Jātaka* frequently uses, this first argument against Mahāyāna theism would look like this:

1. If theism is true then man is not responsible for his actions (because God designed the life of the entire world and man is, then, a mere instrument of God's will).

2. But man is responsible for his actions (all Buddhists assume this).

3. Therefore, theism is false.

My comment is brief enough. The first premise assumes that theism entails an all-powerful God who allows no free will to any of its subordinate creatures because such free will would entail a lack of power in that God. The question then is, Would or could an omnipotent God leave any part of the universe unplanned? The first premise implies that there would be a contradiction between divine omnipotence and human free will such that if one is true the other cannot be true.

There is a plausibility to the argument; if God's power entails no real free choice for man, i.e. no real alternatives to action, and this seems to be what the *Jātaka* says, i.e. in designing the life of the entire world, for all future time, real alternatives to action were left out. For example, you probably feel right now that if you wanted to, you could choose either to continue reading this book or to shut it and do something else. We all feel real alternatives about us all the time; and if there are such real alternatives, and if we can choose one or the other, then we say that we are free and that we are then responsible for whatever alternative we do choose. If there are no real alternatives then we're not responsible for what we do, and man's moral life, which depends on free will, would be rendered meaningless.

The first *Jātaka* argument says that if God exists then God has pre-planned *all* events in the world such that there are no choices, no real alternatives. If God planned it so that you would continue reading this book, as you apparently are, then you could not have chosen not to keep on reading without turning God into something He is not, i.e. something not omnipotent. But if you had no choice, and if you had to do what God intended for you to do or what He knew you would do, then you're not responsible for this choice, viz., to keep on reading, or any choices - for there are no real choices. Therefore, you're not responsible and, as the second premise of the argument implies, this is absurd.

In the end we come down to having to accept either an all-powerful God (who planned everything), or a moral life that accepts free will, but not both. The Hīnayāna Buddhists through their atheism accept the latter while rejecting the former; and the Mahāyāna Buddhists through their theism would appear to accept both alternatives, i.e. they accept an all-powerful Buddha, Buddhas and numerous Bodhisattvas, together with the doctrine of free will; and with both they inherit the theological problem of free will.

b. The Theologial Problem of Evil

The *Jātaka* states the theologial problem of evil as follows:

> If Brahmā is lord of the whole world and creator of the multitude of beings, then why has he ordained misfortune in the world without making the whole world happy; or for what purpose has he made the world full of injustice, deceit, falsehood and conceit; or the lord of beings is evil in that he ordained injustice when there could have been justice.[210]

Stated more elegantly in *modus tollendo tollens* logical form the second argument against Mahāyāna theism would look like this:

1. If theism is true then the world ought to contain neither misfortune nor injustice nor deceit nor falsehood nor conceit, i.e. evil.

2. But the world does contain evil.

3. Therefore, theism is false.

Let me briefly comment on this argument. The first premise assumes that God or Brahmā is all-powerful and all-good and, therefore, that he could prevent evil (he's all-powerful) and that he would want to prevent evil (he's all-good). But, as the second premise assumes and states, there is evil. So, the argument says, if the first premise is true then how can the second be true? or vice versa?

The theological problem of evil has a long history in both the East and West. In the West it was first explicitly formulated by Epicurus (341-270 B.C.E.) in the form of a dilemma:

> God either wishes to take away evils and is unable; or He is able and is unwilling; or He is neither willing nor able or He is both willing and able. If He is willing and unable, He is feeble, which is not in accordance with the character of God; if He is able and unwilling, He is envious, which is equally at variance with God; if He is neither willing nor able, He is both envious and feeble, and therefore not God; if He is both willing and able, which alone is suitable to God, from what source then are evils? or why does He not remove them?[211]

The theological problem of evil has been a puzzle for all those who hold that God is all-good and all-powerful (and all-knowing, some would add) and that evil, the contradictory of good, exists in the world.

Once again, we come down to having to accept either an all-powerful and all-good God, or a world that contains agony, suffering and evil, but not both. The Hīnayāna Buddhists through their atheism accept the latter while rejecting the former; and the Mahāyāna Buddhists through their theism would appear to accept both alternatives, i.e. they accept an all-powerful and all-good Buddha, Buddhas and numerous Bodhisattvas, together with the doctrine that agony, suffering and evil exist in the world; and with both they inherit the theological problem of evil.

In conclusion to the problems of theism let me state the central argument of the critic of theism, once again: Any belief or doctrine that leads to insuperable problems is not true; we have seen that theism does lead to insuperable problems; therefore theism is not true. Of course the defenders of Mahāyāna Buddhism have their responses to the second premise of the argument, not the least of which responses woud be an outright denial that Buddha, the Buddhas or the Bodhisattvas are Gods in any form. So let's look at this aspect of Mahāyāna more closely.

We turn next to the Buddhacentrism of Mahāyāna, and this new Buddhist attitude towards Buddha and the Buddhas.

3. Buddhacentrism

Mahāyāna Buddhism tends to be a Buddhacentric religion. It is Buddhacentric because its tendency to theism found religious expression centered upon the person of the Buddha. Mahāyāna Buddhacentrism did not begin in a vacuum, however. For while the early Hīnayāna believed that the Buddha as well as all Buddhas were merely human, the Mahāsaṅghikas, as we saw, believed Buddha to be superhuman, and the Sarvāstivāda school even regarded Buddha and all Buddhas as heavenly beings much after the manner of the Hindu Gods.

Indeed, it was the Sarvāstivāda who introduced into Buddhism one of the most singularly Buddhacentric notions yet seen in Buddhism, viz., the doctrine of the Buddha's three bodies, trikāya. The trikāya doctrine, trikāyavāda, was subsequently elaborated upon by the Yogācāra school of Mahāyāna in the form familiar to us today, and then adopted by later Mahānāya. The ultimate outcome of the doctrine was to focus philosophic and religious attention on the Buddha or Buddhas making him or them and his or their three forms or bodies the focal point, the center, of the new Mahāyāna Buddhist religion.

Trikāyavāda establishes a series of three metaphysical levels in which the Buddha, or other numerously infinite Buddhas, for that matter, may stand. First, the Buddha was born into this world at a particular time and place with a human body that lived, taught, preached the Dharma, and died. This body is merely an appearance body, the nirmāṇakāya, the physical body of the Buddha. It was believed that the transcendent Buddha or Buddhas merely made or created these illusory bodies for themselves and that they are all subject to the physical and mental ills and agonies to which flesh is heir.

The nirmāṇakāya Buddha experiences suffering and seeks a way out. The way out that is found, and the message that is left behind about that way, constitutes the heart of the eightfold noble path to enlightenment. It is useless, however, for one to pray to the nirmāṇakāya Buddhas or to seek their aid or help, since as persons they have ceased to exist with the death of their created bodies. But Buddhacentrism is exhibited even here; for by recalling and then imitating the noble earthly and physical lives of the Buddhas one can cleanse one's heart and mind, thereby making the way out of suffering more efficacious.

Metaphysically above the physical Buddha is the second level of the trikāya, the body of enjoyment, saṁbhogakāya. The enjoyment body of Buddha, or the Buddhas, is a transcendent body or bodies in a state of nirvāṇic bliss. This body cannot be experienced by the senses but it can be perceived by intuitive or spiritual means when the devotee is in a mystical state brought about by meditational yoga. In other words, what Mahāyāna is offering is Indian mysticism with the bliss body of Buddha forming the central core or object of one's mystical endeavors.

Just as the nirmāṇakāya is different for different Buddhas in different times and places, i.e. there are multiple nirmāṇakāyas, so also the saṁbhogakāya is said to be different in the various transcendent Buddha heavens and heavenly assemblies where it exists; for Buddhas exist in all worlds and universes and they preach to all of the great assemblies of men, Gods, Bodhisattvas and Buddhas. It is in the enjoyment body, however, that the heavenly Buddhas reveal themselves to the Bodhisattvas. But while there are different Buddha bodies on both the nirmāṇakāya and the saṁbhogakāya planes, the message preached by these Buddhas to men (on the first or earthly plane) and to the Bodhisattvas and Gods (on the second or heavenly plane) is essentially the same message.

This uniformity of the earthly and the heavenly message is underscored in the third, final and most important Buddhacentric plane of existence, the dharmakāya, or the body of Dharma. It is the most important of the trikāya for It constitutes the metaphysical support, and ontological origin, of the other two bodies. In truth, It alone is real while the other two bodies of Buddhas only arise, appear and then pass away. We are now at the heart of Mahāyāna Buddhacentric mysticism, dealing with an absolute reality paralleling in many respects the Upaniṣadic doctrine of parā, or highest, Brahman.

The mystical body of dharmakāya is the same for all Buddhas and can be experienced completely only by the enlightened. But while It constitutes the essence of the nirvāṇa experience attained by the very few through mystical prajñā, the rest of us can get a glimpse of It depending on our own level of attainments and insight. For in Its very subtle form It can be experienced as saṁbhogakāya, and in Its more gross form It can be sensed as nirmāṇakāya. The Dharma of the dharmakāya is essentially indescribable, though one Buddhologist, Edward J. Thomas, has aptly, I think, referred to dharmakāya as "the body of the nature of things."[212] The word "Dharma" has here close associations with the universal law and order of the cosmos, *natura naturans* in the Latin sense of nature nurturing, a concept not unlike the Vedic concept of Ṛta, universal order.

The full-blown theory of the trikāya speaks of dharmakāya in three ways: As the Buddha of the law, as the Buddha with the knowledge of a perfect one, and as the perfect one who is the origin or root of all; dharmakāya thereby includes all three bodies in one Buddha body.

D.T. Suzuki has summarized this aspect of the Mahāyāna trikāya most succinctly when he states:

> There is, it is asserted, the highest being which is the ultimate cause of the universe and in which all existences find their essential origin and significance. This is called by the Mahāyānists Dharmakāya. The Dharmakāya, however, does not remain in its absoluteness, it reveals itself in the realm of cause and effect. It then takes a particular form. It becomes a devil, or a god, or a deva, or a human being or an animal of lower grade, adapting itself to the degrees of the intellectual development of the people. For it is the people's inner needs which necessitate the special forms of manifestation. This is called Nirmāṇakāya, that is, the body of transformation. The Buddha who manifested himself in the person

> of Gautama, the son of King Śuddhodana about two thousand five hundred years ago on the Ganges, is a form of Nirmāṇakāya.

Having dealt with dharmakāya and nirmāṇakāya, Suzuki goes on to the third and final element of this "Buddhist trinity", as he calls the "trikāya":

> The third one is called Saṁbhogakāya, or body of bliss. This is the spiritual body of a Buddha, invested with all possible grandeur in form and in possession of all imaginable psychic powers.[213]

But however viewed, and to whatever mystical and metaphysical heights the doctrine of trikāya may take us, the object of attention in that doctrine is, and remains, the Buddha. Whether one views Buddha as an earthly, heavenly or mystically absolute entity one still sees Buddha as the center, the essence, of the new Mahāyāna religion and philosophy.

Trikāyavāda, finally, brought answers to three religious questions about the historical Gautama Buddha Śākyamuni, questions that must have plagued the Buddhacentric, theistically oriented and supernaturally inclined Mahāyāna: First, if Gautama the Buddha was born at a particular time and place then how eternal and how spiritually and religiously worthy of worship was he? The answer according to trikāyavāda was, of course that the Buddha had always existed and that his last earthly appearance as Gautama, prince of the Śākyas, was merely one of many such appearances by the real Buddha, dharmakāya, in his nirmāṇakāya, or earthly body.

Second, if Gautama the Buddha died at a particular time and place then how can I, a prospective worshipper and devotee, ever hope to contact that dead Buddha in my devotions? The answer according to trikāyavāda was, again, that the Buddha's nirmāṇakāya is gone, it was never real in the first place, but the saṁbhogakāya, the heavenly body, exists and is a fitting and most worthy object of worship: "He is risen and he lives."

Third, how could Buddha, if he was born with a physical body and died at the age of eighty, appear in so many places, now in the heavenly planes and then on the earthly, all simultaneously? The answer according to trikāyavāda was that the absolute dharmakāya was able to make bodies in which It could manifest Itself on the two lower planes of existence. Once again, the historical and religious aspects of Buddhism are grounded in, and made consistent with, the metaphysical and mystical aspects of Buddhism, and trikāyavāda made that grounding and consistency possible.

The psychological impetus for Buddhacentrism has been well stated by David J. Kalupahana who says:

> Thus the conception of Buddha in the Mahāyāna caters to the psychological needs of ordinary people who are faced with the hazards of existence, and, in a way, it is similar to the conception of God in many of the theistic religions which emphasize the conception of a father figure. This, therefore, may be taken as the culmination of the religious trend initiated by the Mahāsaṅghikas, who took up the cause of the ordinary man and his religious aspirations.[214]

The Buddhacentrism and theocentrism of the rising Mahāyāna will be touched on further when we come to discuss the Bodhisattva ideal and bhakti. Before moving on, however, let us examine a problem that emerges with respect to this religion and philosophy of Buddhacentrism.

3. The Problem of Buddahcentrism

The problem of Buddhacentrism in Mahāyāna is curiously similar to the problem of anthropocentrism in Hīnayāna. The latter problem involved the Hīnayāna Buddhist in an egocentrism and selfishness that was, to say the least, "not likely to produce the kind of sympathetic and compassionate arhat that Buddhist ethics (or any ethics) would seem to demand." We shall see that, in a sense, Mahāyāna is no better off with the problem of Buddhacentrism.

The doctrine of the trikāya establishes Buddhacentricity at three levels; that is to say, attention is fixed on the Buddha or Buddhas as the object of worship or the object of all endeavors at the bodily, heavenly and mystical planes of existence. The worshipper or devotee or aspirant is invited, as it were, to rise up through these stages or levels until the third stage, the dharmakāya, is reached. This advancing through stages of realization to an ultimate stage of perfection is familiar enough, not only in Hinduism but also in Western mysticism, from Plato to Plotinus to Dionysius the Areopagite and the medieval Jewish Christian and Moslem mystics.

Essentially, even for trikāyavāda, there are two stages involved, viz., a religious stage which has objects of attention and worship such as crucifixes, icons and statues together with such concepts as God, or nirmāṇakāya or saṁbhogakāya Buddhas, objects and concepts about which one can speak, theologize and philosophize. The goal of this stage is heaven, a better birth, and other sorts of benefits for the devotee. And pursuing such goals can be said to be a selfish activity, at best.

But there is a second stage as well, viz., a mystical stage which has no objects for a devotee to fix on and worship, the stage of dharmakāya, that contains no easily identifiable paraphernalia about which one can theologize and philosophize, and that has no goal or end in the ordinary sense of those words. It is the stage of śūnya or Void spoken of previously.

And herein lies the problem of Buddhacentrism: How is it possible to move from the self-centered, self-concerned, religious stage of nirmāṇakāya to the śūnya-centered mystical stage of dharmakāya? We said previously that egotism and selfishness were probable by-products of the anthropocentrism of Hīnayāna. But, now, is Mahāyāna any different at the nirmāṇakāya level of religious worship?

Consider this: Three of the religious reasons that I may have for seeking the nirmāṇakāya Buddha are, first, that I may live happily and unblemished by sorrow in this world today; second, that I may live happily in Buddha heaven or the Pure Land tomorrow; and third, that I may be glorified as a Buddha, myself, someday. But aren't these reasons essentially selfish? And if they are then isn't the first stage, the religious stage, bound to be infected with this selfishness? And if it is then how can one advance from the egocentrism, selfishness and nirmāṇakāya Buddhacentrism of the religious stage to the selflessness, emptiness and dharmakāya Buddhacentrism of the mystical stage? That's the problem of Buddhacentrism.

Is there a way out of the problem of Buddhacentrism? It won't help to say that there is an intermediate stage, the saṁbhogakāya, between the other two stages; for the heavenly stage between the religious stage and the mystical stage, we are told, is merely an extension of the religious stage. Like the religious stage, the heavenly stage possesses objects, Buddhas, bodhisattvas, Gods and selves which stand in relation to sermons preached by Buddhas, sermons with theological and philosophical content, and so on. The problem of leaping from this heavenly stage of objects to the objectless mystical stage would be merely a repetition of the problem of Buddhacentrism.[215]

The problem of Buddhacentrism is merely a species of a much more general problem, "the problem of mysticism," as we might call it. That general problem involves solving the puzzle regarding how to leap the chasm that separates the religious world of metaphysical theism, subjects and objects, of ordinary language and common sense meaning, to the mystical world of metaphysical absolutism of either pure Subject or pure Object, where ordinary language and common sense meanings have no place, where only the Void exists. The mystic has answers to the problem of mysticism and responds, oftentimes, by speaking of yoga, stored merit, special training in Buddha Fields, Heaven or Pure Lands, divine grace, the flight of the Absolute to Itself, of the Alone to the Alone, of myths and symbols, and so on.

Meanwhile, we turn next to the fourth characteristic of Mahāyāna Buddhism, the Bodhisattva ideal.

4. The Bodhisattva Ideal

Mahāyāna Buddhism upholds the ideal of the Bodhisattva as opposed to the arhat ideal of Hīnayāna. Recall that the arhat seeks his own salvation or realization by using the dharma to ferry himself across the stream of delusion and suffering. The vehicle by which the arhat travels, the Mahāyāna critic is quick to point out, carries but one person at a time to nirvāṇa, hence, as we have seen, the name *hīnayāna*, "little vehicle", given to them by the Mahāyāna Buddhists.

In contrast to the arhat of Hīnayāna the Bodhisattva of Mahāyāna delays his own nirvāṇa, reverses his course across the stream of suffering, returns and gathers as many of the suffering as possible into his vehicle and ferries them all across the stream. He returns again and again for as many more as he can take into the boat of the dharma; thus the name *mahāyāna*, "great vehicle", given to Northern Buddhism.[216] The Bodhisattva out of his great compassion resolves to save suffering mankind from agony and delusion before he steps onto the farther shore of nirvāṇa, himself.[217]

The Bodhisattva is a bold, but not necessarily a new, conception for Buddhism. In fact, as we have seen, a transcendental conception of Buddha has been growing for some time, and even within the Hīnayāna tradition the concept of the Bodhisattva was not absent but meant simply "one destined for enlightenment (bodhi)." It was perhaps an easy move for early Mahāyāna Buddhism to apotheosize this Buddha-to-be as one who puts off his own final enlightenment out of love for all other beings, especially given the transcendental tradition that was lurking about in such early schools as Sarvāstvāda (with its trikāya) and Mahāsaṅghika (with its superhuman view of the Buddha). But it is not until we arrive at the *Prajñāpāramitā* literature, and especially the *Aṣṭasāhasrikā Sūtra*, and the *Saddharmapuṇḍarīka Sūtra* that the doctrines of transcendental Buddhas and soteriological Bodhisattvas fully emerge.

In the *Aṣṭasāhasrikā Sūtra, "The Eight Thousand Line Sūtra"*, the oldest *Prajñāpāramitā Sūtra* that we possess, and therefore a Mahāyāna sūtra from about the 2nd century B.C.E.,[218] the doctrine of the Bodhisattva is set forth as follows:

> Doers of what is hard are the Bodhisattvas, the great beings who have set out to win supreme enlightenment. They do not wish to attain their own private Nirvāṇa. On the contrary, they have surveyed the highly painful world of being, and yet, desirous to win supreme enlightenment, they do not tremble at birth-and-death. They have set out for the benefit of the world, for the

> ease of the world, out of pity for the world. They have resolved: "We will become a shelter for the world, the world's place of rest, the final relief of the world, islands of the world, lights of the world, leaders of the world, the world's means of salvation.[219]

We shall have more to say about the pity and compassion of the Boddhisattvas, along with their other moral characteristics, shortly.

In the *Saddharmapuṇḍarīka*, a number of astonishing new doctrines relative to the Bodhisattva ideal are propounded. Here, Lord Buddha tells an assembly of monks and his chief disciple, Śāriputra, that only Tathāgatas, i.e. those *thus gone* to nirvāṇa, i.e. Buddhas, can truly explain things. He declares that a Tathāgata's knowledge far surpasses that of all other beings. Now the arhats who are present at Lord Buddha's lecture are puzzled and not without reason; for the Lord seems to be flying in the face of the older teaching by suggesting that the Tathāgatas are superior to the arhats. Angered and puzzled, the proud arhats rise as a body and leave the assembly, whereupon the Lord remarks that the assembly has been cleared of rubbish.

This new doctrine about the Tathāgatas is then elaborated, with the author of the *Saddharmapuṇḍarīka* underlining the point that this new doctrine is now part of the Buddha's secret teaching,[220] a teaching which had been implicitly present all along for all to see and hear. This move is calculated to grant a measure of orthodoxy to the "new" doctrine which was only now being made explicit.

The secret that is brought forth is really two-fold: First, that there is a level of being, that of the Tathāgata, that is higher than that of the arhat (no wonder they left); and second, that this new level of being can be achieved only through the way of the Bodhisattva.

The Lord had begun the *Sūtra* by reminding Śāriputra of a vow to become a bodhisattva that the latter had taken in a previous life. Through the aeons Lord Buddha, himself, had been preparing and maturing Śāriputra for just that goal and now the further directions for the way to that goal are to be enunciated. Lord Buddha says:

> This my utterance has furnished you with the Bodhisattva counsel and the Bodhisattva secret. You, Śāriputra, do not, through a Bodhisattva's sustaining power, remember your former vow to practice (as a Bodhisattva), nor the Bodhisattva counsel or the Bodhisattva secret.[221]

The Lord continues by telling Śāriputra that the nirvāṇa that he has already achieved as an arhat is not sufficient and that there is a level of being beyond even that. In order to accomplish that end of becoming a Bodhisattva, the Lord will reveal to Śāriputra and the other disciples the discourse of the doctrine contained in the *Saddharmapuṇḍarīka* as a guide to all future Bodhisattvas.

This teaching regarding the way of the Bodhisattva continues as the Lord tells the assembly:

> Beings, because of their great ignorance, born blind, wander about;
> Because of their ignorance of the wheel of cause and effect, of the track of ill.
>
> In the world deluded by ignorance, the supreme all-knowing one,
> The Tathāgata, the great physician, appears, full of compassion.

Buddha then introduces the startling news that there are some three levels of enlightenment. He describes these three levels by calling attention to the three kinds of devotees who inhabit these levels. He begins,

> As a teacher, skilled in means [upāya], he [Buddha] demonstrates the good dharma.

And then he briefly indicate the nature of the three levels. The first is the highest stage:

> To those most advanced he shows the supreme Buddha-enlightenment.

The second level is next:

> To those of medium wisdom the leader reveals a medium enlightenment.

Finally, the third and, presumably, lowest level of enlightenment is mentioned:

> Another enlightenment again he recommends to those who are afraid of birth-and-death.

He continues this startling Mahāyāna revelation with a reference to the first and highest level with its "deathless Nirvāṇa":

> To the Disciple, who has escaped from the triple world, and who is given to discrimination
> It occurs: "Thus have I attained Nirvāṇa, the blest and immaculate."
>
> But I now reveal to him that this is not what is called Nirvāṇa,
> But that it is through the understanding of all dharmas that deathless Nirvāṇa can be attained.[222]

Buddha concludes by exalting the doctrine that there is no other nirvāṇa that transcends "deathless Nirvāṇa." It is only when one comes to see all dharmas, i.e. all process-moment entities, as the same, and therefore as empty, "śūnya", that one sees the Dharmabody and achieves final nirvāṇa.[223]

The remaining chapters of the *Saddharmapuṇḍarīka* continue the attack on the arhat ideal, exhalting the Buddha and the Bodhisattva ideal.

In later Mahāyāna, the Buddha gradually evolves into an all-wise, all-good Father, with the Bodhisattvas likened to Buddha's beloved sons. Both emerge from developing Mahāyāna like the Gods in other theistic religions. While the Bodhisattva is not yet a Buddha, "as a grain of sand compares with the earth", says one text, still his being in the world for the sake of others likens him favorably to the Tathāgatas, i.e. the Buddhas; and it is his compassion which is like theirs that distinguishes the Bodhisattva from all other beings. Here is the *Aṣṭasāhasrikā Sūtra* again:

> He becomes endowed with that kind of wise insight which allows him to see all beings as on the way to their slaughter. Great compassion thereby takes hold of him. With his heavenly eye he surveys countless beings, and what he sees fills him with great agitation: So many carry the burden of a karma which will soon be punished in the hells, others have acquired unfortunate rebirths, which keep them away from the Buddha and his teachings, others are doomed soon to be killed, or they are enveloped in the net of false views, or fail to find the path, while others who had gained a rebirth favourable to their emancipation have lost it again.

Recognizing those in sorrow, seeing the problem, the Bodhisattva puts off his own salvation to become a Savior:

> And he radiates great friendliness and compassion over all those beings, and gives his attention to them, thinking: "I shall become a savior to all those beings, I shall release them from all their suffering!"[224]

I conclude with what is very likely one of the best expressions of the nature of the Bodhisattva. It comes in the work of Śāntideva, a poet and himself a Bodhisattva, of the 7th century C.E. The son of a King, Śāntideva renounced throne and kingdom to take up the vocation of a Bodhisattva. Here are several lines from his monumental work, the *Bodhicaryāvatāra*, "Entrance into Training for Enlightenment", which gives us the flavor of the Bodhisattva from the mouth of a living Bodhisattva:

> My bodies (in all rebirths) as well as all the property and pleasures which I have acquired (and will acquire) in the Three Times (past, present and future), I give away indifferently for the welfare of all beings....
>
> As many (beings) in all regions of the world as are suffering from illnesses of body and mind, may they (all) obtain through my (karmic) merit oceans of happiness and joy.[225]

The love that the Bodhisattva feels for the suffering is further expressed in the same poem as Śāntideva pours out his love for all beings:

> Thus through all the good done by me may I become a tranquilizer of all the pains of all beings.
> May I become medicine for the sick and their physician, their support until sickness comes not again.
> Their pains of hunger and thirst may I quench with showers of food and drink; in the famines at the end of an age may I become drink and nourishment.
> May I become an unfailing store for the wretched, and be first to supply them with the manifold things of their need.
> My own self and my pleasures, all my righteousness, past, present and future, I sacrifice without regard, in order to achieve the welfare of all beings.[226]

But it is precisely the Bodhisattva's compassion and agitation over human suffering that leads to a problem with this very basic and moving Mahāyāna doctrine. We turn next to the problem of the Bodhisattva ideal.

4. The Problem of the Bodhisattva Ideal

The Bodhisattva ideal represents a new level of religious aspiration for Buddhism. Like the tendencies towards theism and Buddhacentrism mentioned previously, the ideal of the Bodhisattva is an attempt to satisfy human religious needs that appear to have been frustrated within the Hīnayāna religious tradition. But in introducing the Bodhisattva ideal a problem emerges that Mahāyāna Buddhists must answer.

The Bodhisattva stands somewhere below the highest level of spiritual realization ("a mere grain of sand", after all). Intuitive insight or prajñā is not yet fully manifested or else the Bodhisattva would be a Buddha. But we know that the Bodhisattva has postponed reaching the state or level of full Buddhahood in order to respond to the suffering he or she (women can aspire to the Bodhisattva ideal, as well) has seen in the world. Indeed, the *Aṣṭasāhasrikā* has told us with what "great agitation" the Bodhisattva surveys the suffering and agony of all mankind.

And here is precisely where the problem of the Bodhisattva ideal lies: How can a being that is not yet fully enlightened lead other beings to full enlightenment?[227] Or put more particularly, How can a Bodhisattva who is subject to desire and agitation show others the way out of desire and agitation to the state of deathless nirvāṇa that transcends such states? In other words, Is the Bodhisattva any better off than those he or she is trying to save? And if not then what kind of ideal is the Bodhisattva ideal? There are innumerable texts describing the virtues and excellences of the Bodhisattva but these virtues must all come to nothing when one realizes that they flow from a heart which is motivated by desire, i.e. love and compassion, however noble. So much for the problem of the Bodhisattva ideal.

The Mahāyāna Buddhists, like all religions with a Savior doctrine, have a solution, of course, which is simply to make a virtue, the highest virtue, out of love and compassion and the desire to help suffering mankind. But, the critic is quick to respond, if those same religions also exhalt the goal of deathless nirvāṇa wherein all desire and attachments are blown out and emptied in the great metaphysical void of śūnya then those religions have a problem of reconciling their highest virtue with their highest goal.

We turn next to the fifth characteristic of Mahāyāna Buddhism, pragmatism.

5. Pragmatism

Mahāyāna Buddhism, like the Hīnayāna which preceded it, is a pragmatic religion whose truth and whose goal, viz., release from suffering, can be tested and proved in one's own lifetime. But another pragmatic side of Mahāyāna Buddhism can also be identified. It is seen most clearly through the person of the Bodhisattva and in the development of what came to be called his "skill-in-means" (upāya). Edward Conze has put the matter this way:

> The Bodhisattva would be a man who does not only set himself free, but who is also skillful in devising means for bringing out and maturing the latent seeds of enlightenment in others.[208]

While not eschewing the practice-the-doctrine-and-see-for-yourself attitude of the Hīnayāna, later Indian Buddhism sets out on a pragmatic path with new practical skills now developed by the Bodhisattva for leading man to salvation.

In the *Saddharmapuṇḍarīka*, Buddha tells Śāriputra a story to illustrate the skill-in-means that may be employed by the Tathāgata to save suffering man. He begins by stating that the Tathāgata must first take account of the different capacities and inclinations of beings in order that he might use the most appropriate and skillful means possible to lead them to enlightenment. These means involve arguments, reasons, definitions and explanations that will produce the desired effect, viz., enlightenment, in the listener:

> But it is precisely the supreme enlightenment that all his demonstrations of Dharma are concerned with, and he instigates all people to use the vehicle of the Bodhisattvas[229]

To illustrate, Buddha tells the following parable: There once was a rich householder who had many sons. One day his fine and beautiful house caught fire. The rich man fled from the burning house but once outside he remembered his sons still inside. The sons were playing and amusing themselves unconcernedly as the house burned around them. Though threatened by the conflagration they made no effort to get out. With great agitation, but with love and concern for the boys at the same time, the father calls to them but they pay no attention to his pleas and cries:

> Then this man thinks again: This house is all ablaze, the great mass of fire is burning it down. How can I prevent further disaster for myself and my boys. Perhaps with my skill-in-means I can drive these boys out of the house.

Knowing the children and their interests the father, who in the parable is, of course, symbolic of the Bodhisattva, calls to them and tells them that all of their fascinating and wonderful toys, which are symbolic of the enticements and promises of the Bodhisattva, have been put out in the yard for them to play with. These toys consist of bullock-carts, goat-carts and deer-carts. He cries out:

> Come here, run out of the house! To each one of you I will give whatever he wants and asks for. Come out quickly, run out so that you can get them![230]

The boys hear their father and come rushing, pell-mell, out of the burning house, inconsiderately pushing and shoving one another in order to get there first and receive the beautiful playthings they thought were there.

The father, upon seeing that the boys are all safe and that they have escaped the burning house, is joyful and jubilant, freed from his anxiety and fear for his sons' lives. But the boys run up to their father demanding the toys, viz., the bullock-carts, goat-carts and deer-carts, that he had promised them. Whereupon the father, out of love for his children, gives to them the most magnificent of all carts, viz., white bullock-carts yoked to white oxen, the most precious carts and animals that money can buy, appointed with the finest embellishments and accoutrements, rather than the carts that he had promised them. And why?

> Because that man is wealthy and very rich, with an abundance of gold, silver, and treasures stored away, and he would not think it right to give second-rate carts to these boys. "For they all are my own sons, they are all dear and precious to me...."[231]

The question then arises, Did the father lie to the children? He promised them what he knew they wanted, bullock-, goat- and deer-carts, and then, finally, he gave them white bullock-carts and oxen, more precious and attractive then all of the rest put together. But has he spoken a falsehood? And does skill-in-means entail using any practical artifice or strategem whatsoever in order to deliver suffering mankind from the flames of desire and saṁsāra? Śāriputra himself replies to the question, Did he lie? and his reply receives Buddha's full acquiescence:

> Not so, O Lord! Not so, O [Tathāgata!]. That man cannot be charged with speaking falsely,

> since it was only a skillful device by which he managed to get his sons out of that burning building, and to present them with life. And it was only because their own bodies were first rescued that they could later on receive all those toys to play with.

Then Śāriputra says something that drives home the pragmatic point once and for all:

> Even if the man had not given any carts at all to the boys, even then, O Lord, he could not be charged with falsehood.

And why not? Because truth is to be measured in terms of the effectiveness or ultimate workability of the skill-in-means employed:

> It was because he had merely considered how to save the boys by some skillful device from that great mass of fire that he was not guilty of falsehood... That man, O Lord, is certainly not guilty of falsehood.[232]

But, Śārputra and Lord Buddha to the contrary notwithstanding, there are at least two senses in which the father-Bodhisattva is surely guilty of falsehood. First, the father promised bullock-, goat- and deer-carts, but delivered white bullock-carts and white oxen instead. If lying consists of not fulfilling a promise, then the father surely lied. One might counter that it was a magnificent lie, nonetheless.

If I promise you a Honda and then give you a Rolls-Royce you're not going to complain; but no one is going to say that I fulfilled my promise. The point, of course, is that the pragmatic theory of truth, or, possibly, the mythic theory of truth, and not the correspondence theory of truth,[233] are what stand behind the entire story with its promising: Skill-in-means measures truth and promises by useful results and not by a one-to-one correspondence between thing promised and thing delivered.

Second, this pragmatic thrust is underscored by the other sense of falsehood in Śāriputra's reply. He says that even if the father had not given any toys at all there still would have been no falsehood. Now on a correspondence theory of truth the father's lie in this second sense is quite blatant. If I promise you a Honda and then give you nothing, I have surely lied. But if I get you to come out of a burning building by such a ruse or necessary subterfuge then on pragmatic grounds there is no lie but only a grand truth measured by extremely successful consequences, viz., I saved your life with a golden lie, i.e. a pragmatically justified "falsehood." So, from the pragmatic point of view, Śāriputra and Lord Buddha are both correct: The father did not lie; he spoke the saving truth.

Buddha goes on to explain the parable, showing that the two inferior carts, the deer-cart and the goat-cart, correspond to the vehicle of the Disciples (śrāvakas), who depend on teachers, and the vehicle of the Pratyekabuddhas, who owe nothing to a teacher but understand causes and conditions (pratyaya) by themselves. These two vehicles are inferior because each contains seekers who long for nirvāṇa for themselves, alone. But the superior cart, the bullock-cart, is like the vehicle of the Bodhisattva and the great vehicle, itself, Mahāyāna:

> ...they hope to win final Nirvāṇa for all beings - for the sake of the many, for their welfare and happiness, out of pity for the world, for the weal, welfare, and happiness of a great mass of people, be they gods or men. They are those who escape the Triple world in the expectation of the great vehicle, and for that reason they are called "Bodhisattvas, great beings." And they correspond to the boys who longed for the finest carts, for bullock-carts.[234]

In this fashion pragmatism is tied to the Bodhisattva's skill-in-means. But an inconsistency appears to loom here in Mahāyāna that relates back to the pragmatism of Hīnayāna. Let me say a word about this apparent inconsistency before we push on to a discussion of the Mahāyāna problem of pragmatism in earnest.

The basic issue here is, Will the Bodhisattva go to any lengths, use any means whatsoever, to secure nirvāna for those he loves? or Will the Bodhisattva ever be guided by other-than-pragmatic principles to secure such a goal? If Buddhism is exclusively pragmatic then, in one sense, all's fair in love and war and salvation; therefore, truth, beauty, goodness and justice are all to be measured wholly and only by the consequences to which they lead, viz., nirvāṇa. So we may ask, Is truth to be equated with usefulness?

Buddhologists, such as K.N. Jayatilleke, argue that it is not, at least not in early Buddhism, i.e. not in Hīnayāna Buddhism. For otherwise critics could point to those liberated beings who have crossed over the river of suffering to the farther shore of enlightenment, and, these critics might argue, the Buddha's dharma would then have ceased to have any value for such enlightened beings: And if it is valueless *then*, according to pragmatism, it must be false.[235] Jayatilleke replies that while the dharma ceases to be useful it does not cease to be true.

So how are the true and the useful related? In early Buddhism,

> ...the Buddha speaks only what is true and useful, whether pleasant or unpleasant. We may sum this up by saying that the truths of Buddhism were considered to be pragmatic in the Buddhist sense of the term, but it does not mean that Early Buddhism believes in a pragmatic theory of truth.[236]

In other words, early Buddhism does not identify truth with utility in the way that many Western pragmatic ("pragmatist" in Jayatilleke's sense) theories of truth would. However, Jayatilleke feels that Buddhism does maintain a limited pragmatism, one that, while not identifying the true with the useful, does claim that what is true must also be useful, but that the useful is not necessarily true. On the other hand, as we have seen, the parable of the father-Bodhisattva from the *Saddharmapuṇḍarīka* appears to uphold an unlimited pragmatism, i.e. one that identifies truth with the useful. There the controversy is joined and we must ask, Who is correct?

In this regard, K.N. Jayatilleke is worth quoting in full in order to get his position of limited pragmatism as straight as possible.

> In the Abhayarājakumāra Sutta, we find statements classified according to their truth-value, utility (or disutility) and pleasantness (or unpleasantness). The

intention of the classification is to tell us what kind of propositions the Buddha asserts.

From these three classifications we can get eight possible combinations:

1. True useful pleasant
2. True useful unpleasant
3. True useless pleasant
4. True useless unpleasant
5. False useful pleasant
6. False useful unpleasant
7. False useless pleasant
8. False useless unpleasant

Jayatilleke then quotes the *Sutta* commentary:

> The Tathāgata does not assert a statement which he knows to be untrue, false, useless, disagreeable and unpleasant to others (i.e. 8). He does not assert a statement which he knows to be true, factual, useless, disagreeable and unpleasant to others (i.e. 4). He would assert at the proper time a statement which he knows to be true, factual, useful, disagreeable and unpleasant to others (i.e. 2).[237]

Hence the reason for rejecting combination 8 and 4 is not that they are disagreeable or unpleasant to others, but that they are either false (untrue, i.e. not factual) or useless. Hence, the pragmatism of the Buddha, if that is what is being demonstrated here, does not entail a hedonism, i.e. the useful truth may pain you but Buddha is going to tell it to you anyway. Thus the pleasant and the unpleasant do not concern us here at all. It remains, then, to discover which of the other six combinations would be determinants for what the Buddha would assert and what he would not assert. The Sutta commentary says:

> He would not assert a statement which he knows to be untrue, false, useless, agreeable and pleasant to others (i.e. 7). He would not assert a statement which he knows to be true, factual, useless, agreeable and pleasant to others (i.e. 3).[238]

While agreeableness and disagreeableness to others are not criteria for the assertableness of statements, the truth (that which corresponds with the fact) and the usefulness of statements seem, or are both, necessary and sufficient to that assertableness:

> He would assert at the proper time a statement which he knows to be true, factual, useful, agreeable, and pleasant to others (i.e. 1) [and, by implication, 2, again].[239]

Possibilities 5 and 6 are omitted from the Sutta, but Jayatilleke believes that the exclusion is probably intentional "because it was considered self-contradictory to say of a statement that it was false but useful or because such statements did not in fact exist."[240] The reason for this is explained by Jayatilleke:

> This (i.e. both these latter alternatives) seems likely not because of any pragmatist theory of truth but because of the peculiarly Buddhist use of the term 'useless'.... Here [useful] is not just 'what is advantageous' in the broad utilitarian sense of the term, but what is morally good in the sense of being useful for the attainment of the goal of Nirvāṇa. Since falsehood or the assertion of a statement which is false...was considered a moral evil, it would have been held to be logically or causally impossible for what is false, i.e. what is morally evil, to result in what was useful in the sense of being morally advantageous or good.[241]

Thus the claimed self-contradiction between the false (the non-factual) and the useful, and the reason for the absence from the Sutta of combinations 5 and 6. Two things follow from this discussion:

First, in establishing the early Buddhist concept of pragmatic truth, the pleasant (the agreeable) as a criterion of that truth has been ruled out once and for all. Rather, the true is now construed as that which is useful for the attainment of nirvāṇa provided that that which is useful not be factually false as well. In other words, the useful assertion must correspond with the factual world, if it is to be considered true, and a factually false statement can never be useful.

Second, the contradiction between the false and useful, pointed out previously, seems to run counter to certain Western notions of pragmatism that say that a factually false, but useful, statement is true. If Jayatilleke is correct then truth by correspondence would, where applicable, be a necessary condition for the useful; and the useful and the true would no longer be equated in the sense that whatever is useful must thereby be true, as well. As a consequence our criticism of the pragmatic theory of truth in Hīnayāna Buddhism [242] would no longer apply. Recall that it was assumed there that pragmatism could be used to justify the most monstrous lies and assertions as long as they were useful in producing nirvāṇa. In other words, if I could have brought you to nirvāṇa by getting you to believe that Buddha was a lady, I would have been justified in doing so. But now the employment of such a falsehood, a moral evil, would make nirvāṇa impossible. So while all might be fair in love and war, all is not fair in Hīnayāna Buddhist salvation and religion.

Now we come to a major difficulty for Mahāyāna. For if, once again, Jayatilleke is correct then neither the Tathāgata nor a Bodhisattva can, without contradiction, successfully assert what is both factually false and useful for nirvāṇa; and lying is asserting what is not or cannot be, or promising what cannot be delivered. Therefore, however useful for nirvāṇa lying may seem to be, it can never be used successfully to lead to nirvāṇa.

But the father-Bodhisattva of the *Saddharmapuṇḍarīka*, as we have seen, is either lying or, as Śāriputra says, he would be justified in lying, in order to get his sons out of the burning house, i.e. he would be justified in promising something he did not intend to deliver. And that's not possible: If he lies they can't (logically) come out, i.e. reach nirvāṇa. The present difficulty results from this apparent inconsistency between the older Hīnayāna sutta quoted and defended by Jayatilleke and the newer text upheld by the Mahāyāna.

The question that seems to arise is this: Which version of pragmatism should the Buddhists support? The Hīnayāna pragmatism supported by Jayatilleke which says truth and usefulness are not identical? Or the Mahāyāna pragmatism supported by the *Saddharmapuṇḍarīka* which says that truth and usefulness are identical?

On the former interpretation, the father-Bodhisattva would not have been successful in getting his sons out of the burning house by promising oxen and carts he doesn't intend to deliver: Lying leads to a frustration of means. Skill-in-means for the Hīnayāna pragmatist must, presumably, stay within the tight boundaries of the facts and the truth.

On the latter interpretation, however, the father-Bodhisattva is not so bound to the facts and the truth; instead, as long as the lie produced the desired consequences the assertion would be true. On the Mahāyāna pragmatic theory, therefore, the pragmatically true might well be the factually false: Lying can lead to success of means. Skill-in-means for the Mahāyāna pragmatist would, presumably, have gotten the sons out of the burning building while the Hīnayāna pragmatist was still fumbling with his facts.

But a problem for the Mahāyāna pragmatist looms large on this interpretation and we turn to it next.

5. The Problem of Pragmatism

Mahāyāna pragmatism, the view that truth and nirvāṇic usefulness are to be identified, introduces a new puzzle into Buddhism. Spurning the seemingly more morally admirable doctrine that says that the *way* to the goal is just as important as the goal itself (and Hīnayāna pragmatism seems to uphold this virtuous admonition), Mahāyāna draws admiration to itself, nonetheless. The task, the Mahāyāna seems to be saying, is to get the occupants of the burning house out of the house, and hang the means! As long as everyone gets out. There is a kind of fittingness and appropriateness in the way in which this attitude seems to meet Gautama Buddha's claim that he taught only two things, viz., suffering and the release from suffering. What we are witnessing in Mahāyāna pragmatism is merely the most direct and resolute practice of that basic Buddhist teaching without the exra-practical paraphernalia and super-moralistic trappings of the view that says that the way to the goal is just as important as the goal.

But this is precisely the problem of pragmatism that the Mahāyāna view would force us to face. If the Bodhisattva's upāya is a skill in employing any means whatsoever as long as they lead the devotees to nirvāṇa then this would seem to place the morality of Buddhism in some jeopardy. In other words, the problem of pragmatism for Mahāyāna Buddhism is a moral problem, for Mahāyāna seems to hold that the end justifies the means, i.e. the use of any means is justified in order to reach enlightenment or heaven or whatever.

For example, would I be justified in lying, stealing and killing, if doing so would lead you to salvation, eternal happiness or nirvāṇa? The question sounds like the old question generally put to utilitarians, viz., Would you kill one man in order to save a thousand men from certain death? To which the utilitarian generally answers, Yes, of course. Whereupon the questioner asks, Well then, would you kill one man to save a hundred men? to save ten? to save two? At which point the utilitarian principle of identifying rightness in action with that action which produces the greatest amount of happiness also appears to be in some jeopardy. But the utilitarian is careful to count the consequences of the means as well as the consequences of the goal in calculating that happiness, hence he cannot be written off as one who argues that the end (happiness) always justifies the use of any means whatsoever. But the Mahāyāna Buddhists are not utilitarians in this sense; they are moral pragmatists and the skill-in-means of the Bodhisattva might appear to entail the use of any means whatsoever to bring about the nirvāṇic end.

Perhaps the analogy used in the *Saddharma-puṇḍarīka* is misleading, and in this sense: What father would not lie in order to get his children out of a burning house? One must have some sympathy with the father in such a situation. But the question remains, How far is the father prepared to go to achieve his ends? Would he kill? Would he kill one man outside the house to save his three sons inside? Would the Bodhisattva employ such means? But wouldn't such means of killing one to save three defeat the very purpose of the Bodhisattva's mission which was to defer his own nirvāṇa until every sentient being had been saved? i.e. you can't save the dead.

So it would seem that there are moral limitations placed on the Bodhisattva, and that, as a consequence, the doctrine that the end justifies the means is not as wide open as it seemed at first glance. But once it is seen that there are such limitations on the Bodhisattva's skilled means we can expand the principle that thus limits those means and say this: Whatever means would tend to defeat the very purpose (nirvāṇa) for which they are employed then those means (killing) should not be employed. Now the question is, Does lying defeat that purpose? And even Lord Buddha, as we have seen, along with Śāriputra, appears to have agreed that the employment of deception (he denies that it is a "falsehood") is acceptable as a means to be employed.

But the problem of pragmatism is not solved by this analysis; it is only refocused. While it may be true that the boys brought out of the burning house will be indifferent to the deception, and that those brought to nirvāṇa will be overjoyed despite the immoral means used, what of those standing and watching the father-Bodhisattva? The other Buddhist or non-Buddhist observers of the world? What effect might this discovery have upon their own future relations with the father-Bodhisattva? Would the awareness of the use of deception defeat all further dealings between those spectators or witnesses and the father or the Bodhisattva? When the Buddhist pragmatist poses the question, What effect will this teaching have on my life?, as both the Hīnayāna and Mahāyāna do, the question becomes especially important for the latter, given their commitment to unlimited pragmatism. I leave the reader to mull the puzzle.

We turn next to the sixth characteristic of Mahāyāna Buddhism, viz., its concern with heaven as a goal of Mahāyāna endeavor, where we shall have more to say about the Bodhisattva and his/her pragmatically applied skill-in-means.

6. Heaven

Mahāyāna Buddhism tends to hold that heaven is the penultimate goal for the Buddhist aspirant or devotee. Mahāyāna thereby disagrees with Hīnayāna not on the ultimate goal, which is and remains nirvāṇa, but it disagrees with Hīnayāna on where the stress and emphasis regarding the goals should be placed; and it seems to disagree with Hīnayāna on the nature of nirvāṇa, itself. The Mahāyāna conception of heaven provides an alternative to both the self-obliterating Hīnayāna conception of nirvāṇa as well as the Upaniṣadic conception of mokṣa. In addition, the Mahāyāna conception of heaven can be seen as a positive response to the influence of popular Hinduism that tended to see heaven as the real goal of liberation.

Technically speaking "nirvāṇa" is "extinction" or "blowing out." To the Hīnayāna this meant, among other things, annihilation and, particularly, the annihilation of sorrow, desire, and, finally, the illusion of self. But such annihilation must have been a scandal to many Hindus and a stumbling block to the Mahāyāna Buddhists who would see nothing enjoyable in pursuing such a nihilistic end.

Indeed, the Hindu world had already wrestled with this problem and had come out, in at least one śruti text and tradition, favoring personal survival as a necessary constituent of mokṣa, or liberation. There is, you will recall, that famous story of Lord Indra's education at the heavenly hands of Lord Prajāpati presented in the *Chāndogya Upaniṣad*. Indra comes to Lord Prajāpati in order to learn the nature of ultimate reality, i.e. the nature of man's goal or final destination. After spending thirty-two years with Prajāpati, Indra is taught that this goal is the Self or Ātman or Brahman (three names for one reality) and that this reality is to be identified with the body and the waking state of the mind. Indra leaves but realizes that if the body were ultimately real then, when the body dies, that reality would necessarily be destroyed as well.

Dissatisfied, he returns to Prajāpati for the second semester of his metaphysical education. After another thirty-two years Prajāpati tells him that the Self is that which is identified with the dream state of consciousness. Once again Indra leaves but rejects this conclusion seeing nothing enjoyable in identifying reality with a dream.

He returns to Prajāpati for a third term of instruction and after another period of thirty-two years he is taught that reality is to be likened to the dreamless state, the state of void and nothingness. Indra is thus brought up through the metaphysical stages of realization, from wakefulness to dreamfulness to dreamlessness, and with the third he has arrived, more or less, at the stage at which the Hīnayāna, themselves, have arrived, viz., an ultimate stage of being, a void that is without thought, memory, consciousness or personality. Indra leaves to return to the other Gods, and the *Chāndogya* registers Indra's sudden reaction to this goal of nothingness:

> Then, even before reaching the Gods, Indra saw this difficulty: "Truly, that dreamless, sleeping man does not know himself, nor that he exists, nor does he know anything at all that exists. He has been completely annihilated. I see no good in such a view."[243]

In a panic, Indra returns to Prajāpati and expresses his objection to this identification of ultimate reality with the state of nothingness. Prajāpati asks him to remain for a fourth semester, a period of five more years. At the end of this time, Prajāpati reveals the great truth to Indra that there is a fourth state beyond the dreamless and it is a state of ānanda, or enjoyment. Lord Prajāpati concludes:

> Truly, those Gods in heaven revere the Ātman. There, all worlds and all desires have been taken over by them. That man receives all worlds and all desires who discovers and understands the Ātman.[244]

Indra's panic at the possibility of self-annihilation in a world of dreamless obliteration is thereby removed. In place of an ultimate world of nothingness, we have a heavenly world of complete enjoyment from which one does not return to saṁsāra ever again.[245]

Indra's panic at self-obliteration is not at all different from the Mahāyāna reaction to the nirvāṇa of annihilation. The alternative to self-extinction as the goal of enlightenment is parallel to the Hindu worlds of the afterlife with their stages of self realization and liberation. There arose, as a consequence, in Mahāyāna those heavens and hells, where selves are rewarded or punished for their deeds, together with those intermediary places where the time between death and rebirth might be passed, and, finally, those Pure Lands or Heavens of the celestial

Buddhas and Bodhisattvas, for beings who are on their way to, or have already reached, nirvāṇa.

In a 1st century C.E. Mahāyāna work (the Greater) *Sukhāvatīvyūha* ("Description of the Happy Land") we have just such a description of a truly happy land. It is a heavenly kingdom of the Buddhas, the Pure Land, or Happy Land, of Lord Amitābha, the Tathāgata. The Buddha describes that rich and prosperous realm to his disciples, a land where there are no hells, no animals, ghosts or demons, where fragrant flowers and succulant fruits abound, where sweet-throated birds and bejeweled trees adorn the landscape.

In fact, one is reminded of the *Chāndogya Upaniṣad* with its description of just such a Hindu happy land. Lord Prajāpati rhapsodizes:

> The wind is bodiless. Clouds, lightning, thunder - these are bodiless. Now as these, when they arise from yonder space and reach the highest light, appear each with its own form, in the same way that serene being within when he rises up from this body and reaches the highest light, appears, too, in his own form. That one is the highest person. There that one goes around laughing, playing, enjoying women or chariots or friends, forgetting this body.[246]

The Buddhist picture of heaven is far more ornate and far more complete than the *Chāndogya* picture. In this bountiful Buddhist realm every desire known to man can be met and satisfied, every delight experienced; one has only to wish and then one gets. The *Sukhāvatīvyūha* states:

> And the beings in the world-system Sukhāvati [heaven or happy land] do not eat gross food, like soup or raw sugar; but whatever food they may wish for, that they perceive as eaten, and they become gratified in body and mind, without there being any further need to throw the food into the body. [The later *Maitreyavyākārana*, on the life of the future Buddha, Maitreya, will identify the three major human evils, viz., relieving the bowels, growing old and eating.] And if, after their bodies are gratified, they wish for certain perfumes, then the whole of that

> Buddha-field becomes scented with just that kind of heavenly perfume. But if someone does not wish to smell that perfume, then the perception of it does not reach him. [Smokers and non-smokers could both be accommodated in the same place.] In the same way, whatever they may wish for comes to them, be it musical instruments, banners, flags, etc.; or cloaks of different colours, or ornaments of various kinds.[247]

The faithful devotee may reach Sukhāvati, or heaven, by a rather complicated route which we shall detail in our discussion of bhakti, below. For the present we can simply say that in virtue of drawing upon the vast amount of stored merit, or good karma, left behind in a sort of cosmic merit bank by previous Bodhisattvas and Buddhas, the devotee can raise his faith and devotion to a point that enables him or her to enter Sukhāvati, or heaven. This merit residue collected from the Bodhisattvas and Buddhas of the past involves the Mahāyāna Buddhists in a doctrine of vicarious atonement in which the sins of the faithful can be abrogated by drawing upon the stored merit from this great moral, borrowing and lending institution. We will have more to say about this doctrine and its place in Buddhism, shortly.

Merit, your own or someone else's, is important for eventually getting you into Buddhist heaven and we might well ask, What's the purpose of going to heaven? Is heaven a permanent solution to saṁsāra for the Buddhists? Is heaven a goal that replaces enlightenment in Mahāyāna Buddhism? The answer to all of these questions is that heaven is merely a training camp or preparatory school for enlightenment. Whoever is reborn in heaven must still reach enlightenment; heaven, or the Pure Land, is simply the best possible place from which to secure that final goal. The *Sukhāvatīvūha* continues:

> And everyone hears the pleasant sound he wishes to hear, i.e. he hears of the Buddha, the dharma, the Saṅgha, or the (six) perfections, and (ten) stages...of emptiness, the signless and the wishless,...of non-production, non-existence, non-cessation, of calm, quietude, and peace...[He hears of] the great

> evenmindedness, of the patient acceptance of things which fail to be produced, and of the acquisition of the stage where one is consecrated [as a Tathāgata].

In this pleasant educational milieu the final goal is achieved:

> And, hearing [all] this, one gains the exalted zest and joyfulness, which is associated with detachment, dispassion, calm, cessation, Dharma, and brings about the state of mind which leads to the accomplishment of enlightenment.[248]

The *Sukhāvatīvyūha* concludes this discussion by noting:

> And all the beings who have been born, who are born, who will be born in this Buddha field, they all are fixed on the right method of salvation, until they have won Nirvāṇa.[249]

Thus the description of the Buddhist heaven and the reason for its existence as a prep school for nirvāṇa.[250]

But several problems arise in connection with the Pure Land and it will be worth our while to point them out.

6. The Problems of Heaven

The ideal of heaven as a penultimate goal in Mahāyāna Buddhism raises some questions regarding this ideal and its relation to the mainstream of traditional Buddhist thought. I mention three such questions and then focus on the third as central to the problem of heaven.

First, while it is apparently true that personal survival in the Pure Land, or heaven, is only the penultimate goal, and that enlightenment, or nirvāṇa, remains the utimate goal, the tendency of Mahāyāna, wherever it has flourished as a religion, is to regard heaven as of much greater importance than that ultimate goal. This tendency has no doubt accounted for the great appeal of Mahāyāna; for Hīnayāna has nothing that can quite compare with the Pure Land nor the infinite other Buddha or Bodhisattva heavens that at leastthis branch of Mahāyāna can call upon. If one is faced with a choice between nirvāṇa and the tendency to the self-obliteration of the Hīnayāna, on the one hand, and heaven and self-exhaltation of the Mahāyāna, on the other, then no doubt one would be ill-disposed, indeed, to choose the former. So, official Mahāyāna pronouncements to the contrary, the penultimate goal of heaven has gradually been turned into the ultimate goal of the ordinary Buddhist's religious yearnings.[251]

Second, while Mahāyāna heaven may officially be a basic training depot for nirvāṇa, it seems, nonetheless, to be more like one of those fleshly pleasure palaces that tend to abound around the outskirts of other basic training camps. If one takes seriously the magic-wishing-cow nature of heaven, it is difficult to see how all those satisfiable, satisfying and satisfied desires can be anything but a distraction and detriment to the official business at hand, viz., the reaching of enlightenment. Desire is and has always been the enemy of nirvāṇa; after all, it's what nirvāṇa "blows out"; and yet in Mahāyāna heaven we find desire soliciting at the very embarkation point to nirvāṇa.

Third, and finally, while Mahāyāna religion populates its heaven with wishers and desirers together with their wishes and desires, Mahāyāna philosophy tends to stress the belief that all that exists is mere phenomena, empty appearance, which includes the Gods, heaven and the Buddhas, as well. Mahāyāna philosophy is generally committed to seeking the truth of the emptiness of all phenomena. We have some inkling of this way of negation in the *Sukhāvatīvyūha* where Buddha mentions in his catalogue of the paraphernalia of heaven such items as emptiness, signlessness, wishlessness, non-production and non-existence; and yet side by side with these negative attributes there is a host of positive elements, viz., lovely rivers, beautiful flowers, haunting perfumes, enchanting jewels, superlative coats, gorgeous ornaments, and so on, and so on.

The problem of heaven comes down to asking, What is the ontological status of the kingdom of heaven? And this leads to what we might call "the dilemma of heaven": If heaven is real then the Mahāyāna philosophers are wrong, and nirvāṇa and emptiness cannot be the ultimate goals of Buddhism. If heaven is unreal then the Mahāyāna philosophers are right, but a great deception has been practiced on the heaven-bent devotees. Either way, the problem of heaven would seem to land us in this rather curious dilemma which concludes by saying that heaven must be either real or unreal; and that, therefore, either nirvāṇa is not the ultimate goal, after all, and Mahāyāna religion is at odds with Mahāyāna philosophy (if heaven is real), or nirvāṇa is the ultimate goal and Mahāyāna religion is deceiving its followers (if heaven is not real). So much for the dilemma of heaven and the problem of heaven.

The Mahāyāna have an answer to the problem of heaven that recalls our discussion of the skill-in-means of the Bodhisattva,[252] and it might be helpful to our further understanding of the problem to see what this attempted solution is like.

The Mahāyāna Buddhists tried mightily to integrate their new popular religion, with its talk of Gods, Bodhisattvas and heavens, into the philosophy of the *Prajñāpāramitā* literature, with its talk of negation, emptiness and the metaphysical void. We know that the Buddhas and Bodhisattvas with their practical skill-in-means always at hand will do anything in their power to provide the most favorable circumstances possible for their devotees' attainment of enlightenment. Mahāyāna has merely multiplied the conditions under which the average person may attain enlightenment by claiming that one of these heavens, the Pure Land, has been established by the Buddha for precisely this purpose.

The Mahāyāna is really continuing a system of heavens previously introduced by the Sautrāntikas and the Mahāsaṅghikas; but the system came to full flower, perhaps under the inspiration of Hinduism, here in the Pure Land religion with the latter's introduction of the notion of a Buddha field or Buddha land. Even now, we are told, the next Buddha, Maitreya, waits in the Tuṣita heaven to be reborn into this world at an auspicious moment. The heavenly followers of Maitreya yearn to be with him and to acccompany him in his final birth into this world from Tuṣita. Maitreya, like the Bodhisattvas before him, uses his skill-in-means to bring all men to enlightenment, even if this skill-in-means involves the use of heavens to accomplish his ends.

Officially, then, the heavens are no more real than the promises of toys given by the father-Bodhisattva to his children in the burning house. The heavens, like the toys, are pragmatically efficacious in providing the necessary incentive for the average person in his or her journey to full and final nirvāṇa: And deception in the pursuit of nirvāṇa is, probably, no deception at all. Thus the problem of pragmatism joins with the problem of heaven to give students of Mahāyāna Buddhism an occasion for philosophical problem solving.

We turn next to the seventh characteristic of Mahāyāna Buddhism and a discussion of bhakti.

7. Bhakti

Mahāyāna Buddhism introduces bhakti, or devotionalism, as one of the chief yogas or ways to enlightenment. The object or objects of devotion, of course, are the numerous Buddhas and Bodhiattvas that populate the Mahāyāna pantheon. Bhaktism became an adjunct to the dhyāna yoga, or meditational yoga, of the Hīnayāna and an alternative to the jñāna yoga, or prajñā, of several of the Mahāyāna philosophical schools. Where the latter attempted by prajñā to seize the emptiness and grandeur of reality and thereby attain nirvāṇa, bhakti provided, from about 250 B.C.E. onwards, an easier and more popular alternative to the more difficult way of prajñā.[253]

The practice of Buddhist bhakti entailed the love for, faith in, and absolute dedication of the devotee to a personal Bodhisattva or Buddha. The result of such utter devotion was, ideally, the complete change or transformation of the devotee, since what he surrendered was life, itself, i.e. its character, direction and goals. With the surrender of the old self in love, adoration, faith and trust, a new self was gradually born, a self that came to be identified with the beloved object of its devotions.

The Mahāyāna religious texts explain this state of affairs through a number of interesting concepts that help to locate bhakti and its place in the new religion. The Mahāyāna religion made four essential claims:[254] First, it claimed that there was a problem and it identified that problem as saṁsāra, i.e. as rebirth and as suffering; second, it claimed that there were causes of the problem, and the causes were ignorance and desire; third, it claimed that there was a solution to the problem, viz., a penultimate solution, heaven, and an ultimate solution, nirvāṇa; and, fourth, it claimed to know the ways to those solutions, viz., devotion (which would conquer desire) and prajñā (which would conquer ignorance), respectively. Let's look briefly at the chains of events that brought about these solutions or goals, and the place of bhakti in those chains.

The ultimate goal for Mahāyāna remains enlightenment, or nirvāṇa, reached through prajñā. But the penultimate goal of the religion is heaven, or the Pure Land, where enlightenment can be reached more easily than in the world. Heaven, in turn, is reached by gaining good karma through the grace, or favor, of the Bodhisattva, and this grace is reached by the devotee's devotion.

It is at this point that Mahāyāna introduces the doctrine of stored merit. The innumerable Bodhisattvas and Buddhas of the past have, through the aeons, produced and accumulated more good karma than could be used up in their own lifetimes. This super-abundance of good karma has been stored, as we mentioned above, in a kind of cosmic merit bank where it can now be tapped and drawn on by devotees seeking that merit in order to reach heaven.

The Bodhisattva has dedicated his own excess merit to the use of his devotees.[255] Through a process of vicarious atonement the Bodhisattva has freely taken the sins of the world upon himself and sacrificed all of his merit to the liberation of the suffering world. In other words, the stored merit is there, it has been paid for, the Owner of it desires that it be used by others, and it can be used by others. Then, in virtue of the merit being requested by the devotee, the grace of the Bodhisattva may then grant that merit and with that the heaven or the Pure Land may be reached. In other words, bhakti is a key to grace, and grace is the key to merit, and merit is the key to heaven, and heaven is the key to final liberation, or nirvāṇa.

Significant in this whole process, of course, is the request for help by the devotee, a request made through bhakti yoga, i.e. by the way of devotion or faith in the Bodhisattva or Buddha. Faith (śraddhā) is the sign that the devotee is ready for the grace and the merit that will carry the devotee to heaven and thence, after proper practice and training, to prajñā and enlightenment. Here is the Bodhisattva Śāntideva (7th century C.E.) speaking:

> Faith is the guide, mother, originator, protector, increaser of all virtues, dispeller of doubts, rescuer from the flood of rebirths. Faith is the signpost to the secure city (of the Buddha paradise)....
>
> Faith creates liking in renunciation, faith creates delight in the doctrine of the victors (i.e. the Buddhas), faith creates distinction in the knowledge of the virtues; it leads in the direction of the Buddha goal.[256]

Faith or devotion, the words are used interchangably by the commentaors, lead to the transfer of the stored merit to the devotee thereby opening the way to heaven or the Pure Land.

The faith or trust was, as often as not, displayed in the form of a simple mantram, repeated over and over again, as the devotee worshipped the Bodhisattva or Buddha who would save him from saṁsāra. Edward Conze mentions one example of these formulas and their use by the faithful:

> One should think of the Buddha while repeatedly pronouncing his name. Since the name contains the power of the Buddhas and the Bodhisattvas, its invocation is an act of the highest virtue. Innumerable formulas of invocation were elaborated. The most famous of all is "Homage to the Buddha Amitabha!" Om Namo Amitabhāya Buddhāya in Sanskrit, Om O-mi-to-fo in Chinese, Namo Amida Butsu in Japanese.[257]

But while the monkish professionals might be involved in ceaseless repetitions of the holy name of Buddha, the ordinary layman could achieve his heavenly salvation by "one single act of devotion", "one single thought of the Buddha", "for one single moment."[258]

In summary, then, the devotee envisions the goal, enlightenment (ultimately) or heaven (penultimately), and then works his way backward to something that can be done here and now to reach that goal. For example, one might reason in this way: In order to reach nirvāṇa I have to achieve heaven; in order to reach heaven I have to achieve sufficient merit; in order to achieve sufficient merit I have to practice good actions, myself, and/or draw down by grace the stored and transferable merit of the Bodhisattvas and Buddhas; and, finally, in order to practice good actions and/or draw down by grace the stored and transferable merit, I must practice the good actions *now* and/or ask for the grace and merit *now* by appropriate moral and religious action, i.e. by behaving rightly to all sentient beings and/or by reciting, for example, the name of Buddha, "Homage to the Buddha Amitabha!", or some such thing. We have reached the final "in-order-to" in our causal chain of things that I can say or imagine that I am going to do. And the final link in that chain brings that imagined scenario of to-be-done's right back to me with an action that I can perform here and now, viz., doing good while uttering the name of Buddha, thereby turning the action into a sacrifice to the Buddha: This is bhakti yoga in Mahāyāna Buddhism.[259]

But this imagined scenario with its causally linked chain of events leads us into several difficulties which the proponent of bhakti must be preared to meet. We turn to those problems next.

7. The Problems of Bhakti

There are four problems for the bhaktas (the practitioners of bhakti) of Mahāyāna. We mention three of them for openers and then move on to a final major problem.

a. The Problem of Parsimony

First, we have seen that "a portion of [the Bodhisattva's] immeasurable merit is transferred to the believer, if asked for in faith"[260] and that to ask for something in faith presumably brings the grace, that brings the merit, that brings the heaven, that brings the nirvāṇa. The problem here is one of a lack of simplicity in the entire procedure; let's call it "the problem of parsimony."

The problem of parsimony is that the route to heaven is strewn with too many steps and stages, i.e. the stages are multiplied beyond necessity. Wouldn't it be simpler, and wouldn't things be neater and more elegant, the critic might say, if faith and merit were reduced to a single stage, grace left out of the picture entirely, and heaven removed as a penultimate step? The Mahāyāna bhaktas could simply say, Those beings who show sufficient faith and have merit, alone, will be able to achieve enlightenment. For isn't this precisely what the Mahāyāna religion is trying to say, anyway? Or if this leans too closely to Hīnayāna Buddhism then couldn't the problem of parsimony be solved by keeping heaven but abolishing enlightenment? Or if this leans too closely to certain dvaita (dualistic) or viśiṣṭadvaita (pluralistic) schools of Vedāntic Hinduism then couldn't the problem of parsimony be solved by keeping both heaven and enlightenment but abolishing one or another of either faith or grace or merit entirely and letting the other two or the other one take over the tasks that all three seem to perform now?

The Mahāyāna Buddhist has a response to all of these suggestions for parsimony, of course, not the least of which is the reply that none of these suggestions for parsimony is what the texts, themselves, suggest. However that might be, and 'So much the worse for the texts', the parsimonious critic might say, the feeling must remain that too many stages are doing too many similar jobs here and that some of them are obviously repetitive; hence, they ought to be either expunged or reduced.

b. The Problem of Second Best

Second, another feeling that must remain is that bhakti leads only to the second best, i.e. heaven, and not the first best, i.e. enlightenment. And if bhakti leads only to the second best then bhakti must really be a "second best", in some sense, as well.

There is surely a common sense law or principle somewhere that must say, Things that lead to the best are themselves the best; hence a corollary must exist, viz., Things that lead to the second best are themselves second best, that allows us to conclude that bhakti is, indeed, second best. If the critic is correct then such a conclusion surely jeopardizes the role that bhakti is called upon to play in Mahāyāna Buddhism; for no one wants to be second best or to use second best ways to arrive at second best goals.

The Mahayana Buddhist has a response to this "problem of the second best", as we might call it. He simply reminds the critic that heaven is only the penultimate goal, that enlightenment remains the ultimate goal and prajñā remains the ultimate way to that goal; that bhakti and heaven, far from being a second best way and goal, respectively, are both first best, for there is another principle that says, Things that lead to the best, whether ultimately or penultimately, whether now or later, are, themselves, the best. Since bhakti yoga gets you to the place where enlightenment is attainable, that makes it one among at least two "bests", i.e. it's just as good, finally, as prajñā. So much, perhaps, for the problem of the second best.

c. The Problem of Selfishness

Third, there is a recurring problem of selfishness that comes up throughout this entire discussion of Mahāyāna. Seeking heaven is selfish because to get heaven *I* have to get merit; seeking merit is selfish because to get merit *I* have to get grace; and seeking grace is selfish because it entails *my* doing bhakti in order to get grace and good karma for *myself*, and the latter is surely an instance of selfishness. There must be some other law or principle, surely, that says, If the means to a goal is selfishly sought then the goal will be infected with selfishness. Furthermore, the critic maintains, the practice of selfishness is guaranteed to deliver nothing but bad karma, for selfishness tends to reduce merit and to make the whole selfish enterprise of seeking enlightenment turn upon itself and end in one glorious and inevitable defeat. In other words, if the means to the goal (attaining enlightenment) involves selfishness then the goal cannot be reached because this particular goal can only be reached when one is free of selfishness.

The Mahāyāna Buddhist has a response to the problem of selfishness, of course. He reminds the critic that merely because behavior is goal-directed does not make it selfish. For example, I may want to reach enlightenment but I know that to do that I must reach heaven, and to reach heaven I know that I must have merit, and to get that merit I must obtain the grace of the Bodhisattva; and to get that grace I know that I must practice bhakti; but none of this means that my behavior is selfish or practiced at the expense of anyone else. In fact, the Mahāyāna may continue, since the ultimate goal is extinction of all notions of the self then working for that goal must surely be non-selfish. Finally, the self, as all good Buddhists know, is a false concept anyway, so ultimately there can't be any self-centered actions if there is no self to center them on. Thus Mahāyāna Buddhism's answers to the problem of selfishness.

But the last answer must prove to be the least satisfactory to the critic; for the latter has merely to remind the Mahāyāna Buddhist that whether one is working for self-extinction or whether one knows now that the self is not real are both quite beside the moral point which is that there are selfish actions that can retard grace and merit and heaven and enlightenment. The Mahāyāna is on strongest ground when he admits this and argues that selfishness is a problem, alright, but that not all behavior need be selfish; and that it is the task of a good Buddhist to seek grace and merit and heaven and enlightenment unselfishly. And it is here, in debating the possibility of unselfish behavior, that the critic and the Buddhist meet head on.

d. The Problem of Merit

Fourth, and finally, we come to a major problem entailed by the doctrine of bhakti which we can call "the problem of merit." The problem of merit is major because it points to what appears as an attempt to nullify a central doctrine of Buddhism, viz., the law of karma.

Recall that Mahāyāna believes that an excess of unused good karma can be accumulated and stored, and that this stored merit can be transferred by grace to worthy selves in order that they might enter heaven. The problem of merit can be seen as a problem in two senses, then, first, as a problem of the storage of excess merit, and second, as a problem of the transfer of what has been stored: Both senses seem plainly inconsistent with the traditional understanding of the law of karma.

The law of karma, as we have noted, is really a principle of justice modelled after the ancient Vedic concept of Ṛta, the principle of cosmic and moral ordering. The law of karma says simply that everyone gets what's coming to him, i.e. sooner or later everyone gets his due. To those who do the good, rewards will come, and those who do the wicked, punishments will come.

But consider; the notion of the storage of good karma, or merit, would be quite inconsistent with this law: To store the good without rewarding the doer of the good is flatly contradictory to the law of karma. For example, to transfer my merit to you means that my merit is no longer my merit; and to say of my excess stored merit that it's not going to lead to a reward for me (because it's been transferred to you) is again to say that my merit is not my merit.

Furthermore, even if you deserve my stored merit, the fact of your deserving it means that you, too, have done good actions which have produced merit that now demand to be rewarded. So what has happened to your deserved merit? To say that it has been topped off with someone else's stored merit entails either of two things: First, that someone else didn't get his reward, i.e. he got less than he deserved, which is unjust; or, second, that you have gotten more than you deserved, which is also unjust.

The critic is quick to point out that stored merit is not ruled out *per se* by the law of karma, provided only that it is stored and then used by the same one who stored it, i.e. storer and user must be the same in some sense. For example, I might do many good works in this life but not be rewarded until the next life.[261] So in some sense my good karma has been "stored." However, if I reach nirvāṇa, and if my good karma is not used up or exhausted by being rewarded, then this would be inconsistent with the law of karma.

The critic is quick to point out, again, that transferred merit is not ruled out *per se* by the law of karma, provided only that the person to whom it is transferred is the same person who made it, i.e. transferer and transferee must be the same in some sense. For example, I might do many good works in this life, accumulate merit, but not be rewarded until the next life.

To repeat, if my stored merit is transferred to me then there is no problem; however, if I reach nirvāṇa and my stored merit is transferred to another, there is a problem that we might call "the dilemma of stored merit": If that other person deserves my stored merit then, since he has a reward of his own coming that doesn't involve my merit, his being deserving makes the transfer of my merit unnecessary. If that other person does not deserve my stored merit then such a transfer of my merit to him would be unjust. Now, he either deserves my merit or he does not. Therefore, either the transfer is unnecessary or it is unjust. Thus the dilemma of stored merit, the problem of merit, and the critic who concludes that the storage and transfer of merit is inconsistent with the ancient law of karma.

If the dilemma of stored merit is not solved then bhakti yoga is in trouble, since it is said to be efficacious in leading one to heaven only if the stored merit is transferable. And if the problem of merit, which is generated from the merit being transferable, is not solved then the law of karma is in trouble. On both counts, it must appear, bhakti yoga and the law of karma are in trouble.

But the Mahāyāna Buddhist is quick to point out that the law of karma need not be contradicted by the storage and transfer of merit. The latter merely calls for an extension of the law of karma. And that extension, far from being inconsistent with the original law, is, rather, a logical deduction from it. The original formulation of the Hindu law of karma was merely too narrowly stated and too narrowly applied (to single individuals and persons); what Mahāyāna did was merely to resist that narrow and personal interpretation of the law of karma and draw out its wider implications (to apply it to whole societies and communities).

Edward Conze gives a fine defense of this Mahāyāna point as he speaks, first, about the original and narrow belief in the law of karma:

> The original belief seems to have been that each one of us has his own series of karma, that the punishment for his misdeeds must be suffered by him, and that the rewards for his good deeds are enjoyed only by him. This excessive individualism was not essential to the karma doctrine, and just as historically the notion of collective responsibility preceded that of individual responsibility, so, in the Vedas it had been assumed that

> the members of a family or clan all share one common karma.

And then concludes with this objection to that original belief about the law of karma:

> The individualistic interpretation of the law of karma throws each individual on his own resources, and seems to deny any solidarity between the different persons as regards the more essential things of life, i.e. as regards merit and demerit.[262]

The Mahāyāna interpretation of the law of karma is, according to Conze, less individual-oriented, and more community-oriented: Merit is made to be shared in a community. As such it would allow, according to Mahāyāna, the storage and the transfer of merit to other bhaktas, to other members of the bhakta community.

A good deal of what Mahāyāna has to say about the problem of bhakti is determined by the Buddhist concept of the individual or the self. We turn next, therefore, to the eighth characteristic of Mahāyāna Buddhism, viz., the tendency to reify the self.

8. Ātmavāda

Mahāyāna Buddhism tends to reintroduce the notion of a self back into Buddhism, and it does it in a most curious manner. The reality of the self had been denied vigorously by the Hīnayāna, and there is not one passage in the Canon in which a real self is ever clearly maintained. But in the Mahāyāna we find a compromise being struck somewhere between the positive Ātman doctrine of Hinduism and the negative anātman doctrine of Hīnayāna Buddhism. Mahāyāna adopts a middle way *par excellence*. Let us review the "official" Buddhist doctrine of anātman as it came out of the earlier Hīnayāna and Abhidharma traditions, traditions which may go back to about 300 B.C.E.[263]

Recall that the so-called "self" can be reduced to five sets, complexes or skandhas of momentary dharmas and that anything relating to "person" must be analyzed in terms of these five skandhas:

1. body - the physical body and the various appendages that we identify with it

2. feelings - pleasant, unpleasant and neutral sensations
3. perceptions - judgments of sound, sight, taste, touch and smell
4. willings - love, hate, greed, faith and other dispositions
5. consciousness - the rational awareness of the preceding skandhas

The so-called "self" is a "construction" from these five skandhas.

In reality, of course, there is no self but only these five heaps of momentary, ever-changing dharmas. Out of ignorance we come to believe in an unchanging, permanent, real self and, in our delusion, we become attached to that self. From this delusion and attachment come egotism, selfishness, competition, greed, envy, jealousy and the myriad other vices that depend on the belief in a self. And from all this comes suffering, anxiety and pain.

The great Mahāyāna philosopher, Vasubandhu, put the matter in this fashion:

> Do we not see that certain people, ignorant of the true nature of the conditioned Dharmas which constitute their so-called 'Self', attach themselves to these Dharmas by force of habit - however completely these Dharmas may be devoid of personality - and suffer a thousand pains because of this attachment?

The object, of course, is to recognize the self as a fiction, which is what the Bodhisattva has done, and to teach this recognition to others, which is what he or she does:

> Likewise, one must admit that the Bodhisattvas, by the force of habit, detach themselves from the Dharmas which constitute their so-called "Self', do no longer consider these Dharmas as 'I' or 'mine', [grow] in pitying solicitude for others, and are ready to suffer a thousand pains for this solicitude.[264]

Since avidyā, ignorance, is the cause of this delusion with its attendant suffering then the way out of the delusion and the suffering is through prajñā. But prajñā, as we have seen, is best practiceable in heaven or the Pure Land, though heaven is not the only realm or plane or place where prajñā can be practiced; the earthly plane could be just as good a place or plane for some persons as heaven is for others for the release from the delusion, i.e. for enlightenment. Now, since avidyā stays with one until enlightenment is reached, and since avidyā is responsible for the false belief in the reality of ātman, then we must conclude that this false belief in the self can exist on both the earthly and the heavenly planes. In other words, to repeat, the delusion about the self remains until enlightenment is reached: The self is a fiction.

What we are about to witness in this new doctrine of Mahāyāna is really a revival of the heretical belief in the pudgala. Recall Pudgalavāda for a moment; it was the view that maintained the reality of the pudgala, or self, a heresy that was invented some 200 years after the Buddha's parinirvāṇa. Pudgalavāda was roundly rejected in the *Kathāvatthu* and later by Vasubandhu in his *Abhidharmakośa* where he devoted an entire chapter to its refutation. The Pudgalavādins had argued that the pudgala is a "real" entity that underlies, or exists separately from, and in addition to, the skandhas.

These Pudgalavadins, or "Personalists", as they have been called, were seeking an answer to a very important question: If the person, or self, and the skandhas were identical then who or what bears the burden of bondage and suffering? That is to ask, How can there be bondage and suffering unless there is a subject, a person, who is in bondage and suffers?

To answer by saying that the skandhas bore the burden seemed patently absurd for it would mean that the skandhas were serving the function of being both subject and object of bondage, and it is clear that the Personalists were looking for a more *bona fide* subject than that, a subject who was in bondage, who sought release from bondage, and who was, finally, released from bondage.

In the famous *Burden Sūtra* the Personalists seized upon the answer that Buddha gave to the question concerning the self:

> I will teach you the burden, its taking up, its laying down, and the bearer of the burden (*bhāra-hāram*). The five skandhas (which are the range) of grasping are the burden. Craving takes up the burden. The renunciation of craving lays it down. The bearer of that burden is the person....[265]

The self may be a "fiction" but it is surely a convenient fiction for it allows us to introduce a subject that is identifiable from the womb to the tomb in this life, and it allows that subject to continue in an identifiable chain over many lives that continue up to the point of enlightenment, itself.

Further, Pudgalavāda can answer several rather common sense questions arising from such diverse concepts and topics as rebirth (What is it that migrates from one body to another?), stored merit (What is it that seeks and receives the merit stored by the Bodhisattvas?), ethics (What is it that must be punished for wicked deeds? and What is it that is to be held morally responsible?), memory (What is it that remembers past events?) and personal identity (What is it that makes the differentiation of skandhas into separate and identifiable individuals possible?), questions that, previously, may have proved difficult or unanswerable.

The existence of the self or person, however "unreal" such a fiction may be, provides a useful locus, therefore, for bondage, for the means out of bondage, for language, for memory, for the virtues as well as the vices, and, finally, for liberation, itself.

The middle way compromise that the Personalists struck lay in holding that while this convenient entity had no permanent substantiality, for at enlightenment it passed out of existence (thereby agreeing in part with the Hīnayāna), it was, nonetheless, capable of having a semi-permanent and limited existence (thereby agreeing, in part, with ātmavādins like the Hindus). This useful fiction of the token-person remained in the closet in Buddhism, biding its time until Mahāyāna, at last, made it tolerable, respectable and even necessary.

Later Buddhism found it extremely difficult to maintain the official anātman doctrines of the earlier

Hinayana. Hence we find personalist or ātman doctrines creeping back everywhere, even in orthodox Hīnayāna circles. For example, later Hīnayāna advanced a life-continuum (bhavaṅga) theory which maintained that a common thread connects a series of lives at the subconscious and subliminal level; the Sautrāntikas and the Mahāsaṅghikas put forward a theory of subtle consciousness to the same end; and the Saṁkrāntikas taught that the skandhas themselves transmigrated to accomplish this same purpose, viz., to give some cogency to the rather common, intuitive belief in an empirical self. Edward Conze has said of all these attempts to dodge the canonical and orthodox Abhidharma rejection of the self:

> In spite of their professions to the contrary, the Buddhists were constantly, drawn to the belief in a 'true self', which would act as a permanent constituent (*dhatu*) behind the ever-changing 'continuity'.[266]

The point to all of this discussion, of course, is that the Mahāyāna, themselves, were closet Pudgalavādins, who believed that, up until the time of enlightenment, a fictional self (as opposed to a non-existent self or a permanent Self) exists. That is to say, given our previous discussion about bhakti and heaven, it would seem to follow that they necessarily believed that a fictional self exists on the earthly, the heavenly and Pure Land planes, and that such a self continues to exist until dispelled by prajñā and enlightenment.

When we come to a discussion of the philosophic schools of Mahāyāna philosophy and, in particular, to the Yogācāra school we shall discover that Mahāyāna does, indeed, boldly and unashamedly attempt to smuggle back into Buddhism a substantial and permanent Self.

There are several questions that arise with this Mahāyāna belief in a self enduring through time until enlightenment, not the least of which is simply getting clear on what this self is. There are probably three notions of a self floating about in the literature and they seem to be variously affirmed or denied depending on the school, the text, or the spirit of the times under which the discussion of the self takes place. Let me delineate these three selves and identify each one very briefly. Call them $self_r$, *self$_p$, self $_s$*:

self$_r$ - the real Self, or Ātman, of Upaniṣadic Hinduism and Yogācāra Idealism

self$_p$ - the pudgala, or person, of the Sammitīyas and "unofficial" Mahāyāna Buddhism (as argued above)

self$_s$ - the saṁtāna or momentary self of Hīnayāna and "official" Mahāyāna Buddhism

The claim that we made previously was that self$_p$ is a kind of middle way between self$_r$ and self$_s$; the former, self$_r$, is real, i.e. it is unchanging, independent and eternal; while the latter, self$_s$, is unreal, i.e. it is changing, dependent and temporal. Further, self$_p$, it was argued, is a middle way self, for while it is not real, neither is it unreal, i.e. it doesn't exist forever but it exists for an awfully long time with self-identity, memory and consciousness, all rather intact: Self$_p$ is a self that is busy evolving from self$_s$, a process-self, to self$_r$, a substance self. Upon attaining nirvāṇa, self$_p$ ceases to exist, at least according to one interpretation of nirvāṇa (recall Indra's panic).

Finally, we call self$_p$ the self of "unofficial" Mahāyāna Buddhism because while both Mahāyāna and Hīnayāna Buddhism dogmatically deny the reality of any self whatsoever, Mahāyāna manages, nonetheless, to smuggle a self, self$_p$, out from the metaphysical closet. In the last analysis, it may very well be the case that self$_s$, the process-self, is not altogether different from self$_p$, the personal self: For process-self, after all, has prāpti to hold its traces together long enough to make it indistinguishable from a pudgala.

But now the critic of this unofficial doctrine of Mahāyāna self$_p$ arrives to point to the problem of ātmavāda. We turn very briefly to that problem next.

8. The Problem of Ātmavāda

There is a major problem for the defenders of self$_p$, those closet Pudgalavādins who boldly support a doctrine of the relative reality of the personal self, a doctrine that seems eminently common-sensical and intuitively obvious. This problem pits the pragmatic justification of $self_p$ against the phenomenalistic and introspective justification of $self_s$.

The best argument against $self_p$ is based on a kind of introspective empiricism and it is offered by the Hīnayāna critic-defender of $self_s$ against the Mahāyāna defender of $self_p$. It demonstrates the very central problem of ātman, the problem that at no time in any of our experiences do we ever come across a thing, entity, pudgala, ātman, ego, subject or whatever that we could ordinarily call a "self."

Recall, once again, the observation made by the 18th century British phenomenalist, David Hume. Hume was performing an introspective experiment, trying, unsuccessfully, through the direct inspection of his mind and its contents, to discover the self:

> For my part, when I enter most intimately into what I call *myself*, I always stumble on some particular perception or other...I never catch *myself* at any time without a perception, and never can observe anything but the perception.[267]

Hume's phenomenalistic remarks could equally well have been made by a Hīnayāna Buddhist defending $self_s$, and they constitute an interesting argument against any pragmatic proclivities that the Mahāyāna may have for defending $self_p$.

Now, I invite you to perform the same brief experiment. I want you at this moment to peer into your own mind, memory and consciousness in order to see if you can honestly experience any thing there, any thing at all, that you could call "a self." *Please try it*. Could you really apprehend anything other than particular bits and pieces of present or past experiences, e.g., bits and chunks of sights, sounds, touches, smells and tastes? These phenomena are all that experience can contain or ever will contain, and phenomenalists, i.e. those philosophers who defend this view, defy you to find a continuous, relatively permanent and unchanging $self_p$ in all these phenomena. In other words, a self can be neither introspectively experienced in the mind nor anywhere else. The critic would conclude that $self_p$ is a fiction; and however useful it might be for meeting arguments or solving puzzles it remains a fiction. So much for closet Pudgalavādins masquerading as Mahāyāna Buddhists.

We have not finished with the problem of ātman, however, nor with self$_p$. It remains to say more about this self that exists up until nirvāṇa, and Mahāyāna Buddhism will demonstrate further its belief in self$_p$ in the ninth characeristic inclination of Mahāyāna Buddhism, viz., the doctrine of transmigration.

9. Rebirth (As Transmigration)

Mahāyāna Buddhism is committed, it would seem, to a doctrine of transmigration, wherein "something passes over."[268] This commitment probably follows logically from the commitment to the pudgala, or person, theory dealt with above: In other words, if there is a self$_p$, i.e. a person that exists until nirvāṇa is achieved, then this self$_p$ must transmigrate from one body or place to another. We have argued in the previous section that Mahāyāna seems to accept such a self$_p$. Therefore, this self$_p$ must transmigrate from one body or place to another until liberation is reached. In other words, if self$_p$ is the case then, as far as rebirth is concerned, transmigration must be the case, as well.

Again, that which transmigrates is neither an absolutely permanent psychological self nor an ultimately real, Hindu Ātman; but it is, nonetheless, a relatively stable, relatively real, being, self or person, the product of avidyā, and a congeries of memory, consciousness and desire. That is to say, self$_p$ is the bearer of self identity and it exists as a being only as long as its desires and avidyā last, i.e. until nirvāṇa. As the Buddha of the *Sukhāvatīvyūha* has said:

> And all the beings who have been born, who are born, who will be born in this Buddha-field [heaven or the Pure land] they all are fixed on the right method of salvation, until they have won Nirvāṇa.[269]

The Mahāyāna, by introducing self$_p$ as the vehicle of self identity, can solve the problem of personal identity that proved to be such a difficulty for reincarnation under Hīnayāna Buddhism; however, it raises other problems that might not be so neatly handled. Perhaps we ought to get clear on precisely what transmigration really is before we turn to those problems. If, to begin with, we were to analyze the logic of transmigration by laying out the various rules and assumptions (the necessary and sufficient conditions) of transmigrations we might get a clearer picture of that to which the Mahāyāna theory of rebirth seems committed. And we might discover that what seemed so very simple a notion is in fact quite complex.

In Table VI, below, we identify the four assumptions (A) which would seem to be necessary and sufficient to any theory of transmigration:

Table VI: The Logic of Transmigration

A_1 A self (selves) exists.

A_2 Places for self (selves) to exist.

A_3 Movement of self (selves) between places is possible.

A_4 Rules governing the movement of self (selves) between places exist.

Let me speak briefly to each of these assumptions:

A_1 A self (selves) exists

Transmigration assumes that $self_p$ exists complete with memory, consciousness and desire. The self is, therefore, a stuff that bears an identifiable stamp that distinguishes it from other selves and their stamps, and it is identical with itself through time. The memories that $self_p$ has, for example, of childhood and youth, give a kind of continuity to that self, and consciousness of those memories is what gives an awareness of that self. The desires that are had, even the Hīnayāna would agree, are what keep those memories and the consciousness of them alive, active and functioning. It is, then, this desiring $self_p$ that seeks out new places in which to exist, e.g. bodies and heavens, and to which it carries its memories and consciousness. Mahāyāna Buddhism, as we have seen, seems perfectly capable of accepting this first assumption of transmigration.[270]

A_2 Places for self (selves) exist

Transmigration assumes that $self_p$, described above, must exist in some place, usually some space-time locus, and most frequently, this place is a physical body. The body is the mechanism by which the self acquires experiences and then memories, by which it manifests its desires and without which memory and desire would both be impossible. Mahāyāna Buddhism accepts places for $self_p$ and it also accepts places for these places to be in, e.g. the world and the various heavens are places where, presumably, bodies of some sort, physical, mental or spiritual, can reside.

A_3 Movement of self (selves) between places is possible

Transmigration assumes that $self_p$ is mobile. If it were not mobile, if it were incapable of leaving one place for another, the Mahāyāna might end up with some animistic or hylozoic universe with selves as permanent occupants all over the place, with the consequence that we certainly would not have transmigration. Mahāyāna Buddhism in its Pure Land religious phase accepts this mobile $self_p$ travelling from this world to the Pure Land, the Buddha fields or heaven, for final instructions on nirvāṇa from the Bodhisattvas and Buddhas.

A_4 Rules govern the movement of self (selves) between places

Transmigration assumes the law of karma as the chief governing principle by which selves go to the places that they go. The law of karma may be elaborated by rules regarding the divine grace of the Bodhisattva, vicarious atonement and stored merit, as we have already seen, but the central principle governing the mobile self remains this principle of moral causation. Mahāyāna Buddhism, as we have seen, accepts the law of karma as the principle by which rebirth is governed.

Having laid out the four assumptions of the logic (the rules) of transmigration to which the Mahāyāna Buddhist seems committed, we turn next to an examination of the several problems generated by this logic and by the doctrine of transmigration.

9. The Problems of Transmigration

There are four putative problems which the defender of transmigration must face and all of them are connected with the logic of transmigration. Let me take the problems one at a time, state them briefly and then just as briefly state what would very likely be a Mahāyāna response to the putative problem.

A_1. <u>The Problem of the Self</u>

The problem of the self arises from assuming A_1, that a $self_p$ exists. The Hīnayāna critic would claim that A_1 is heterodox, i.e. A_1 violates one of the basic beliefs of Buddhism. For, the critic says, the Buddhist commitment to the reality of a self was rejected long ago when the Pudgalavādins tried the same move with their belief in the self; and that belief has been summarily rejected ever since. Hence, the problem of the self states that A_1 cannot be an assumption within Buddhism.

In response, let me simply say that this first objection to the doctrine of transmigration is nonsense. The Buddhists may have rejected Pudgalavāda as heterodox at the Third Buddhist Council sometime around 247 B.C.E., but pudgala in one form or another had been creeping back into Buddhism ever since. Consequently, there is nothing heterodox about A_1 unless one is measuring orthodoxy by 3rd century B.C.E. standards.

A_2. <u>The Problem of the Places of the Self</u>

The problem of the places of $self_p$ arises from assuming A_2, that those places exist. The critic may claim that three things are wrong with A_2: First, the critic might claim that the places that the self occupies are just as unreal as the self. The body, heaven, hell, the Pure Land, and so on, are ever-changing, caught up in anitya or māyā or śūnya,[271], and that they are, consequently, unfit ephemeral locations for anything.

In response, let me say that this objection is similar to the first objection, above, and can be met in the same way, viz., by pointing to the manner in which Mahāyāna Buddhism has evolved from the Pristine Buddhism of the Founder and Hīnayāna Buddhism. The temporality, ephemerality and fluxious nature of the body, or the world, or the Happy Lands beyond this body and world, are not matters of momentous concern to the new religion of Mahāyāna.

Second, the critic might say that the places of $self_p$ and their reality were not talked about by Buddha, hence any commitment to $self_p$, the loci for $self_p$, or movement between loci by $selves_p$, and so on, are completely negated or śūnyafied, in the grand silence of the Buddha.

In response, let me say that the Buddha's silence on matters of the reality of the world, and the self after death, will be of momentous concern in shaping one of the later schools of Mahāyāna thought, viz., Mādhyamika.[272] But, further, even the Mādhyamikas, despite the commitment to this silence and its implications, were not prevented from accepting the logic of transmigration in some form or other, complete with Buddha fields, Happy Lands and heavens. So where's the problem? What is needed in meeting the critic's objection to A_2 in some perspective that would lay out the relative importance of the elements in A_2, and that perspective will be provided in our discussion of Mādhyamika, below.[273]

Third, the critic might then say that if the places are real then we are involved in a metaphysical pluralism of a most radical and heterodox sort and this pluralism runs counter to official Buddhist orthodoxy.

In response, let me say that there is no implication whatsoever of the loci for $self_p$ being real. The assumption merely states that places for $self_p$ exist, without committing itself to any notion that those loci are real. The loci, consequently, when seen with the metaphysics of the Mahāyāna tradition present no problem to that tradition.

A_3. <u>The Problem of the Movement of Selves</u>

The problem of the movement of $selves_p$ between places arises from assuming A_3, that such movement is possible. The critic has only to point out that the statement about this movement or travel is woefully incomplete and being incomplete all sorts of questions must surely arise. For example, what makes or forces $self_p$ to move on from one locus to another? Is that matter decided for $self_p$ rather than by $self_p$? Can two or more $selves_p$ move into the same locus? Ordinarily such double occupancy is referred to as "possession"; now what rules govern possession? Can $selves_p$ exist and move and occupy no locus? i.e. be "nowhere"? Why do $selves_p$ move at all? If one answers, Because the conditions for their occupancy change, then the critic might ask, So what? Why can't a self occupy, for example, a dead body and refuse to move on? Further, what stops the movement of $self_p$ between loci? What holds $self_p$ in one locus rather than another? And finally, what stops the movement of $self_p$, totally and completely? Is it nirvāṇa? Where is $self_p$, then, after nirvāṇa? Thus the rules for A_3 are woefully incomplete until these questions are satisfied.

In response let me say that this objection with its series of rather formidable questions is not insurmountable. If the problem of the movement of $selves_p$ between places is a matter of incompleteness of rules then that problem can be met by simply expanding the rules. Part of that expansion is accomplished by merely augmenting the law of karma, by showing that movement between loci is governed by the law of karma that specifies when and how and from where and to where such movement shall take place. We turn, therefore, to that law and one of the problems that it raises.

A_4. The Problem of the Rules

The problem of the rules that govern the movements of $selves_p$ between places is, essentially, the problem of the law of karma that arises from assuming A_4. The critic is quick to point out that even with an expanded A_4 the problem remains, i.e. even if we meet the objections and questions raised above under the problem of the movement of selves, there remains a fundamental problem with the law of karma, *per se*. That problem is simply that the status of the law of karma is not at all clear. What is the nature of this law whose viability we are assuming? It is clear that it is not an empirical law and the result of an inductive generalization. The law of karma, as we have seen, is a metaphysical principle of universal moral justice that guarantees that everyone gets his due, everyone gets what's coming to him: Bad behavior is punished, good behavior is rewarded, necessarily and everywhere. And the critic asks, How do you know this? And then hastens to point out that you don't. When you believe that good $selves_p$ move to fortunate places after the destruction or death of the place that they are now in, and that wicked $selves_p$ similarly move to unfortunate places, the critic states that you have no worthwhile, i.e.

unimpeachable, evidence for this belief. Thus the problem of the rules that govern the movements of selves_p between places is that those rules are unverifiable or unconfirmable or untestable. And if the rules cannot be justified then neither can any of the other three assumptions be accepted: If the rules fail then transmigration fails.

In response let me point out first of all that none of these assumptions, A_1 to A_4, are meant to be grounded in any kind of sensory verification. Their empirical untestability is not what is at issue here; they are assumptions and assumptions are not the kinds of things about which philosophers seek empirical confirmation. But assumptions do need justification and the critic raises this issue when he questions the lack of clarity in the status or nature of the law of karma, i.e. what is its justification?

I would suggest, once again, that the law of karma is one of our "useful fictions", those ideas, concepts, beliefs, principles or laws that are unverifiable or unconfirmable by any of the ordinary and usual empirical tests; hence they are fictions under the correspondence theory of truth. Further, they are not the result of deduction from another set of verified or confirmed set of principles; hence, they are fictions, once, again under the coherence theory of truth.[274] Penultimately, these "fictions" when believed or accepted can be said to accomplish certain goals or ends and can be said to be true, consequently, under the pragmatic theory of truth. Ultimately, then, belief in them accomplishes or leads to metaphysical realization or enlightenment, hence they are true under what we have been referring to as the mythic theory of truth. The convenience, then, of accepting convenient fictions like the law of karma is that such assumptions lead to desired metaphysical ends: And that is the justification for the law of karma and that is the answer to the critic. This ends our discussion of the problems of transmigration.

We turn next to the tenth and final characteristic of Mahāyāna Buddhism, viz., the tendency towards the philosophies of absolutism and idealism. In this final section we shall attempt a reconstruction of the philosophic history of the two major schools of Mahāyāna Buddhism, viz., Mādhyamika absolutism and Yogācāra idealism.

10. The Philosophies of Absolutism: Śūnyatā and Vijñaptimātra

Mahāyāna Buddhism tends to be anti-realist in its approach to the worlds of minds and things, but absolutist in its metaphysics. The two schools of Mahāyāna philosophy that we are going to examine have this in common: Each school questions and then rejects both metaphysical materialism, the view that matter alone is real, and metaphysical body-mind dualism, the view that body and mind are both real, and in rejecting these commonly accepted reals, they are said to be "anti-realist."[275]

But each school seems to accept views that lead ultimately to metaphysical absolutism, the view that an indescribable ultimate reality exists, transcending the mental and physical worlds, and that It can be known. Metaphysical absolutism appears under the guise of "Buddha nature" and other names in both schools such as "Śūnyatā", or "Absolute Emptiness", in the Mādhyamika school, and as "Vijñaptimātra", or "Absolute Mind", in the Yogācāra school.

The first school, the Mādhyamika, rejects metaphysical materialism, metaphysical idealism and metaphysical body-mind dualism. It argues to these rejections by means of a philosophical method that has been referred to as "nihilistic." At times the reference seems appropriate, despite claims to the contrary by defenders of Mādhyamika. But to refer to Mādhyamika, in genreal, as nihilistic[276] is to confuse its method with its metaphysics, its means with its conclusions. In its methodology and means Mādhyamika emerges as a rigorous philosophical nihilism, a "dialectical nihilism" would be a good name for it; but in its conclusions and ends, and despite the protests of its founders and its defenders, it has something quite positive to say. It argues that the methodology that shows the utter emptiness of both material and mental things, entities and beings, leads ultimately to the realization that that Emptiness is the Absolutely Real: And this realization constitutes enlightenment. Since the methodology involves the rejection of the reality of the material and mental worlds, we can say, therefore, that Mādhyamika seems to be an anti-realist philosophy.

The second school, the Yogācāra, rejects common sense realism, as well. Yogācāra is the Buddhist version of metaphysical idealism. It argues that all things, entities and beings are part of Mind, that Mind is the Absolutely Real, and that Mind can be known: And knowing that everything is Mind, and realizing the nature of Mind, constitutes enlightenment. Since the methodology involves the rejection of the reality of the empirical and material world, we can say, therefore, that Yogācāra, too, seems to be an anti-realist philosophy.

In what follows, our concern will be with these two anti-realist, but absolutist, schools of Mahāyāna, viz., Mādhyamika and Yogācāra Buddhism.

During the period from 200 B.C.E. to 200 C.E. there occurred a profound change in Buddhist philosophy. The profound change essentially amounted to a move from a philosophical realism to a philosophy of anti-realism. The chief cause of this revolution in metaphysics is unknown but it has been conjectured that one cause may have lain in the growing influence of Hinduism.[277] If this conjecture is correct, it would mean that the Vedic tradition and, in particular, the Upaniṣadic tradition shaped and may have been shaped in return by Mahāyāna Buddhism. Finally, the *Prajñāpāramitā* literature, itself, from which our two Mahāyāna schools trace their origin, appears to exhibit some rather obvious parallels to the Upaniṣadic literature. Thus both literatures propound at least two similar doctrines: First, both the *Prajñāpāramitā* and the *Upaniṣads* warn against the human tendency to talk about that which is ultimately indescribable, i.e. that which is ultimately śūnya ("empty") or neti, neti ("not this or that"); and second, both warn against the all-too-human proclivity to impose human, all-too-human, categories upon the Real, turning concepts into things, thereby reducing the Real to the unreal, reducing śūnya to dharmas, or Brahman to māyā. The result is that our two Mahāyāna schools, Mādhyamika and Yogācāra, might easily, and mistakenly, be taken for two Upaniṣadic schools of philosophy.

But, conjectural or not, I would suggest that the reader keep in mind what's already been said previously about the similarities between Mahāyāna, the Hindu *Upaniṣads* and the concepts generated in the latter texts. Recall especially higher and lower Brahman and the identity between Ātman and higher Brahman, the function of the māyā (magic power) of higher Brahman in the creation of lower Brahman, the nature of saṁsāra (māyā, this world, suffering and rebirth), bondage by avidyā, or ignorance, and finally, jñāna yoga, or intuitive knowledge, as the way to mokṣa, or liberation, from saṁsāra.[278]

We begin our discussion of anti-realism by examining at some length the extremely important school of Mādhyamika Buddhism. Mādhyamika was probably the first important Mahāyāna school to turn its critical attention to the Abhidharma philosophic literature and the problems created therein by the realist metaphysics of the dharmas.

a. The Mādhyamika (Śūnyavāda) School

The founder of the first great Mahāyāna Buddhist school of philosophy was a second century C.E. south Indian brahmin by the name of Nāgārjuna who studied the four *Vedas* and knew all of the commentaries and sciences. He is said to have been born beneath an arjuna tree, hence part of his name "Nāgārjuna." His biography was translated into Chinese in 405 C.E. by Kumārajīva who states that Nāgārjuna had been a great Sorcerer whose wishes were satisfied by an army of familiar nāgas, i.e. serpents, that he commanded. Hence, the rest of his name. Kumārajīva also tells us that Nāgārjuna could make himself invisible. One time, accompanied by three companions, he secretly entered the royal palace and found, and began to molest, the women of the palace. The four were discovered and arrested but, while his three friends were sentenced to death, Nāgārjuna managed to escape after vowing to become a monk. Kumārajīva relates that he did become a monk, that he studied and absorbed the meaning of the whole of the *Tripiṭaka* in just 90 days but that he was unsatisfied with what he learned. His dissatisfaction remained until about 150 C.E. when an aged monk in the Himalayas gave him the whole of the *Mahāyāna Sūtras* (the *Prajñāpāramitā*, the *Saddharmapuṇḍarīka*, the *Lalitavistara*, the *Aṣṭasā hasrika*, the *Laṅkāvatāra*, the *Gaṇḍavyūha* and four other texts). Another story has it that Nāgārjuna visited the underworld of the Nāga, the serpents, the traditional bearers of wisdom in the world's mythology (recall *Genesis* I), and there he was given the Large *Prajñāpāramitā Sūtra* which had been entrusted to the serpents by Lord Buddha, himself. And the rest is history (or legend).

Nāgārjuna and the school that he founded were strongly influenced by the *Prajñāpāramitā* literature. That influence may have justified the common belief that he was 'a mystic of high attainment' who had practiced meditation assiduously and at death had been raised up to heaven, without the serpents, to the Pure Land of Sukhāvatī. It is important to remember throughout the discussion of these philosophical systems that their primary purpose was, after all, a religious, and not an aesthetic or intellectual, one.

Though he never used the term, himself, the school that Nāgārjuna founded came to be called "Mādhyamika" (from *mādhya*, "middle") which hearkens back to the "middle way" championed by the Buddha.[279] Where the Buddha had stressed the middle path between the moral extremes of self-pleasure and self-mortification (recall the history of his life), the Mādhyamikas attempted to steer a middle and moderate philosophical course between the metaphysical extremes of existence and nonexistence, between self and non-self, between the eternal and the non-eternal.

The chief work attributed to Nāgarjuna, and the one that will launch us into his extremely exciting and challenging philosophy, is the *Mūlamādhyamika-kārikā* or *Mādhyamika-kārikā*, for short. The work beautifully illustrates Nāgārjuna's methodology as well as his doctrines and we shall be quoting extensively from it, below.

In the *Mādhyamika-kārikā* Nāgārjuna sets out to explain causation and to explore śūnya and nirvāṇa in the process. And in the work the author seeks to devastate the two principle realist schools of Buddhism, viz., the Sarvāstivāda and the Sautrāntika schools, and along the way to take a crack at the Sāṁkhyas, the Jains, the materialists and a host of other philosophers, theologians and skeptics, to boot.[280]

Our rather lengthy examination of Madhyamika will center around the presentation of four central topics: First, causation, its nature, its analysis and its importance; second, truth, and with it the apparently paradoxical dictum that all truth is inexpressible; third, Śūnyavāda, the view that everything is dependent and relative; fourth, and finally, nirvāṇa and with it the apparently inconsistent dictum that saṁsāra isn't different from nirvāṇa, and vice versa.

Following the presentation of each of these four topics we shall, in keeping with our theme of philosophic history, indicate a problem or problems connected with each. Our first topic is causation.

1). Causation: Its Nature, Its Analysis and Its Importance. Nāgārjuna attempted to demolish not only the theories of causality espoused by two of the Hīnayāna schools but he sought to demolish several other theories of causality, as well, which depended on enduring substances to explain change. In the process of demolition he gave birth to a new movement in Buddhist thought, a movement with a new methodology and a new doctrine.

We turn, first, to an examination of "causation" and its meaning; second, we'll see how and why Nagarjuna, in attacking Hīnayāna realism, rejected four rather famous theories of causation belonging to the Sāṁkhyas and the Sarvāstivādins, to the Sautrāntikas, to Jainism, and to the materialists and skeptics; third, and last, we'll attempt to demonstrate why a theory of causation is so crucial to Buddhism and to any religion that believes in the possibility of liberation from bondage.

a) The Nature of Causation. We ordinarily say that a causal relationship exists when, for example, we take some milk and by treating it properly we turn that milk into cheese. Here the milk is the cause and the cheese is the effect. It seems fairly innocuous then to ask, What caused the cheese? and it must seem altogether bizarre to go on to ask as the Buddhists did, Is there something *new* produced in the effect that wasn't in the cause? i.e. Is what is produced, the cheese, different from the cause, the milk? What interest or significance could possibly turn on questions as seemingly trivial or far out as these?, and why have so many Indian philosophers been so concerned about them, anyway?[281]

Any causal relationship can be extremely complicated if one wants to take the time to think about the matter (and the Buddhists did). Customarily we say that C causes E whenever, in order to have E, you have to have C first; and milk and cheese work causally just like that. Now C, milk, is not a *sufficient* causal factor for producing cheese, i.e. milk is not enough, alone and by itself, to bring about cheese; but it is a *necessary* causal factor, i.e. without milk there would be no cheese even if all of the other necessary conditions, such as heat, pressure, stirring, and rennet, were present. So a cause can be either a necessary condition or a sufficient condition for an effect to occur.

Further, we know that, generally speaking, a causal condition, whether necessary or sufficient, must come before its effect; in other words, and generally speaking, C temporally precedes E in a causal relation in the sense that the milk is there before the cheese and not the other way around. But this "generally speaking" sense is about to be violated, for an effect, E, can exist simultaneously with its cause, C, and not be preceded by it at all.

Let's examine the relationship between cause and effect in the four theories of causality current during Nāgārjuna's time, and subsequently rejected by him.

b) The Analysis of Causation. In his *Mādhyamika-kārikā* Nāgārjuna attempts to refute the following four theories of causation:

1. Self causation which maintains that the cause and the effect are *identical* (satkāryavāda held by Sarvāstivāda).
2. External causation which maintains that the cause and the effect are *different* (asatkāryavāda held by Sautrāntika).
3. Both self causation and external causation which maintains that the effect can be both the same as well as different from its cause (held by Jainism).
4. Neither self causation nor external causation which maintains that things are produced by chance (held by materialism and skepticism).

The first theory, the identity theory, would maintain that the cheese was pre-existent in the milk and that the cause was, therefore, identical with the effect. Hindu Sāṁkhya philosophers, like Īśvarakṛṣṇa (4th century C.E.), and earlier Buddhist Sarvāstivādins have both maintained that fundamentally nothing new is created when the cheese is produced from the milk. This example of satkāryavāda (the view that the effect pre-exists in the cause) entails the view that the cheese is only a mere transformation of the milk, a view that the Sāṁkhyas call pariṇāma-vāda, or transformation-ism. In pariṇāmavāda some basic stuff or substance simply alters its superficial characteristics in changing from milk to cheese, but the basic stuff or substance does not really change.[282]

Nāgārjuna rejected this satkārayavāda view of the Buddhist direct realists, such as the Sarvāstivādins, by pointing out that in maintaining a belief in a basic and unchanging underlying stuff or substance (svabhāva), the satkāryavādins had advocated a covert form of the ātman doctrine which they had doctrinally professed to reject. Hence, the Sarvāstivādins are inconsistent in their metaphysical realism. In a crucial passage Nāgārjuna rightly observes that "the substance (svabhāva) of the existents (bhāva) is not to be found in the different causal factors or correlations (pratyaya)";[283] and for Nāgārjuna svabhāva was as much an illegitimate metaphysical entity as was ātman; hence, if the latter is rejectable then so is the former. Furthermore, as Candrakīrti, a later Mādhyamika commentator on Nāgārjuna, has rightly said, if one were to take the identity theory and satkāryavāda literally and seriously, any kind of production, other than mere self-duplication, such as milk causing milk, would be impossible. Hence, on all counts satkāryavāda, as a theory of causation, fails.

The second theory, the difference theory, would maintain that the cheese was not pre-existent in the milk and that the cause was quite different from the effect. Consider that according to the Hīnayāna Buddhists when I whirl a fire stick or torch in a wide circle the impression given is that of a wheel, a wheel of fire.[284] But the cause of the fire-wheel is the torch at several successive moments in space as it is whirled about in a circle. These successive but individual moments of fire are the causes of the wheel, and the entire wheel, an illusion, is wholly distinct from the separate and individual moments of fire which are its cause. This is an example of asatkāryavāda, the view that the effect does not pre-exist in the cause, but is wholly and totally different from it.

Nāgārjuna also rejected this asatkāryavāda view of the Buddhist representative realists, such as the

Sautrāntikas, by pointing out that without a permanent and self-identical substance through time there cannot be any concept of difference (parabhāva), for one can speak of difference only if one recognizes and accepts svabhāva, or substance, to begin with. There is a certain plausibility to this, to be sure. I can't recognize C as different from E unless I know E in some sense. And I can't know E unless it has its "own nature," a svabhāva, an identical and permanent nature, the same through time. But if the doctrine of difference depends on the doctrine of sameness, i.e. if asatkāryavāda depends on satkāryavāda, and if the latter has failed (it has, see the first theory, above) then the former fails, as well. The reasoning is tricky but curiously compelling.

The third theory of causation would maintain that the cheese was both identical with and different from the milk, and it all depends on whether you put your attention on the substance or its qualities. When we attend to the underlying milk substance then the satkāryavāda view is correct for the svabhāva is identical from one moment to the next. But when we attend to the qualities of the milk substance then the satkāryavāda view is correct for the milky quality is replaced by, and is different from, the cheesy quality of the milk substance. Hence, both views are correct in a certain sense, and it all depends on your point of view.

This theory, which is attributable to Jainism, is also rejected,[285] though it is barely criticized in the Mādhyamika literature and for good reason: The Jain theory merely multiplies difficulties by joining together two theories already refuted; hence the third theory fails.

The fourth theory of causation would maintain that the cheese is not produced according to either of the first two theories but that it comes about uncaused and at random. This materialist and skeptical view[286] is rejected as a philosophical view because it is either a dogmatic assertion with no reasons behind it at all or, if it has reasons, it contradicts itself: For if the proposed philosophic view has no arguments to support it then it is no view at all; if it has arguments then those arguments must have premises and conclusions; but then any materialist - skeptical conclusion (an effect) must come from those premises (a cause); but if it is the conclusion (or effect) to a set of premises (or cause) then it is the result of the very thing it denies, and the view is self-contradictory. Thus on both counts the fourth theory of causation fails.

Below we find Nāgārjuna, in his great *Mādhyamika Sūtra* or *kārikā* setting out to examine both the nature of causality and the nature of the things that are said to be causally related. The technique or method by which he analyzes causes and things is the dialectical method which he made famous. That method, essentially, is *reductio ad absurdum*, which reduces all theories, as above, to contradictions or to absurdities, showing that no cause or thing can exist in isolation, in separation or absolutely, from other causes or things.

He begins in I by stating the now familiar four theories of causation and he will, in what follows, deny that each, viz., the self-caused, the not-self-caused, i.e. the caused-by-others, the caused by both self and not-self, and the randomly-caused, i.e. the without-cause, is possible.

I

> Existing things have never been found to come into existence, either from themselves, from something else, from both or from neither.

He shows in the verses that follow the reasons why these four theories for generation, or causation, all fail.

In II he states the four necessary conditions that any causal situation must possess:

II

> There are only four conditions (pratyaya)
> (For anything that is said to be produced):
> Its cause (hetu), its object, its foregoing moment [and]
> Its most decisive factor. There is no fifth.

Then the self-caused is attacked by denying that there is a self-nature in the conditions:

III

In these four conditions we can find
no self-nature (svabhāva).
Where there is no self-existence,
There can be no relational existence [parabhāva] either.

Next, the caused-by-others is attacked in IV to V:

IV

There are no energies [kriyā] in causes,
Nor are there energies outside them.
There are no causes without energies,
Nor are there causes that possess them.

V

Those things will be "causes"
From which co-ordinated other things arise.
And they will be "non-causes"
In so far as other things do not arise from them.

Then, the both caused, i.e. the self caused and the other caused, is denied in VI to VII:

VI

Neither non-Being (an unreal thing) nor Being (a real thing)
Can have a cause.
If it was for non-Being, a cause would be silly.
If it was for Being, a cause would be redundant.

VII

Therefore, when no dharma (entity) is turned out,
From neither a Being nor a non-Being,
Nor from both Being-non-Being,
How can we then assume
The possibility of a cause?

And, finally, the randomly caused or non-caused is denied in VIII to IX:

VIII

A mental Being is reckoned as a dharma,
Separately from its object of cognition.
Now, if it [begins] by having no objective counterpart,
How can it get one afterward?

IX

If [separate] dharmas do not exist,
Then it is not possible for them to disappear.
The moment which immediately precedes
Is thus impossible. And if 'tis gone,
How can it be a cause?

In the remainder of the passages, X to XIV, Nāgārjuna sweeps the field clear of all absolutes and, thereby, reveals the truly relative and dependent character of all causality and things:

X

If existing things have no self nature (svabhāva)
Then they have no real existence.
The [formula] "this being, that appears"
Then loses every meaning.

XI

Neither in any of the single causes [individually],
Nor in all of them together [collectively],
Does the (supposed) result reside.
Therefore, how can you extract an effect out of them
If it never did exist in them?

XII

Supposing that from these causes does appear
What never did exist in them,
From out of non-causes then
Why does it not appear?

XIII

The result [effect[is a cause-possessor,
But causes are not even self-possessors
[they don't consist of themselves].
So how can a result be a cause-possessor,
If of nonself-possessors it be a result?

XIV

There is, therefore, no cause-possessor,
Nor is there an effect without a cause,
If altogether no effect arises,
[How can we then distinguish]
Between the causes and non-causes?[287]

It's not easy reading. But the conclusion is that nothing new appears and nothing old disappears; and that if everything is relative and causally dependent then everything is śūnya, i.e. void and empty. All of this constitutes Nāgārjuna's recasting of pratītyasamutpāda ("dependent origination"). The argument goes something like this: Pratītyasamutpāda had held, in effect, "This being, that becomes; from this arising, that arises; from this not becoming, that does not become; from this ceasing, that ceases."[288] But Nāgārjuna now interprets this to mean what has come to be called his famous "Eight Noes": No birth nor death; no annihilation nor persistence; no unity nor plurality; no coming in nor going out.[289] The Eight Noes constitute the doctrine of śūnya. In other words, from pratītyasamutpāda, interpreted now as the Eight Noes, and from the confirmation of these Noes following the destruction of his opponents' views of causation by the above dialectic, Nāgārjuna is led ultimately to Śūnyavāda, the view that everything is dependent, relative and empty; that is to say, nothing is self-dependent, self-existent or real.

Nāgārjuna's method of rejection of all theories, as we have said, is by a kind of dialectic that employs the technique of *reductio ad absurdum* on the grounds that any position that leads to an absurdity must, itself, be absurd. But as T.R.V. Murti has pointed out, this dialectical demolition of one theory does not entail the establishment of its opposite.[290] The Mādhyamika seeks to refute all theories without proving any. Murti states:

> How does the Mādhyamika reject any and all views? He uses only one weapon. By drawing out the implications of any view he shows its self-contradictory character. The dialectic is a series of *reductio ad absurdum* arguments (prasangāpādanam).

And Murti concludes:

> Every thesis is turned against itself. The Mādhyamika is a...dialectician or free-lance debater. The Mādhyamika *disproves* the opponent's thesis, and does *not* prove any thesis of his own.[291]

We shall return to this apparently paradoxical claim shortly.

c) The Importance of Causation. But why was the discussion of the nature of causation so singularly important and why did so much turn on the refutation of all views of causation? What significance hung on this seemingly trivial and innocuous concept? and the rather bizarre questions raised on its behalf? Well, a great deal of significance is tied up with causality, as it turns out. The concept is introduced by Gautama in the second of the four noble truths that states that there is a cause of suffering; furthermore, the doctrine of causation is identical with the doctrine of pratītyasamutpāda, i.e. the Buddhist theory of causation, itself. Murti again:

> There is a particular reason why the Mādhyamika should pay particular attention to causality. The entire Buddhist thought revolves on the pivot of Pratītya Samutpāda; the Mādhyamika system is the interpretation of Pratītya Samutpāda as Śūnyatā [Emptiness].[292]

Causation, it turns out, is central not only to the Buddhist doctrine of Pratītyasamutpāda, and to Mādhyamika śūnya, but it is essential to any philosophy or religion that uses "causal concepts" such as the law of karma, saṁsāra, the yogas and nirvāṇa, and that holds that bondage is caused but that release from bondage can be caused, as well.

And this brings us to the heart of the causal issue for Buddhism. For if the causal relation between the events that led me to, and that now holds me in, bondage is too strong, i.e. if it is necessitated or fated in some inexorable or unalterable sense, then I could never break the causal chain, and as a result, release from bondage would be impossible. On the other hand, if the causal relation between the events that led me to, and holds me in, bondage is too weak, i.e. if chance rules or the causal relation holds loosely and willy-nilly at one moment and then becomes unglued at the next, then the causal chain is too easily broken, and bondage, itself, and the law of karma, the yogas and nirvāṇa, would all be impossible, if not useless or meaningless. But, the Buddhist continues, release from bondage is possible, Gautama did it; and bondage is possible, Gautama was in it. Therefore, this *modus tollens* argument concludes, the causal relation must not be too strong nor too weak.

The alternatives denied in this conclusion are precisely the problems faced by the satkāryavādin (who holds that the effect pre-exists in the cause) where the causal relation is, indeed, too strong; and by the asatkāryavādin (who holds that the effect does not pre-exist in the cause) where the causal relation is, indeed, too weak. There are a number of questions which this discussion of causation naturally raises and we shall turn to examine those questions next.

15. The Problem of Causation. The discussion of causation must strike the modern reader as archaic if not downright silly. It's just plain illogical and it's certainly eccentric to talk about an effect being pre-existent in its cause, or not being pre-existent in its cause, or both, or neither. Further, saying, "The cheese is in the milk," is not something designed to hold sense or interest for anyone, except the dedicated antiquarian. Philosophers and other normal people just don't say these sorts of things. And to go from milk-cheese talk to bondage-liberation talk is to make the most curious leap, yet. Errors in analogy abound; cheese and liberation, physical causes and metaphysical causes are mixed up in a most unprofessional way. Finally, while it may be important for the Buddhists to know whether bondage is present or not, and while it may be important, subsequently, to discover how to break the chain that binds, surely the topics of causation, and bondage and liberation, can be treated in a far simpler way than the

Abhidharma apologists together with the Sarvāstivāda and Sautrāntika Buddhists and their attackers, the Mādhyamikas, have chosen to do. Thus the modern critic, craving sense and simplicity.

The critic of all this is probably in a rather secure position with centuries of what he considers as fairly sound Western philosophy of science behind him. He knows that causal talk is outdated having been profoundly analyzed and criticized by David Hume[293] and the 19th and 20th century empiricist tradition.[294] Meaningful causal talk, he knows, is always reducible to talk about future expectations based on past similarities, statistical frequencies, the logics of induction and deduction, general laws, and the nomological deductive theory of explanation and prediction. Consequently, all talk about C causes E, in itself obscure, is reducible to a wholly different set of empirical concepts and descriptions, none of which have anything to do with the metaphysics of the dharmas and pratītyasamutpāda. Thus the modern critic, once again, who refuses to play the causality game laid out before him by the Buddhists.

In a sense the Mādhyamika has also refused to play the causality game, but for entirely different reasons. In analyzing and criticizing the theories of causality of his predecessors and in unleashing massive dialectical destruction on his opponents' views, he arrives at a conclusion that is pretty much echoed by our modern critic who also seems to be saying that all these theories of causality are pretty unintelligible. And in claiming absurdity or unintelligibility for these causal theories, the Mādhyamika claims that he is proposing no theory of his own. If he is right then, of course, he differs from the modern Humean who reduces all causal talk to either talk about past constant conjunction and present expectability, or to inductive generalizations, laws and statistical frequencies, i.e. the modern critic has a theory of causality. Whether Nāgārjuna really has a theory of his own or not is a topic that we shall take up shortly in discussing the silence of the Buddha.

In a sense, then, there is no problem of causation, at least not of the type described above, and for the very simple reason that, until further notice, Nāgārjuna has no theory of causation - so how can there be a problem with it?

It is well to keep in mind that the purposes that the Humean and the modern Western philosopher of science have for discussing causality at all differ appreciably from the purposes of Nāgārjuna and the Mādhyamika: The Western philosopher of science seeks, *inter alia*, to control the world and its physical processes by understanding the natural laws of that world; Nāgārjuna and the Mādhyamika seek to control ignorance and desire by understanding that everything is śūnya. This latter understanding, that all is śūnya, leads to a basic Buddhist belief, viz., that there is really nothing that one can do to reach enlightenment, a topic that we shall touch on below in discussing the paradox of nirvāṇa. And it leads to a question about truth, viz. What truths remain, what Buddhism or what Mahāyāna or what Mādhyamika remains, if all is ultimately śūnya? We turn, therefore, to the second topic of Mādhyamika Buddhism, viz., truths.

2) Truths. The dialectical method leading to the total rejection of all theories has prompted some critics to suspect an outright nihilism, if not a covert double dealing, at work in Nāgārjuna's philosophy; but this suspicion is probably mistaken. Nāgārjuna, for all his dialectical and nihilistic maneuverings, remains a Buddhist. As it turns out, his own negative philosophical method found deep and positive religious inspiration through the doctrine of śūnya in the earlier Mahāyāna *Prajñāpāramitā* tradition. T.R.V. Murti again states:

> The Mādhyamika system is the systematised form of the Śūnyatā doctrine of the *Prajñāpāramitā* treatises; its metaphysics, spiritual path...and religious ideal are all present there, though in a loose, prolific garb. With the *Prajñāpāramitās* an entirely new phase of Buddhism begins.

We enter now upon the positive side of Nāgārjuna's Buddhist philosophy. Murti continues:

> A severe type of Absolutism established by the dialectic, by the negation (śūnyatā) of all empirical notions and speculative theories, replaces the pluralism and dogmatism of the earlier Buddhism. The *Prajñāpāramitās* revolutionized Buddhism, in all aspects of its philosophy and religion by the basic concept of Śūnyatā.[295]

Part of that revolution is found, first of all, in the putative return to the original Buddhism of its founder and to a kind of agnosticism attributed now to Gautama and expressed in numerous places in the literature. For example, in the *Majjhima Nikāya*, in the *Samyutta Nikāya*, in the *Mahānidāna* and *Brahmajāla Suttas*, in the *Mahāli Sutta*, in the *Milindapañha*, in the *Abhidharma Kośabhāṣya*, and elsewhere, Buddha declares certain questions to be unanswerable.[296] And this silence of the Buddha on certain seemingly crucial philosophic questions in several of the earliest Hīnayāna texts is confirmation, the Mādhyamikas say, for *their* own negative conclusions.

The questions upon which Buddha's silence was directed are traditionally four in number, but each of the first three questions was stated as a tetralemma (Greek "four assumptions") or catuṣkoti (Sanskrit), i.e. each of the first three questions has four parts to it while the last question had two parts such that the total number of inexpressibles or unanswerables (avyākṛta) was fourteen in all. Thus where 'x' is a variable and 'A' is a predicate we have the following schema of the catuṣkoti:

<u>Catuṣkoti (Tetralemma)</u>
All x is A.
No x is A.
Some x is A, and some X is not A (both).
No x is A, and no x is not A (neither).

The catuṣkoti is extremely important for it contains the four possible assumptions of any doctrine; and it is upon these that Nāgārjuna practices his famous dialectic, reducing his opponents' doctrines to a logical absurdity, as we have seen with causation and as we shall see with nirvāṇa. At all events, what Buddha is saying with the avyākṛta and what Nāgārjuna is saying with the catuṣkoti would seem to come to the same thing in the end: Some questions are unanswerable; and if you should try to answer them you will either be wasting your time (Buddha) or you will end in absurdities (Nāgārjuna).

Here are Buddha's fourteen avyākṛtas:

1. Whether the world is eternal, or not, or both, or neither?
2. Whether the world is finite (in space),

2. Whether the world is finite (in space), or infinite, or both, or neither?
3. Whether the Tathāgata exists after death, or does not, or both, or neither?
4. Whether the soul is identical with the body or different from it?

On all these questions the Buddha was "silent", i.e. he refused to commit himself and encouraged his followers to do likewise. In the *Majjhima-Nikāya* Buddha gives typical expression to this silence:

> To hold that the world is eternal or to hold that it is not, or to agree to any other of the propositions you add ce, Vaccha, is the jungle of theorising, the wi derness of theorising, the tangle of theorising, the bondage and the shackles of theorising, attended by ill, distress, perturbation and fever; it conduces not to detachment, passionlessness, tranquility, peace, to knowledge and wisdom of Nirvāṇa. This is the danger I perceive in these views which makes me discard them all.[297]

Buddha rejected all theories and theorising because they did not lead to enlightenment.[298] And Nāgārjuna agreed and went on to give dialectical voice to his agreement.

Another part of that revolution lay, secondly, in the adoption by Nāgārjuna and the Mādhyamikas of a positive doctrine, taken from the Prajñā literature, that postulated an absolute and ultimate metaphysical Reality. It was a Reality wholly and totally beyond description, a Reality labeled simply as "śūnya" and empty or void of all content and properties; it was an Absolute to which no predicates or descriptive terms were applicable. Consequently, the appropriation and adoption of the Prajñāpāramitā philosophy of relativity and emptiness proved to be a singularly significant move for Mādhyamika Buddhism.

These two parts of the Mādhyamika revolution, i.e. first, its return to the putative silence of the Buddha on theoretical and philosophical questions, and second, its discovery of an Absolute beyond description, conjoined with the devastating method of the dialectic, led nonetheless to four "truths" which the Mādhyamika Buddhists, themselves, seem to hold or to which they appear to be committed:

1. All existence is ultimately śūnya.

That is to say, everything is relative and conditioned by everything else, there are no "absolutes" and no final ultimate truths. It follows that if all is śūnya then nothing can be finally and absolutely named or explained. And this śūnyafication, the dialectical reduction of everything to relativity, applies to this world of ever-changing dharmas as well as to any world beyond.

2. The two truths doctrine.

While all is śūnya and all truths are relative, there are nonetheless higher truths to be known following the attainment of bodhisattvahood and Buddhahood and nirvāṇa. On one level, the philosophical (rational) and worldly (empirical) level, only relative truth obtains. But on a higher level there are "truths" and an Absolute which can be known but only through prajñā, even though to enunciate these "truths" is to place them and oneself back into the lower realm of relativity and māyā. Nāgārjuna expresses the matter of two truths in this fashion:

> The teaching of the Dharma by the many Buddhas is based on two truths: Namely, the relative and lower truth, on the one hand, and the absolute and highest truth, on the other. Those who are ignorant of the difference between the two truths cannot understand the profound nature of the Buddha's teaching.[299]

3. The Truth is inexpressible.

One hardly dares call it a "truth" since inexpressible truths are not what we ordinarily mean by "truths." The Truth that Nāgārjuna has in mind, of course, is ultimate Reality, and that Reality cannot be talked about, it is śūnya (truth 1, above), but it does exist as the Absolute (truth 2, above), and it can be directly experienced in this life (truth 4, below). So we are invited to experience this ultimate Reality and the Buddhist way is the way to attain that experience. As Kenneth Inada has said of Nāgārjunian Truth:

> Truth does not lend itself to mere rational accounting however subtle or refined that may be. It is rather the result of *prajñā*, the so-called "eye of wisdom", the instrument which cuts open and at once reveals reality for what it is.[300]

4. Saṁsāra is nirvāṇa and nirvāṇa is saṁsāra.

This dictum serves to remind the Mādhyamika Buddhist that whatever problems there are to be solved in this life, problems relating to ethics, the dharma and desire, must be solved *in this life*, and not by theorizing and philosophizing but by living: Nirvāṇa is here and now, not in some future life or time or place, but here and now in saṁsāra. The problem of saṁsāra, the problem of pain, suffering and human agony, is to be solved where the problem is met, in this life. The solution to that problem lies in living the eightfold path: Buddhism is a day-to-day living religion, and living that religion day to day is what nirvāṇa is. And that is one of the Buddhist meanings of the identity of saṁsāra with nirvāṇa. We shall return to this most important truth of Mādhyamika below.[301]

There are a number of problems and questions that our discussion of truths has raised and we shall turn to examine these questions and some tentative answers to them, next.

2') The Problems of Truths. There are two problems that I wish to take up in this examination of the problems of truths:

a) The problem of universal śūnyafication.

The discussion of truths leads naturally into the question: If everything is śūnyafied or emptied, refuted and silenced by Buddha, or by Nāgarjuna, or by whomever, then what kinds of truths remain? And, more importantly, What happens to Buddhism, itself, its doctrines, its dogmas and truths?

Nāgarjuna, himself, speaks to this question when he answers the following objection:

> If everything is empty, there is no origination or destruction. That would be to accept the nonexistence of the four Noble

> Truths.... If these are nonexistent, then also the four noble 'fruits' do not exist. In the absence of the four noble 'fruits', there would not be those who have attained the fruits nor those who have attained the path [leading to them].

If all this is so, the objector concludes, then the Buddha, the dharma and the Order of monks would be destroyed:

> In the absence of these...types of people, there would be no Order. From the nonexistence of the Noble Truths, the true *dharma* also does not exist. Without the *dharma* and the Order, how can there be Buddha? Consequently, what you assert also destroys the Three Treasures [i.e. the Buddha, the *dharma* and the Order].

A good objection. For, if Nāgarjuna is right then isn't Buddhism destroyed? And, further, if Buddhism is destroyed then why have a Buddhist philosophy, such as Mādhyamika, to begin with? And, even further, isn't it self-contradictory to even promulgate the Mādhyamika philosophy of śūnya? Finally, and even more devastating, isn't it paradoxical to say what Nāgārjuna is saying? For if he's right then he must be wrong, i.e. if Śūnyavāda is true then it is open to the very critique that is being set against the other philosophies.

Nāgārjuna answers the objector's question about Buddhism and the Three Treasures but he does not answer all of the questions that we've raised, above. He begins by reminding the objector that whatever exists is relative, i.e. śūnya. He puts his reply into the language of causation (causality is nothing but relativity, i.e. śūnyatā or emptiness). To put it otherwise is to be led into an absurdity:

> Since there is no *dharma* whatever which is not causally conditioned [i.e. not relative], no *dharma* whatever exists which is not empty. If all existence is not empty [i.e. if it is not causally conditioned], there is neither origination nor destruction. You must therefore wrongly conclude that the four Noble Truths exist.[302]

This reply is quite simple and rather ingenious. Nāgārjuna assumes that every dharma (truth) is relative or śūnya, i.e. causally conditioned by a particular time and place. But if a dharma is relative then it is not absolute, i.e. not transcendent to time and place, and not ultimately Real or unconditioned. But if the dharma is not absolute then it is empty, as are all existences because they are caused and conditioned in space and time. For if existence were non-empty then it would not be subject to origination, or coming into existence, or destruction, or going out of existence, i.e. such existence would be absolute, unconditioned and unchanging. But then, Nāgārjuna concludes, in effect, that the four Noble Truths would not exist, i.e. would not have come into existence, which is absurd, for they have! Look, there they are! Therefore, since the position of the objector leads to an absurdity, his position must be absurd. Therefore, the conditioned, the relative, i.e. śūnyatā or emptiness, is real. In other words, if śūnyatā weren't real then the four Noble Truths wouldn't exist; but the four Noble Truths do exist; therefore, śūnyatā is real.

But what has Nāgārjuna really said? All that he's said is something that Western philosophers in the Protagoras-Hume sceptical and empirical tradition have been saying for centuries: Man is the measure of all things; and once he starts measuring, he can be mistaken; so watch out! Further, the questions that we raised, above, regarding the application of śūnya and relativity to Mādhyamika, itself, can now be answered in this same language: Nāgārjuna is the measure of Mādhyamika; once he starts measuring he can be mistaken; so watch out! And I think Nāgārjuna would have approved of this formulation, if he hadn't found another way out. For there are two ways of facing the problem of truth, i.e. the embarrassing problem of having to accept the consequences of having said that all theories are relative, which makes even the theory that says that all theories are relative also relative.

One way, the way mentioned above, is to follow the sceptics, Protagoras or Hume, and admit that you ought to be sceptical even about scepticism, i.e. in Nāgārjunian terms, Śūnyavada is relative, too. The other way is to say that you have no theory to offer. The Mādhyamikas, hoping to avoid embarrassment, and inconsistency or paradox, seemed to favor this second way and we'll turn to it next.

The first question of the problems of truth with which we began appears to be answered: If everything is śūnyafied..., what kinds of truths remain? The answer is, Relative truths, truths relative to man, made by him and for him, remain; and while some may be better than others, watch out!

b) The problem of Nāgārjuna's silence.

The discussion of truth leads naturally to the question, In analyzing and attacking other theories and truths by the dialectical method, isn't Nāgārjuna offering us a theory or view of his own?

Nāgārjuna, or the Mādhyamika, claim they are putting forward no theory or view of their own. But in one very simple sense, he or they are just plain wrong. Nāgārjuna's claim (if it was his claim) seems to come down to two possible claims: First, that he's offering no positive theory of his own (which is false as I shall show); or, second, he's offering no theory of any sort of his own (which is also false). Let's examine each of these claims.

First, let's assume that the Mādhyamika, using the catuṣkoti, practices dialectical *reductio* on causal theory t and in the process he shows, first, that t is false, inconsistent or absurd. Second, he then goes on to show, let's assume, that not-t, by the same destructive method, is also false; and, third, that both t and not-t, and fourth, that neither t nor not-t, as well, are both false. Now what has he done? I would suggest that he's advanced a theory, and a positive theory at that, about t, viz., that t is false, and that not-t is false, and that both t and not-t are false, and that neither t nor not-t are false. For suppose that we let T stand for what has been shown about t in the above conjunction. But then T is a positive theory containing four conjuncts. But then we have a positive theory, T, advanced by Nāgārjuna. And it's false to say that Nāgārjuna is advancing no positive theory of his own.

It may be that Nāgārjuna did not intend to offer or advance a theory of his own, or that he did it unconsciously. However, I think nothing is gained by an analysis of the psychological interpretations of "offer" or "advance." We'll leave it as it stands and say that it appears that Nāgārjuna, in criticizing all four theories, did advance, whether he intended it or not, a positive theory of his own.

Second, Nāgārjuna, in using the method of dialectic as a method of reducing the opponent's position to an inconsistency or an absurdity, is offering us a theory about a methodology: For if you use a philosophic method successfully then, whether you intend it or not, you are advocating its use by others; and then you are offering or advancing or putting forth a theory of your own. Furthermore, not only does he offer a theory of methodology to his followers but in the very practice of that methodology Nāgārjuna arrives at yet another theory, viz., the doctrine or view of relativity or emptiness. That is to say, śūnyavāda, too, is a theory and Nāgārjuna arrives at it; and any theory that one arrives at can, unless one is playing *advocatus diaboli*, certainly be said to be offered or advocated.

Nāgārjuna loses on both claims, therefore: He has put forward a positive theory, T, regarding a conjunction of other theories. And he has advocated a successful methodology, the dialectic and *reductio ad absurdum*, a theory about argument. And, finally, he has arrived at a theory, śūnyavāda, to which his successful methodology has led him. Nāgārjuna, or the Mādhyamika, are dead wrong when they say that they are putting forward no theory of their own.

So why would anyone make the claim that they have put forward no theory or view? I suspect that one reason might be that Nāgārjuna, knowing that one of the major causes of suffering in this world is attachment, clinging, tṛṣṇa (Pāli taṇhā), realized that theories and views can be clung to just as surely as things. Republicans and Democrats, Communists and Capitalists, Christians and Buddhists, can become as attached to their theories and views and dogmas as surely as they can become attached to motor cars, houses, wealth and heaven. Nāgārjuna is, in effect, cleansing himself, and what later came to be called 'Mādhyamika', by saying, I have no theory, no view, and, therefore, there's nothing to cling to here. But then what is Nāgārjuna doing when he does analyze and criticize? What Nāgārjuna is doing is rather like shouting "Be quiet!!" in a crowded and noisy room; and shouting in order to get everyone to be quiet. Let's look at this claim.[303]

At first glance, shouting "Be quiet!!" seems at odds with trying to quiet everyone down, i.e. there's an initial practical contradiction in making noise in order to stop noise. But the practical contradiction accomplishes its end when people quiet down. In the same way, the success of the dialectic and Śūnyavāda lies in the quieting that they accomplish for whatever goal they may have. And the point of the analogy between "Be quiet!!" and Śūnyavāda, Nāgārjuna might say, is that, first, "Be quiet!!" is not a positive theory; and, second, "Be quiet!!" is not a theory of any sort; so you can't cling to it.

We seem to have arrived at an inconsistency (which might please Nāgārjuna) in trying to determine whether Nāgārjuna advocated a view of his own or not: On the one hand, Nāgārjuna, in using the dialectic and, in arriving at Śūnyavāda, does advocate views or theories (to which his followers can cling!); and on the other hand, Nāgārjuna does not advocate views or theories for he merely uses the dialectic and Śūnyavāda to shout "Be quiet!!" (to which his followers can't cling!).

One way out of the inconsistency would, of course, be to argue that "Be quiet!!" is just as much a positive philosophy, or that it can be made so, as any theory about methodology or śūnya. To make this clearer, let's turn to an examination of that positive philosophy, the philosophy that, in part at least, made Nāgārjuna an absolutist and kept him a Buddhist. At the conclusion to that examination we shall return to the question of Nāgārjuna's positive philosophy, Śūnyavāda, and to whether *it* is relative, contradictory and false, i.e. the question will be raised and answered, Is Śūnyavāda a lot of śūnya?

We turn, therefore, to the third topic of Mādhyamika Buddhism, viz., Śūnyavāda.

3) Śūnyavāda. Nāgārjuna attempted to establish the thesis of Śūnyavāda, i.e. that everything is empty of reality, there are no absolutes and no final ultimate expressible truths. It follows that if all is śūnya then nothing can be finally and absolutely real, named or explained. And this śūnyafication, this reduction of everything to relativity, applies to this world of ever-changing dharmas, moments, as well as to any worlds beyond. Śūnyavāda, at this stage, seems to be employing several familiar notions that we

encountered earlier in our discussion of the *Upaniṣads*. Thus the concept of māyā and the Upaniṣadic phrase *neti, neti* ("*not* this, *not* that") are expressive of saṁsāra (the world) and Brahman and have, it would seem, some rather interesting parallels in Śūnyavāda.[304]

But more importantly, if Nāgārjuna's metaphysical view can be seen as similar to the monistic metaphysics of the *Upaniṣads* then it ought to be possible to reconstruct from the Mādhyamika writings something analogous to the Upaniṣadic way to mokṣa. Consider the following sorites (chain) argument, compiled from the *sūtras* and Candrakīrti's 7th century C.E. commentary on the *Kārikās*, his *Prasannapadā*, that claims to lead one from knowledge of śūnya to deliverance (nirvāṇa):

> [1] One who is convinced of the emptiness of everything is not captivated by worldly dharmas, because he does not lean on them.

The premise has the sense of, If one knows śūnya then one is not captivated by the world of dharmas (i.e. one does not store up one's treasure where moths and rust doth corrupt, if one knows the way the world really is).

> [2] One who in such a way is not captivated by the worldly dharmas is said to be one who knows emptiness.[305]

The premise has the sense of, If one is not captivated by the world of dharmas then one knows śūnya i.e. the first premise is reinforced and, if being convinced of emptiness and knowing emptiness are the same, we have a biconditional from the first two premises, i.e. one knows the emptiness of everything if and only if one is not captivated by the world. Both of the first two premises are necessary to the complete argument.

> [3] Karma and the defilements...are stopped by [knowing] emptiness.[306]

The premise has the sense of, If one knows śūnya then karma and the defilements are stopped (i.e. intuitive knowledge, viz., jñāna or prajñā, leads to the extinction of karma, a Upaniṣadic way, pure and simple).

[4] From the extinction of karma and defilement results deliverance.[307]

The premise has the sense of, If karma and the defilements are stopped then deliverance (nirvāṇa) results.

The completed chain of premises looks like this:

1. If one knows śūnya then one is not captivated by the world of dharmas.

2. If one is not captivated by the world of dharmas then one knows śūnya.

3. If one knows śūnya then karma and the defilements are stopped.

4. If karma and the defilements are stopped then nirvāṇa results.

The conclusion follows:

5. Therefore, if one knows śūnya then nirvāṇa results.

The argument is the important matter here and I don't wish to belabor the parallels with Upaniṣadic philosophy. But one final hypothetical observation: If one replaces "śūnya" with "higher Brahman", and "dharmas" with "māyā", and "deliverance" or "nirvāṇa" with "mokṣa", and "knowledge" or "prajñā" with "jñāna", then the Mādhyamika Buddhist parallel with the Upaniṣads becomes rather obvious. We conclude, that Nāgārjuna or the Mādhyamikas can, indeed, be seen as in agreement with Upaniṣadic metaphysics and with one of the ways to liberation associated with it.

We turn next to an examination of the problems of Śūnyavāda.

3) The Problems of Śūnyavāda. There are two puzzles that I wish to take up in this examination of the problems of Śūnyavāda. The first is familiar, having been introduced in our discussion of the problems of truths, but the second will be new.

a) The problem that Śūnyavāda may be a lot of śūnya?

Think back for a moment to the question raised above, viz., If everything is śūnyafied (applying the dialectic to a catuṣkoti of doctrines) then what kinds of truths remain? If Śūnyavāda is a truth then does it, itself, survive the dialectical onslaught that constitutes śūnyafication? In other words, if everything is śūnya i.e. void, empty and relative, and if the truth of śūnya, itself, is ultimately inexpressible, and if any attempt to express that truth involves one in contradiction, relativity and falsehood, then what about Nāgārjuna's own Śūnyavāda? Isn't it also contradictory, relative and false? Or does Nāgārjuna mean to imply that Śūnyavāda escapes the net of śūnyafication?

Nāgārjuna boldly and consistently admits that Śūnyavāda is, itself, relativistic and enmeshed in śūnya. But then we must ask, What's the use of adopting or accepting or paying attention to Śūnyavāda or Mādhyamika?

Recall that Nāgārjuna claims that his system is wholly destructive of all views but that it is not meant to be a replacement or substitute for the views that it demolishes. However, while Śūnyavāda, too, is deceptive if one attempts to take it as a positive philosophy by which to lead one's life, it is nonetheless a useful deception and Nāgārjuna would have to admit that it is more useful than any other usefully deceptive system.

Recall the man who shouts "Be quiet!" in a noisy room in order to silence the noise while at the same time adding to that noise. Nāgārjuna's own noisy system attempts to accomplish its goal of silencing all philosophers in order that the quiet and tranquility of enlightenment might be attained.

Recall the father with the sons in the burning house; Nāgārjuna's epistemological upāya, his philosophic skill-in-means, entails getting Buddhists to give up desiring, grasping and lusting. Once they are outside the burning house of the worldly dharmas, brought out by Śūnyavāda, then they, too, can experience for themselves that which cannot be described or talked about but is known only through prajñā. In this sense the upāya of śūnya is really a "convenient fiction", a theory "which is undemonstratable but useful in interpreting experience", as Eliot Deutsch has defined such fictions, or "a convenient and effective pedagogical instrument", as Heinrich Zimmer has said of useful fictions.[308]

A useful or convenient fiction, such as Śūnyavāda, functions like a myth. In a religious context such philosophic fictions are best interpreted in terms of the mythic theory of truth where the truth of the expression or story is determined by what is accomplished rather than by any correspondence to fact or by any logical coherence among other existing expressions or stories. It is in this context that all such "convenient and useful fictions" must be seen, not as fictions in the ordinary sense but as forceful devices for producing the conditions necessary for ultimate happiness. This is, I suggest, what Edward Conze means when he says regarding śūnyatā:

> As salt flavours food, so *śūnyatā* or emptiness, should pervade the religious life, and give flavour to it. By themselves neither salt nor emptiness are particularly palatable or nourishing. When 'emptiness' is treated as a philosophical concept by untutored intellects which have no wisdom, it causes much bewilderment and remains barren of spiritual fruit. All that it is then good for is to produce futile assertions of the type that 'emptiness is not nothingness', and so on. As soon, however, as the spiritual intention behind this doctrine is considered, everything becomes perfectly clear. The aim is to reveal the Infinite by removing that which obscures it.... The Void is brought in not for its own sake, but as a method which leads to the penetration into true reality.[309]

In this light, Nāgārjuna's Śūnyavāda emerges religiously and mythically as one of the most powerful of all "convenient fictions."[310]

Thus the answer to our question, Is Śūnyavāda a lot of śūnya? must be Yes, it is, but it is a very useful, and an extremely salutary, lot of śūnya.

We turn now to our second puzzle under the problems of Śūnyavāda.

b) The paradox of śūnya.

There is one very practical question that is bound to arise regarding Candrakīrti's valid argument displayed above, viz., How does one go about knowing śūnya, or How does one go about not being captivated by the dharmas (the first two premises of that argument) so that one can climb the ladder to deliverance (the final premise and the conclusion)?

In response to this question, the Mādhyamikas would probably recommend the tried and tested ways of Mahāyāna, viz., dhyāna, bhakti and prajñā, i.e. the yogas and ways that were seen at work in our discussion of Mahāyāna above.[311]

However, an interesting puzzle develops for Śūnyavāda when one attempts to *do* anything, e.g. using meditation, devotion or knowledge, in order to achieve liberation. This puzzle we might call "the paradox of śūnya."

The paradox of śūnya can be put in this fashion: Any attempt to know śūnya, or any attempt to escape being captivated by the dharmas, is doomed to frustration and failure, for both attempts employ the very means that any success in the attempt would appear to contradict. It is like trying to attempt the unattemptable, to grasp the ungraspable, know the unknowable or desire the non-desirable. Contradictions abound in seeing śūnya, the void, the empty, the indescribable, or in seeing escape from the dharmas, as a goal, an end or an object. But if it's not an object, a something, then one will never be able to meet the condition of the first premise of the argument, above, and climb the ladder to nirvāṇa: How can you put your foot on the first rung of the ladder when there's no damned rung...and no damned ladder...?

The paradox of śūnya has other dimensions, as well. Not the least of which is the puzzle known as "the paradox of nirvāṇa" which says, in effect, that those who earnestly seek after nirvāṇa are those who are least likely to achieve it.[312] The reason is that all effort in avoidance or pursuit of certain goals affects the goal making it unattainable. Thus if I desire nirvāṇa, I'll never get it. And if I don't desire nirvāṇa, I'll never get it either. No matter what I *do*, I'll never reach nirvāṇa: All *effort* leads to frustration.

We shall attempt to solve both paradoxes, below, under the section, "the paradox of desire."[313] But in order to do any of that solving we must temporarily leave the paradox of śūnya.

We turn, therefore, to the fourth and final topic of Mādhyamika Buddhism, viz., nirvāṇa.

4. Nirvāṇa. In chapter 25 of his famous *Mādhyamika-kārikā* Nāgārjuna takes up the topic of nirvāṇa and says something so startling in it that the reader might at first glance believe that the great Sorcerer, himself, had fallen somehow into darkest śūnya:

> There is no difference at all
> Between Nirvāṇa and Saṁsāra.
> There is no difference at all
> Between Saṁsāra and Nirvāṇa.[314]

In what follows I shall attempt to clarify this assertion that nirvāṇa is saṁsāra and saṁsāra is nirvāṇa, and, at the same time, come to some understanding of what "nirvāṇa" means within Śūnyavāda.

In order to do this I want to examine chapter 25 of the *Mādhyamika-kārikā*, taking the exposition and arguments step by step to develop our topic, viz., nirvāṇa, and the curious assertion about its non-difference from saṁsāra. I shall make four summary comments on this rather lengthy but extremely important chapter as we move through it, and then conclude, fifth, with an analysis of the assertion that saṁsāra is nirvāṇa and nirvāṇa is saṁsāra.

The chapter begins:

I

[Opponent:]
> If every thing is śūnya
> [With] no [real] origination, no [real] annihilation,
> How is Nirvāṇa then conceived?
> Through what deliverance (from suffering), through what annihilation (of illusion)?

II

[Nāgārjuna]

Should every thing be aśūnya,
[With] no [new] creation, no [new] destruction,
How would Nirvāṇa then be reached?
Through what deliverance, through what annihilation?

First, (in I) playing the Opponent, Nāgārjuna asks, If all is relative and śūnya then how, since there could be no real ending of bondage and no real beginning of nirvāṇa, is nirvāṇa possible?; then (in II) Nagarjuna asks, If on the other hand, all is absolute and real then how, since there could be no new states or conditions and no change from bondage to nirvāṇa, is nirvana possible? What emerges from I and II is what we might call "the dilemma of nirvāṇa", and it goes like this:

1. If all is relative then no permanent state such as nirvāṇa is possible.
2. If all is absolute then no change to nirvāṇa is possible.
3. But everything must be either relative or absolute.
4. Therefore, either no permanent state such as nirvāṇa is possible or no change to nirvāṇa is possible.
5. In either case, nirvāṇa is impossible.

The dilemma of nirvāṇa is reminiscent of a similar dilemma we encountered in Plato's *Sophist*.[315] The discussion in *Sophist* was about "knowledge", in the course of which both being (the unchanging and absolute) and becoming (the changing and relative) were discussed. What emerged was what we might now call "the dilemma of knowledge" and it goes like this:

1. If all is becoming and changing then there is no being known and knowledge is impossible.
2. If all is being and unchanging then there is no becoming known and, once again, knowledge is impossible.
3. But everything must be either in a state of becoming or being.
4. Therefore, either there is no being known or no becoming known.

5. In either case, knowledge is impossible.

I mention the parallel between the dilemma of nirvāṇa and the dilemma of knowledge in order to illuminate the former by the latter. Plato's way out of his dilemma was momentous and led to the theory of forms; Nāgārjuna's way out, equally momentous, led to the doctrine of śūnya. Nāgārjuna's way out is designed to discourage any and all speculation on and about nirvāṇa, and the technique that he employs to drive this point home is the now familiar method of the dialectic combined with the catuṣkoti.

The catuṣkoti had the following general form for any proposition *p*: *p*; not *p*; both *p* and not *p*; neither *p* nor not *p*. When we combine the catuṣkoti with the dialectic we produce the following powerful form of destructive argument for any proposition *p*: If we suppose *p* then we are led to problems; if we suppose not *p* then we are led to more problems; if we suppose both *p* and not *p* then we are led to further problems; and, finally, if we suppose neither *p* nor not *p* then we are led to still further problems. The catuṣkoti dialectic, i.e. "śūnyafication", is designed to force one's opponent to give up all the possible logical positions generated by a proposition. It is used in the first two parts of the selection below in examining the suppositions that nirvāṇa and Buddha are existing things.

If we suppose that nirvāṇa is an existing thing then problems develop (in IV to VI):

IV

Nirvāṇa, first of all, is not an ordinary
existing thing,
It would then have decay and death.
For there is no existing thing
Which is not subject to decay and death.

V

If Nirvāṇa is an ordinary existing thing,
It is produced by causes.
Nowhere and none the entity exists
Which is not produced by causes.

VI

If Nirvāṇa is an ordinary existing thing,
How can it lack dependence on something else?
There cannot be an existing thing
Which is not subject to dependence.

And if we suppose that nirvāṇa is not an existing thing then problems also develop (in VII to X):

VII

If Nirvāṇa is not an ordinary existing thing,
Will it be then a non-existing thing?
Whenever there is found no existing thing
There cannot be a [corresponding] non-existing thing.

VIII

Now, if Nirvāṇa is a non-existing thing,
How can it then exist without dependence on something else?
For surely an independent non-existent thing
is nowhere to be found.

IX

This world is going into and out of existence
For it is both dependent and caused.
That which is not dependent and not caused
Is Nirvāṇa.

X

[The Buddha] has declared
That existing things as well as non-existing things
Should all be rejected. Nirvāṇa, therefore, is
Neither an existing thing nor a non-existing thing.

And if we suppose that nirvāṇa is both an existing thing and a non-existing thing then problems develop (in XI to XV):

XI

If Nirvāṇa were both an existing and a non-existing thing,
Final deliverance would be also both
Reality and unreality together.
And this is impossible.

XII

If Nirvāṇa were both an existing and a non-existing thing,
Nirvāṇa could not be uncaused.
For both existing and non-existing things
Are dependent on causation.

XIII

How can Nirvāṇa be
Both an existing and a non-existing thing?
Nirvāṇa is, indeed, asaṁskṛta [uncaused and uncausing].
While existing and non-existing things are saṁskṛta.

XIV

How can Nirvāṇa be
Both an existing and a non-existing thing?
As light and darkness [in one spot]
They cannot both be simultaneously present.

Finally, if we suppose that nirvāṇa is neither an existing thing nor a non-existing thing then problems also develop (in XV and XVI);

XV

It would be valid to say, "Nirvāṇa is neither
An existing nor a non-existing thing",
Provided that it would also be valid to say,
"It is an existent thing and a non-existent thing."

XVI

But if Nirvāṇa is neither existing nor non-existing
No one can really understand such

A doctrine which proclaims at once the
Negation of them both together.

The catuṣkoti dialectic on nirvāṇa is completed.

Second, there is a discussion of the unanswerability of the questions regarding the Buddha and the Buddha's nirvāṇa and his nature while he was alive and using the catuṣkoti (in XVII to XVIII).

XVII

What is [the Buddha] after his Nirvāṇa?
Does he exist or does he not exist,
Or both, or neither?
It cannot be understood.

XVIII

What is [the Buddha] then during his lifetime?
Does he exist, or does he not exist,
Or both, or neither?
This [also] cannot be understood.

Third, and most significantly, we come to the startling kārikās or verses, where Nāgārjuna seems to identify nirvāṇa with saṁsāra (in XIX to XX):

XIX

There is no difference at all
Between Nirvāṇa and Saṁsāra.
There is no difference at all
Between Saṁsāra and Nirvāṇa.

XX

What makes the limit of Nirvāṇa
Is also the limit of Saṁsāra.
Between the two we cannot find
The slightest shade of difference.

Fourth, Nāgārjuna gives the all-important reason for this curious identification (if that is what it is - note that he only says that they are not different!); and he gives the rationale for his entire dialectical attack on the now-familiar unanswerable questions, viz., What exists beyond nirvāṇa? and What is the end of the world like?, together with the rationale behind his attack on the possibility of knowledge about the following, viz., the finite and the infinite, negation, identity and difference, permanence and impermanence (in XXI to XXIII):

XXI

The contradictory views concerning life after death
And whether it is limited by a beginning and an end,
Depend on Nirvāṇa and
Being limited by a beginning and an end.

XXII

Since all dharmas are śūnya
What meaning do finite and infinite have?
What meaning do both finite and infinite have?
What meaning do neither finite and infinite have?

XXIII

What is identity, and what is difference?
What is permanence and impermanence?
What is both permanence and impermanence?
What is neither permanence and impermanence?

The all-important reason for the identity of nirvāṇa and saṁsāra is that both are śūnya; recall that bliss and enlightenment are found only in the stoppage of all thought, the giving up of the search for a higher unity, a higher reality, altogether, since all categorizing and labeling, the attempt to reduce the many to a one, is vain, sorrowful, frustrating, empty and useless, indeed (in XXIV):

XXIV

Bliss consists in the cessation of all thought,
In the quiescence of plurality.
No Dharma was ever preached at all,
Nowhere and none, by Buddha![316]

But we haven't yet cleared the great Sorcerer of the charge of having fallen into darkest śūnya, himself. We shall attempt that clearing next.

Fifth, and finally, return for a moment to the third summary comment above, viz., that there is no difference between nirvāṇa and saṁsāra. This remains the most celebrated, outrageous and curious conclusion yet reached by a Buddhist philosopher. If Nāgārjuna is not espousing a doctrine then in the light of what we have learned up to this point about Śūnyavāda we know that he is probably shouting something like "Be quiet!" And the shout on this occasion has had a profound influence on later Buddhist thought, most notably on Zen Buddhism. In fact, the cornerstone of Zen might fairly be said to be this dictum that nirvāṇa is saṁsāra and saṁsāra is nirvāṇa. For this reason I propose to have a closer look at it because its puzzling presence in Śūnyavāda, as well as its extraordinary later influence on Zen, are puzzles of some magnitude. So, what does it mean?

If we assume that the utterance is not self-contradictory then, in the light of what we have said previously about Śūnyavāda, I think that there are at least four possible interpretations that the expression might be said to have:

First, to say that saṁsāra and nirvāṇa are not different means, as we have said, and as Nāgārjuna plainly intends, that both are śūnya, i.e. relative and empty; therefore, one should stop thinking about both, stop philosophizing about both, and get on with what is really important, viz., becoming a Bodhisattva, becoming a Buddha, and not becoming a philosopher, a sophist, a manipulator of words, concepts and ideas. The dictum plainly functions in the same manner as a myth, viz., to urge the devotee along the path to enlightenment. It is true, consequently, in a mythic sense, i.e. it is true according to the degree to which it leads to, facilitates or helps to accomplish, metaphysical realization. On the first interpretation, then, both nirvāṇa and saṁsāra are empty and to say this is to urge the devotee on to enlightenment in the manner of a myth.

But, one might well ask, How is one to become a Bodhisattva or a Buddha without becoming a philosopher first? Even the Mahāyāna admit that in these latter days it's tough to practice the bhakti, in order to achieve the grace, in order to achieve the merit, in order to achieve heaven, in order to achieve Bodhisattva-instruction, in order to achieve prajñā, in order to achieve nirvāṇa.[317] Buddha was no simple-minded bumpkin but a philosopher of the keenest intelligence, at least according to the Mādhyamika. The request to stop philosophizing is misleading, indeed. The shout that we're hearing is a shout that urges us at least to become careful observers and analysts, i.e. philosophers. And part of what needs analyzing is the conclusion that nirvāṇa and saṁsāra are both sunya.

Second, to say that saṁsāra and nirvāṇa are not different means that both are a product of māyā and that each is an illusion. In the *Mahāyāna Viṁśaka*, a work at one time attributed to Nāgārjuna, we are told that ignorance creates illusion:

> IX. Like unto things magic-created,
> so are the deeds of sentient beings
> who take the external world for reality...
>
> IV. The self-nature of all things is
> regarded as like shadows....[318]

Reaching enlightenment is like awakening from a dream; one looks back on the shadows and the baseless fabric of both saṁsāra and nirvāṇa and sees them then for what they truly were, viz., illusions created by magic:

> XVI. Thus regarded, saṁsāra and nirvāṇa have no real substance...
>
> XVIII. When things created by magic are seen as such, they have no existence; such is the nature of all things.

On the second interpretation, then, to say that saṁsāra and nirvāṇa are identical means that both are illusions, phantoms, part of the dream of māyā in which the dreamer is exhorted to wake up:

> XXI When the ignorant wrapped in the darkness of ignorance conceive eternity or bliss in objects as they appear or as they are in themselves, they drift in the ocean of transmigration.[320]

But, one might well ask, If everything is a dream, then what practical sense does it make to assert that everything is a dream? Hasn't the Mādhyamika simply overstated his case now? And isn't this really a lot of nonsense? In other words, to declare that "śūnya" means "dream" and to state that we're all living in that dream is to overstate the case beyond all reason. For then one can simply reply to such a universal claim, "So what?" and dismiss the entire outrageous declaration and with it, unfortunately, the very subtle and significant point that the Mādhyamika is trying to make.

For consider: Suppose that I ask you, How do you know you're not dreaming right now? i.e. that you're not home in bed, sound asleep and dreaming that you're reading this book, turning its baffling pages, and so on? How would you be able to prove that you weren't? Any proof to the contrary that you could muster, e.g. pinching-yourself, closing the book, splashing cold water on your face, and so on, would all be dream-proof, i.e. dreaming that you were pinching yourself, dreaming that you were closing the book, and so on. But if there's no way of knowing the difference between waking and dreaming states, then what difference could it possibly make to assert that you're dreaming right now or that all life is a dream? If it's not a difference that makes a difference then it's no difference at all.

Consequently, the Mādhyamika claim that śūnya is māyā, and the creator of universal dream, illusion and appearance, is nonsense, because to make the universal claim that that's the way all life is can make no practical difference to one's life. And the Mādhyamika certainly wants to claim that śūnya and śūnyavāda make a practical difference to one's life. Thus an inconsistency and thus the critic, if one assumes that everything, saṁsāra and nirvāṇa included, are all products of māyā and that they are illusions or dreams.

Third, to say that saṁsāra and nirvāṇa are not different means that one should stop worrying about both, stop being afraid of saṁsāra, i.e. suffering and rebirth, stop being anxious at not attaining release and enlightenment, and get on with what is really significant, viz., living one's life according to the dharma. In the words of the great Yogācāra work of about 350 C.E., the *Laṅkāvatāra Sūtra*, the text that was to become the foundation of later Zen Buddhism:

> Those who, afraid of the suffering arising from the discrimination of birth-and-death (*saṁsāra*), seek for Nirvāṇa, do not know that birth-and-death and Nirvāṇa are not to be separated from one another; and, seeing that all things subject to discrimination have no reality (they) imagine that Nirvāṇa consists in the future annihilation of the senses and their fields.[321]

But they have no reason to fear, for "what has never arisen does not have to be annihilated." So let go of your fear and calm down. Thus Nāgārjuna's shouting out the identity of saṁsāra and nirvāṇa quiets the frantic fear that comes in attempting to flee saṁsāra into the arms of nirvāṇa. Emphasizing that nirvāṇa and saṁsāra are identical says in effect, Calm down; fear not; there's no place to go for the nirvāṇa you seek is right here and now.

Fourth, and finally, to say that saṁsāra and nirvāṇa are not different means that there is a way to enlightenment and it lies in stopping desire, in stopping the striving to escape from the suffering in saṁsāra and in stopping the lusting after the bliss and peace of nirvāṇa. This fourth interpretation of the identity is expressed most succinctly by Alan Watts when he says:

> These are not the idle speculations and sophistries of a system of subjective idealism or nihilism. They are answers to a practical problem which may be expressed thus: "If my grasping of life involves me in a vicious circle, how am I to learn not to grasp? How can I try to let go when trying is precisely not letting go?" Stated in another way, to try not to grasp is the same thing as to grasp, since its motivation is the same--my urgent desire to save myself from a difficulty. I cannot get rid of this desire, since it is one and the same desire as the desire to get rid of it![322]

Nāgārjuna, with his simple formula of the identity of saṁsāra with nirvāṇa, solves that practical problem by reminding all Buddhists that there is nothing to grasp because there are no reals, no absolutes, no goals, no ends to be achieved; hence desiring, grasping and lusting are useless. And only when one has understood that fearing and desiring are, indeed, useless, only then will that tranquility come of which the Buddhists and Nāgārjuna both speak so eloquently.

To this extent, then, the dictum, "Saṁsāra is nirvāṇa and nirvāṇa is saṁsāra" is a convenient fiction and joins company with a number of other useful fictions that we have had occasion to meet throughout this study, e.g. pratītyasamutpāda,[323], general or abstract words,[324] the concept of the self,[325] heaven[326] and the law of karma.[327] We shall return to this topic of useful fictions and their function in Buddhism, again.[328]

Perhaps the third and fourth interpretations of our dictum that saṁsāra is nirvāṇa and nirvāṇa is saṁsāra come closer in meaning to what was intended by this shout from Nāgārjuna. The shout means, Don't be afraid, all effort is bound to be frustrated, anyway, and fear and worrying are simply by-products of that effort. (Thus the third and fourth interpretations.) But he's also saying that there is something that can be done in order to see the emptiness of all fear and effort (the first interpretation), and that is to become philosophers, wise abandoners of ignorance and desire, in order to see the illusions of the world (the second interpretation). The multiple meanings of the dictum, provided that it is not overstated to the point of creating the curious problems we discovered in the first and second interpretations, constitute a cry that warns the devotee and guides him along the right and fruitful path to enlightenment. If the great Sorcerer is right, perhaps he had not fallen into darkest śūnya, afterall, when he said that there is no difference at all between nirvāṇa and saṁsāra.

But the test of all of Nāgārjuna's dialectical efforts is to be found in the way in which the Mādhyamika philosophers have handled a particular philosophic paradox, viz., the paradox of desire, the solving of which leads to enlightenment. We turn next to that paradox as we discuss the problem of nirvāṇa.

<u>4') The Problem of Nirvāṇa</u>. There is one puzzle that I wish to take up next in this examination of the problem of nirvāṇa, viz., the paradox of desire. Following the presentation of this paradox I shall

attempt to show that Mādhyamika provides a solution to it and, as a consequence, a solution is similarly available for two other paradoxes as well, viz., the paradox of śūnya and the paradox of nirvāṇa.[329] I shall make the claim that the practice of philosophy, itself, can overcome these paradoxes and that in solving the paradox of desire the devotee is gently led to nirvāṇa. In that successful leading Nāgārjuna's Mādhyamika tradition proves that the great Sorcerer apparently was right in all that he said and meant about the non-difference of nirvāṇa and saṁsāra.

a) The paradox of desire.[330]

If one of the chief aims, if not the only aim, of Buddhism is the stopping of desire and desiring then two questions immediately arise: First, what is the nature of this desire that is to be eliminated? and, second, How does one go about the business of eliminating it? Both questions are central not only to the Buddhist and even the Hindu traditions but to any philosophy or religion that holds that desire *per se* is a barrier to ultimate human happiness. Furthermore, all of these traditions face the same paradox in their endeavors to explain the process of the elimination of desire, namely, the paradox of desire.

The paradox of desire points to the practical contradiction or frustration involved in the desire to stop all desiring and states simply that those who desire to stop all desiring will never be successful.

Let me begin by distinguishing between three types of desire to which the paradox of desire seems to be pointing. First, there is the most important desire, namely, the desire for desirelessness ("desire$_1$"). Second, there is the desire in desirelessness, namely, the desire we are trying to eliminate ("desire$_2$"). Finally, there is the desire that is the result of desiring desirelessness, that is, the type of desire that the desire$_1$ for desire$_2$-lessness produces, viz., "desire$_3$". Thus, we have the first of four statements in our explication of the paradox of desire:

1) Desire$_1$ for Desire$_2$-lessness leads to desire$_3$.

Desire$_1$ may be intense (a lust), or it may be weak (a need), depending on the perseverence, passion, and history of the devotee. $Desire_2$ includes the lusts, cravings, and needs of ordinary existence that lead to the suffering and misery about which the Buddha spoke so eloquently. The condition that $desire_1$ attempts to achieve, of course, is the eradication of this $desire_2$. But this $desire_1$ for $desire_2$-lessness leads in turn to $desire_3$, a species of desire that is merely the result of the juxtaposition of the two previous desires. The question that remains to be answered now, of course, is: What is the nature of $desire_3$?

The paradox of desire would lead us to believe that $desire_1$ is not ultimately different from $desire_2$ and that the resultant desire, $desire_3$, is also not ultimately different from $desire_2$. Hence, the paradox of desire assumes that no matter what I do I can never completely eliminate some species or other of $desire_2$, that is, the desire that we wanted to eliminate in the first place. Of course, one way out of the paradox would be to argue strenuously that $desire_1$ and $desire_3$ are ultimately different from $desire_2$; or, more to the point, that $desire_1$ or $desire_3$ are not desires at all, or not really bad desires, but rather good and useful desires. But I reject this, primarily because the Buddhists themselves seem to reject it: A desire by any other subscripted name would still smell of desire.

Another way out is simply to accept the paradox of desire and then see what happens. And what happens involves us with two other statements necessary to our philosophic explication of the paradox:

2) $Desire_1$ is a species of $desire_2$.

That is to say, $desire_1$ for the condition of desirelessness is really a $desire_2$, pure and simple.

3) $Desire_3$ is a species of $desire_2$.

That is to say $desire_3$ that results from $desire_1$ for $desire_2$-lessness is also just another $desire_2$, pure and simple. But then the paradox is shown fully and completely by this fourth step:

4) But if $desire_1$ and $desire_3$ are merely species of $desire_2$ then $desire_2$-lessness is impossible.

Thus the paradox of desire which says that it is impossible to eliminate $desire_2$ since it would continue to exist as either $desire_1$ or $desire_3$. The "impossibility" spoken of here may be a logical impossibility, that is, it may be self-contradictory to desire a condition of desirelessness; or it may be a practical impossibility, that is, it may be self-frustrating to desire a condition of desirelessness. In what follows I want to focus on this practical impossibility or practical contradiction entailed by the paradox of desire and show that, for Buddhism, this is a very useful contradiction, indeed.

b) The solution to the paradox of desire.

Let me try an historical approach to the paradox and focus on the essential frustration involved in desiring to eliminate desire and the representation of that frustration in $desire_3$. The English utilitarian philosopher, Henry Sidgwick (1838-1900), identified and named a similar puzzle which he called "the fundamental paradox of Hedonism."[331] The fundamental paradox of hedonism bears such a close resemblance to the paradox of desire that what Sidgwick had to say about the former can, I believe, give us some insight into the approach we ought to take to the latter.

The fundamental paradox of hedonism, according to Sidgwick, is the consequence of observing that the impulse toward pleasure, if too predominant, defeats its own aim.[332] Following a discussion of self-love in his classic work, *The Methods of Ethics*, Sidgwick observes:

> I should not, however, infer from this that the pursuit of pleasure is *necessarily* self-defeating and futile; but merely that the principle of Egoistic Hedonism, when applied with a due knowledge of the laws of human nature, is *practically* self-limiting; i.e. that a rational method of attaining the end at which it aims requires that we should to some extent put it out of sight and not directly aim at it.[333]

In the same way the pursuit of desirelessness, that is, the desire for desirelessness tends in practice to be self-limiting, that is, it tends to defeat its own end. Please note that the paradox of desire in 1) to 4), above, leads to a conclusion similar to Sidgwick's about a practical impossibility (a rather weak claim) rather than to a logical impossibility (a much stronger claim) regarding the attainment of desirelessness through desiring.

Understanding the practical contradiction that desirelessness can never be attained because desiring desirelessness produces desire then leads to two consequences: In the first place, understanding the practical contradiction produces frustration in the devotee. Lusting after or needing that which is practically (that is, in practice) impossible to attain produces frustration, and with it misery and suffering. The devotee has backed himself into a corner from which there is no practical way out.

If there is no practical way out, and if the frustration that results is a sign of there being no way out, then of course it makes no sense to advise devotees to stop desiring or to remove the objects of desire in order to stop the desiring. What then can a devotee do? And what is the use of Buddhism if it merely points out the contradictions, logical and practical, in the paradox of desire and then leaves one in the paradox? In other words, even if we grant the contradictions in the paradox of desire, what is to be done? The answer is: Nothing is to be done; there is nothing one can do because nothing can be done, and that is precisely what Mādhyamika Mahāyāna Buddhism has been saying all along.

In the second place, understanding the practical contradiction (that is, truly understanding the import of 4), viz., that there is no solution to the paradox of desire) leads to nirvāṇa. The conclusion to our philosophical explication of the paradox of desire would then be:

5) Understanding the truth of 4) is tantamount to achieving nirvāṇa.

That is to say, seeing that there is no way out of the paradox of desire, one "lets go" of the way and the goal. And that "letting go" leads to, or is, nirvāṇa: For, once the devotee realizes that there is nothing that he can do then there is nothing left to be done.

"Letting go," after all, is the condition of desirelessness, and it is achieved following the frustration of knowing that it cannot be achieved, that is, it cannot be regarded as a goal to be striven for, worked for, sought after--in a word, desired. Hence it is not a question of "damned if you do and damned if you don't" but rather 'damned if you do but saved if you don't.' And that 'don't-ing' is not the result of conscious lusting or needing. It is the result of giving up altogether. It is the essence of śūnya.

The impatient critic might ask, again, at this juncture: What, then, is the point of all the Buddhist texts, philosophies, theories, and injunctions, if at the end we are told, 'Let it all go'? The point, of course, is that these were all necessary and useful fictions, shouted out in order to bring one to the realization that they were not at all necessary to nirvāṇa - something the devotee could not know until he had been through all the texts, philosophies, theories and injunctions.

The texts, the philosophies and theories all helped to back me into the corner that I found myself in; in other words, the paradox had to be experienced before escape from it was possible. The philosophic understanding was necessary before the rational insight was possible; and that rational insight, namely, that there is no way out, was necessary before "letting go" could occur; and "letting go" was necessry before nirvāṇa was possible.[334]

<u>c) The solution to the paradox of śūnya and the paradox of nirvāṇa.</u>

If what has been said above with respect to the paradox of desire makes any sense, i.e. if it is true that desirelessness to be got must be forgot, then it follows, since śūnya and nirvāṇa are similar impossible "goals" and may be of a species with pleasure, happiness and desirelessness, that śūnya and nirvāṇa to be got must also be forgot: For the realization of desirelessness, śūnya and nirvāṇa, we can see, are by-products of doing other things well. And realizing that striving for, working for, and seeking for that which is only a by-product leads to the same practical frustration that we met with in the paradox of desire.

What must I do then? the frustrated devotee cries, knowing that if he tries to do anything directly to realize desirelessness, śūnya or nirvāṇa, he's lost. The Mādhyamika Mahāyāna Buddhist can however point to certain indirect doings or activities that don't aim at goals but can be done for their own sakes, e.g., meditation and devotion. He might even point to philosophic activity, the activity of philosophic analysis that leads to the insight that there is nothing to be done.[335] The Zen Buddhist answers the same question, viz., What must I do then?, by simply saying, Eat when you're hungry, drink when you're thirsty.

Faced with these three paradoxes and the inevitable conclusion to which they lead, there's not much else that one can do. But it's no easy thing, either to know when one is hungry or thirsty, and it's an even more difficult thing to know how to eat and how to drink. (And have you ever tried getting a plumber on weekends?)

b. The Yogācāra (Vijñānavāda) School.

The second great Mahāyāna school of philosophy to draw its spiritual sustenance from the *Prajñāpāramitā* literary corpus was the school of Yogācāra or Vijñānavāda. The word "yogācāra" means "the practice or way of yoga"; however, the word does not really differentiate the school from other Buddhist schools of philosophy since they all, one way or another, regarded the practice of meditational yoga as essential to the effectiveness of their disciplines. A more descriptive term for this school would be vijñānavāda or "the consciousness view" i.e. the view that consciousness alone is real. We shall, however, use the more common, but less descriptive term "yogācāra", for the school that we are about to discuss.

Yogācāra thought evolved slowly from the second century C.E. side by side with the Mādhyamika school. But it was not until the fifth century C.E. that it reached maturity through the works believed to have been written by two of the greatest Yogācārins, Asaṅga and Vasubandu.[336]

They were brothers and are traditionally taken to be the founders of Yogācāra, though prior to their time there was already a struggling school in existence founded by Maitreyanatha (270-ca.350 C.E.). Asaṅga and Vasubandhu were both born in the fourth century C.E. in Peshawar in Gandhara in Northwest India. Asaṅga is said to have studied Śūnyavāda but gave it up because he could not understand it. He then studied Hīnayāna thought and then gave it up before turning, finally, as a disciple to Maitreyanatha and to the school to which he was to devote the rest of his life, Yogācāra. It is said that his conversion came about in this fashion. Becoming dissatisfied with the Hīnayāna master, Mahīśāsaka, he went to the forest to meditate. Twelve years later he received a vision of Maitreya, He who was to be the future Buddha. Maitreya thereupon dictated to Asaṅga the texts of Yogācāra named for Himself, the future Savior, the *Maitreyanātha* texts. Asaṅga subsequently wrote a series of books and commentaries on the texts of his vision. But, most important of all, he converted his younger brother, Vasubandhu, to Yogācāra.

At the time of his conversion, Vasubandhu was a convinced Sautrāntika who had made important contributions to that Hīnayāna School. He was, after all, the Sautrāntika - leaning author of one of the greatest philosophic books of the 4th century C.E., the *Abhidharmakośa*. This work had elegantly explained the entire Sarvāstivāda system and then, in the commentary to that explanation, had just as elegantly completely demolished the Sarvāstivādas. In addition, Vasubandhu had been the powerful philosophical opponent of the Vedic brahmins, the Sāṁkhya dualists, and, even, the Mahāyāna Buddhists.

But then Vasubandhu saw the light and was converted to Mahāyāna. His biographer, Paramārtha (499-569 C.E.), tells us that Vasubandhu regretted his former attack against the Mahāyāna so much that he sought to cut out his tongue. But his brother, Asaṅga, persuaded him to use his talents, and his tongue, in defense of Mahāyāna. Vasubandhu did as he was instructed and, after his brother's death, wrote many of his greatest works including the two superb, short treatises on idealism, viz., the *Viṁśatikā*, which we will analyze below, and the *Triṁśikā*. In these two compositions Vasubandhu succeeds in denying the reality of the external world and at the same time defends the ultimate reality of pure Consciousness, Vijñāptimatrā.

Vasubandhu died at the age of eighty and Paramārtha says of the long and productive life of this St. Augustine of Mahāyāna:

> The sense conveyed in his compositions is fine and excellent; there is no one who, on hearing and seeing it, does not believe and pursue it. Therefore all those who study the Mahāyāna and Hīnayāna in India and in all the frontier countries use the works of Vasubandhu as their text-books. There are no teachers of any other schools (of Buddhism) or of the heretical sects who, on hearing his name, will not become quite nervous and timid.[337]

We shall try to control ourselves as we look at one of his grandest and most popular compositions.

Yogācāra, or what came to be called "the doctrine of consciousness only", i.e. vijñānamātra or vijñāptimātra, argued that ideas, or consciousness, were, or was, the only reality. As with Mādhyamika, Yogācāra, too, has some interesting parallels in the Hindu tradition of the *Upaniṣads* where, for example, we find such assertions as the following:

> He knew that vijñāna is Brahman, for from vijñāna all beings are born, when born they live by vijñāna, and at the end they enter into vijñāna.[338]

But while vijñāptimātra may have Upaniṣadic similarities, the direction that Asaṅga and Vasubandhu gave to it was distinctly Buddhist.

One of the schools that the Yogācārins were seeking to combat was the Sautrāntika school of Hīnayāna Buddhism, the school to which Vasubandhu had previously belonged. Sautrāntika, recall, had maintained that the external, dharma-composed world was in some sense "real", and in the enormous Sarvāstivāda work, the *Abhidharma*, the groundwork had been laid for an atomic metaphysics. The *Abhidharma* had argued, in effect, that all the objects and entities in the universe, time and matter as well as the "self", could be reduced to their "atomic" constituents, to a series of real, dharma-atomic moments of force. Mahāyāna Buddhism, initially, had been willing to put up with what had evolved into a curious atomic metaphysics. They seemed to have thought, Why bother to refute a theory that was ultimately going to be śūnyafied, anyway? But it was here, on this metaphysical issue, that Yogācāra took its stand and turned to combat the representative realism and atomism of Sautrāntika.[339]

The task that Vasubandhu set for himself is very roughly parallel to the task that the British idealist philosopher, George Berkeley (1685-1753), set for himself when he established the philosophical idealism for which he became so justifiably famous. It might help our understanding of the *Viṁśatikā* if we reconstruct that very rough parallel in order to see in perspective what the issues were between the idealists, like Vasubandhu and George Berkeley, and the direct, or naive, realists, like the Sarvāstivādins, and the indirect, or representative, realists, like the Sautrāntikas, and, for comparative purposes, the Hindu Vedāntist Śaṁkarācarya (693-725 C.E.). Finally, to really anger those who have no use whatsoever for comparative studies, let's add to the list the English indirect, or representative, realist, John Locke (1632-1704).[340]

1) "Utterly Absurd, Utterly Irrefutable"

Look at your hand for a moment. Now let me ask you, What do you see? You'd probably answer, I see my hand; and if I asked you, Where is your hand located? you'd probably say, It's out here, and you'd point to the hand and its general environs. All this is pretty straightforward and familiar stuff to us by now for it's precisely the stuff out of which metaphysical realism and epistemological realism are made. The metaphysical realist assumes, as we have already noted, that what is real is out there someplace, and the epistemological realist states that it can be known or is knowable.[341] And when you're not looking at your hand, the hand continues to exist out there in some fashion or other; that's what makes the hand real, viz., the continued and independent existence of the object even when no one is looking at it or thinking about it; and that's what turns this metaphysical position into a metaphysical realism, the belief in the continued or continuing (think of the saṁtāna of dharmas) existence of unperceived physical objects.

There are two perceptual views that metaphysical realism can take, viz., direct realism and indirect realism. The first, you'll recall,[342] contends that physical objects are exactly what they look like, so that if your hand looks brown then by heavens your hand is brown.

This *direct* or *naive realism* is refuted, however, if we recall that the brownness is mental, or mind dependent, and not out there in the world at all. That real world out there consists of light waves, the physicist tells us, and it's those light waves out there that cause me to see brown. The color is mental and it's the result of those light waves striking my retina which transmits an electrochemical message along the optic nerve to the occipital lobe of the brain where the actual brown color is perceived. That's why we say that color is mental. But a host of other so-called sense qualities like smells, tastes, feels and sounds are also mental.

The realist might maintain, in the light of this criticism of his original naive view about your hand, that while the sense qualities are all mental, that while the pink, black or brown look, the papery odor from handling this book, the inky taste, the smooth feel, and the fleshy sound it emits when struck, are all in the mind, there is, nevertheless, something out there that must cause those sense qualities to appear when they do, and that that is what exists, independent of the mind.

The criticism of direct realism brings us, you'll recall,[343] to the second perceptual view that metaphysical realism can take, viz., indirect or representative realism.

Indirect realism contends that perceptions or sensations while not identical with that something out there, as the direct realist had maintained, are representations or copies of external objects. It is this indirect or representative realism (bāhyanumeya-vāda) that occupied the Sautrāntika and that led directly to the idealism of Yogācāra.[344]

The Sautrāntikas (and Śaṁkarācarya in India and John Locke in the West) argued, in effect, that while I never know the external object directly, I do know directly the mental copy of the object in my mind; and, therefore, I know indirectly by it the thing out there of which it is a copy. Hence, knowledge of the external world through perception is possible because I have indirect knowledge of that world through direct knowledge of a copy of that world. The hand that I see or experience is a representation caused by that external hand. The brownness is mental, the representative realist may concede, but its cause, the external hand, is not mental.

In summary, then, we might say that both the direct realist and the indirect realist believe that in perception an independent external object causes the mental internal object. They both believe that that external object exists even when it is not being perceived. The naive realist believes that the internal mental object is identical with the external physical object, while the representative realist believes that the relation between internal and external object is one, not of identity, but of resemblance, i.e. resemblance between the copy in my mind and the physical something or other out there that it copies.

At this point the idealist critic steps in demanding to know what that "something out there" can be that causes you to have the sense perceptions that you have. Is it ever observed? If it is then it can only be observed through the sense qualities that we have already discussed. If it is never observed then, the idealist asks, how do you know that it's there? The idealist concludes that if physical objects can all be reduced to or identified with sense qualities, i.e. sights, feels, tastes, etc., and if all of these sense qualities are mental then the object must be mental as well. And this is precisely what *metaphysical idealism* contends, viz., that whatever is real is mental and vice versa.

Further, all that we ever really know are ideas, i.e. colors, tastes, sounds, desires, memories, and so on. We never know physical objects or external bodies until they are transformed into ideas of color and size for our minds. And this is precisely what *epistemological* or *perceptual idealism* contends, viz., that all that we can ever know are minds and ideas.

Finally two wierd consequences are deducible from this idealist philosophy. Consider the following argument which follows from idealist common sense:

1. All that I ever know are mere ideas. (Epistemological idealism)
2. I know physical objects. (Common sense says so)

3. Therefore, physical objects are mere ideas. (Metaphysical idealism)
4. Ideas are experiences. (Common sense says so)
5. Experiences cannot exist unexperienced. (Common sense says so)
6. Therefore, ideas cannot exist unexperienced. (By logical deduction from 4 and 5)
7. Therefore, physical objects cannot exist unexperienced. (And there's logic for you!, again)

The argument has been called "utterly absurd but utterly irrefutable!"

Some idealists believe that minds together with their ideas are both knowable and ultimately real (thereby combining epistemological with metaphysical idealism); such a position is called *subjective idealism*. Some idealists contend that it is only one's own mind together with its own ideas, that are knowable and ultimately real; such a position is called *solipsism*, i.e. "self alone-ism". Some idealists believe that there is one mind or Mind which is God or the Absolute Who thinks divine thoughts, and that man and the world are simply those thoughts or ideas in God's mind or in the Absolute Mind; such a position is called *absolute idealism*. Finally, the idealist who believes that there are real and knowable ideas without minds, without "selves", is a *phenomenalist*.[345]

In what follows we shall try to locate Vasubandhu in the Buddhist idealist tradition as a phenomenalist with traces of absolute idealism, with no commitment to solipsism, and with a position which may be irrefutable but which cannot, given his overall metaphysical and religious goal, be said to be absurd.

2) Idealism.

Vasubandhu's enormously influential *Viṁśatikā* constitutes the first part of his longer *Treatise on Vijñapti-Only*. In the portions of the translation of the *Viṁśatikā* that follow, I have made several minor alterations. First, I have left out the first two kārikās, or verses, of the translation, replacing these with a brief summary, instead. In the first of these two verses, Vasubandhu, pretending to be a realist, presents four objections to idealism (marked as "O_1", "O_2", "O_3" and "O_4"). In the second kārikā he then gives his own idealist answers to each of these objections (marked as "A_1", "A_2", "A_3" and "A_4"). Second, I have made a minor change at some points in the translation. The translator had rendered "vijñapti" (literally, "information", "report" or "indication") as "representation". But "representation" suggests that there is some thing out there being represented, and that is not what the Yogācāra idealist wants to say at all. Consequently, in place of "representation" I have used instead either "ideas", i.e. mental objects, or "consciousness" whichever seemed appropriate since those are plainly what Vasubandhu intends.

Vasubandhu begins with a summary of the idealist position (see below). In I, following this brief introduction, the hypothetical realist presents his objections: If there are no physical objects outside my mind, i.e. if there are no real representations of something out there, and only consciousness is real, then (O_1) space, (O_2) time, (O_3) the public observability of objects, and (O_4) the obvious usefulness or workability or activity of objects would all be impossible, meaningless or unfounded. But (O_1 and O_2) space and time are objective and meaningful, the objector says; further, (O_3) we all have the same perceptions of physical objects which we could not have if the objects were mental and private rather than objective and public; and, finally, (O_4) since mere, mental water could never satisfy a raving thirst then the usefulness of objects., e.g. the ability of food, knives and poison to feed, to cut and to kill, could never be explained if everything were merely mental.

In II Vasubandhu answers these four objections and follows it up by elaborating on his answers somewhat as follows: The objections are without merit for we all know that (A_1, A_2) both space and time appear in our dreams where they are entirely mental and that they appear in exactly the same fashion in waking experience; so they must be mental there, as well.

Further, we all know that (A_3) all ghosts in hell see and will be immersed eventually in the same river of pus as just punishment for their sins, and that these mental projections are common to all these ghosts; yet these projections do not exist outside the mind; and exactly the same kinds of projections occur in sense experience; so they must be mental there, as well.

Finally, we all know (A_4) in our dreams the usefulness or workability or activity of objects is accomplished, e.g. erotic dreams produce nocturnal seminal emissions, dream beasts produce real fear, and so on; so the usefulness of objects can be explained even if they all were mental. Hence, the objections to the Yogācāra view of consciousness-only come to nothing.

The plan of the first fourteen verses in the *Viṁśatikā* is to set forth the logical arguments supporting idealism and attacking the reality of matter. Kārikās I to IX argue, in effect, that the picture that we have of the world is the same whether we assume external objects or mere internal sources as causes for our ideas. Kārikās X to XIV attack the atomism to which realism had been driven, and they argue that the infinite divisibility of matter demonstrates that the atom must be mere idea.[346] Kārikās XV to XVIII take up the curious commitment to pre-established harmony between minds. Kārikā XX introduces the problem of other minds and how one knows that there are other minds. Kārikā XXI concludes the work with a comment on the incompleteness of human knowledge. Following each of the above five divisions, I shall make a brief critical comment on one or another of the arguments presented in that division.

Here now is Vasubandhu's *Viṁśatikā*, without Kārikās I and II. It begins with a summary of Buddhist idealism.

The Treatise in Twenty Stanzas
On Consciousness-Only[347]

In the MAHĀYĀNA it is established that the three worlds are consciousness. According to the scriptures it is said that the three worlds are only mind. Mind, thought, consciousness, discernment are different names. What is here spoken of as mind includes mental activities also in its meaning. "Only" excludes external objects; it does not do away with mental associates. When inner [so-called] "representations"

> arise, *seemingly* external objects appear; [but that's just like] persons having bad eyes seeing hairs and flies...[for these are only in the mind].

There follows the realist's four objections and Vasubandhu's answers.

3) The Buddha's upāya.

Vasubandhu moves on to playing the realist objector, once again; he objects that if Buddha had been an idealist then he ought to have said so and he ought not to have misled us with all that realist talk about "bases of cognition", i.e. external, physical object sources of consciousness; that is to say, Why did Buddha speak as if there were physical objects, if there weren't any? To which Vasubandhu answers in VII that Buddha had a secret intention in talking like a realist while believing like an idealist:

> [Objector]...if it is only consciousness which appears as if colored, etc., and there is no separate colored, etc., object, then the Buddha ought not to have said that there are "bases" of cognition, visual, and so on.
>
> [Answer] This teaching is not a reason, for it has a different meaning....
>
> VII. Conforming to the creatures to be converted
> The World-honored One with secret intention
> Said there are bases of cognition, visual, etc....

In other words, the Buddha using his upāya, his skill-in-means, put his message in such a way that those beings he came to convert would understand it, i.e. he intentionally spoke their language.[348] After all, the idealism proposed is, on the face of it, utterly absurd; hence skill in the use of useful fictions, such as talk about external objects as if they were real, is necessary at the beginning of the conversion. Later, as wisdom grows, these bases can be seen for what they are, viz., fictions.[349]

Vasubandhu continues in VIII to argue that consciousness of apparent external objects is really consciousness of a gradually unfolding and independently developing series of mental phenomena. This view is phenomenalism, viz., perceptions without a perceiver, thoughts without a thinker, ideas without a self; and this view is the "inner meaning", the secret meaning, of the Buddha's pronouncements, as IX then goes on to explain:

> VIII. [Perceptive] consciousness is born from its own seed
> And develops into an apparent object aspect.
> To establish the distinction of inner and outer bases of cognition,
> Buddha says there are ten of these.
>
> [Objector] What advantage is there in this teaching of an inner meaning?
>
> IX. By reason of this teaching one enters into
> [The doctrine] of the egolessness of the individual:
> The asserted non-substantiality of elements
> One enters again by reason of the remainder of the teaching....

In other words, as IX explains, this phenomenalistic idealism leads to the conclusion that the self is just as the physical world was previously, unreal, and unreal because it, too, lacks substance, i.e. it is not unchanging, independent and eternal. Vasubandhu is not espousing subjective idealism, because lying behind the mental phenomena that is ever-flowing through consciousness there, is, as far as this argument goes, no real subject. The best label available for Vasubandhu here would probably be "subjective-idealist-without-a-subject", i.e. Vasubandhu's a phenomenalist.

Comment

My comment is brief enough. To claim that the Buddha's upāya is always directed to the needs and understanding of his pupils is nonsense, on the one hand, and it could lead to endless confusion, on the other: First, when Buddha preached to large groups, as he frequently did, would anyone care to maintain that his message was geared to the individual levels of everyone's needs and understandings? That would be nonsense. Second, if Buddha's message was always pitched to the level of understanding of his listeners then this would have to produce as many messages as there were listeners, which would lead to an endless profusion, and therefore confusion, of doctrines of the Buddha. If nothing else, upāya bids us keep our wits about us when we are interpreting it.

4) The Dilemma of Atomism.

Vasubandhu now turns to the attack. First, he strikes out at the doctrine of atomism (paramāṇuvāda), a realist view which had come to roost in both later Sarvāstivāda and Sautrāntika. His argument in X states that if there are external bases of cognition which become objects of sense representation then one of three things must be the case: Either that outer realm must be one thing, or it must be many separate atoms, or it must be many atoms in agglomeration or combination.

But, Vasubandhu begins, it can't be one thing for no one can perceive or grasp a one, a whole, apart from its parts? and everything can, after all, be parted, i.e. divided into its parts. In other words, I could never perceive an atom without perceiving its right side part, its left side part, its up part, its down part, and so on. Therefore, that outer realm, if it is one, could never be perceived as one, and if it could never be perceived, it is unknowable. But, then, that outer realm must be many separate atoms.

But, as Vasubandhu goes on to show in both X and XI, the outer world is neither many separate atoms nor a combination, or agglomeration, of atoms because we cannot apprehend the atoms separately (X) but only as a whole, i.e. as one (XI); for one separate atom in an aggregate is always going to exist in relation to the others that it joins in that aggregate and they will exist simply as parts of that one whole aggregate (XI); but either of these last alternatives carries us back to perceiving that outer realm as a whole, as one, which was shown previously to be unknowable.

Next, Vasubandhu goes on in XII to consider a realist's reply that the atoms can't join together to make one aggregate because they don't join together at all. The realist is now trying to save himself by arguing that there are aggregates, or molecules, or real objects which don't necessarily result from joined atoms; because, if they did then, as XI showed, we are back to wholes and ones and Vasubandhu has shown that that is impossible because we can't know the whole apart from its parts. The assumption throughout here is, of course, that knowledge comes by analysis of parts. So, the realist argues now that atoms have no spatial divisions; for example, no right side or left side, no top or bottom, no back or front. Vasubandhu objects to this curious defensive move, as well he might. Here, now are X, XI and XII, beginning with the realist's question about the Buddha's intention in his upāya where he spoke as if physical objects were real:

> [Objector] Again, how do we know that Buddha intended such an inner meaning when he said there are bases of sense cognition? Are there not separate, really existing, outer elements, having color-and-form, etc., which become severally the objects of visual, etc. consciousness?
>
> X. That [outer] realm is neither one [thing],
> Nor is it many atoms;
> Again, it is not an agglomeration, etc.,
> Because the atom is not proved.
>
> ...the external object cannot logically be one, because we cannot grasp the substance of the whole apart from the parts. Also it logically is not many, because we cannot apprehend the atoms separately....
>
> XI. One atom joined with six others
> Must consist of six parts.
> If it is in the same place with six,
> The aggregate must be as one atom.
>
> If one atom on each of its six sides joins with another atom it must consist of six parts, because the place of one does not permit of being the place of the others. If there are six atoms in one atom's place then all the aggregates must be as one atom in quantity, because though revolving in mutual confrontation they do not exceed that quantity; and so aggregates also must be invisible.

XII. Since [the realist replies] atoms do not join,
Of what, then, is the joining of the aggregates?
If joining is not proved [of the latter]
It is not because they have no spatial divisions.

If you [the realist]...say that aggregates also do not join one another, then you should not say that atoms are without combination because of having no spatial divisions. Aggregates have spatial divisions, and yet you do not grant their combination. Therefore the non-combining of atoms is not due to their lack of spatial division. For this reason the single real atom is not proved. Whether atomic combination is or is not admitted, the mistake is still as we have said. Whether spatial division of atoms is or is not admitted, both views are greatly in error....

In other words, there can be no really existing outer elements, and one must understand Buddha's realist upāya accordingly.

Vasubandhu now concludes the discussion about the spatial divisibility of atoms on which so much turned, above. In XIII he poses the following dilemma to the atomistically inclined realist. Let's call it "the dilemma of atomism":

1. If the atom (or an aggregate) has spatial divisions then it cannot be a unity, a one.

2. If the atom (or an aggregate) has no spatial divisions then there wouldn't be shadows or the concealing of one thing behind another.

3. But the atom (or an aggregate) either has spatial divisions or it has no spatial divisions.

4. Therefore, either it cannot be a unity, which is absurd, or neither shadows nor concealings are possible, which is also absurd.

5. Therefore, the atomists position leads to an absurdity in either case.

In XIV, Vasubandhu goes on to show the absurdity of assuming that there is a unity; for if all is one, if space is uniform, single and one, then any kind of change of that absolute space, such as the walking in it or the changing or altering of it, would be impossible, and these results are both absurd.

The conclusions to both XIII and XIV point up, once again, the absurdities that abound in atomism and realism:

> XIII. If the atom has spatial divisions,
> It logically should not make a unity.
> If it has none, there should be neither shadow nor occultation;
> Aggregates being no different would likewise be without these two.
>
> ...The fault of multiplicity is as explained before. Unity also is irrational.
>
> XIV. Assuming unity, there must be no walking progressively,
> At one time, no grasping and not grasping,
> And no plural, disconnected condition;
> Moreover, no scarcely perceptible, tiny things.
>
> ...if one step is taken it reaches everywhere...a unitary thing cannot at one time be both obtained and not obtained. A single place, also, ought not to contain disconnected things such as elephants, horses, etc. If the place contains one, it also contains the rest. How can we say that one is distinguished from another? Granting two [things present], how comes it that in one place there can be both occupancy and non-occupancy, that there can be a seeing of emptiness between?...

It is assumed then, that any philosophical view which leads to an absurdity is, itself, absurd. This ends the attack on atomism and Vasubandhu's opening defense of idealism.

Comment

The realist defender of atoms, whoever he may be, is in a good position to attack the apparently devastating dilemma of atomism with a plausible and sensible counter-dilemma of his own. Let's call it "the counter-dilemma of atomism":

1. If the atom (or an aggregate) has spatial divisions then there would be shadows, etc.

2. If the atom (or an aggregate) has no spatial divisions then it can be a unity.

3. But the atom (or an aggregate) either has spatial divisions or it has no spatial divisions.

4. Therefore, either there are shadows, etc., or there is a unity, either of which is perfectly sensible.

5. Therefore, the atomist's position is perfectly sensible and not absurd.

As things stand, who is to say which dilemma or counter-dilemma, Vasubandhu's or the atomist's, is the most defensible? Thus the atomist's possible reply to Vasubandhu.

5) Pre-established Harmony.

An objector now raises the all-important query, If there are no external objects then how can I be presented with ideas as if there were? Vasubandhu answers, first, with a now familiar ploy by drawing attention to similar immediate experiences in dreams where there are ideas without external objects; and, second, by drawing attention to the obvious time lag between the presence of an object and the perceiver's idea of it; this move challenges the entire notion of immediacy in perceptions:

> [Objector] The existence or non-existence of anything is determined by means of proof. Among all means of proof immediate perception is the most excellent. If there are no external objects, how is there this

awareness of objects such as are now immediately evident to me?...

XV. Immediate awareness is the same as in dreams, etc.
At the time when immediate awareness has arisen,
Seeing and its object are already non-existent;
How can it be admitted that perception exists?

[According to] those who hold the doctrine of momentariness, at the time when this awareness arises the immediate objects, visible [tangible, audible] etc., are already destroyed. How can you admit that at this time there is immediate perception?...

If you wish thus to prove the existence of external objects from "first experiencing, later remembering," this theory also fails....

We will return to a closer examination of this issue when we take up the problem of idealism, below.

Following XVI, next, the objector raises a most interesting question that plays on the analogy between dream life and waking life, leading into a discussion of "solipsism"[350] in XVII to XVIII where, because it is possible for streams of consciousness to intermingle, solipsism is explicitly denied:

XVI. [first part] As has been said, the apparent objects are ideas.
It is from this that memory arises.

[Objector] If, in waking time as well as in a dream, ideas may arise although there are no true objects, then, just as the world naturally knows that dream objects are non-existent, why is it similarly not naturally known of the objects in waking time?...

XVI. [second part] Before we have awakened we cannot know
That what is seen in the dream does not exist.

After this, the purified knowledge of the world which is obtained takes precedence; according to the truth it is clearly understood that those objects are unreal. The principle is the same.

[Objector] If for all sentient beings ideas arise as apparent objects because of transformation and differentiation in their own streams of consciousness, and are not born from external things acting as objects, then how explain the fact that those sentient beings through contact with good or evil friends, or through hearing true or false doctrines, are determined to two kinds of ideas since there are neither friends nor teaching?....

XVII.[first part] By the power of reciprocal influence the two kinds of ideas become determined.

That is to say, because distinct ideas in one stream of consciousness occasion the arising of distinct ideas in another stream of consciousness, each becomes determined, but not by external objects.

XVII.[second part] The mind by sleep is weakened:
Dream and waking retributions are not the same.

[Objector] If only ideas exist...then how are sheep, etc., killed by anybody?

XVIII.Because of transformation in another's mind
The act of killing and injuring occurs;
Just as the mental power of a demon, etc.,
Causes another to lose his memory.

In other words, Vasubandhu concludes, all of our separate streams of consiousness are ordered, harmonized, timed and inter-faced such that they seem, but only seem, to be externally and causally interrelated.

Comment

My comment is brief enough. From what we are told here about some form of pre-established harmony between minds, a harmony that coordinates my impressions and ideas with yours, or a sheep's, an obvious question arises: Who does the harmonizing?

i.e. who or what establishes the coordination between my consciousness of stabbing the sheep and the sheep's consciousness of pain and death? How seriously are we to take the suggestion that a demon could pre-program the sheep and myself in such a way that our separate experiences would indeed be coordinated and harmonized? The problem is that there is a yawning gap between minds; and where common sense would bid us bridge the gap with physical objects and sense experiences, Vasubandhu bids us turn to some other coordinating and harmonizing source, perhaps demons, perhaps Buddha or Absolute Mind. Common sense must blush at this spectacle of Yogācāric pre-established harmony.

6. Other Minds.

Penultimately, Vasubandhu turns to the problem of other minds. The objector doubts that knowledge of another's mind is possible and Vasubandhu hedges in his answer, a hedging which leads him ultimately into a discussion in XX of ignorance, wherein he reminds the listener-reader that, in the end, only Buddhas can have pure knowledge. Raising the issue of minds and other minds seems to lead us back into subjective idealism (with minds), on the one hand, and into external objects (with other minds), on the other. But by "other mind" all that Vasubandhu means is a flow or stream of mental phenomena that supposedly can be separate from one's own stream, i.e. this mental stream here and now. He is not necessarily committed to subjects and non-mental, external objects by this move, though some interesting questions are raised by it, nonetheless:

> [Objector] If only ideas exist, does knowledge of another's mind know another's mind or not?....
>
> If it cannot know, why speak of knowledge of another's mind?
> If it can know, the view of consciousness-only is of necessity not proved.
> [Answer] Although it knows the mind of another it does not know exactly....
> XX. How does knowledge of another's mind
> Know its object inexactly?
> Just as the knowledge in knowing one's own mind
> Does not know [it] as the Buddha's knowledge would.

> [Objector] Why is this knowledge of one's own mind not an exact knowing of its object? [Answer] Because of ignorance. Both knowledges of the object, because each is covered over and darkened by ignorance, do not know it as the ineffable object reached by the pure knowledge of a Buddha. These two, in their objects, do not know exactly because of the false appearing of seemingly external objects; and because the distinction between what is apprehended and the apprehender is not yet discontinued.

In other words, the possibility of pure knowledge exists even though for all those who would become Buddhas, themselves, that condition does not now obtain.

Comment

Vasubandhu is courageous to say that at our present stage of ignorance we know neither our own mind nor the minds of others, and that only enlightened minds and the Buddha can know both. But while one must admire his courage (after all, how many philosophers do you know who would ever admit that they didn't know something or other?), one must conclude that his courage doesn't help one whit in solving the problem of the knowledge of other minds. Nor does it help to say that when this ignorance is removed we shall know - that's a teasing and trivial tautology. Nor does it help to suggest, as Vasubandhu does next, that there is a species of enlightened but silent beings who could enlighten us on the matter of other minds but won't...or can't.

7. The Verification of Idealism.

In the conclusion Vasubandhu reminds the listener-reader that the view of consciousness-only can be fully understood only by one who has pure knowledge. This is not an irrational cop-out and a refusal to face philosophic problems rationally, but a reminder to his audience that the philosophic enterprise on which he is set is sacred, involving, as it must, ultimate metaphysical transformation, if all would be understood:

> The doctrines and implications of the view of consciousness only are of kinds infinitely diverse for decision and

selection; difficult is it to fathom their profundities. Without being a Buddha, who is able to comprehend their total extent?

XXI. I, according to my ability,
Have briefly demonstrated the principles of consciousness only;
Among these all [other] kinds,
Difficult to think, are reached by Buddhas [alone].

And on that nirvāṇic note the *Viṁśatikā* ends.

Comment

My comments here are of a kind with the comment made previously about our knowledge of other minds. To say that the final verification of Yogācāra idealism must rest with minds and intelligences as enlightened as the Buddha is to put forward a rationally indefensible principle, viz., only those theories are true which are verified by the enlightened. I have two comments on this principle and its implications: First, the principle would leave every theory dangling until an enlightened person should appear to give it a final blessing; while such dangling might cause us all to become perspicacious and humbly open-minded, it would make an already overly-wary species, i.e. philosophers, paranoically super-cautious. Second, from what the Mahāyāna have said about the enlightened ones, I don't think they care two pins for philosophic theories; therefore, those who wait for Buddhistic verification of their theories must wait in vain, which must all seem patently absurd. In other words the above principle is rationally indefensible. But is this philosophically depressing conclusion all that there is to the great *Viṁśatikā*?

I would like to hypothesize that the philosophic discourse presented in the *Viṁśatikā* can have the same purpose as the utterances in a myth; further, that the mythic theory of truth can comprehend philosophic works like the *Viṁśatikā* as well as myths of the kind that began this entire volume. Recall the definition of truth under that theory: The mythic theory of truth states that a story, legend or account is true if and only if the recitation or hearing or reading of the story, legend or account leads to metaphysical transformation. Similarly, we might now say that a sound[351] philosophic argument is right, or more to the point here, that a philosophic view is true, if and only if understanding it leads to metaphysical realization of the very sort that Vasubandhu seems to be inviting in his conclusion to the *Viṁśatikā*.

Furthermore, the above hypothesis, that philosophic discourse can lead to enlightenment, could now augment the mythic theory of truth such that we can now say that a story, legend, account or philosophic view is true if and only if the recitation or hearing or reading or understanding of the story, legend, account or view leads to metaphysical realization. That this is precisely the measure of philosophic truth in Buddhist philosophy can be seen, below, in the philosophy of the Buddhist logicians;[352] and it is from the Buddhist logicians that final confirmation of our hypothesis shall be given: Understanding philosophic views, through doing philosophic history, can be yogas to liberation.

Using metaphysical idealism as a base, Yogācāra established an absolute idealism by first, positing an entity called "Ālayavijñāna", literally "the storehouse of consciousness." The karmic seeds laid in Ālayavijñāna give rise to all the experiences in the individual and Ālayavijñāna is said to be the One, the single Whole, the Unconscious Mind. Ālayavijñāna has been likened to both Brahman and Ātman in Hindu thought and the similarity, if not outright identity, between them is not accidental, i.e. the Hindu influence seems obvious.

Further, Ālayavijñāna, in its purest state, is Vijñaptimātra, pure Consciousness; as such It is unchanging, independent and eternal.[353] It is a spiritual energy actively dwelling in all beings of which the imperfect and illusion-ridden and idea-filled conscious mind, that sees a duality of subject and object everywhere, is a mere fragment. The Yogācāra practices meditation in order to raise or bring pure Consciousness, Vijñaptimātra, into realization, hence the importance of dhyāna yoga to this Mahāyāna school.

Further, the Absolute or pure Consciousness is ultimately śūnya and Tathatā (Thatness); for, though nothing can be spoken truly about It, It can be known by yoga and through prajñā, thereby effecting enlightenment and Buddhahood.

Finally, those Bodhisattvas who practice the great way recommended by Yogācāra are said to have the following four qualities: First, the *realization* that everything is really a manifestation of pure Consciousness; second, the *freedom* from those false ideas of duality that claim that external objects are real; third, the *understanding* that all external objects are non-existent; and, fourth and finally, the *knowledge* that prajñā and enlightenment are to be attained within pure Consciousness.

In his great work, *Triṁśikā*, Vasubandhu explains the rationale of this enlightenment as follows:

> 28. But when cognition no longer apprehends an object, then It stands firmly in [pure] Consciousness, because, where there is nothing to grasp there is no more grasping.[354]

The point is the same one made by the Mādhyamika in their solution to the paradox of desire: Where desiring (grasping) is impossible, one gives up trying to desire (to grasp); one then stands firmly in śūnya (pure Consciousness) and enlightenment is reached.

Vasubandhu commenting on his own verse, brings out the Śūnyavāda point beautifully:

> The reason for this is that 'where there is nothing to grasp; there is no more grasping.' Where there is one object there is a subject, but not where there is no object. The absence of an object results in the absence of a subject, and not merely in that of grasping.[355]

In pursuing his goal, the Yogācāra chooses to deny object first and then subject, thereby making Vijñaptimātra (pure Consciousness) the Absolute. The Mādhyamika chose to deny subject first and then object, thereby making Śūnyatā (Emptiness) the Absolute. The result was the same: Where there is nothing to grasp there is no grasping; where there is no grasping there (one) abides (in) the Vijñaptimātra, pure Consciousness, and the peace of enlightenment.[356] Vasubandhu has probably found that for which Gautama Buddha, himself, had been searching:

Without any grasping and beyond thought
Is the supra-mundane wisdom [of bodhisattvahood].
This is the realm of passionlessness or purity,
Which is beyond description, is good, and is eternal,
Where one is in the state of emancipation, peace and joy,
The Dharma-body of the great Buddha.[357]

That is a rather bare philosophic outline of the Yogācara system with its variously intermingled Hindu and Mādhyamika elements. It remains for us to focus our attention now on one problem with the system and I have chosen a single puzzle implicit in the Yogācāra theory of perception. We turn next to the problem of Yogācāra.

b′) The Problem of Yogācāra.

An objector in the *Viṁśatikā* had asked, "If there are no external objects, how is there this awareness of objects such as are now immediately evident to me?"[358] Vasubandhu had answered by saying that in dream life we are also conscious of objects which we believe to be external but on waking we discover that they were all the internal products of our own consciousness. The problems raised by this answer are manifold not the least of which is the difficulty that if Vasubandhu is right then we'd never be able to distinguish dream life from waking life. And that's absurd, the critic might say, for we do it all the time. But this sort of idealism *is* absurd; we have suggested that several times, and it solves nothing, perhaps, to continue to reiterate its absurdity.

Certainly, the only way to counter absurdity is with common sense. One of the most common sense philosophers, as far as knowledge of this world is concerned, was Śaṁkarācārya, the Hindu Vedāntist who lived from 693-725 C.E. Śaṁkara attacked Buddha and Buddhism in a philosophically most vigorous way in his commentary on the text of the *Vedānta-* or *Brahma-Sūtras*. In that commentary, besides laying out his own advaita or non-dualistic metaphysical system, Śaṁkara chased after the idealism of the Buddhists, combating absurdity with what he thought was common sense, as we shall see, below. The reader will have to determine for himself or herself whether this "irrefutable" idealist doctrine falls under the common sense onslaught of the great Śaṁkara. As with Vasubandhu's *Viṁśatikā*, Śaṁkara's work consists of short verses (sūtras) followed by his commentary. In the *Vedānta Sutras* these verses were composed earlier by the third century B.C.E. Vedānta philosopher Bādarāyana, and it is upon them that Śaṁkara comments:

> II. ii. 28. The non-existence (of external things) cannot be maintained, because we are conscious of (external things).

Samkara now comments and in such a way as to give the impression that for his opponent he had someone exactly like Vasubandhu in mind. We pick up Śaṁkara as he begins his attack:

> To all this we [the Vedāntins] make the following reply.---The non-existence of external things cannot be maintained, because we are conscious of external things. In every act of perception we are conscious of some external things corresponding to the idea, whether it be a post or a wall or a piece of cloth or a jar, and that of which we are conscious must exist. Why should we pay attention to the words of a man who, while conscious of an outward thing through its approximation to his senses, affirms that he is conscious of no outward thing, and that no such thing exists, any more than we listen to a man who while he is eating and experiencing the feeling of satisfaction avers that he does not eat and does not feel satisfied?

Śaṁkara has argued that the existence of external objects is supported by our always being conscious of them in perception. The consciousness-of-physical-objects argument says, in effect:

1. If there were no external objects then we shouldn't be conscious of external objects in perception.

2. But we are all conscious of physical objects in perception.

3. Therefore, there are external objects.

This is common sense at its best.

Having argued that the existence of external objects is supported by our being conscious of them in perception, Śaṁkara now goes on to show that their existence is further proved by the way we talk. Calling attention to ordinary language, i.e. to the way we speak, Śaṁkara uses the following ordinary language argument:

1. If there were no external objects then we wouldn't use expressions that refer to external objects.

2. But we do use expressions that refer to external objects.

3. Therefore, there are external objects.

He continues:

> That such is the consciousness of all men, appears also from the fact that even those who contest the existence of external things bear witness to their existence when they say that what is an internal object of cognition appears like something external. For they practically accept the general consciousness, which testifies to the existence of an external world, and being at the same time anxious to refute it they speak of the external things as 'like something external.' If they did not themselves at the bottom acknowledge the existence of the external world, how could they use the expression 'like something external'?

The Yogācāra could counter the ordinary language argument by saying that we use many "referring" expressions, for example, "There is a pink elephant" and "There is a rabbit with horns," that simply don't refer to external objects because we were dreaming or hallucinating. And with respect to the consciousness argument used previously, the Yogācāra could counter in the same fashion that consciousness could be mistaken in confusing an external object with a dream object or with an hallucinated object, since I would be indistinguishably conscious of both.

To buttress common sense Śaṁkara must give some attention to the difference between waking ideas and dream ideas. So he attacks the Yogācāra notion that dream ideas and waking ideas are fundamentally indistinguishable:

> 29. And on account of their difference of nature (the ideas of the waking state) are not like those of a dream.
>
> We now apply ourselves to the refutation of the [declaration] made by the Buddhist that the ideas of posts, and so on, of which we are conscious in waking state, may arise in the absence of external objects, just as the ideas of a dream, both being ideas alike.--The two sets of ideas, we maintain, cannot be treated on the same footing, on account of the difference of their character. They differ as follows.--The things of which we are conscious in a dream are negated by our waking consciousness. 'I wrongly thought that I had a meeting with a great man; no such meeting took place, but my mind was dulled by slumber, and so the false idea arose.' In an analogous manner the things of which we are conscious when under the influence of a magic illusion, and the like, are negated by our ordinary consciousness. Those things, on the other hand, of which we are conscious in our waking state, such as posts and the like, are never negated in any state....

Śaṁkara next asks, What is the cause or the origin of new impressions or ideas in the mind? He argues that on the Yogācāra Buddhist theory no satisfactory account can be given:

> 30. The existence (of new mental impressions) is not possible (on the Yogācāra view) on account of the absence of perception (of external things).
>
> We now proceed to that theory of yours, according to which the variety of ideas can be explained from the variety of mental impressions, without any reference to external things, and remark that on your doctrine the existence of mental impressions

> is impossible, as you do not admit the perception of external things. For the variety of mental impressions is caused altogether by the variety of the things perceived. How, indeed, could various impressions originate if no external things were perceived? The hypothesis of a beginningless series of mental impressions would lead only to a baseless regressus ad infinitum, sublative of the entire phenomenal world, and would in no way establish your position....[359]

This new-impressions argument says, in effect:

1. If there were no external objects then I would never have any new ideas (e.g., how would I know about Buddhism unless someone out there told me about it?).

2. But I do have new ideas.

3. Therefore, there are external objects.

The Yogācāra counters, as we have seen, with the docrine of Ālayavijñāna, that unconscious repository of new and different mental seeds that are forever germinating into new impressions and ideas.

This ends our discussion of the problem of Yogācāra and with that we bring to an end our presentation of Yogācāra Buddhism as well as Mahāyāna Buddhism.

Chapter Five: Summary of Hīnayāna and Mahāyāna Buddhism

We turn next to a brief summary of our discussions of Mahāyāna and Hīnayāna Buddhism. To aid the reader I append below a comparative guide which may be useful in this summary.

Table VII. A Comparison of Hīnayāna and Mahāyāna Buddhism

Hīnayāna tends toward:	Mahāyāna tends toward:
1. Naturalism	1. Supernaturalism
2. Atheism	2. Theism
3. Anthropocentrism	3. Buddhacentrism
4. Idealization of the arhat	4. Idealization of the Boddhisattva
5. Pragmatism	5. Pragmatism
6. Nirvāṇa as the goal	6. Heaven as the goal
7. Meditation as the means	7. Bhakti as the means
8. Anātmavāda	8. Ātmavāda
9. Reincarnation	9. Transmigration
10. Realism in philosophy	10. Absolutism in philosophy

Let me summarize very briefly our investigations into Hīnayāna and Mahāyāna Buddhism. I would, once again, caution the reader to look upon this summary as an indication of general trends, propensities and inclinations of these two philosophies and religions of Buddhism rather than as a set of hard and fast, absolute and non-exceptionable, characteristics. For, not only in practice but also in the texts themselves, there is, in many instances, an overlapping of the properties of the two Buddhisms. For example, we find the Pāli Nikāya texts of Hīnayāna speaking about Gods, heavens and Bodhisattvas in ways that would seem, *prima facie*, at least, to make those texts indistinguishable from the Sanskrit *Prajñāpāramitā* texts. We are not, therefore, dealing with defining characteristics and logical differences of and between the two divisions of Buddhism so much as we are speaking about major tendencies and general differences between them. A warning such as this is necessitated by the fact that the Buddhist literature and Buddhist practices, themselves, tend oftentime to blur, blend and overlap in the many instances where theory and practices are involved. Having sounded this caveat, once again, I shall now lay on with a heavy hand to summarize those general tendencies that seem to differentiate the two Buddhisms discussed in our investigation.

1. <u>Naturalism and Supernaturalism</u>

The metaphysics, the theories about ultimate reality, would seem to differ for the two Buddhisms. Hīnayāna appears committed to a naturalism that ultimately wipes away the very things that Mahāyāna seems willing to accept. It was this difference in metaphysical commitment, as a matter of fact, that led to the other differences that defined and separated these two schools, as a glance at the remaining items in Table VII plainly shows.

It is no doubt a truism in religion and philosophy that to know the metaphysics that a person or a religion or a philosophy maintains is to know everything else about that person, that religion or that philosophy That truism is especially applicable here. To know that Hīnayāna is committed to a naturalistic metaphysics is tantamount to knowing, by implication, that it will be atheistic and, generally, man-centered in its religious views; non-self or non-soul oriented in its psychology; and realistic and, generally, empirical in its philosophy.

Further, to know that Hīnayāna is committed to naturalism in its metaphysics is tantamount to knowing, again by implication, that it will reject Buddhacentrism and the idealization of supernatural beings such as the Bodhisattvas; that it will, consequently, reject bhakti as a means to heaven; that it will reject heaven as the proper goal of yogic endeavors; that it will reject the doctrine of the self and transmigration; and, finally, that it will reject the emptines and idealism that Mahāyāna, itself, upholds.

What we discovered in our investigation showed, at any rate, that while Hīnayāna held to a generally strict naturalistic metaphysics and empirical epistemology, Mahāyāna committed itself to a theory of reality that transcended mundane nature and carried on an easy association with a monistic metaphysics rather similar to that in Hinduism. For example, Mahāyāna developed a commitment to a Hindu-like religion in its leanings towards theism, in its Buddhacentrism, in its idealization of the Bodhisattva, and in its doctrine of heaven as a goal for human endeavors with bhakti devotionalism as the chief means to that goal; and Mahāyāna developed a commitment to a monistic psychology in its own version of the doctrine of the self and in its rebirth theory of transmigration; finally, Mahāyāna developed a commitment to a monistic philosophy of transcendent emptiness together with an objective idealism that strongly parallels similar monistic strains of Hinduism. In what follows, we shall speak briefly to each of the remaining nine general characteristics of Hīnayāna and Mahāyāna Buddhism that flow from these two quite distinct metaphysical foundations.

2. Atheism and Theism

The theories about the Gods and their significance for human beings would seem to differ for the two Buddhisms. Again, this follows logically from their distinct metaphysical commitments. We discovered that the attitudes towards these super-human agents differed profoundly, with Hīnayāna generally denying their significance in human affairs while Mahāyāna adopted a much more positive and active commitment to such beings.

3. Anthropocentrism and Buddhacentrism

The beliefs about man and his place in the universe would seem to differ for the two Buddhisms. The Hīnayāna took Buddha's final words to his disciples literally and seriously. Those words, "Seek out your own salvation with diligence" and "Be lights unto yourselves" formed the foundation of the man-centered philosophy of Hīnayāna, and this followed logically from the metaphysical commitment, once again. Only man can save himself; not the Gods, not the Bodhisattvas and not the Buddhas or the Buddha. This Hīnayāna anthropocentrism would seem to have been abrogated or modified by the Mahāyāna discovery of the permanent availability of the Buddha. This discovery went hand in hand with the belief in the super-human qualities of the ever-compassionate Buddha, qualities of omnipotence or omniscience, that turned the Buddha into an object of adoration from whom favors and grace could be obtained.

4. Idealizations of the Arhat and the Bodhisattva

The commitments to what man should become would seem to differ for the two Buddhisms. The arhat worked for his own salvation; he achieved nirvāṇa and was released once and for all from saṁsāra and from all that saṁsāra implied, viz., anxiety in this life and the rebirth of desires in the next. The Hīnayāna arhat was characterized by the Mahāyāna, rightly or wrongly, as an essentially selfish individual who sought only his own welfare to the possible exclusion of the heavenly and nirvāṇic welfare of others.

To this ideal of the arhat the Mahāyāna juxtaposed the ideal of the Bodhisattva, that compassionate being who somehow goes to the very brink of nirvāṇa but declines to make the final leap until all beings have been saved. This nirvāṇic brinksmanship follows from the nature of the Bodhisattva, a nature so filled with compassion for suffering mankind that the goal that the potential arhat sought becomes an unacceptable goal for the Bodhisattva. The career of a Bodhisattva now becomes the goal sought by serious devotees within Mahāyāna, a goal necessitated by the power of love which is manifested by all true devotees. Again, seeking Bodhisattvahood is a general tendency in Mahāyāna; it is not the final nor even a necessary stage, however, for the Mahāyāna Buddhist does not deny that nirvāṇa remains the ultimate goal, and that it is achievable without passing through the penultimate stage of becoming a Bodhisattva. Thus the two idealized goals of the arhat and the Bodhisattva stand in opposition to each other in the two Buddhisms.

5. Pragmatism

The commitment to pragmatism seems to be the one common characteristic that runs through both Hīnayāna and Mahāyāna Buddhism. The test of truth in all spheres of Buddhist philosophy would seem, in the end, to come down to one thing and one thing only, viz., successful activity, i.e. activity that leads to liberation. We have noted this practical aspect of Buddhism from the beginning of this book and I shall reserve further comment on it until we come to the Conclusion, below.

6. Nirvāṇa and Heaven

The commitments to nirvāṇa and heaven as the ultimate and penultimate goals, respectively, would seem to differ for the two Buddhisms. They differ, however, only in terms of emphasis. Ultimately and finally all Buddhists hold that nirvāṇa is the goal being sought. But while Mahāyāna agrees with this contention it places the greater emphasis upon the attainment of heaven and becoming a Bodhisattva, feeling that nirvāṇa is not the proper and final end until all beings have been raised out of saṁsāra into heaven. For Mahāyāna, heaven becomes the place to train for nirvāṇa, a place where the Gods, the Buddhas and the Bodhisattvas can instruct the devotee in the art of making the leap into nirvāṇa. The commitment to heaven, therefore, would appear to follow from, and to be consistent with, the previous commitments to the Bodhisattva ideal, Buddhacentrism, theism, and the general supernaturalism that appears to pervade Mahāyāna. The goal of nirvāṇa in Hīnayāna appears to follow from and to be consistent with their previous commitments to the arhat ideal, anthropocentrism, atheism and naturalism, and it stands, then, in rather sharp contrast to the heaven-directed activities of Mahāyāna.

7. Meditation and Bhakti

The commitments to meditation and bhakti as the means or ways to nirvāṇa and heaven, respectively, would seem to differ for the two Buddhisms. Hīnayāna viewed nirvāṇa and arhatship as possible, primarily within the confines of the Saṅgha, for only in the Saṅgha could the way to nirvāṇa be followed. That way, of course, was meditation. The noble eightfold path taught that meditation was the way to enlightenment and the Saṅgha provided the necessary conditions for the pratice of meditation. But it was the exclusivity of the Saṅgha and the exclusivity of meditation as the chief way to enlightenment that probably led to the dissatisfaction among reformers and heretics, alike, and which led, in turn, to heresy, to schism and, eventually, to Mahāyāna.

With Mahāyāna and its doctrine of the Bodhisattva as the holder of the keys to the kingdom of heaven, meditation gave way to bhakti, i.e. dedication to one's life to, and loving devotion for, a Bodhisattva. The doctrines of vicarious atonement and the storehouse of merit increased the significance of bhakti as the chief way of tapping the good karma stored by the numerous Buddhas and Bodhisattvas of the past; these beings had willingly and compassionately developed, and then given, that karma in order that others might benefit from their merit-making acts.

Mahāyāna also made use of means other than bhakti to gain heaven, e.g., the devotee's own good deeds; but once the devotee had gained heaven the process of seeking nirvāṇa began in earnest. Then prajñā, or intuitive knowledge, was brought into play on the heavenly plane and under the guidance and instruction of the heavenly teachers, the Gods, the Buddhas and the Bodhisattvas, until nirvāṇa was reached. Prajñā was also used on the earthly plane; thus bhakti was not the only way for the Mahāyāna Buddhists to transcend worldly sorrows and anxiety.

At all events, the ways out of suffering for the Hīnayāna and Mahāyāna Buddhists differ both in the very nature of the means employed, viz., saṅghaic (monastic) meditation versus extra-saṅghaic (secular) devotionalism and intuitive knowledge, as well as in the goals sought, viz., nirvāṇa and heaven.

8. Anātmavāda and Ātmavāda

The views on the nature of the self and its identity through time would seem to differ for the two Buddhisms. Of the two, Hīnayāna is perhaps the most boldly consistent with its doctrine of anātmavāda which follows logically from the assumption of the doctrine of the momentariness of all dharmas. But logical consistency is not sufficient for the Mahāyāna and we find early in the history of Buddhism a persistent striving to make the person into either a semi-permanent self or a permanent Self. It was this rather common-sensical, and rather human, urge to maintain one's self in existence which went on to bolster the self-doctrine of Mahāyāna. The consequence of this fight between logic, on the one hand, and a rather common human urge, on the other, points up one of the more outstanding differences between Hīnayāna and Mahāyāna.

9. Reincarnation and Transmigration

The two views on the nature of saṁsara would also seem to differ for the two Buddhisms. The reincarnation doctrine of Hīnayāna holds that no thing, substance or person, moves from one physical body to another when the body dies or disintegrates, and this doctrine follows logically, once again, from their view of the nature of the self. Since nothing transmigrates, we are not speaking about a substance or stuff here but rather a process, an ongoing, ever-changing flow of moments of energy that make up what we conventionally call a "self."

This doctrine stands in sharp contrast to the Mahāyāna self which upholds a substance view of the person, viz., a being rather than a process, identical and identifiable through time, who suffers on earth, who gains heaven and who eventually, in nirvāṇa, enjoys eternal and indescribable bliss for all eternity (on one interpretation) or who, eventually, in nirvāṇa is absorbed unto the Absolute or the Void or Mind (on another interpretation). Again, each view or doctrine about rebirth follows from the two differing views about the self and the goals and means to which that self is dedicated within Hīnayāna and Mahāyāna.

10. The Philosophies of Realism and the Philosophies of Absolutism

The philosophc views on the nature of the world, physical objects, the self and the universe would seem to differ for the two Buddhisms. The Hīnayāna schools of Sarvāstivāda, direct realism, and Sautrāntika, indirect realism, had both held to the common view that objects or processes exist outside the mind and independently of that mind. But they differed in their doctrines of perception regarding what the mind can actually know about those independently existing extra-mental objects: Sarvāstivāda held that what seems apparent to consciousness is identical with what is outside that consciousness; while Sautrāntika held that what seems apparent to consciousness is not identical with what actually is, but is only like, or similar to, what actually exists.

The Mahāyāna schools of Mādhyamika (or Śūnyavāda) and Yogācāra (or Vijñānavāda), on the contrary, held that the perceptual and metaphysical realisms of Hīnayāna were both quite mistaken: Śūnyavāda held that reality is not characterizable at all and that the only thing that we can say about the real is that it is a void, a no-thing; while Yogācāra held that reality is characterizable as mental, as ideas in one Mind, as claimed by absolute idealism, or in many minds, as claimed by "subjective" or phenomenalistic idealism. Thus, for Yogācāra, perceptual and metaphysical idealism become the dominant philosophic views, while for Śūnyavāda we have a rejection of all philosophic views.

The philosophic views about reality held by each Buddhism are consistent, as a little attention will show, with the other nine characteristics or "tendencies", as we have called them, of Hīnayāna and Mahāyāna. And this ends our summary of the tendencies of, and the apparent differences between, Hīnayāna and Mahāyāna Buddhism.[360]

We turn, finally, to the conclusion of this study of Buddhist thought. In that conclusion I want to call brief attention to another late philosophic school that we have neglected to mention in this work, viz., the Mahāyāna school of the Buddhist Logicians. The Buddhist Logicians in their epistemology have underscored and accentuated one of the themes with which we have been dealing since the myth of the future Buddha first started us on our long journey into Buddhist thought, viz., the pragmatic theme of useful fictions. In order to bring together the many common elements of this theme it will help us to see how the Logicians in their epistemology made use of this doctrine that we have found so often in our own investigations.

III. CONCLUSION

Swami Vivekananda, the 19th century Bengali missionary of Hinduism and foremost disciple of the Hindu mystic and saint, Ramakrishna, speaking to the World Parliament of Religions in Chicago in 1893, said in defense of the practice of "idol worship":

> If a man can realize his divine nature with the help of an image, would it be right to call that a sin? Nor even when he has passed that stage, should he call it an error. To the Hindu, man is not traveling from error to truth, but from truth to truth, from lower to higher truth.[361]

In this study of Buddhist thought we have witnessed many such useful images or idols at work within the Buddhist tradition. They served as ladders and vehicles that enable the devotee to attain certain goals or ends that constitute the Buddhist version of man's "realizing his divine nature."

The Buddhist's useful images included such diverse items as the myth of the future Buddha[362], pratītyasamutpāda[363], general or abstract words[364], the concept of the self[365], heaven[366], the law of karma[367], the Mādhyamika doctrine that saṁsāra is not different from nirvāṇa[368], the Mādhyamika concept of śūnya[369], the Buddha's upāya[370], his secret intentions or inner meanings[371], and, finally, philosophy, itself, interpreted as myth.[372] We referred to these concepts collectively as "useful and convenient means or fictions", and they were often treated as "useful and effective pedagogical instruments" (Heinrich Zimmer), as "theories which are undemonstratable but useful in interpreting experience" (Eliot Deutsch)[373], and as "useful for the attainment of the goal of nirvāṇa" (K.N. Jayatilleke).[374]

But to call them "fictions" or even "undemonstratable" does not really do justice to what is actually going on in the employment of such idols or images. In other words, there is nothing ultimately "fictional" or "undemonstratable" about such useful images when they are employed successfully. To refer to them as "fictions" (or as "sins" or "errors" following Vivekananda) is inappropriate; for if the image is employed successfully to attain heaven, or to attain nirvāṇa then there is nothing fictional about it.

The two principal theories of truth at work throughout Buddhism are both versions of the pragmatic theory of truth. The first takes into account all of the useful images and idols mentioned previously, and it is a theory that we referred to as the theory of useful or skillful means.[375] That theory stated that any means to an end is right, true or useful (depending on the nature of the means) if and only if it leads to liberation.

The second theory at work throughout Buddhism is, of course, the mythic theory of truth which stated that a story, legend or account is true if and only if the recitation or the hearing or the reading of the story, legend or account leads to metaphysical realization or enlightenment.[376]

Subsequently, following our discussion of Mādhyamika, we suggested that philosophy, itself, could be included as one of the useful means that could lead to liberation. In other words, a philosophy, i.e. a philosophic activity, philosophic argument, philosophic history of a philosophic view is right or true if and only if it leads to liberation. Put more elegantly, and somewhat shortened, the hypothesis we advanced would state that a philosophic view, V, is right or true for a person, P, if and only if P understands V and V leads P to liberation. Thus philosophy becomes a yoga leading to liberation.

That this seems to be what Buddhism is suggesting is made plain among a group of Buddhist philosophers who lived from the 4th century C.E. to the 9th century C.E., philosophers known collectively as "the Buddhist Logicians." These Logicians were, as their name implies, concerned with the nature of inference and with the fallacies that resulted from its misuse. This logical concern was applied to the very important activity of discovering knowledge in order that human conduct might be guided by that knowledge.

Dharmakīrti, one of the 7th century leaders of this school, has stated in the opening lines of his famous *Nyāya-Bindu* ("short work on logic"):

> All successful human action is preceded by right knowledge. Therefore, this (knowledge will be here) investigated.[377]

It was important, as the logicians saw it, to get one's rules of inference straight, in order to get one's knowlege straight, in order to get one's conduct straight, and all of this in order to ultimately seek and find liberation. In other words, logic would be necessary to epistemology, epistemology would be necessary to ethics, and both would be necessary to the ultimate goal of all Buddhist thought, viz., nirvāṇa.

Dharmakīrti, like the earlier founder of the school of Buddhist Logic, the philosopher Dignāga (4th century C.E.), was born in South India of brahmin parents sometime in the 6th or 7th century. He was converted to Buddhism and after journeying to Nālandā, the great university town of the ancient world, he studied under a pupil of Vasubandhu's. His interest in logic then carried him to work with a direct pupil of Dignaga's, a man whom he shortly surpassed in logical abilities. He then began his own teaching and writing career until, finally, he died at Kalinga in a monastery that he, himself, had founded, surrounded by his devoted disciples.[378]

Dharmakīrti's famous commentator, the Buddhist Logician Dharmottara (8th-9th century C.E.), explains the above passage from the *Nyāya-Bindu* stating that right knowledge is knowledge which is not contradicted by experience:

> In common life we likewise say that (a man) has spoken truth when he makes us reach the object he has first pointed out. Similarly (we can also say) that knowledge is right when it makes us reach an object it did point to.[379]

In other words, truth and knowledge are useful because human activity is purposeful, and truth and knowledge help us to attain our purposes. The true test of any putative knowledge, then, is that it helps us to attain our purposes. The term the Logicians use as the test for a true judgment is *arthakriyātva*, "the character of doing things", i.e. efficiency:[380] And all this is pragmatism, pure and simple.

Consequently, useful fictions cease to be fictions and become knowledge when they help us to attain our purposes; and if those purposes or desires involve, as they do for all Buddhists, the reduction of bad karma or the increase of good karma, or obtaining a better life in the next birth, or reaching the heavenly worlds of the Buddhas and Bodhisattvas, or becoming a Bodhisattva or a Buddha, or attaining nirvāṇa, then all the "fictions" we have dealt with in this book, from the myth of the future Buddha to philosophy, itself, cease to be fictions and become knowledge or "right" knowledge (samyagjñāna or pramāṇa). The Buddhist Logicians simply made clear what we have been at pains to point to throughout this book.

I don't know whether Swami Vivekananda would approve of all the useful idols and images that we have conjured and catalogued. Indian philosophy in general would approve, however, of our concluding discovery that philosophy, the practice of philosophy, can lead to knowledge of one's "divine" nature. And just as the myth of the future Buddha can incite Buddhists to go off in search of their own higher nature, a search that leads to peace, tranquility and the cessation of anxiety and suffering so also, it would seem, Buddhist philosophy has as its goal that same laudable end.

FOOTNOTES

1. The propitious constellation of Puṣya shone brightly, we are told, proclaiming the birth of the Savior.

2. Following in part the Sanskrit text and translation by E.H. Johnston *The Buddhacarita* (New Delhi: Oriental Books Reprint Corporation, 1972/1936), Part II, pp. 1-23, and the *Nidāna-Kathā* in *Buddhism A Religion of Infinite Compassion* Edited by Clarence H. Hamilton (Indianapolis: The Bobbs-Merrill Company, Inc., 1952), p. 3.

3. Joseph Campbell, *The Hero With A Thousand Faces* (New York: Bollingen Foundation, Inc., Pantheon Books, 1949), p. 3.

4. Heinrich Zimmer recalls one such revelation:

> Some years ago I paid a visit to the Musée Guimet in Paris to see this work of art which the museum had then just acquired. I was already familiar with its myth. And as I stood before it, suddenly there dawned on me an awareness of something which I immediately recognized as characteristic of other Hindu monuments and symbols-a peculiar phenomenon of style-an aesthetic effect which I have encountered nowhere except in certain of the most remarkable and significant Hindu creations. I should like to call it "the phenomenon of the growing, or expanding, form." Heinrich Zimmer, *Myths and Symbols in Indian Art and Civilization*, edited by Joseph Campbell (New York: Bollingen Foundation, Inc., Pantheon Books, 1946), p. 130.

Zimmer continues, focusing on the sculpture, a prodigious liṅgam, or phallus, with a niche carved in its side through which Śiva, the Lord of the liṅgam, is suddenly revealed. The work is significant in its portrayal of Śiva, the Supreme Power of the universe, for it commemorates Śiva's first appearance among the Gods as he emanates from the liṅgam, growing and expanding, filling infinite space with his presence:

> This piece of sculpture might be said not merely to commemorate or signify a mythical event, but actually to exhibit the process of its taking place. In this respect, this piece of sculpture is more like a motion picture than a painting. (*Ibid.*, p. 131)

Zimmer later concludes by commenting in general on the relation of Indian art to myth and philosophy:

> Indian symbols of art voice the same truth as Indian philosophy and myth. They are signals along the way of the same pilgrim's progress, directing

human energies to the same goal of transmutation. Our task, therefore, as students of Indian myth and symbol, is to understand the abstract conception of India's philosophical doctrines as a kind of intellectual commentary on what stands crystallized and unfolded in the figures and patterns of symbolism and art, and conversely, to read the symbols as the pictorial script of India's ultimately changeless wisdom. (*Ibid*, pp. 195-96)

5. The sources for the life of Gautama Siddhārtha Śākyamuni, called "the Buddha", are the Pāli accounts: the Introduction to the *Jātaka Stories* (I. 49- I. 76); the *Mahāvagga* I; the *Mahā-Parinibbāna Sutta* (V and VI) of the *Digha-Nikāya*; the *Aṅguttara-Nikāya I*; the *Digha-Nikāya XIV* for the myth of the four signs; and the *Majjhima-Nikāya XXVI* for the myth of the Great Renunciation. In addition there are the later Sanskrit accounts: The *Mahāvastu* ("the great story"), the *Lalitavistara* ("the account of the leisure" of the future Buddha), the life of Buddha from his decision to be born into the world down to his first sermon; the *Adhiniṣkramaṇa Sūtra*, lost in Sanskrit but preserved in a Chinese translation as a continuous story from the Buddha's birth to his ministry; and the *Buddhacarita* of Aśvaghoṣa. See also Edward J. Thomas, *The Life of Buddha as Legend and History* (London: Routledge and Kegan Paul Ltd., 1969/1927), for what may still be the best history in English of the life of Buddha.

6. This date is arrived at by using three fairly reliable assumptions: That Buddha lived for eighty years; that the great Indian emperor, Aśoka, was crowned in 265 B.C.E.; that a Ceylonese text is accurate when it says that Aśoka's coronation took place 218 years after Buddha's death. Some simple arithmetic then gives us 563-483 B.C.E. as the most likely dates for Buddha's life. However, Hīnayāna Buddhism generally adopts 624-544 B.C.E. in this matter.

7. And yet it has been suggested that we now possess the technology to live from womb to tomb without ever experiencing the pangs of suffering. Consider the following remarks by J.W.N. Sullivan, a distinguished scientist and musicologist, writing more than half a century ago:

   To the modern mind suffering is essentially remediable. Suffering is primarily due to physical and moral maladjustment, and with the spread of science and correct social theories, we shall be able to abolish it. For an increasing number of people suffering is already practically abolished.

They may go through life without meeting one problem they cannot evade until they reach their death bed.... J.W.N. Sullivan, *Beethoven, His Spiritual Development* (New York, Vintage Books, 1927), p. 43.

Sullivan, in his sanguine view of the future, overlooks the very point which the myth of the four signs highlights: The role that anxiety plays in our understanding of suffering. Recall that Gautama does not feel the suffering of age, sickness or death. How could he? He is young (though 29 may have been more like middle age in 534 B.C.E.), healthy and very much alive. But he is able, as we all are, to feel anxiety; and were Sullivan to suggest to us that soma or bromides could always cure anxiety, we reply that anxiety must first appear in some fashion or other in order that one knows when to take these drugs. That "duḥkha", anxiety, is always with you, is the great truth that Gautama learned.

8. Aśvaghosa: *Buddhacarita* in *Buddhist Scriptures*, Selected and Translated by Edward Conze (Penguin Books, 1959), p. 39.

9. It is more or less in the tradition of the āśrama dharma, the Hindu law of the stages, *āśramas*, of life. Ideally, these āśramas function somewhat as follows: The span of a human life is taken to be 100 years in length. These years are divided into approximately four 25 year segments and these four segments are the āśramas or "stages" to be passed through as a human being travels from birth to death. The passage through these stages, however, is designed only for those who are the twice-born, or dvija, in the Hindu varṇa, or vocational, system. Thus only brahmins (the priests and teachers of the *Vedas*), kṣatriyas (the warriors and political rulers) and vaiśyas (the merchants and farmers) of the varṇa system are eligible to trod the āśrama path, while śūdras (the servants and serving class) and outcastes and untouchables are excluded from this path.

10. See A.L. Herman, *An Introduction to Indian Thought* (Englewood Cliffs, NJ: Prentice-Hall, Inc., 1976), pp. 218-19.

11. However, there is another and quite different story in which Buddha tells his disciples:

> Then I brethren...when I was a young lad, a black-haired stripling, endowed with happy youth, in the first flush of manhood, against my mother's and father's wish, who lamented with tearful eyes, I had the hair of head and face shaved off, I donned the saffron robes and I went forth from my home to the homeless life.(*Majjhima-Nikāya* 1.163 in *Some*

Sayings of the Buddha According to the Pāli Canon Translated by F.L. Woodward. Oxford University Press, 1973/1925, p. 3).

Just where the saffron of the saffron robes came from is not clear.

12. Paul Gauguin (1848-1903) was a French painter who deserted his wife, family and commercial affairs to lead a bohemian-hippie life in Paris as an artist before charging off to the South Seas, Tahiti, romance and immortality as one of the world's great *artistes* and, ultimately, as the hero of W. Somerset Maugham's picaresque novel, *The Moon and Sixpence.*

13. Cf. Sir Mortimer Wheeler, *Civilizations of the Indus Valley and Beyond* (New York: McGraw-Hill, 1966); and A.L. Herman, *Indian Thought, Op. Cit.,* pp. 9-19.

14. T.R.V. Murti is bolder than most of the older and more conservative Buddhologists (see, for example, T.W. Rhys Davids, *Buddhist India* (New Delhi: Motilal Banarsidass, 1971/1902), pp. 162-63). Murti comments: "Buddha of the Nikāyas [the Canonical or orthodox texts of later Hīnayāna Buddhism] appears to be well acquainted with all the philosophical systems and trends of thought current before and during his time. He rejects them because they are at variance with the path of perfection elaborated by him." T.R.V. Murti, *The Central Philosophy of Buddhism* (London: Unwin Paperbacks, 1980/1955), p. 30. Whether the sophisticated Buddha of the *Nikāyas* can be identified with the young Gautama of some three hundred years earlier is conjectural. But a word of caution. At least one other modern Buddhologist would be reluctant to accept Murti's and our sanguine assumption regarding Buddha's philosophic awareness of traditions and texts before his time; especially is this the case with regard to the *Upaniṣads* whose secret teachings would have made them unavailable to the uninitiated. Like Rhys Davids before him, Edward Conze observes:

> But it should never be overlooked that the *Upaniṣads* were a secret doctrine taught to groups of pupils who "sat near" their teacher, and there is no real reason to believe that the early Buddhists were in contact with just these groups of persons who were instructed in the Vedānta. Edward Conze, *Further Buddhist Studies.* (Oxford: Bruno Cassirer, 1975, p. 155).

My only comment is this: Gautama did not live in a philosophic vacuum. He had a quick and inquiring mind, as evidenced by his Renunciation. He had teachers and companions who shared his concerns and views. It is difficult to believe that even these "secret teachings" would have escaped him.

15. Franklin Edgerton, *The Bhagavad Gītā* (New York: Harper Torchbooks, 1964), p. 111. See also the discussion of the role that the *Brāhmaṇa* texts played in the development of the word "Brahman" from "spell" or "holy word" to "holy Power" in Arthur Berriedale Keith's *The Philosophy and Religion of the Veda and Upanishads,* Two Volumes (Delhi: Motilal Banarsidass, 1970/1925); Vol. II, pp. 442-54. Keith comments:

    It is a very easy step from the conception of the Brahman as the prayer, which brings into operation the activity of the gods, or as the spell which is the cause of results aimed at by men...to develop the use of the term to cover the idea of holy power generally, and this rendering is applicable in many passages of the Brahmanas.... (p. 446)

16. *Bṛhadāraṇyaka Upaniṣad* II. 3.1 Author's translation of all Śanskrit works unless otherwise specified .

17. *Muṇḍaka Upaniṣad* I. 1. 4-7.

18. It is important to remember that the early Buddhist, Pāli Canon, or scriptures, never mention Brahman nor the way of reaching Brahman nor becoming one with Brahman. See Edward J. Thomas, *The History of Buddhist Thought* (London: Routledge & Kegan Paul Ltd., 1971/1933), p. 87. But while the Pāli *Tripiṭaka* is silent on these matters, it will be left to the Sanskrit Mahāyāna tradition to rediscover what, I am assuming, Gautama Buddha, himself, may have known, viz., what the Upaniṣadic ṛṣis believed.

19. *Bṛhadāraṇyaka Upaniṣad* IV. 4.5.

20. *Chāndogya Upaniṣad* V. 10.7.

21. The principle or doctrine of pratītyasamutpāda, the law of dependent origination, can be seen, in part, as a law of moral causation, i.e. as the law of karma, reflected through Buddhist categories.

22. A.L. Herman, *Indian Thought, Op. Cit,* pp. 142 ff. for a discussion of the *Gītā's* place in Hinduism.

23. The following table might help to summarize the view that we have been discussing above, viz., that religions are social institutions established to solve certain kinds of human problems. We indicate the two religions, together with the

five elements which are identifiable in any religion, viz., the human problem that the religion attempts to solve, the chief cause of that problem, the nature of the solution to the problem, the way (or ways) adopted to reach that solution, and finally, the law or ordering principle that guarantees that these ways will be effective.

Table I: The Religions of the *Ṛg Veda* and the *Upaniṣads*

	Ṛg Veda	*Upanisads*
Problem	Fear of not getting happiness in this life or the next	Saṁsāra
Cause	Lack of divine aid or power	Avidyā and confusing māyā with reality
Solution	Getting the goods of this world and getting into heaven	Mokṣa
Way	Ritual Sacrifice	Jñāna yoga
Ordering Principle	Ṛta	Law of karma

24. By "early Buddhism" here I mean the Buddhism probably espoused by Gautama Buddha and by Hīnayāna or Southern Buddhism. The rejection of these three concepts will not be as clear with later Mahāyāna Buddhism.

25. *Majjhima-Nikāya* I. 165 in *Buddhism in Translations* by Henry Clarke Warren (New York: Antheneum, 1963/1896), p. 336.

26. "Nothingness" is the seventh of the eight attainments of later Buddhist meditation. See Edward J. Thomas, *The Life of Buddha, Op. Cit.*, pp. 62-63 for a discussion of Gautama's teachers and their levels of attainment. Thomas says of the goals of "nothingness" and "neither consciousness nor non-consciousness", the seventh and eighth attainments of later Buddhism, and here the goals of Āḷāra Kālāma and Uddaka: "The compiler is using the only terms he knew to express the imperfect efforts of Buddha's predecessors." p. 184.

Curiously enough, T.R.V. Murti says of these two teachers of Gautama: "The teachers of Buddha, Āḷāra Kālāma and Uddaka Ramaputta, were Sāṁkhya philosophers." T.R.V. Murti, *Op. Cit.*, p. 60.

27. See Edward J. Thomas, *The Life of Buddha, Op. Cit.*, pp. 113 ff., for the legends connected with the twenty years of wandering and preaching following enlightenment.

28. Debiprasad Chattopadhyaya, *Lokāyata, A Study in Ancient Indian Materialism* (New Delhi: People's Publishing House, 1959), p. 486. The *Sandaka Sutta* calls the six systems "abrahamacariya" or "immoral (unchaste)" systems.

29. The sources from which our knowledge of the six heretics comes are: *The Teachings of the Six Heretics* by Claus Vogel (Wiesbaden:Kommissionsverlag Franz Steiner GMBH, 1970) which contains a translation from two Tibetan and Chinese sources of the teachings. The original Sanskrit versions of these teachings existed in three separate groups: First, the *Pravrajyāvastu* of the *Mūlasarvāstivāda Vinayavastu* whose Sanskrit is now lost, but which still exists in Tibetan and Chinese translations; second, the *Saṁghabhedavastu* of the same *Mūlasarvāstivāda Vinayavastu* which exists in sizable portions in the original Sanskrit and in Tibetan and Chinese translations, as well; finally, Tibetan and Chinese translations of the *Mūlasarvāstivāda Vinayavibhanga*, the latter Sanskrit text being completely lost. In addition to these sources there is also the Pāli source which contains the longest and most picturesque account of the six heretics, *Sāmaññaphala Sutta* or "the discourse (sutta) on the results (phala) of becoming a monk (samana)" of the *Digha-Nikāya* I. 47. The teachings of the first four heretics are also given in the *Majjhima-Nikāya* I. 513.

29. Our principal source for the Pāli account will be T.W. Rhys Davids, *Dialogues of the Buddha*, Three Volumes (London 1899-1921), Vol. I, pp. 69-95 which contains the *Sāmaññaphala Sutta*.

30. T.W. Rhys-Davids, *Op. Cit.*, Volume I, p. 66.

31. For the account of the enlightenment and the sources see especially Edward J. Thomas, *The Life of Buddha, Op. Cit.*, pp. 61-80.

32. See *Saṁyutta-Nikaya* V. 420 in Edward J. Thomas, *The Life of Buddha, Op. Cit.*, pp. 87-88; and *Majjhima-Nikāya* iii, 248-52 in *Further Dialogues of the Buddha*, II, translated by Lord Chalmers, *Sacred Books of the Buddhists*, VI (London: Oxford University Press, 1927), pp. 296-99, both quoted in *A Source Book in Indian Philosophy*, edited by Sarvepalli Radhakrishnan and Charles A. Moore (Princeton University Press, 1957), pp. 274-78.

33. In reality, there are two things here because there are two truths in this epigraph: There is suffering, is one; and there is release from suffering, is the second.

34. Edward J. Thomas, *The Life of Buddha, Op. Cit.*, p. 87. Thomas is translating throughout from the 'Sutta of Turning the Wheel of the Doctrine', *Samyutta-Nikāya* V. 420, which agrees in all essentials with *Lalita-Vistara* 540 (416) and the *Mahāvastu* iii 330, the Sanskrit versions of the same story. Thomas translates duḥkha or dukka as "painful", which I have rendered as "suffering."

35. See above p. 35 and footnote 23 and our discussion of religion as a social institution.

36. Edward J. Thomas, *The Life of the Buddha, Op. Cit.*, p. 87.

37. *Ibid.*

38. See *Matthew* 11:28 and *Jeremiah* 31:25.

39. Edward J. Thomas, *The Life of the Buddha, Op. Cit.*, p. 87.

40. *Further Dialogues of the Buddha*, II, translated by Lord Chalmers, in *A Source Book in Indian Philosophy, Op. Cit.*, pp. 277-78. The four ecstasies, or trances, constitute stages or levels of awakening leading to nirvāṇa. The first trance or dhyāna (Pāli jhāna) entails detachment from sensual craving, and being filled with enthusiasm, pleasure and tranquility; the second trance entails detachment from the craving for the first trance and discursive thought, and being filled with zest, enthusiasm, pleasure and tranquility; the third trance entails detachment from craving for the second trance, and being filled with pleasure, dispassion and equanimity, and being mindful and aware; the fourth trance entails detachment from craving for the third trance, being freed from all opposites such as pleasure and pain, the ups and the downs, and being filled with equanimity and full awareness. The fourth trance leads to the six superknowledges, viz., 1. magic powers; for example, levitation, becoming invisible, and walking on water; 2. the divine ear, enabling one to hear all human and heavenly sounds at whatever distance; 3. the knowledge of the thoughts of others; 4. the memory of one's former lives (acquired during Buddha's first watch of the night); 5. the divine eye enabling one to know of the past and future births and deaths of all being according to their karmic conditions (acquired during the second watch at midnight); 6. the final extinction of the āsravas (pains or afflictions), viz., sensual desire, the desire for future

existence, wrong views and ignorance (acquired during the third watch of the night). Finally, with dawn, the fourth watch, there was nirvāṇa. For more on the jhānas, dhyānas and trances see Stephen Beyer, *The Buddhist Experience, Sources and Interpretation* (Belmont, California: Dickenson Publishing Company, Inc., 1974), pp. 85-89, 107-08; Richard H. Robinson and Willard L. Johnson, *The Buddhist Religion, A Historical Introduction*, Second Edition (Belmont, California: Dickenson Publishing Company, Inc., 1977), pp. 28-29. See below pp.147-50 for a discussion of meditation and its place in Hīnayāna Buddhism.

41. Ananda K. Coomaraswamy puts the matter most succinctly when he observes:

> The way of the Buddha is not, indeed, concerned directly with the order of the world, for it calls on higher men to leave the market-place. Ananda K. Coomaraswamy, *Buddha and the Gospel of Buddhism* (New York: G.P. Putnam's Sons, 1916), p. v.

Coomaraswamy places the matter even more directly when he states in another context:

> The philosophy of the Upanishads, the psychology of Buddhism, indeed, were originally meant only for those who had left behind them the life of a householder, and were thus in their immediate application anti-social. "Yakṣas", in Smithsonian Miscellaneous Collections, LXXX, No. 6 (Washington, DC: Smithsonian Institute, 1928). p. 1.

42. Of course, living in a monastery constitutes "living in a world", i.e. a monastic world, wherein social rules resting on moral precepts are bound to be necessary. A true follower of the noble three fold path would probably have to be a non-social hermit or anchorite.

43. See below, pp. 263-269, the discussion regarding the Bodhisattva who puts aside his or her religious duty to achieve nirvāṇa in order to exercise the ethical norm of compassion to all beings. See also the criticism below, pp. 144-47, of the arhat ideal with its putative essential selfishness and egoism as the arhat pursues his religious duty to the apparent exclusion of the ethical norm.

44. From *samutpāda*, "arising", and *prati + i + ya*, "after getting", i.e. literally "an arising after getting"; also *pratītya* "dependent", *sam* "together", *utpāda* "to come into existence", i.e. literally "to come into dependent existence together", i.e. interdependent origination or causation. Either etymology is instructive.

45. Pratītyasamutpāda thus enables one to explain how ignorance causes suffering: Because ignorance causes karma which causes consciousness...which causes birth which causes suffering and despair; and it enables one to explain how suffering causes ignorance. Thus the links in the chain are interdependent, really, for the chain of causation is cyclical not linear.

46. The triadic nature of pratītyasamutpāda is best expressed by the familiar formula: "When this exists, that occurs; when this does not exist, that does not exist; when this is destroyed, that is destroyed."

47. But see below fn. 87. Just how important any set of propositions is to being or defining a Buddhist as opposed to achieving enlightenment is moot. Perhaps the following will help: Surely, Buddhists differ from Christians by virtue of their adherence to some set of propositions called "dogmas." So Buddhism has dogmas. But believing in or adherence to these propositions is not necessary to achieving nirvāṇa. So Buddhism has no dogmas.

48. For a discussion and summary of all the "useful or convenient fictions" that we are going to find at work in Buddhism see below p. 361.

49. A. L. Herman, *Indian Thought, Op. Cit.*, pp. 151-52.

50. See below pp. 265-66 for a discussion of bondage as ignorance in Mahāyāna Buddhism.

51. Accounts differ as to whether Yasa's mother and his former wife were the first female lay disciples or not. Thus compare:

> The first two women to become lay disciples were the mother and former wife of Yasa, at whose house Buddha accepted a meal. Edward J. Thomas, *The Life of Buddha, Op. Cit.*, p. 90.

with:

> Buddha also allowed Sujātā, the woman who had offered him food when he abandoned his austerities, to take refuge in him, thus becoming the first female lay disciple *(upāsikā)*. *Buddhism: A Modern Perspective*, Edited by Charles S. Prebish (The Pennsylvania State University Press, 1975), p. 13.

52. See Edward J. Thomas, *The Life of Buddha, Op. Cit.*, pp. 81-123 for these and other details.

53. Buddha spent the last twenty-five rainy seasons out of his forty-five year ministry in the city of Śrāvastī. See *Buddhism: A Modern Perspective, Op. Cit.*, p. 14.

54. Edward J. Thomas, *The Life of Buddha, Op. Cit.*, p. 91.

55. See below pp. 143-44 for a discussion of the Fire Sermon.

56. See Charles S. Prebish in *Buddhism: A Modern Perspective, Op. Cit.*, p. 16.

57. See *Mahāvastu* ii.234 for the story of the aphrodisiac sent to the Buddha and the consequences.

58. *Cullavagga* X. 1:3-4 in *Buddhism in Translations, Op. Cit.*, p. 447. Winternitz draws attention to an even harder misogynist strain in Buddha's temperament as he quotes from the *Aṅguttara-Nikāya* wherein Buddha replies to Ānanda's question, "What is the reason, Lord, (that) women have no place in the public assembly, pursue no business, and do not earn their livelihood by some (independent) profession?":

> (Hot-tempered), Ānanda, is womankind; jealous, Ānanda, is womankind; envious, Ānanda, is womankind; stupid, Ānanda, is womankind. That, Ānanda, is the cause why women have no seat in the public assembly, pursue no business, and do not earn their livelihood by some (independent) profession. M. Winternitz, *A History of Indian Literature*, Two Volumes (New York: Russell & Russell, 1971/1933), Vol. II, p. 64. Other great religions fare no better in their attitudes towards women. See A. L. Herman, *Indian Thought, Op. Cit.*, pp. 92-97.

59. Edward J. Thomas, *The Life of Buddha, Op. Cit.*, p. 111.

60. *Ibid.*, p. 146.

61. See *Buddhism: A Modern Perspective, Op. Cit.*, p. 40. One ought to consider carefully what is lost when a scripture is written down and what is protected when the oral tradition is maintained. The Druids, the ancient Celtic priests, were well aware of the implications of the introduction of writing. Julius Caesar reports of them:

> The Druids are by custom not present during war nor do they pay taxes; indeed, they have immunity from military service and exemption from all public duties. Inspired by such rewards many persons assemble together for instruction from the

> Druids, sent there by parents and kin. There they are said to learn by heart a great number of sacred verses. And some remain thus in study for 20 years. Nor do the Druids regard it as right to commit these verses to writing, while in other matters, in private and public business, they use the Greek script. I think that they have established this oral tradition for two reasons: They do not wish the sacred discipline to be carried off by the masses, and they do not wish those who do learn to trust more to writing than to memory. For it usually happens to very many when they have the support of writing that they neglect both the diligence of thorough learning and the cultivation of their memories. (J. Caesar, *De Bello Gallico* VI. 14, translated by Arthur Herman, Jr.).

A sound insight but a bit late to be of much use in these super-literate days of torrential writing and blitzkrieg publishing.

62. Actually, some eight places of pilgrimage have been identified by Buddhists: 1. Lumbini, Buddha's birthplace, in the modern village of Rummindei in Nepal; 2. Buddhagaya, near modern Gaya where Buddha achieved nirvāṇa under the Bodhi tree; it is the most famous and important pilgrimage site of all the eight; 3. Sarnath, near Banaras, where Buddha gave his first sermon, the first turning of the wheel of the law; 4. Kusinārā, near Kasia just east of Gorakhpur, where Buddha died; 5. Rājagṛha, the modern Rajgir, seventy miles from Patna where Buddha's first monastery stood; 6. Nalanda, eight miles from Rajgir, the birthplace of Sariputta and Moggallana, two of Buddha's greatest disciples; 7. Śravasti, where Buddha spent twenty-four rainy seasons; 8. Sanchi, which enshrines the relics of the two disciples mentioned above.

63. *Mahā-Parinibbāna Sutta* of the *Digha-Nikāya* in *Buddhism in Translations, Op. Cit.*, p. 109.

64. The Pāli account of the first two Councils is contained in chapters XI and XII of the *Cullavagga* of the *Vinaya Piṭaka (Sacred Books of the East*, Vol. XX, pp. 409 ff). There has been much scholarly debate as to whether these first Councils did in fact meet at all. I see no good reasons to deny that such Councils did occur, and since we are more concerned with what Buddhists believed happened than what in fact did happen, we shall assume their historical occurrence and get on with the philosophic details of the Councils. The one exception to common Buddhist belief that might be made

is in drawing attention to the second Second Buddhist Council. Modern scholarship seems to leave no doubt now that there was such a Council. As early as 1912 Moriz Winterniz indicated the probable existence of such a fourth Council among the traditional three of early Buddhism:

> As a matter of fact, it is probable that even more than three councils were held. Singhalese and North Indian records of a "great council" (Mahāsangīti) which is said to have led to the schism of the Mahāsaṅgītikas or Mahāsaṅghikas would seem to indicate that the council of the orthodox Buddhists at Pataliputra was preceded by a great assembly of the schismatics. (M. Winternitz, *Op. Cit.*, p. 7)

Sources for this second Second Buddhist Council are from the *Mahāprajñāpāramitā Śāstra*, probably by Nāgārjuna and the *Samayabhedoparacanacakra* of Vasumitra, among others. (See *Buddhism: A Modern Perspective, Op. Cit.*, pp. 21-22); sources for our Third Buddhist Council are the Pali texts, *Dīpavaṁsa, Mahāvaṁsa, Mahābodhivaṁsa* and *Samantapāsadikā. (Ibid.)*

65. See the old but good account in L. De La Vallée Poussin, "The Buddhist Councils," *The Indian Antiquary*, Volume XXXVII, 1908, p. 2; also for the first, second and third Councils see Edward J. Thomas, *The History of Buddhist Thought, Op. Cit.*, pp. 27-41; for the second Second Buddhist Council see Charles S. Prebish, "Buddhist Councils and Divisions in the Order" in *Buddhism: A Modern Perspective, Op. Cit.*, pp. 21-28; and Charles Prebish, "A Review of Scholarship on the Buddhist Councils," *The Journal of Asian Studies*, 33, 2 (February 1974), pp. 239-54.

66. Ānanda's faults, for which he was officially censured, probably included the following: all but the first must seem trivial, if not downright silly:
    1. Not having informed himself concerning the nature of the lesser and minor precepts.
    2. Having stepped upon Buddha's robe during the rainy season when wishing to sew it.
    3. Having allowed Buddha's body to be visited by women who then profaned it with their tears.
    4. Not encouraging Buddha to go on living as he lay dying.
    5. Not having given Buddha something to drink at one time in spite of Buddha's thrice-repeated request for a drink.
    6. Having obtained from Buddha the admission of women to the order. Quoted in part by L. De La

Vallée Poussin, "The Buddhist Councils," *The Indian Antiquary, Op. Cit.*, p. 4.

67. *Saṅgha*, "council", is from *sanghiti*, "a chanting together."

68. *Buddhism in Translations, Op. Cit.*, pp. 302-03.

69. See Edward J. Thomas, *The Life of Buddha, Op. Cit.*, pp. 257-75, and Edward J. Thomas, *The History of Buddhist Thought, Op. Cit.*, pp. 265-74 for two general summaries of the five *Nikāyas*. Also see M. Winternitz, *Op. Cit.*, pp. 34-165 for a more complete discussion of each of the *Nikāyas* and their contents.

70. *Digha-Nikāya* II. 156 in Edward Conze, *Buddhism: Its Essence and Development* (Harper Torchbooks, 1959), p. 16.

71. *Majjhima-Nikāya* 130, in *Buddhist Scriptures*, translated by Edward Conze, *Op. Cit.*, pp. 224-25.

72. *Devattā-Saṁyutta* 1.2.9 of the *Samyutta-Nikāya* in M. Winternitz, *Op. Cit.*, p. 57 with a little smoothing out on our part of Mrs. Rhys Davids' translation.

73. *Aṅguttara-Nikāya* III. 129 in M. Winternitz, *Op. Cit.*, p. 63.

74. *Udāna* vi. 4 of the *Khuddaka-Nikāya* in M. Winternitz, *Op. Cit.*, pp. 87-88.

75. See Edward J. Thomas, *The Life of Buddha, Op. Cit.*, p. 169.

76. What seems certain is that the first Second Buddhist Council at Vaiśālī was instigated, as Andre Bareau notes, "by the mere quest for gold and money"; while what seems equally certain is that the second Second Buddhist Council at Pāṭaliputra was established to deal with "the first true schism in the saṁgha," brought about by the Mahāsaṅghikas and directed against the Sthaviras. The central unresolved issue left over from the First Council was the issue of "authority" and where it resides. For a fine summary of both Second councils see, once again, Charles S. Prebish, "A Review of Scholarship on the Buddhist Councils," *Op. Cit.*, pp. 246-53.

77. For a brief but excellent discussion of the Mahāsaṅghika heresy see Edward Conze, *A Short History of Buddhism* (London: George Allen & Unwin, 1980), pp. 33-35. The language of the Mahāsaṅghika was probably prakrit, the popularized form of Sanskrit used in towns and villages. The movement flourished in Magadha and Pāṭaliputra, in

particular, and it was the first Buddhist sect to speculate seriously on the nature of the Buddha. Information about this sect is found in the Pāli *Kathāvatthu* (ca. 250 B.C.). One of their own works, written in hybrid Sanskrit, the *Mahāvastu*, survives.

78. See below pp. 229-35 for a discussion of the Bodhisattva.

79. See below pp. 264-71 for a discussion of the ātman doctrine and its denial.

80. The 13th Rock Edict, quoted in A. L. Basham, *The Wonder That Was India* (New York: The Grove Press, Inc., 1959), pp. 53-54. See also *The Edicts of Aśoka*, Edited and Translated by N.A. Nikam and Richard McKeon (The University of Chicago Press, 1959).

81. See A. L. Basham, *Op. Cit.*, pp. 54-55 for a discussion of Aśoka's political, social and cultural influence on 3rd century B.C.E. India.

82. See below p. 271 for a discussion of the self and its place in transmigration; and see below pp. 151-62 for a discussion of the anātman (non-self) doctrine of Hīnayāna Buddhism.

83. See below pp. 187-89 for a discussion of the Hīnayāna Abhidharma tradition which continued in India to 1200 C.E. It gave rise to Sarvāstivāda Buddhism and Theravāda Buddhism and provoked opposition from Sautrāntika Buddhism which tried to remain faithful to the original sūtra tradition in the face of all this new-fangled philosophy, metaphysics and psychology from the Abhidharma. But as Edward Conze has said of this new-fangled philosophy, the philosophy which began to play the implication-intention game (see above pp. 96-97): "The creation of the Abhidharma was one of the greatest achievements of the human intellect." Edward Conze, *A Short History of Buddhism*, *Op. Cit.*, p. 55.

84. M. Winternitz, *Op. Cit.*, p. 170.

85. T.R.V. Murti quotes the Buddha as saying of himself, "I am not a generaliser (dogmatist); I am an analyser (Vibhajjavādi)." *Majjhima-Nikāya* II, *Subha Sutta* 99 in T.R.V. Murti, *Op. Cit.*, p. 3.

86. See Charles S. Prebish, "Major Schools of the Early Buddhists: Theravāda" in *Buddhism: A Modern Perspective, Op. Cit.*, pp. 39-40 for details.

87. I see nothing sinister in the use of the word "dogma" ("established point of view") to describe a fundamental precept, a definitive or authoritative tenet. Many Buddhists like to believe that they are dogma-free. I would suggest that no one is dogma-free, and to believe differently is to believe in at least one dogma.

88. *Aṅguttara-Nikāya* III. 134 in *Buddhism in Translations, Op. Cit.*, p. viii. Two other dogmas are also presented in this same passage, viz., duḥkha, i.e. anxiety or misery, and anātman, i.e. non-self. See below pp. 151-62 for a discussion of anātman.

89. *Digha-Nikāya* II. 198 in *Some Sayings of the Buddha According to the Pāli Canon, Op. Cit.*, p. 126.

90. Plato, *Clatylus* 402 A in G.S. Kirk and J.E. Raven, *The Pre-Socratic Philosophers* (Cambridge University Press, 1963), p. 197.

91. Aristotle, *Physics* θ 3,253b 9, *Ibid.*

92. The metaphor of *becoming* is beautifully stated in the image of the river in the *Chāndogya Upanisad* VI. 10: "All these rivers flow, my son...they flow from the ocean (of Being) and back again." Anitya is reflected in saṁsāra, as well.

93. Aristotle, *Metaphysics* Γ 5,1010a 13, in Kirk and Raven, *Op. Cit.*, p. 197.

94. *Majjhima-Nikāya* III 248 ff. in Lord Chalmers', *Further Dialogues of the Buddha* quoted in *A Sourcebook in Indian Philosophy, Op. Cit.*, p. 276.

95. Two modern Western authors have illustrated the connection between change and misery in a way that, I'm sure, the Buddhists would applaud. The American novelist, Thomas Wolfe, in a remarkably moving passage, comments on man's youth and his fruitless attempt to stay the hand of time and change, beginning,

> Man's youth is a wonderful thing; It is so full of anguish and of magic and he never comes to know it as it is, until it has gone from him forever,

and ending,

> ...we yet know that we can really keep, hold, take and possess forever - nothing. All passes: nothing lasts: the moment that we put our hand upon it it melts away like smoke, is gone forever, and the snake is eating at our heart

again; we see then what we are and what our lives must come to. Thomas Wolfe, *Of Time and the River, A Legend of Man's Hunger in His Youth* (Garden City, New York: The Sun Dial Press, 1944). p. 454.

Alvin Toffler, in an enormously popular book on change and suffering, says in his opening sentence, "This is a book about what happens to people when they are overwhelmed by change." Toffler defines change as "the process by which the future invades our lives." (Alvin Toffler, *Future Shock* (New York: Bantam Books, 1971), p. 1), and he uses the term "future shock" to describe "the shattering stress and disorientation that we induce in individuals by subjecting them to too much change in too short a time." (*Ibid.*, p. 2): Future shock, in other words, is duḥka. Summarizing research on what happens to people subjected to repeated change Toffler states:

> ...those with high life change scores were more likely than their fellows to be ill in the following year. For the first time, it was possible to show in dramatic form that the rate of change in a person's life - his pace of life - is closely tied to the state of his heatlh. (*Ibid.*, p. 330)

One of the researchers whom Toffler quotes had said that the results of their work were so spectacular that "at first we hesitated to publish them." The findings which inexplicably startled the investigators were released in 1967. Toffler then concludes, perhaps a bit incautiously (depending on what he means by "established") but certainly enthusiastically:

> In every case, the correlation between change and illness has held. It has been established that "alterations in life style" that require a great deal of adjustment and coping, correlate with illness - whether or not these changes are under the individual's own direct control, whether or not he sees them as desirable. Furthermore, the higher the degrees of life change, the higher the risk that subsequent illness will be severe. (*Ibid.*)

The physiological relationship between change (anitya) and illness (duḥkha) has been known for some time in both the East and West. The experiments that Toffler cites give dramatic reconfirmation to that previous knowledge.

96. *Digha-Nikāya* II. 198 in *Some Sayings of the Buddha, Op. Cit.*, p. 126.

97. The interpretations of change espoused by Heraclitus and Cratylus remarkably parallel similar interpretations given by the early Buddhists with the concept of anitya and later Buddhists with the concept of kṣaṇikatva, momentariness. Where both Heraclitus and the early Buddhists focused on the fact of change, that *panta rei*, "everything flows", Cratylus and the later Buddhists adopted a more radical and extreme view of the flow that focused on the velocity or rate of change, moment to moment. Thus S.N. Dasgupta in mentioning Śāntarakṣita, an 8th century Mādhyamika of the Mahāyāna school, comments on this concept of kṣaṇika and the rate of change it measures:

> The word *kṣaṇika*, which is translated as "momentary", is, according to Śāntarakṣita a technical term. The character in an entity of dying immediately after production is technically called *kṣaṇa*, and whatever has this quality is called *kṣaṇika*.... It means the character of dying immediately after being produced. Surendranath Dasgupta, *A History of Indian Philosophy*, Five Volumes, 1922-1955 (Cambridge University Press, 1965/1932), Volume II, p. 182 n. 1.

98. Later Mahāyāna Buddhism found it extremely difficult to maintain both the orthodox anitya and anātman dogmas of earlier Buddhism, as we shall see below, pp. 264-69.

99. See Plato's *Sophist* 249 a-d; and *Theaetetus* 179 ff. Also see below pp. 309-10 for a further discussion of the dilemma of knowledge.

100. See the devastating diatribe against the use of "Northern and Southern Buddhism" delivered, with reasons, by T.W. Rhys Davids in his *Buddhist India, Op. Cit.*, pp. 171-73. The use is defensible not because of the origins of either the religions or their texts, but because of their subsequent geographical locations.

101. Recall the use of "philosophic history" in the Preface above, pp. xii-xiii and xvi-xvii.

102. See Richard Gombrich, *Precept and Practice, Traditional Buddhism in the Rural Highlands of Ceylon* (Oxford: Clarendon Press, 1971). pp. 16-17, 46, 71, 121, 151.

103. *Therīgāthā* 240-41 quoted in K.N. Jayatilleke, *Early Buddhist Theory of Knowledge* (London: George Allen and Unwin Ltd., 1963). p. 409.

104. *Aṅguttara-Nikāya* iii. 18 in *Buddhism in Translations, Op. Cit.*, p. 424.

105. *Ibid.*

106. *Ibid.*

107. Modern Theravāda Buddhists in theory, i.e. cognitively speaking, do not worship Buddha nor even pray to him. They do kneel before images of Buddha but this kneeling is an expression of their gratitude to one who had found the Way and had then selflessly revealed it to others. However, "Our general conclusion must therefore be that cognitively the Buddha is dead and without further power, but that even this...is not consistently maintained in the ritual context...but that affectively the Buddha is felt still to be potent, even when an image is not present." Richard Gombrich, *Precept and Practice, Op. Cit.*, p. 142. See Gombrich pp. 80-82 and especially, "However, the Buddha has long since become the victim of a personality cult." *Ibid.*, p. 82.

108. *Jātaka*, v. 238 quoted in K.N. Jayatilleke, *Op. Cit.*, p. 411.

109. *Ibid.* Both of these arguments, the Designer Argument and the Good God Argument, will receive a more complete analysis under Mahāyāna Buddhism and "The problem of theism", below. See pp. 218-23 as we take up the theological problem of free will and the theological problem of evil.

110. *Aṅguttara-Nikāya*, iii. 37, *Buddhism in Translations, Op. Cit.*, p. 424.

111. *Ibid.*, p. 425.

112. *Ibid.*, pp. 425-26.

113. See Bruce Kuklick, *The Rise of American Philosophy, Cambridge, Massachusetts, 1860-1930* (Yale University Press, 1977). p. 251. Kuklick can find no confirmation for this delightful legend which, I must conclude, probably means that it is, in some sense, merely "mythically true."

114. *Dhammapada* viii in *Buddhism, A Religion of Infinite*

Compassion, Op. Cit., p. 73.

115. T.R.V. Murti, *Op. Cit.*, p. 23n. Murti is translating from the *Mahāparinibbāna* text.

116. *Vinaya Mahāvaggya* viii. 26 in *Some Sayings of the Buddha, Op. Cit.*, pp. 84-85.

117. *Avadāna Śataka* II. 348 in Edward Conze, *Buddhism Its Essence and Development, Op. Cit.*, p. 94.

118. *Saṁyutta-Nikāya* III. 25 in *Some Sayings of the Buddha, Op. Cit.*, p. 177.

119. *Bhagavad Gītā* XII. 13, 15; XIV. 24, 25.

120. *Bhagavad Gītā*, XII. 16, 17, 19.

121. *Majjhima-Nikāya, Sutta* 63 in *Buddhism in Translations, Op. Cit.*, pp. 120-21.

122. *Ibid.*, p. 122. Recall the parable of the blind men and the elephant.

123. *Ibid.*

124. A great Buddhologist reminds us, "Buddhism is not an orthodoxy, a coherent system of dogmas; it is rather a practical discipline, a training." L. De La Vallée Poussin, *The Way to Nirvana* (Cambridge, 1917), p. 124.

125. *Chāndogya Upaniṣad* VIII. 11.1.

126. *Ibid.* VIII. 12.5.

127. Guy Welbon, *The Buddhist Nirvāṇa and Its Western Interpreters* (The University of Chicago Press, 1968), p. viii.

128. Walpola Rahula, *What the Buddha Taught* (New York: Grove Press, Inc., 1974), pp. 37-38.

129. *Mahāvagga* I. 21. in E.J. Thomas, *Buddhist Scriptures* (London: John Murray, 1931), pp. 54-56, quoted in *Buddhism, A Religion of Infinite Compassion, Op. Cit.*, pp. 49-50.

130. Walpola Rahula, *Op. Cit.*, p. 40.

131. *Ibid.*

132. *Aṅguttara-Nikāya* III. 88 in *Buddhism in Translations, Op. Cit.*, p. 288.

133. *Samyutta-Nikāya* XXXVI. II[5], *Ibid.*, p. 384.

134. See the fascinating work of the late Abraham Maslow and his attempts to identify, phenomenologially, the empirical elements in "peak experiences", which are something like "mystical or liberating experiences." Peak experiences may come as close as we're probably ever going to get to nirvāṇa, mokṣa, or satori, in this kali yuga (iron age). Some of the identifiable properties of peak experiences recognized by Maslow are: Peak experiences have nothing to do with religion; they are natural and humanistic rather than supernatural; they are very common; they tend to be alike among people; they come unexpectedly, but mental passiveness, openness of mind and letting things happen can bring them on; and they are beautiful, wonderful and creative experiences in which the perception is that whatever *is, ought* to be just that way. However, the peak experience is temporary and transcient which may not permit it to be identified with the more permanent, ultimate goals of Hinduism and Buddhism. See Abraham Maslow's early paper, "Lessons From Peak-Experiences," *Journal of Humanstic Psychology*, v. 2, 1962, pp. 9-18.

135. Buddhaghoṣa's commentary to stanza 57 of the *Dhammapada*, *Buddhism in Translations, Op. Cit.*, pp. 381-82. The same story appears in *Saṁyutta-Nikāya* I. 122-23, *Buddhist Texts Through the Ages*, Edited by Edward Conze, *et al.* (New York: Harper and Row, 1964), pp. 42-44.

136. The monasteries were formed for other reasons as well; initially they may have been established for the very simple purpose of keeping monks, bhikṣus (Pali bhikhus), dry during the monsoon. See Sukumar Dutt, *Buddhist Monks and Monasteries of India* (London: George Allen & Unwin, Ltd., 1962), who states:

> Vihāras (monasteries) were built for the Sanghas and originally they were vassas (rain retreats) for wandering monks. (p. 214)

Dutt observes that the monasteries were also formed in order that the laity might visit the monks since the monastery now prevented the latter from wandering about. (p. 26) Much later, many of the larger monasteries were transformed into the great universities of India, e.g., Nālandā University, near the city of Rājagṛha, which was turned in the 5th century C.E. into a Mahāvihāra, had initially been a group of five monasteries. So monasteries evolved from vassas to vihāras to mahāvihāras to universal centers of learning.

137. See footnote 41 above for a defense of the position that Buddhism was originally meant only for those who had already renounced the world, and that it was, in its immediate application, "anti-social." And compare that with Richard Gombrich's extremely interesting discussion regarding the tension between the ideals of *śānta danta* ('self restraint'), the original monastic ideal, on the one hand, and the *karuṇāvanta* ('love'), the religious ideal of the laity, on the other, in not only traditional Hīnayāna and Mahāyāna Buddhism, respectively, but also with modern Ceylonese Buddhism, as well. Gombrich distinguishes between the 'cognitive religion' (where the goal is nirvāṇa and the means to it is by self-restraint) and the 'affective religion' (where the goal is heaven and the means to it are by love and acts of merit). In the tension between these two religions it is doctrine that has had to come to terms with emotional needs as self-restraint has accommodated itself to love:

> The monks [in Ceylonese Buddhism] are all supposed to be 'salvation strivers', and the laity interested mainly in heaven attained by faith and good works. This finds some justification in the texts [the source of the cognitive religion] but none in social reality. Richard Gombrich, *Precept and Practice, Traditional Buddhism in the Rural Highlands of Ceylon, Op. Cit.*, p. 324.

138. *Aṅguttara-Nikāya* III. 134[1] in *Buddhism in Translations, Op. Cit.*, p. viii. Emphasis added. Warren renders "self" as "Ego."

139. *Anattalakkhaṇa Sutta* in *Saṁyutta-Nikāya* III. 66 in *Buddhism, A Religion of Infinite Compassion, Op. Cit.*, p. 33 with some minor changes.

140. The above classification of the skandhas is as reported by Vasubandhu in the late fourth century C.E.; see Edward J. Thomas, *The History of Buddhist Thought, Op. Cit.*, pp. 162-63; and Stefan Anacker, "The Abhidharma Piṭaka" in *Buddhism, A Modern Perspecive, Op. Cit.*, pp. 59-64.

141. David Hume, *A Treatise of Human Nature* (Oxford At the Clarendon Press, 1888), p. 252.

142. B.F. Skinner, *About Behaviorism* (New York: Alfred A. Knopf, 1974), p. 171.

143. B.F. Skinner,*Beyond Freedom and Dignity* (New York: Alfred A. Knopf, 1971), p. 200, 201.

144. See Gilbert Ryle's classic *The Concept of Mind* (1949) in which he introduces the phrase "the dogma of the Ghost in the Machine", a dogma which he describes as "a philosopher's myth" about the self.

145. *Milindapañha* 25-27, in *Buddhism in Translations, Op. Cit.*, pp. 129-31. I have put scare quotes around "designation" and "name" to indicate that the words are *not* used in their ordinary sense here to designate and to name - that's the whole point of Buddhist nominalism.

146. *Buddhist Scriptures*, Selected and Translated by Edward Conze (Penguin Books, 1959), p. 149. In place of "used" Conze has "applied" which word, of course, misses Nāgāsena's entire point. "Chariot" cannot be applied to anything for there is nothing for it to apply to.

147. See A.J. Ayer, *The Foundations of Empirical Knowledge* (New York: Macmillan and Company, 1940), pp. 240 ff.

148. See Edward Conze, *Buddhist Thought in India* (The University of Michigan Press, 1973), p. 102.

149. See David Hume, *Op. Cit.*, I. vi.

150. D.T. Suzuki, *The Field of Zen* (London: Buddhist Society, 1969), p. 58.

151. The Buddhists, however, have a number of parables to explain why a man is responsible for his actions even though there is no unchanging, continuous, identifiable ātman. One such parable from the *Milindapañha* tells of a man who steals some mangoes and is siezed by the owner of the mangoes who then brings him to the king for judgment. To the charge of theft the thief says, drawing more perhaps on the dogma of anitya than on the dogma of anātman:

> "Your majesty, I did not steal this man's mangoes; the fruits which he planted, and those which I took away, were not the same fruits; I deserve no punishment."

But the king judges that the man is guilty:

> "Because, whatever the man may say, he would be punished on account of the last mango which undeniably would not be there, had it not been

for the former one." *Milindapañha* in *Sacred Books of the East*, Volume 35, p. 72, quoted in M. Winternitz, *Op. Cit.*, p. 180.

The argument shows that the mango changed and not the man, hence theft was impossible. That is to say, if I took that which belonged to no one then I was not stealing; but the mango I took belonged to no one (by anitya it was a different mango than the one planted and owned by the mango planter-owner); therefore, I was not stealing. This argument from the mango's side of anitya would be parallel to the same argument from the ātman's side: If someone else committed this theft then I cannot be charged with the theft; but someone else committed this theft (by anitya I'm not the same person today that I was yesterday); therefore, I cannot be charged with the theft. Presumably, the king in his argument is saying that if the owner owns, and is responsible for, the first planted mango then he owns and is responsible for the second fully grown tree of mangoes. And, *pari passu*, if the thief owns and is responsible for the first self who stole the mango yesterday then he must own and be responsible for the self who stands here charged with the theft today.

152. Śaṁkara, *Brahmasūtrabhāṣya* I. 1.1.

153. *Ibid.*, *Preamble*.

154. Eliot Deutsch, *Advaita Vedānta: A Philosophical Reconstruction* (Honolulu: East-West Center Press, 1969), p. 51.

155. Śaṁkara has an even closer "cogito" version of the argument at *Brahmasūtrabhāṣya* II. 3.7 when he says "...to refute the Self is impossible, for he who tries to refute it is the Self." And a 14th century advaitin, Vidyāraṇya, in his *Pañcadaśī* III, 23-24 comments *a la Descartes*:

> No one can doubt the fact of his own existence. Were one to do so, who could the doubter be?

And Vidyāraṇya concludes, using common sense as his guide:

> Only a deluded man could entertain the idea he does not exist. (Quoted in Eliot Deutsch, *Op. Cit.*, pp. 50-51.

156. Buddha in the *Majjhima-Nikāya* refers to ātmavāda as a 'doctrine of fools':

> Since neither self nor aught belonging to self, brethren, can really and truly be accepted, is not the heretical position which holds 'this is the world and this is the self, and I shall continue to be in the future, permanent,

immutable, eternal, of a nature that knows no change, yea I shall abide to eternity', is not this simply and entirely a doctrine of fools? *Majjhima-Nikāya* I. 138 quoted in S. Radhakrishnan, *Indian Philosophy* Two Volumes (New York: The Macmillan Company, 1956/1929), Vol. I, p. 385.

157. Think also of the analogy of the wave: When a volume of water is raised up as a wave, the mass of water seems to move on, but it does not really move. Its motion is simply communicated to another volume of water.

158. *Milindapañha* 71.16 in *Buddhism in Translations, Op. Cit.*, p. 234.

159. See above pp. 4-6 for a discussion of myth and symbolic meaning.

160. *Visuddhi-Magga*, Chapt. XVII, in *Buddhism in Translations, Op. Cit.*, p. 238.

161. *Ibid.*, pp. 238-239.

162. *Ibid.*, p. 239.

163. *Ibid.*

164. John Locke, *An Essay Concerning Human Understanding*, edited by Alexander Campbell Fraser. Two Volumes (New York: Dover Publications, 1959), Volume I, pp. 450-51.

165. *Ibid.*, Volume I, p. 449.

166. Recent scholarship has cast some doubt on the traditional treatment of Hīnayāna, as a whole, as a realistic philosophy. For example, David J. Kalupahana has forcefully argued, with respect to the dharma theory of early Buddhism upon which Buddhologists had generally rested the charge of "realism" against Hīnayāna,

> The conception of dharma in early Buddhism, as depicted in the Pāli Nikāyas, the Chinese Āgamas, and the Theravāda *Abhidhamma* as represented by the *Kathāvatthu*, would therefore be much different from the Sarvāstivāda conception. Hence we maintain that it was the Sarvāstivādins who propounded a theory of the substantiality of dharmas [hence they are "realists"] and that there is no justification for extending that criticism to the other Hīnayāna schools. David J.

Kalupahana, *Causality: The Central Philosophy of Buddhism* (Honolulu: The University Press of Hawaii, 1975), p. 80.

I think that we shall find, however, that Hīnayāna, in general, is a rather bold realist philosophy and that this realism does rest entirely in the dharma theory: Kalupahana's warning ought not to mitigate the attribution of realism to Hīnayāna. On the other hand, the (dual) substance doctrine that Kalupahana does use to characterize Sarvāstivāda realism is undoubtably not attributable to the earlier Hīnayāna; and to this extent we have two kinds of realism working in the Hīnayāna tradition. That is to say, there are realisms and there are realisms.

167. See below pp. 278, 294f. for a discussion of metaphysical agnosticism in Mādhyamika Buddhism and in the philosophy of Gautama the Buddha, in particular.

168. See above footnote 97 for a brief discussion of kṣaṇa.

169. Quoted in David J. Kalupahana, *Causality, Op. Cit.*, p. 81.

170. It is clumsy and unpoetic, even if it is correct, to have to keep saying "Sarvāstivādin" where "Sarvāstivāda philosopher" is meant. It is as clumsy as "Mahāyānist", "Hīnayānin", "Yogācārist", etc. For this reason I shall use "Sarvāstivāda" throughout and try to use similar collective nouns without their clumsy, though correct, suffixes in the later sections of this work. Also see the excellent summary and bibliography of texts in Charles S. Prebish, "Major Schools of the Early Buddhists: Sarvāstivāda" in *Buddhism, A Modern Perspective, Op. Cit.*, pp. 42-45.

171. Th. Stcherbatsky has summarized the doctrine of the dharmas in the following way:

> The [dharmas] of existence are momentary appearances, momentary flashings into the phenomenal world out of an unknown source.... They disappear as soon as they appear, in order to be followed the next moment [kṣaṇa] by another momentary existence. Thus a moment becomes a synonym of a [dharma], two moments are two different dharmas. A [dharma] becomes something like a point in time-space. Th. Stcherbatsky, *The Central Conception of Buddhism* and *The Meaning of the Word Dharma* (New Delhi: Motilal Banarsidass, 1974/1923), p. 37. In place of "dharma" Stcherbatsky uses "element", throughout.

172. David J. Kalupahana, *Causality, Op. Cit.*, p. 75.

173. Edward Conze, *Buddhist Thought in India, Op. Cit.*, pp. 139, 140.

174. See Hans Wolfgang Schumann, *Buddhism, An Outline of Its Teachings and Schools* (Wheaton, IL: The Theosophical Publishing House, 1974), p. 86; and Edward J. Thomas, *The History of Buddhist Thought, Op. Cit.*, pp. 136-64.

175. David J. Kalupahana, *Buddhist Philosophy, Op. Cit.*, p. 100. In what follows I draw rather heavily on Professor Kalupahana's very fine book.

176. The *Vibhāṣaprabhāvṛtti* of the *Abhidharmadīpa* quoted in David J. Kalupahana, *Buddhist Philosophy, Op. Cit.*, pp. 102-03.

177. Consider Surendranath Dasgupta's claim: "According to Guṇaratna, the Vaibhāṣikas [the more orthodox Sarvāstivāda] held that things existed for four [unchanging] moments, the moment of production, the moment of existence, the moment of decay and the moment of annihilation." Surendranath Dasgupta, *A History of Indian Philosophy, Op. Cit.*, Vol. I, p. 114). See also David J. Kalupahana, *Buddhist Philosophy, Op. Cit.*, pp. 97-107.

178. St. Augustine in the *Confessions* Bk. XI. Ch. 14-28 muses about time.

179. For James the *auditory* specious present lasts between six to twelve seconds. See William James, *Principles of Psychology*, Two Volumes (New York: 1890), Vol. I, p. 613; "...the prototype of all conceived times is the specious present [the term was invented by E.R. Clay], the short duration of which we are immediately and incessantly sensible." The specious present has "a vaguely vanishing backward and forward fringe" (p. 613), and through it "we look in two directions into time." (p. 609) For a parallel in Buddhism see *addhā paccupanna*, "the enduring or long present" in David Kalupahana, *Buddhist Philosophy, Op. Cit.*, pp. 108-09.

180. This argument tries to refute the Sarvāstivāda concept of prāpti by an infinite regress argument somewhat after the fashion of the infinite regress argument used by Śaṁkarācarya to refute the inherence doctrine of the Nyāya-Vaiśeṣika. See Karl H. Potter, *Presuppositions of India's Philosophies* (Prentice-Hall, Inc., 1963), pp. 126-29. The Navyanyāya attempted to answer Śaṁkara's objection by the theory of svarūpasambandha, which Potter ingeneously translates as "self-linking connectors". If one could show

that prāpti was capable of either being or having a self-linking connector to join it to the dharmas, perhaps the regress could be avoided by the Sarvāstivāda. Incidentally, changing the diagram as a way out doesn't help, for the problem springs up wherever prāpti touches or inheres the dharmas.

181. The *Vibhāṣaprabhavṛti* of the *Abhidharmadīpa* quoted in David J. Kalupahana, *Buddhist Philosophy, Op. Cit.*, p. 103.

182. According to Vasumitra, a second century C.E. chronicler, the "original doctrines held in common by all members of the Vātsīputrīya, the Personalist or Pudgala, school" were:
    1. The Pudgalas are neither the same as the skandhas nor different from the skandhas...
    2. Some saṁskāras exist for some time while others perish at every moment. [Shades of sthitikṣaṇa!]
    3. Things (dharmas) cannot transmigrate (saṁkrānti) from one world to the other apart from the Pudgala. They can be said to transmigrate along with the Pudgala. *Origins and Doctrines of Early Buddhist Schools*, A translation of the Hsuan-Chwang Version of Vasumitra's Treatise by Jiryo Masuda (Leipzig: Verlag der Asia Major, 1925), pp. 53-55.

183. Why not "Godhika's razor" after the monk who took the supreme, parsimonious step by cutting out the extraneous world entirely when he committed suicide to maintain his nirvāṇa? See above pp. 149-50.

184. Recall our discussion of Buddhist nominalism in the *Milindapañha*. Vasubandhu offers a tempered version of that nominalism, call it "moderate Buddhist nominalism," which says that words refer to changing, phenomenal patterns of dharmas, but they don't refer to, designate or name things or objects. "Extreme Buddhist nominalism," on the other hand, the nominalism of the *Milindapañha* says that names do not refer at all, they are empty.

185. Vasubandhu, *Abhidharmakośa* IX in *Buddhist Logic* by F. Th. Stcherbatsky, Two Volumes (New York: Dover Publications, Inc., 1962/1930), Volume II, pp. 344-47.

186. The reader who may wish to anticipate some of the differences in the tendencies between Hīnayāna and Mahāyāna might consider the following remarks by a Northern Buddhist monk, Bhikshu Sangarakshita:

The Hinayana being conservative and literal-minded, scholastic, one-sidedly negative in its conception of Nirvāṇa and the Way, over-attached to the formal aspects of monasticism, and spiritually individualistic, the Mahāyāna, as a movement of reaction against the Hīnayāna, was naturally compelled to emphasize the importance of whatever qualities and characteristics were the exact opposite of these. It was therefore:

(a) Progressive and liberal-minded, caring more for the spirit than for the letter of the Scriptures, willing to write fresh ones whenever the need of recasting the outward form of the Teaching arose;

(b) More highly emotional and devotional in attitude, with a deeper understanding of the value of ritual acts; and

(c) More positive in its conception of Nirvāṇa and the Way;

(d) While continuing to cherish the monastic ideal it gave increased importance to a dedicated household life; and

(e) It developed the altruistic aspect of Buddhism and preached the Bodhisattva Ideal.

Bhikshu Sangharakshita, *A Survey of Buddhism* (Boulder: Shambala, 1980/1957), p. 227.

187. At least one interpreter of Mahāyāna argues that the origins of the new religion are modern and recent: "If we take ["genuine"] to mean the lifeless preservation of the original, we should say that Mahāyānism is not the genuine teaching of the Buddha, and we may add that Mahāyānists would be proud of the fact...." D.T. Suzuki, *Outlines of Mahayana Buddhism* (New York: Schocken Books, Inc., 1963/1907), p. 14. And, we might add, that no one plays the implication-intention game with more ingenuity and zeal than the Mahāyāna. See above pp. 96-97.

188. Modern scholarship remains in controversy over the question of the influences of Buddhism on Hinduism and vice versa, i.e. over who (Hinduism or Buddhism) owes what to whom (Buddhism or Hinduism). See the *Encyclopedia of Indian Philosophies, Advaita Vedānta Up to Śaṁkara and His Pupils*, edited by Karl H. Potter (Princeton University Press, 1981), p. 604, fns. 29 and 31.

189. See below pp. 207, 224, 225 for a discussion of the Dharma as real.

190. See below pp. 223-27 for a discussion of the Buddha as real.

191. See below pp. 215-18, 229-35 for a discussion of the Buddhas and Bodhisattvas as real.

192. See below p. 346 for a discussion of Ālayavijñāna as real.

193. See above p. 176 for a discussion of "real."

194. Lewis R. Lancaster, "The Rise of the Mahāyāna" in *Buddhism: A Modern Perspective, Op. Cit.,* p. 66. See also D.T. Suzuki's apt remark in footnote 187. The Mahāyāna literature is vast and I refer the reader to the excellent bibliography that stands at the end of *Buddhism: A Modern Perspective*.

195. Edward Conze, *Buddhist Wisdom Books Containing the Diamond Sūtra and the Heart Sūtra* (London: George Allen & Unwin, 1958). p. 28; see also *Buddhist Mahāyāna Texts*, edited by E.B. Cowell (New York: Dover Publications, Inc., 1969/1894) Part II, p. 109.

196. *Ibid.*, p. 29.

197. *Ibid.*, p. 28.

198. *Ibid.*, p. 54.

199. David J. Kalupahana, *Buddhist Philosophy, Op. Cit.*, p. 134.

200. Perhaps the reader can see at this stage why we are speaking of these ten characteristics as "tendencies." For in many respects the Hīnayāna is surely committed to the transempirical in metaphysics as well as a rationalist position in epistemology; and one has only to recall the philosophy of the dharmas to realize how true this is. Therefore, it must seem unfair to even hint that the Hīnayāna Buddhists are "empiricists" and not rationalists. Furthermore, in characterizing the Mahāyāna as intuitionist and rationalist the attribution is surely simplistic if not downright false, e.g., prajñā has nothing to do with locating books behind refrigerators. But if we keep in mind that we are talking about tendencies and that the differences between the two Buddhisms are just that, differences in tendencies, general attitudes and characteristics, I think that this will help us to look beyond what must at times seem unfair, simplistic and even false in those characterizations.

201. "In the first centuries many of the monks had aspired directly for Nirvāṇa. Only the laity and the less ambitious monks were content with the hope of winning a better birth. But from ca. 200 B.C. onward, almost everybody felt that conditions were too unfavorable for winning enlightenment in this life." Edward Conze, *Buddhism: Its Essence and Development, Op. Cit.*, p. 116. For the modern Theravāda attitude on the same matter see Richard Gombrich, *Precept and Practice*. "Rebirth the Buddha considered misery; the peace of nirvāṇa was the only good worth having. But most Singhalese villagers do not want nirvāṇa-yet.... They say they want to be born in heaven; some of them would even like to be reborn in a favorable station on earth." *Op. Cit.*, pp. 16-17: The great and little traditions, i.e. the cognitive and affective traditions, clash. But then no one has a corner on consistency in the Buddhist traditions. See Richard Gombrich, *Op. Cit.*, pp. 154, 320-22.

202. S. Radhakrishnan, *Indian Philosophy, Op. Cit.*, Volume I, pp. 589-90.

203. Francis H. cook, "The Sūtra Piṭaka" in *Buddhism: A Modern Perspective, Op. Cit.*, p. 57.

204. Edward J. Thomas, *The History of Buddhist Thought, Op. Cit.*, p. 185.

205. *Saddharmapuṇḍarīka* 5, p. 61f. (*Bibliotheca Indica*, ed. by N. Dutt. Work NO. 276, Calcutta, 1953), quoted in H. Wolfgang Schumann, *Buddhism, Op. Cit.*, pp. 98-99.

206. Quoted in Mark Ehman, "The Saddharmapuṇḍarīka-Sūtra" in *Buddhism: A Modern Perspective, Op. Cit.*, p. 102. See also Edward Conze, "The Lotus of the Good Law" in his *Thirty Years of Buddhist Studies* (London: Bruno Cassirer, 1967), pp. 111-13. For more on the three yānas as levels, devotees and Buddhas, see below pp. 232-33 and 240.

207. Mark Ehman, *Ibid.*

208. See above p. 123 for a very brief discussion of the theological problem of free will and the theological problem of evil in what we there called "The Designer Argument" and "The Good-God Argument," respectively, arguments that attempted to prove that God does not exist.

209. *Jātaka* V. 238 quoted in K.N. Jayatilleke, *Early Buddhist Theory of Knowledge, Op. Cit.*, p. 411.

210. *Jātaka* VI. 208, *Ibid.*

211. Epicurus as quoted by Lactantius (260-340 C.E.) in the latter's *On the Anger of God*. See A.L. Herman, *The Problem of Evil and Indian Thought* (New Delhi: Motilal Banarsidass, 1976), p. 10.

212. Edward J. Thomas, *The History of Buddhist Thought*, *Op. Cit.*, p. 226. The earlier Pāli tradition had identified dharmakāya with the "body of doctrine," the spoken word. But the Mahāyāna has changed the meaning of the concept entirely:"As the trikāya doctrine is based upon a dogmatic teaching about the nature of a Buddha, it is natural that earlier doctrines should be included in it. But these are not necessarily anticipations of it. When *dhammakāya* occurs occasionally in the Pāli, it is merely the body of doctrine." *Ibid.*, p. 243. See also the discussion of trikāyavāda in Lewis R. Lancaster, "Doctrines of the Mahāyāna" in *Buddhism: A Modern Perspective*, *Op. Cit.*, p. 74.

213. D. T. Suzuki, *Outlines of Mahāyāna Buddhism*, *Op. Cit.*, pp. 73-74.

214. David J. Kalupahana, *Buddhist Philosophy*, *Op. Cit.*, p. 121.

215. Recall the mind-body problem in our discussion of Sarvāstivāda realism. See above pp. 188, 201ff. The problem was generated because mind dharmas and body dharmas flowed from two metaphysically distinct substances; and since likes can only interact with likes, it followed that mind and body, while they may intra-act, cannot interact: Thus the mind-body problem. I would suggest that we have a similar problem with the problem of Buddhacentrism, call it "nirmaṇakāyadharmakāya problem", where, once again, intra-action, but no interaction, is possible and for very nearly the same metaphysical reasons, viz., there exists a metaphysical dualism with an unbridgable ontological gulf separating the two parts of the dualism.

216. But see the discussion of *yāna* as "career" rather than "vehicle" in Edward J. Thomas *The History of Buddhist Thought*, *Op. Cit.*, pp. 177-78 where Thomas states, "...but *hīnayāna*, which very rarely occurs, is used generally for 'low or base career.' 'Career' is *yāna*. This was first pointed out by Dr. Dasgupta. There is no reason to translate it 'vehicle', merely because Burnouf did so nearly a century ago." The fact is that *yāna* is used by many Buddhologists to mean "vehicle", and, in addition, using it in this way helps to explain the very common and popular ferrying analogy used above.

217. "Nirvāṇa is not the ultimate abode of Buddhahood, nor is enlightenment. Love and compassion is what essentially constitutes the self-nature of the All-Knowing One (Sarvajñā)." Daisetz Taitaro Suzuki, Tr., *The Laṅkāvatāra Sūtra* (London: George Routledge and Sons, Ltd., 1932), p. xii.

218. The *Aṣṭasāhasrikā Prajñāpāramitā Sūtra* was the first philosophical Mahāyāna sūtra to be translated into Chinese (179 C.E.). It was also the text most widely used by the Chinese Taoists. See Lewis R. Lancaster, "The Prajñāpāramitā Literature" in *Buddhism: A Modern Perspective, Op. Cit.*, p. 69. But see Hajime Nakamura, "The first appearance of the Bodhisattva-idea must be placed between the beginning of the 1st century B.C. and the middle of the first century A.D., that is to say, after the Bharhut sculptures and before the appearance of the early Mahāyāna scriptures." *Indian Buddhism* (Kansai: University of Foreign Studies, 1980), p. 154.

219. *Prajñāpāramitā (Aṣṭasahasrikā* XV.293) quoted in Edward Conze, *Buddhism: Its Essence and Development, Op. Cit.*, p. 128.

220. This Mahāyāna statement is in clear contradiction to the Canonical Hīnayāna statement that, "I have taught the Doctrine without making any inner and outer differentiation, and herein the Tathāgata has not the closed fist of a teacher with regard to doctrines." See above p. 80. It is essential, of course, that the new religion hint at the closed fist in the Canon, the secret teaching in the tradition, in order to make room for paying the implication-intention game and for its own innovative doctrines. And recall another innovator, playing the same game, and preaching to his disciples, "Think not that I am come to destroy the law, or the prophets: I am not come to destroy, *but to fulfill*." *(The Gospel According to St. Matthew* 5:17).

221. *Saddharmapuṇḍarīka* translated by Edward Conze in *Buddhist Texts Through the Ages, Op. Cit.*, p. 124.

222. *Ibid.*, pp. 124-25.

223. *Ibid.*, pp. 126-27.

224. *Ashṭasāhasrikā* translated by Edward Conze in *Buddhist Texts Through the Ages, Op. Cit.*, pp. 127-28.

225. *Bodhicaryāvatāra*, quoted in H. Wolfgang Schumann, *Buddhism, Op. Cit.*, p. 111.

226. *Bodhicaryāvatāra* quoted in Edward J. Thomas, *The History of Buddhist Thought, Op. Cit.*, pp. 196-97.

227. The assumption is, of course, that the Bodhisattva has not yet reached nirvāṇa. This assumption is fudged a bit in the literature. The question is, Has the Bodhisattva reached nirvāṇa? or merely put it off? See Bhikshu Sangharakshita, *Op. Cit.*, pp. 250 and 397 for a positive answer to the first question, and pp. 235 and 395 for a positive answer to the second.

228. Edward Conze, *Buddhism: Its Essence and Development, Op. Cit.*, p. 128.

229. *Saddharmapuṇḍarīka* in *Buddhist Scriptures, Op. Cit.*, p. 203.

230. *Ibid.*, p. 205.

231. *Ibid.*, p. 206.

232. *Ibid.*

233. See above pp. 4-10 for a discussion of the mythic theory of truth which says that a story (or statement) is true if and only if the recitation or the hearing or the reading of the story (or statement) leads to metaphysical realization; and see above pp. 137-38 for a discussion of the pragmatic theory of truth which says that a statement is true if and only if believing or accepting the statement leads to fruitful, useful or practical consequences for the believer; the correspondence theory of truth says, in effect, that a proposition is true if and only if it corresponds with the facts, such that, for example, 'There are toys outside the house for you' is true if and only if there are toys outside the house for you.

234. Edward Conze, *Buddhist Scriptures, Op. Cit.*, pp. 209-10.

235. The Buddha agreed, but not to the conclusion that the critics desire: "I preach you a dharma comparable to a raft for the sake of crossing over and not for the sake of clinging to it...." (*Majjhima-Nikāya* I, 134 quoted in K.N. Jayatilleke, *Early Buddhist Theory of Knowledge, Op. Cit.*, p. 357.

236. *Ibid.*, p. 358.

237. *Ibid.*, p. 351.

238. *Ibid.*, pp. 351-52.

239. *Ibid.*, p. 352. The Sutta appears in *Majjhima-Nikāya* I. 395.

240. *Ibid.*, p. 358.

241. *Ibid.*, pp. 358-59. K.N. Jayatilleke uses A.D. Woozley's definition of the "Pragmatist" theory of truth throughout, viz., "...a belief is true if and only if it is useful, and false if it is not; or more widely..., a belief is true if 'it works.'" A.D. Woozley, *Theory of Knowledge* (New York: Barnes & Noble, Inc., 1966), p. 134. It might be noted that Jayatilleke has here stated a version of what we have earlier referred to, with more flourishes and trumpets, as "the mythic theory of truth."

242. See above pp. 137-38 for a discussion of the problem of pragmatism in Hīnayāna.

243. *Chāndogya Upaniṣad*, VIII. 11.1.

244. *Chāndogya Upaniṣad*,VIII. 12.6. Compare this early Hindu view of heaven with this from the *Milindapañha*; "Like the wishing jewel, Nirvāṇa grants all one can desire, brings joy, and sheds light...." in *Buddhist Scriptures, Op. Cit.*, p. 157. The Pāli tradition did hold a positive conception of nirvāṇa, but the overwhelming tendency, in the light of their anātman metaphysics, as we have argued, was to take the negative way. More typical of the Pāli texts is the Fire Sermon and what happens following Buddha's recommendation of indifference to all that is on fire;

> And being indifferent he becomes free from passion, by absence of passion he is liberated, and when he is liberated, the knowledge 'I am liberated' arises. Rebirth is destroyed, a religious life is lived, duty is done, and he knows there is nothing more for him in this state. *Mahāvagga* 1.21 in E.J. Thomas, *Buddhist Scriptures, Op. Cit.*, p. 56.

There is no mention here of peace, tranquility and the satisfaction of all desires.

245. *Chāndogya Upaniṣad*, VIII. 15.

246. *Chāndogya Upaniṣad* VIII. 12. 2-3.

247. *Sukhāvatīvyūha*, the *Greater Sukhāvatīvyūha* is meant, in Conze's *Buddhist Scriptures, Op. Cit.*, pp. 234-35.

248. *Ibid.*, p. 234.

249. *Ibid.*, p. 235.

250. The Buddha Amitābha, who has established and now presides over The Happy Land, was worshipped in China where his cult flourished between 647-715 as part of The Pure Land School of Amidism. Cf. Edward Conze, *A Short History of Buddhism, Op. Cit.*, pp. 87-88.

251. See Mark A. Ehman, "The Pure Land Sūtras," who comments that the popular religion connected with these sūtras arose in 100 B.C. to 100 C.E. in Northwest India. Its appeal was to a laity who sought "an easy way to salvation." *Buddhism: A Modern Perspective, Op. Cit.*, p. 119. And David J. Kalupahana commenting on the conception of Buddha in this context observes:

> Thus the conception of Buddha in the Mahāyāna caters to the psychological needs of ordinary people...similar to the conception of God in many of the theistic religions which emphasizes the conception of a father figure.

And he concludes:

> Later Mahāyāna texts like the *Sukhāvatīvyūha Sūtra*...[combine] the conception of gods and heaven in early Buddhism with the conception of Buddha, [thereby] producing parallels to the Christian conceptions of God and Heaven.... It is this conception of 'Pure Land' that dominated the religious life of many of the people in the Far Eastern countries where Buddhism flourished. David J. Kalupahana, *Buddhist Philosophy, Op. Cit.*, p. 121. On the popularity of the new religion with its heavens and Gods see also H. Wolfgang Schumann, *Buddhism, Op. Cit.*, pp. 104-06.

252. See above pp. 236 ff. for a discussion of the Father-Bodhisattva's upāya, skill-in-means, in using any means at his disposal, including lying, to save his sons-devotees.

253. The way of bhakti as an alternative to other more difficult ways may be what is intended in the seventh Rock Edict of Aśoka, issued in about 256 B.C.E. That edict states in part:

> For [men] all seek mastery of the senses and purity of mind. Men are different in their inclinations and passions, however, and they may perform the whole of their duties or only part. Even if one is not able to make lavish gifts [yet] mastery of the senses, purity of mind, gratitude

and steadfast devotion are commendable and essential. *The Edicts of Aśoka, Op. Cit.*, p. 51.

A.K. Warder, for one, assumes that this is the intent of the edict:

People vary greatly; perhaps, then, different sects' teachings suit them accordingly? For the weakest of them all, it seems, mere devotion (*bhakti*) is better than nothing, if it is 'firm.' A.K. Warder, *Indian Buddhism* (Delhi: Motilal Banarsidass, 1970), p. 259.

See also Edward J. Thomas, *The History of Buddhist Thought, Op. Cit.*, p. 178 for a discussion of the introduction of bhakti into Buddhism. And see Har Dayal, *The Bodhisattva Doctrine in Buddhist Sanskrit Literature* (London: 1932) who argues that "bhakti" first appears in a Buddhist treatise: "In fact, the very word *bhakti [bhatti]*, as a technical religious term, occurs for the first time in Indian literature in a Buddhist treatise *[Therāgathā]* and not in Hindu scripture." (p. 32)

254. See footnote 23 for a summary and discussion of five such essential elements and their place in the religion of the *Vedas* and *Upaniṣads*. Similarly, see footnote 360 for a complete summary and discussion of all five essential elements in Hīnayāna and Mahāyāna Buddhism.

255. "The idea of sharing in the merits of a saintly being is not peculiar to Mahāyāna or even to Buddhism. And it contains an element of truth. No being is morally self-made." Edward J. Thomas, *The History of Buddhist Thought, Op. Cit.*, p. 254. As the *Bodhicaryāvatāra* of Śāntideva puts it, the aim of the Bodhisattva was "...to turn over, or dedicate, their merit to the enlightenment of all beings." Edward Conze, *Buddhism, Its Essence and Development, Op. Cit.*, p. 149. And see Bhikshu Sangharakshita: "A nonindividualistic interpretation of the law of karma is provided by the doctrine of *pariṇāmanā* or "turning over" of merits. According to this doctrine, the merits which one person has acquired by the performance of good actions can, if he so wishes, be transferred to another who is desirous of benefiting from them." (*Op. Cit.*, p. 338) In the end, pariṇāmanā means that "...a more powerful karma has canceled out one that was weaker" (*Ibid.*) It is this canceling out of karma that leads to problems.

256. *Śikṣāsamuccaya* quoted in H. Wolfgang Schumann, *Buddhism, Op. Cit.*, p. 133. An interesting comparison with Hīnayāna on the matter of faith is found in the following remarks about the latter religion: "The Buddha praises disciples not for their faith but for their wisdom.... His

[Vikkali's] excessive faith was a hindrance to salvation. Faith likewise is not a characteristic of an Arahant." K.N. Jayatilleke, *Early Buddhist Theory of Knowledge, Op. Cit.*, p. 384.

257. Edward Conze, *Buddhism: Its Essence and Development, Op. Cit.*, p. 158.

258. *Ibid.*

259. At least this is the Mahāyāna of the Pure Land school. Commenting on the history of bhakti, Sukumar Dutt locates the bhakti movement within lay Buddhism and even argues that lay bhaktism and the adoption of the image of Buddha were responsible for the development and popularity of Mahāyāna. It's an interesting claim and Dutt is worth quoting:

> In spreading among the people, Buddhism developed to some extent a popular aspect; its impress is indelibly left on the stupa [temple] sculpture of Sanchi, Bhilsa and Barhut. It is striking in its difference from the religion of the canon [Hīnayāna] as monks understood and interpreted it. Folk elements abound. ...from the lay mind the Bhakti movement spread into the monk mind. Its ferment is seen in the growing concept of the Lord as Savior rather than as instructor (sattha) or pathfinder.... The Bhakti movement first mainfests itself round the stupas of Sanchi, Bhilsa and Barhut....

And he concludes:

> In the centuries immediately following the adoption of the Buddha-image, the Mahāyāna appeared. The Mahāyānists represented in respect of prayer and worship a pole opposite the [Hīnayāna]. They stressed Bhakti as a cardinal virtue. From the Mahāyānists, image-worship received a premium which the [Hīnayāna] were loth to give. Sukumar Dutt, *Buddhist Monks and Monasteries of India, Op. Cit.*, pp. 116, 193.

260. Edward Conze, *Buddhism: Its Essence and Development, Op. Cit.*, p. 149.

261. The Indian tradition has provided for such things as deferred karma:

> "A man reaps that at that age, whether infancy, youth or old age, at which he had sowed it in his previous birth...
> A man gets in life what he is fated to get, and

even a god cannot make it otherwise." *The Garuḍa Purāṇa*, Edited by Manmatha Nath Dutt (Calcutta: Society for the Resuscitation of Indian Literature, 1908) in *The Pocket World Bible*, Edited by Robert O. Ballou (London: Routledge and Kegan Paul, Limited, 1948), p. 68.

Further, karma can be divided between aravdha karma, on the one hand, which is the result of actions that have begun to produce effects, and anaravdha karma, on the other, which is the result of actions that have not yet begun to produce effects. The latter is, in turn, divided into praktana karma, the results of actions done in previous incarnations which have not yet begun to produce effects; and kryamana karma, the results of actions done in this incarnation which have not yet begun to produce effects. See Troy Wilson Organ, *Hinduism, Its Historical Development* (Barron's Educational Series, Inc., 1974), p. 188. And Richard Gombrich, *Precept and Practice, Op. Cit.*, pp. 214-17 for a grand discussion of karma and merit in modern Ceylon.

262. Edward Conze, *Buddhism: Its Essence and Development, Op. Cit.*, p. 148.

263. The date is a bit conservative for the Hīnayāna. One commentator claims, "The Dhammasaṅgani, first book of the *Theravāda* [Hīnayāna] *Abhidhamma*...may date in part from about 380 to 330 B.C.E." Stefan Anacker, "The Abhidharma Piṭaka" in *Buddhism: A Modern Perspective, Op. Cit.*, p. 60.

264. *Abhidharmakośa* II. 191-92, quoted in Edward Conze, *Buddhism: Its Essence and Development, Op. Cit.*, p. 126.

265. Edward Conze, *Buddhist Thought in India, Op. Cit.*, p. 124.

266. *Ibid.*, p. 133. See above footnote 144. Furthermore, in the dash back to self the Sautrāntikas postulated an unchanging "seed of goodness" and an asraya, substratum; the Mahāsaṅghikas postulated mula, or basic consciousness; the Sarvāstivādins propounded prāpti and saṁtāna; and the ālayavijñāna, store-consciousness, of a minority of Yogācārins was, according to Conze, the monstrous climax of the Buddhist search for an acceptable "self."

267. Recall also that certain recalcitrant critics might perform Hume's experiment, as Śaṁkarācarya apparently has done, and find what Hume could not, viz., the Self. See above p. 165.

268. See above p. 170 where transmigration is identified in the *Milindapañha* when something has "passed over." The *Milinda*

rejected transmigration, however, in favor of reincarnation where nothing passed over.

269. *Buddhist Texts through the Ages, Op. Cit.*, p. 205.

270. To an extent even Hīnayāna could accept such a "self." The dharmas maintained by prāpti in a saṁtāna could, depending on how forceful a glue prāpti is, produce a self no different from self$_p$. Furthermore, if prāpti could be made sufficiently gluey not only would self$_s$ be indistinguishable from self$_p$ but each could be made indistinguishable from self$_r$: And that is doctrinally insupportable. See above pp. 193-94 where it was argued that prāpti was, to say the least, an embarrassing expedient in Hīnayāna realism.

271. See below pp. 253,297f., 302 for a discussion of Mādhyamika Buddhism where just such a claim is made that body, self, heaven, hell, Pure Land and so on are all, ultimately, śūnya, i.e. void and empty.

272. See below pp. 294ff. for a discussion of the role played by Buddha's silence in Mādhyamika Buddhism.

273. Curiously enough, the Mādhyamikas need not deny Buddha fields, Happy Lands and heavens as reals; their only concern, after all, is to deny *doctrines about* the real. Cf. T.R.V. Murti, *The Central Philosophy of Buddhism, Op. Cit.*, p. 218. On the other hand, they do admit, along with all other Mahāyāna Buddhists, that ultimately, in the final showdown with religious and soteriological doctrine, all heavens, hells, worlds, Saviors, Gods, Buddhas and Bodhisattvas are "mere fictions and images in a dream" that have come forth from the Void as mere projections of human consciousness. Cf. Edward Conze, "Buddhist Saviors" in *The Savior God*, edited by S.G.F. Brandon (Manchester University Press, 1963), p. 79.

274. The coherence theory of truth maintains that a statement is true if and only if it is logically deducible from a set of previously-existing statements.

275. See above pp. 177-78 for a discussion of metaphysical materialism and metaphysical body-mind dualism. Note the change here from metaphysical realism, which Mādhyamika accepts, to philosophic realism, which it rejects.

276. See above p. 179 for a discussion of metaphysical nihilism. T.R.V. Murti, one of the most active of the defenders of Mādhyamika against the older claim that it was "nihilistic"

in general, observes:

> The middle path [Madhyamā pratipad] is the avoidance of both the dogmatism of realism (the reality of objects) [our metaphysical materialism, idealism and body-mind dualism] and the scepticism of Nihilism (the rejection of objects and consciousness both as unreal) [our metaphysical nihilism and scepticism]. T.R.V. Mutri, *The Central Philosophy of Buddhism, Op. Cit.*, p. 8.

But the way is left open for both metaphysical agnosticism, see above p. 179, which we shall attribute to the Buddha, and metaphysical absolutism, see above p. 178, which we shall attribute to Mādhyamika.

277. See T.R.V. Mutri who cites some of the evidence for this admittedly challengeable conjecture regarding influence:

> External (Brahmanical) influence on the rise of Mahāyāna has been surmised by some scholars, e.g., Kern [citing parallels between the *Bhagavad Gītā* and the *Saddharma Puṇḍarika*], Max Müller [Vedic as well as Christian and Greek influences], Keith, Stcherbatsky ["That the Mahāyāna is indebted to some Upaniṣad influence is probable" *Buddhist Nirvana*, p. 51] and others. Possibly, the influence exerted was with regard to the conception of Godhead and Bhakti and the absolute as the transcendent ground of phenomena, an idea which is well-defined in the Upaniṣadic conception of Brahman.

But then Mutri adds, more cautiously, regarding borrowing:

> The question is difficult to decide as there is little direct evidence. If there was any borrowing, it was indirect and circumstantial. More probable it is that by its own inner dynamism Buddhist thought too was heading towards Absolutism in metaphysics and Pantheism in religion. T.R.V. Murti, *The Central Philosophy of Buddhism, Op. Cit.*, p. 81.

That "inner dynamism" produced other parallels between Hinduism and Buddhism, as well, reaching a climax during the Gupta Period, 300-550 C.E., when, as Sukumar Dutt observes:

> The Buddhist (Mahāyānist) rites of worship [of the Gupta Period] are described in Çanto II. vv. 10 ff. of the Bodhicaryāvatāra of Śantideva (eighth century A.D.). They are practically the same as those performed in Brahmanical image worship - bathing the image with scented water, vocal and instrumental music, offering of flowers, food and clothes, swinging censers and burning incense,

etc. Sukumar Dutt, *Buddhist Monks and Monasteries of India, Op. Cit.*, p. 196.
And it was only two hundred years earlier, in the 7th century C.E., that the Buddha was celebrated as an avatār of Viṣṇu.

278. See footnotes 14, 188, 253, 277 and 304 for a discussion of the conceptual parallels between Buddhism and Hinduism. For a recent bibliography on the parallels see *Encyclopedia of Indian Philosphies, Advaita Vadanta Up to Samkara and His Pupils*, Edited by Karl H. Potter, *Op. Cit.*, p. 604, fn.29.

279. 'Mādhyamaka' is used by the followers of Nāgārjuna to denote his philosophy while calling themselves 'Madhyamika.' Non-Buddhist writers generally employ "madhyamika' to denote both followers and philosophy.

280. In what follows I have relied heavily and gratefully on T.R.V. Murti's classic, *The Central Philosophy of Buddhism, A Study of the Mādhyamika System, Op. Cit.*; David J. Kalupahana's excellent *Buddhist Philosophy, Op. Cit.*; Douglas D. Daye's very informative, "Major Schools of the Mahāyāna: Mādhyamika" in *Buddhism: A Modern Perspective, Op. Cit.*; Frederick J. Streng's moving *Emptiness, A Study in Religious Meaning* (Nashville: Abingdon Press, 1967); and Richard H. Robinson's beautifully terse *Early Mādhyamika in India and China* (Madison: The University of Wisconsin Press, 1967); together with the excellent translations and bibliographies contained in these works. Primary texts and translations will be discussed as we proceed.
For biographical information about the great Sorcerer see M. Winternitz, *A History of Indian Literature, Op. Cit.*, Vol. II, pp. 342-43 from whom the Kumārajīva account given above comes.
Five other works also attributed to Nāgārjuna, with important commentaries by his pupils Āryadeva (ca. 180-200 C.E.) and Candrakīrti (early 7th century C.E.), complete the most imporant early phases of the system. See T.R.V. Murti, *Op. Cit.*, pp. 87-103.

281. See Karl H. Potter's fine analysis and history of the entire problem of causality in his *Presuppositions of India's Philosophies, Op. Cit.*, pp. 93 ff.; and see Kenneth Inada, who protests, with some justification, that pratyaya, "causality" ought to be rendered "relational condition" in *Nāgārjuna* (Tokyo: The Hokuseido Press, 1970), p. 37; see also David J. Kalupahana's extremely good *Causality: The Central Philosophy of Buddhism, Op. Cit., passim*. Buddhism has had more "central philosophy" claims made for it than any other philosophic or religious system.

Recall T.R.V. Murti's *The Central Philosophy of Buddhism* (he thought it was Mādhyamika, of course). And earlier, the man who probably started the entire hunt for "centrals", Th. Stcherbatsky in his *The Central Conception of Buddhism* (he thought it was the dharmas). And not to be outdone by my betters, I have modestly suggested (see p.108, above) that the "central concept of Buddhism" was anitya: Central-philosophy hunting can become a mania.

282. See above pp. 187ff. for a discussion of the doctrine of substance and the two substance dualism in Sarvāstivāda.

283. *Mūlamādhyamakakārikā* 1.3 quoted in David J. Kalupahana, *Buddhist Philosophy, Op. Cit.*, p. 130.

284. See p.202 for a discussion of Sautrāntika causality and the analogy with the moving flame of the lamp as the self. Similarly, whirling a flashlight in a wide circle in the dark can create the same illusion of a solid wheel of light

285. See above p. 52 for a discussion of Jainism and its founder, Mahāvīra.

286. See pp.48-52 for a discussion of materialism and skepticism

287. *Mādhyamika-śāstra* chapter I, in Th. Stcherbatsky, *The Conception of Buddhist Nirvāṇa* (Leningrad: Academy of Sciences of the USSR, 1927), in *A Source Book in Indian Philosophy, Op. Cit.*, pp. 341-42, with some changes and additions by this author. Stcherbatsky uses "ens" and non-ens" for "Being and "non-Being." The translation is not always very good, but I have been unable to find any more readable translation in the existing literature nor do I believe that I could do better myself. Translators, unfortunately, are often trained to duplicate what the text says rather than what the text means. The results, as frequently as not, are stilted, formal and dependent on the linguistic conventions of the particular period and place of the translator. Meanings, on the other hand, as every good Platonic realist knows, are opposed to the literal and historical conventions, and have a way of being eternal, true and beautiful. Some disillusioned sexist has put the matter in the following way: Translations are like women; the beautiful ones are not faithful, and the faithful ones are not beautiful. Unfortunately, it is in striving for faithfulness that we get translations like Stcherbatsky's. See also two other better and more recent translations of the *Mūlamādhyamakakārikā* Kenneth K. Inada, *Nāgārjuna, Op. Cit.*, and Frederick J. Streng, *Emptiness, A Study in Religious Meaning, Op. Cit.*

288. See *Majjhima-Nikāya* II. 32 and *Samyutta-Nikāya* II.28.

289. The Eight Noes are from the opening verses of the *Mādhyamika Sūtra*. See the commentaries by Christmas Humphreys, *Buddhism* (Penguin Books, 1976), pp. 54-55; S. Radhakrishnan *Indian Philosophy, Op. Cit.*, Vol. I, p. 655.

290. See below pp. 294ff. for a discussion of the Buddha's apparent agreement with Murti's assertion that demolishing theory T does not mean the support for non-T, and the silence of the Buddha which this assertion entails.

291. T.R.V. Murti, *The Central Philosophy of Buddhism, Op. Cit.*, p. 131.

292. *Ibid.*, p. 166. Earlier Murti had written

> Pratītyasamutpāda [*sic*], the cardinal doctrine of Buddhism, means, according to Mādhyamika, the dependence of things on each other, their having no nature or reality of their own. *Ibid.*, p. 122.

293. See David Hume, *A Treatise of Human Nature*, Book I, Part 3, and *An Enquiry Concerning Human Understanding* Sections 4 to 7; both are well worth looking into. Here is David Hume on the psychological nature of "cause" in the *Treatise* (1739):

> A CAUSE is an object precedent and contiguous to another, and so united with it, that the idea of the one determines the mind to form the idea of the other, and the impression of the one to form a more lively idea of the other. Book I, Part III, Section xiv, p. 170 in *A Treatise of Human Nature* (Oxford at the Clarendon Press, 1888).

The psychological nature of cause refers, in effect, to the fact that cause is something we read into or put into events, it is not something already there. Hume later expanded on this idea of cause in the *Enquiry* (1748) where he juxtaposes it to the popular idea of cause as a necessary connection or power between events, or some power in one event

> by which it infallibly produces the other and operates with the greatest certainty and strongest necessity.

Nothing could be farther from the truth of what "cause" is, and Hume concluded that such ideas as power and necessary connection are "absolutely without any meaning" for there is no sensory experience to which they can be associated.

> ...after a repetition of similar instances, the mind is carried by habit, upon the appearance of one event, to expect its usual attendant, and to

believe that it will exist.

This expectation, which we feel and read into empirical events, constitutes "cause" and nothing else. Necessary connection, itself, is nothing more than a sentiment or impression of the mind:

> This connection, therefore, which we *feel* in the mind, this customary transition of the imagination from one object to its usual attendant, is the sentiment or impression from which we form the idea of power or necessary connection. Nothing further is the case.

Cause can only be something which the mind puts into experience. Hume finally states:

> ...we may define a cause to be an object, followed by another, and where all the objects similar to the first are followed by objects similar to the second.... The appearance of a cause always conveys the mind by a customary transition, to the idea of the effect. David Hume, *An Enquiry Concerning Human Understanding* Section VI, Part II in *The English Philosophers From Bacon to Mill*, Edited by E.A. Burtt (New York: The Modern Library, 1939), pp. 630, 631.

In other words, causes are not out there. Only phenomena are out there. The causes are in our minds and we, in our ignorance, impose them on those phenomena.

294. "As has been pointed out by Mach, Russell and others, the word "cause" does not occur in the physicist's formulations of the laws of nature at all. The laws of mathematical physics are laws of functional dependence, not causal laws.... Causation...is a relation of uniform succession holding between observable changes...." Arthur Pap, *An Introduction to the Philosophy of Science* (The Free Press of Glencoe, 1962), p. 313.

295. T.R.V. Murti, *Op. Cit.*, p. 83.

296. *Ibid.*, p. 36, n.2.

297. *Majjhima-Nikāya*, quoted in T.R.V. Murti, *Ibid.*, p. 47.

298. See above pp. 135-37 for a discussion of Buddha's pragmatism in the face of mounting theoretical questions. It is interesting to speculate on the question: What if a theory did lead to enlightenment; would the great Sorcerer reject it? The mythic theory of truth, extended to include possible philosophic theories along with myths, would seem to answer strongly in the affirmative.

299. *Mūlamādhyamaka Kārikās* XXIV. 8-9. Kenneth Inada, *Nāgārjuna, Op. Cit.*. For a fascinating study of the problem see *The Problem of Two Truths in Buddhism and Vedanta*, Edited by Mervyn Sprung (Dordrecht, Holland: D. Reidel Publishing Company, 1973).

300. Kenneth Inada, *Nāgārjuna, Ibid.*, p. 20.

301. See below pp. 315-19. Strictly speaking the Mādhyamika claim is that nirvāṇa and saṁsāra are non-different. The reader should be warned that I am making a logical leap, at times, by way of Leibniz' identity of indiscernibles, from the non-difference of S and N to the identity of S and N.

302. *Mūlamādhyamaka-kārikā* 24. 1-6 in David J. Kalupahana, *Buddhist Philosophy, Op. Cit.*, pp. 136-37.

303. Candrakīrti, the 7th century Mādhyamika, comments that a man who clings to a theory is like a man who, upon hearing that a merchant has nothing to sell, hopes nonetheless to buy that nothing from the merchant. Emptiness, Candrakīrti adds, is like a good laxative: It purges everything, including itself. See Hans Wolfgang Schumann, *Buddhism, Op. Cit.*, p. 143. On the "Be quiet!" analogy, I can turn up no source for it. It appears in my notes as follows, but without documentation:

> In a room with loud noises, one may shout, "Make no noise." This is self-contradictory but it accomplishes its purpose: As a means, then, śūnya is valid.

However, see *The Dialectical Method of Nāgārjuna* (Vigrahavyavartani) translated by Kamaleswar Bhattacharya, critically edited by E.H. Johnston and Arnold Kunst (Delhi: Motilal Banarsidass, 1981) in which Nāgārjuna argues:

> "You may think: When somebody says: 'Do not make a sound' he himsef makes a sound and that sound prevents the other sound; in just the same manner, the void statement that all things are void prevents the intrinsic nature of all things. - To this we reply: This also is not valid." p.8. See also p. 20.

For a fine *critical* discussion of Nāgārjuna's philosophy together with a fine summary and current bibliography of the issues involved, see L. Stafford Betty, "Nāgārjuna's masterpiece - logical, mystical, both or neither," *Philosophy East and West*, Vol. XXXIII, No. 2, April 1983: "My thesis is that Nāgārjuna *resorts* to views in *destroying* views, and that therefore his *kārikās* are self-contradictory - in other words, that *it* and not the *dṛṣṭi* of the rival schools stands self-convicted." (p. 128)

304. See above footnote 278 and pp. 125, 132, 207-08, 209, 216, 264, 279-80, 303, 327, 346 for a discussion of the *Upaniṣads* and their parallels with Buddhism. See also Klaus J. Klostermaier, "Hindu Views of Buddhism" in *Developments in Buddhist Thought: Canadian Contributions to Buddhist Studies*, edited by Roy C. Amore (Waterloo, Ontario: Wilfrid Laurier University Press, 1979), who states, quoting the great 13th century dvaitin, Madhva, "both (Advaitins and Śūnyavādins) speak of two kinds of truth and the *brahman nirguṇa* is not different from the śūnya." (p. 71) See also Surendranath Dasgupta, *A History of Indian Philosophy, Op. Cit.*, Vol. IV., p. 69. One must be careful in not attributing too much of a Upaniṣadic or Hindu influence on Mahāyāna, as opposed to Hīnayāna, Buddhism. Particularly in light of travelers' accounts like that of Hsüan-tsang in the 7th century C.E. In about 640 C.E. this eager Mahāyānist reported that half the monks of India were definitely Hīnayāna, while less than a fifth had strong Mahāyāna convictions. See Sukumar Dutt, *Buddhist Monks and Monasteries of India, Op. Cit.*, p. 169, n. 3. If that's true then one may well ask, If the Upaniṣadic influence was what made the Mahāyāna what it was, and thereby made it different from Hīnayāna, then why wasn't Hīnayāna similarly influenced, especially since their numbers were so much greater than the Mahāyāna?

305. *Śikṣāsamuccaya* 264 (*Dharmasangīti Sūtra*) in *Buddhist Texts Through the Ages, Op. Cit.*, p. 163.

306. The full passage reads: "Karma are the defilements derived from discrimination. They spread as a result of discursive ideas, they are stopped by emptiness." Candrakīrti, *Prasannapadā, Ibid.*, p. 167.

307. *Ibid.*

308. See Eliot Deutsch, *Advaita Vedānta, Op. Cit.*, p. 69, and Heinrich Zimmer, *Philosophies of India* (Princeton University Press, 1969), p. 523.

309. Edward Conze, *Buddhist Thought in India, Op. Cit.*, p. 243.

310. See below pp. 319ff. for a description of the philosophical application of śūnyatā to philosophy, itself, as we take up the paradox of desire.

311. See above pp. 247-52 and pp. 255-58 for a discussion of heaven and bhakti and the place of dhyāna, bhakti and prajñā therein.

312. See A.L. Herman, *Indian Thought, Op. Cit.*, pp. 99-100 for a discussion of the same paradox in Hinduism where it appears as "the paradox of mokṣa."

313. See below pp. 319-25 for a discussion of the paradox of desire and its solution.

314. *Mādhyamika-śāstra*, Chapter XXV.XIX in Th. Stcherbatsky, *The Conception of Buddhist Nirvāṇa*, in *A Source Book in Indian Philosophy, Op. Cit.*, p. 344.

315. See above p. 115 for a discussion of knowledge in Plato's *Sophist*.

316. *Mādhyamika-śāstra*, Chapter XXV in Th. Stcherbatsky, *Op. Cit.*, in *A Source Book in Indian Philosophy, Op. Cit.*, pp. 342-45. I have made some changes in Stcherbatsky's rather awkward translation. We have left out kārikā III in the above analysis but I append it here for the curious reader who also enjoys order and completeness:

III

Nirvāṇa is that which
Is never annihilated nor reached;
Is never ended nor eternal;
Never disappears nor originates.

317. See above p. 258 for a discussion about developing this chain of 'in order to's' in order to achieve enlightenment.

318. *Mahāyāna Viṁśaka* attributed to Nāgārjuna, translated by Susumu Yamaguchi: "Nāgārjuna's *Mahāyāna Viṁśaka*," *The Eastern Buddhist* (IV, No. 2, Kyoto, 1927) in *A Source Book in Indian Philosophy, Op. Cit.*, p. 338. Scholars now believe that the work may be by another Nāgārjuna who lived in the 7th century C.E. See T.R.V. Murti, *Op. Cit.*, p. 91.

319. *Ibid.*, p. 339. Recall Prospero's lines from Shakespeare's *Tempest*:

...These our actors,
As I foretold you, were all spirits and
Are melted into air, into thin air;
And, like the baseless fabric of this vision,
The cloud-capped towers, the gorgeous palaces,
The solemn temples, the great globe itself,
Yea, all which it inherit, shall dissolve,
And, like this insubstantial pageant faded,
Leave not a rack behind. We are such stuff
As dreams are made on, and our little life
Is rounded with a sleep. (*Tempest*, Act IV. Scene i.)

320. *Ibid.*, p. 339.

321. *Laṅkāvatāra Sūtra* II. 18, translated by D.T. Suzuki (London: Routledge, 1932, Repr. 1956), p. 55, quoted in Alan Watts *The Way of Zen* (New York: Pantheon Books, Inc., 1957), p. 61. Later the *Laṅkāvatāra* has the Buddha saying of the non-dualistic interdependence of nirvāṇa and saṁsāra: "There is no Nirvāṇa except where there is Saṁsāra; there is no Saṁsāra except where there is Nirvāṇa; for the condition of existence is not of a mutually exclusive character. Therefore it is said that all things are non-dual as are Nirvāṇa and Saṁsāra." *Laṅkāvatāra Sūtra* II. 28 in Suzuki, p. 67, quoted in Watts, p. 64.

322. Alan Watts, *Op. Cit.*, *Ibid.*, p. 62.

323. See above pp. 69-70 for a discussion of pratītyasamutpāda as a useful fiction.

324. See above p. 158f. for a discussion of abstract words as useful fictions.

325. See above pp. 174, 264ff. for a discussion of the self as a useful fiction.

326. See above pp. 253, 239-40 for a discussion of heaven and the upāyas, in general, as useful fictions.

327. See above p. 277 for a discussion of the law of karma as a useful fiction.

328. See below pp. 361-62 for a discussion of the relation between the theory of useful and skillful means and the mythic theory of truth. Finally see below p. 361 for a grand slam conclusion summarizing all of the useful fictions mentioned in this volume.

329. See above pp. 307-08 for a discussion of the paradox of śūnya and the paradox of nirvāṇa.

330. Earlier versions of this section and the one that follows have appeared as "A solution to the paradox of desire in Buddhism" *Philosophy East and West*, 29, No. 1 (January, 1979), and "Ah, but there is a paradox of desire in Buddhism - A reply to Wayne Alt" (*Philosophy East and West* 30, No. 4 (October, 1980), by A.L. Herman.

331. Henry Sidgwick, *The Methods of Ethics* (London: Macmillan & Co., Ltd., 1874/1963), p. 48. The paradox of hedonism, fundamental or not, can probably be traced back to

Aristotle's *Nichomachean Ethics*. (Plato at *Laws* 733b states that pleasure can be desired, and sees no problem in doing so). Aristotle argues that pleasure is the result of an activity and in doing so he asks and answers an intriguing question:

> How, then, is it that no one is continuously pleased? Is it that we grow weary? Certainly all human things are incapable of continuous activity. Therefore pleasure also is not continuous: for it accompanies activity. Aristotle, *Nichomachean Ethics* 1175, 3-6 in *The Basic Works of Aristotle*, Richard McKeon ed. (New York: Random House, 1941), p. 1099.

Now, one can aim at or desire an activity (or its cessation), but it is problematic whether one can in the same sense aim at or desire pleasure. In a similar fashion, John Stuart Mill, the philosopher who undoubtedly led Sidgwick to the paradox in the first place, has said:

> But I now thought that this end (happiness) was only to be attained by not making it the direct end. Those only are happy (I thought) who have their minds fixed on some object other than their own happiness.... Aiming thus at something else, they find happiness along the way.... Ask yourself whether you are happy, and you cease to be so. John Stuart Mill, *Autobiography* in *The Harvard Classics*, Charles Eliot Norton, ed. (New York: P.F. Collier & Son Company, 1909), Volume 25, p. 94.

It is, perhaps, an easy move from seeing pleasure or happiness as that which can only follow from an activity to seeing pleasure as that which to be got must be forgot, the conclusion to the paradox of hedonism. And it is perhaps an easy move from Aristotle, Mill and Sidgwick to the Buddhist conclusion, as we shall see, that desirelessness to be got must be forgot.

332. Henry Sidgwick, *The Methods of Ethics*, *Op. Cit.*, p. 48.

333. *Ibid.*, p. 136; italics mine.

334. Thus one of the claims of this book (see the Preface p. xiv and pp. 319-20, 324-25, 346, 362, 364) was that philosophic activity, philosophic argument, or a philosophic history can lead to enlightenment.

335. Recall the Buddha's remark, "I am not a generaliser (dogmatist); I am a [philosophic] analyser (Vibhajjavādi)." *Majjhima-Nikāya* II, *Subhu Sutta* 99 in T.R.V. Murti, *The Central Philosophy of Buddhism*, *Op. Cit.*, p. 3.

336. The most philosophically important of the early but inchoate Yogācāra compositions are the *Sandhinirmocana Sūtra* (ca. 150 C.E.) and the *Laṅkāvatāra Sūtra* (ca. 350 C.E.); one later composition by Vasubandhu, the great *Vijñapti-matratā-siddhi, The Treatise on Vijñapti-Only* (ca. 400 C.E.), which is in two parts, the *Viṁśatikā* and *Triṁśikā*, and, finally, Asanga's *Mahāyānasaṁgraha* (ca. 400 C.E.). See also Edward Conze, *Buddhist Thought in India, Op. Cit.*, p. 251 for a list of additional influential Yogācāra texts; and finally see also the fine introduction to Yogācāra by Stefan Anacker, "Major Schools of Mahāyāna: Yogācāra" in *Buddhism: A Modern Perspective, Op. Cit.*, pp. 97-101.

337. M. Winternitz, *A History of Indian Literature, Op. Cit.*, Vol. II, pp. 361-62.

338. *Taittirīya Upaniṣad*, III. 5.1.

339. See David J. Kalupahana, *Buddhist Philosophy, Op. Cit.*, pp. 103-04.

340. In Indological studies there are the *purists* who refuse to admit that comparative studies can do anything but harm since all attempts at seeking parallels and similarities between traditions as foreign as those of the West and the East are misleading and false. The *parallelists*, on the other hand, find likenesses and parallels everywhere; they find the purists overly-cautious, shrewish and ill-tempered on the whole matter of philosophical similarities. If T.R.V. Murti is a parallelist then, perhaps, Edward Conze is a purist. Humble Western teachers of matters Indological find themselves, as often as not, and for simple pedagogical reasons, running with the parallelists while hunting with the purists, all the time trying, as best they can, to follow Conze's otherwise sound advice:

> The search for philosophical parallels is fraught with many pitfalls. Some parallels are fruitful [Conze finds very few], others incidental and fortuitous. Edward Conze, "Buddhist Philosophy and Its European Parallels" in *Thirty Years of Buddhist Studies, Op. Cit.*, p. 210.

It might be wise to employ parallels as one would employ a convenient fiction: Use them but don't cling to them.

341. See above pp. 177-79 for a discussion of the various metaphysical positions of both realism and idealism.

342. See above p. 181ff. for a discussion of direct realism in Sarvāstivāda.

343. See above p. 195ff. for a discussion of indirect realism in Sautrāntika.

344. "The Sautrāntika by his insistence on the creative work of thought and the doctrine of Representative Perception directly led to the Idealism of the Yogācāra." T.R.V. Murti, *Op. Cit.*, p. 82.

345. See above p. 156 for a brief discussion of phenomenalism in David Hume's philosophy and in Hīnayāna anātmavāda.

346. Th. Stcherbatsky, *Buddhist Logic, Op. Cit.*, Vol. I, pp. 526-27 provides this summary for these first two sections of the *Viṁśatikā*.

347. The *Viṁśatikā* of Vasubandhu (4th century A.D.), translated by Clarence H. Hamilton: *Wei Shih Er Shih Lun*, or *The Treatise in Twenty Stanzas on Representation-only*, American Oriental Series, XIII (New Haven: American Oriental Society, 1938) in *A Source Book in Indian Philosophy, Op. Cit.*, pp. 328-33.

348. In the same way in which Vasubandhu speaks about the Buddha's upāya to a Vātsīputrīya, a Pudgalavādin, who demands to know why Buddha declined to answer the question, *inter alia*, whether the self was identical with the body. It was, "Because he took into consideration the intention of the questioner...(and) the questioner's state of mind...." T.R.V. Murti, *Op. Cit.*, p. 42. In other words, Buddha teaches in conformity with the mental capacity of his students - that's upāya and that's also good pedagogy.

349. Even the revered Bodhisattvas, apparently, must be seen in precisely this way: "One may ask, 'How, in the absence of an object, can Bodhisattvas, whose thought is unperverted, be born at will for the service of beings?' In answer, things are compared to a magical creation. - A magical creation is not a real thing.... The personality which a Bodhisattva assumes is not real...." Asanga's *Mahāyānasaṁgraha* II. 27 with *Vasubandhu's Comments* in *Buddhist Texts Through the Ages, Op. Cit.*, p. 216. The Yogācāra must be wary here, of course, lest he throw out the Bodhisattva with the bath.

350. Strictly speaking, again, neither "self-alone-ism" (solipsism) nor subjective idealism can be accurately attributed to Vasubandhu since in his metaphysical idealism there is neither self nor subject but only ideas and mental phenomena.

351. A sound argument is both valid, i.e. it follows the rules of logic, and its premises (and conclusion) are true.

352. See below pp. 362-63 for a brief discussion of the Buddhist logicians. There we shall point out that understanding philosophic views is, indeed, a straight and sure way to nirvāṇa.

353. Edward Conze refers to it as "a kind of Buddha-self, and the substratum of our quest for Nirvāṇa." *Buddhist Thought in India, Op. Cit.*, p. 134. See also Conze pp. 251-57 for a discussion of absolute idealism in Yogācāra. See Edward J. Thomas, "There is an ultimate reality, real beyond anything that can be asserted of what comes within the range of experience. This is thought (*citta*) or mind, not mind as existing in the variety in which it is experienced, but without any differentiation, and called store-consciousness (*ālaya-vijñāna*).... It is suchness, the Tathāgata, Buddhahood and mind, but mind stripped of everything transcient and phenomenal." *The History of Buddhist Thought, Op. Cit.*, pp. 233-34. But ālayavijñāna does many other things; it serves many other functions; and can be mistaken for an object or a self; thus a happier term for that ultimate reality is probably vijñaptimātra. Karl H. Potter says, "Freedom [for the Yogācāra] is the laying bare of this pure consciousness [what we are calling "vijñaptimātra"], in which state it is unsullied by the particular manifestations of consciousness [from ālayavijñāna] which characterize the waking or the dream states." *Presuppositions of India's Philosophies, Op. Cit.*, p. 138. In other words, vijñaptimātra is what exists when ālayavijñāna has been cooled and quieted by yoga.

354. Vasubandhu, *Triṁśikā* 28, in *Buddhist Texts, Op. Cit.*, p. 210.

355. *Ibid.*

356. Mādhyamika and Yogācāra are verbally indistinguishable in many of their texts. For example, to which school would you attribute the following?

XVIII. When things created by magic are seen as such, they have no existence; such is the nature of things.

XIX. They are all nothing but Mind, they are established as phantoms; therefore a blissful or an evil existence is matured according to deeds good or evil.

Mahāyāna Viṁśaka (of Nāgārjuna?), *A Source Book in*

Indian Philosophy, Op. Cit., p. 339. See above footnote 318.

357. Vasubandhu, *Triṁśikā* XXIX-XXX translated by Wing-tsit Chan in *A Source Book in Indian Philosophy, Op. Cit.*, p. 337. The last line employs Conze's translation from *Buddhist Texts, Op. Cit.*, p. 211. See David J. Kalupahana, *Buddhist Philosophy, Op. Cit.*, p. 149; "It is significant that *vijñaptimātra*, or the ultimate undifferentiated reality, is equated with the *dharma* of the Buddha" wherein the striving Bodhisattva "becomes one with the Ultimate Reality."

358. See above pp. 340-41 for the objector's question which is, in effect: Isn't it absurd to say that there are no physical objects when every sense that I have tells me that there are? Even Bishop Berkeley got back his external world.

359. *The Vedānta Sūtras of Bàdarāyana with the commentary by Śaṁkara*, translated by George Thibaut, Two Volumes (New York: Dover Publications, Inc., 1962/1896), Volume , pp. 418, 420-21, 422, 424-25, 425-26, with some changes.

360. Let me conclude this summary of the two Buddhisms by briefly recapitulating the religious tendencies of each school. I shall call attention to the five essential elements present in these religions in a manner similar to that employed above in Table I (see above footnote 23) for the religions of the *Vedas* and *Upaniṣads*. Please refer to Table VIII, below, and the brief remarks which follow:

Table VIII. The Religions of Hīnayāna and Mahāyāna Buddhism

	Hīnayāna	*Mahāyāna*
Problem	Saṁsāra-suffering (duḥkha) and reincarnation	Saṁsāra-suffering (duḥkha) and transmigration
Cause	Desire	Desire and Ignorance
Solution	Nirvāṇa	Nirvāṇa and Heaven
Way	Dhyāna yoga	Dhyāna yoga, Bhakti yoga and Jñāna yoga
Ordering Principles	Pratītyasamutpāda, Law of Karma	Pratītyasamutpāda, Law of Karma, and the Bodhisattva

My comments shall be brief enough. Please remember, once again, that we are talking about *tendencies* and that we are still assuming that religions are social institutions established to solve human problems.

On the *problem*, both religions recognize that saṁsāra, i.e. suffering, is the chief problem that Buddhism was established to solve. Hīnayāna augments the problem by adopting reincarnation wherein another being continues to suffer even after "my" saṁtāna of dharmas ends; and Mahāyāna supplements the problem by adopting transmigration, wherein I continue to suffer into my next existence even after this body dies.

On the *cause* of the problem, both religions recognize desire as the cause of saṁsāra, for it is desire that fuels the fires of saṁsāra. However, Mahāyāna posits, in addition an even more fundamental cause, viz., ignorance. It is ignorance that prevents the realization that bondage is illusory; hence, desire continues and with it saṁsāra.

On the *solution*, both religions recognize that nirvāṇa is the only permanent solution to the problem of saṁsāra. However, Mahāyāna tends to adopt an intermediate stage, a place where instruction in the dharma can continue and where the final goal may be more easily attained.

On the *way*, both religions recognize that meditation is significant and necessary for meeting the cause of the problem. However, Mahāyāna places the stress on jñāna yoga, largely because the principal cause of bondage is ignorance. In addition, in order to get into the place, heaven, where instruction in jñāna may be carried out at all, bhakti yoga is also stressed.

On the *ordering principle*, both religions recognize that it is pratītyasamutpāda, as well as the law of karma, that guarantees that the ways to the solution of the problem will be effective. However, Mahāyāna seems to recognize that the Bodhisattva has the power to mitigate or abrogate the power of the law of moral causation for the benefit of his or her bhaktas.

361. Vivekananda, *Complete Works of Swami Vivekananda*, 8 volumes (Calcutta: Advaita Ashrama, 1962/1907), Volume I, p. 17.

362. See above pp. 4, 10 for a discussion of the myth of the future Buddha as a useful means.

363. See above p. 70 for a discussion of pratītyasamutpāda as a useful fiction.

364. See above pp. 158f. for a discussion of general or abstract words as useful conventions.

365. See above pp. 174, 264ff. for a discussion of the concept of the self as a useful fiction.

366. See above pp. 254f. for a discussion of heaven as a useful fiction.

367. See above p. 277 for a discussion of the law of karma as a useful fiction.

368. See above pp. 315-19 for a discussion of the non-difference of saṁsāra and nirvāṇa as a useful fiction.

369. See above p. 306 for a discussion of the concept of śūnya as a useful fiction.

370. See above pp. 239-40 for a discussion of the Buddha's upāya as a useful fiction.

371. See above pp. 334-35 for a discussion of Buddha's secret doctrines or secret meanings as useful fictions.

372. See above pp. 305, 324-25, 345-46 for a discussion of philosophy, itself, as myth and a useful means.

373. See above pp. 305-06 for the quotations from Heinrich Zimmer and Eliot Deutsch regarding "convenient and useful fictions."

374. See above p. 243 for the quotation from K.N. Jayatilleke regarding what is "useful for the attainment of the goal of nirvāṇa."

375. See above the Preface p. xiv for a discussion of the theory of useful or skillful means.

376. See above the Preface p. xiv and p. 4 for versions of the mythic theory of truth and footnote 233.

377. F. Th. Stcherbatsky, *Buddhist Logic, Op. Cit.*, Vol. II, p. 1.

378. See F. Th. Stcherbatsky, *Buddhist Logic, Op. Cit.*. Volume I, pp.34-35; several other useful volumes on the Buddhist Logicians are A.K. Warder, *Indian Buddhism, Op. Cit.*, pp. 447-70; Karl H. Potter, *Presuppositions of India's Philosophies, Op. Cit.*, pp.68-72,140-42;188-97 Surendranath Dasgupta, *A History of Indian Philosophy, Op. Cit.*, Volume I, pp. 151-58 on the logical works of this school see the *Pramānasamuccaya* and *Nyāyapraveśa* (about 400 C.E.) of

Dignāga, and the *Pramāṇavārttika Kārikā* and *Nyāyabindu* (about 650 C.E.) by Dharmakīrti.

379. F. Th. Stcherbatsky, *Buddhist Logic, Op. Cit.*, Vol. II, p. 4.

380. Karl H. Potter, *Presuppositions of India's Philosphies, Op. Cit.*, p. 191.

BIBLIOGRAPHY

Anacker, Stefan, "The Abhidharma Piṭaka" in *Buddhism: A Modern Perspective*, edited by Charles S. Prebish.

Anacker, Stefan, "Major Schools of Mahāyāna: Yogācāra" in *Buddhism: A Modern Perspective*, edited by Charles S. Prebish.

Ayer, A.J., *The Foundations of Empirical Knowledge* (New York: Macmillan and Company, 1940). One of the best introductions to contemporary Western empiricism by one of its 20th century apologists.

Basham, A.L., *The Wonder That Was India* (New York: The Grove Press, Inc., 1959). Without a doubt the best introduction in English to Indian culture and civilization from the earliest period to 1200 A.D. Required reading for all serious students of Indian culture.

The Basic Works of Aristotle, Richard McKeon, ed. (New York: Random House, 1941).

Betty, L. Stafford, "Nāgārjuna's Masterpiece - Logical, Mystical, Both or Neither," *Philosophy East and West*, Vol. XXXIII, No. 2, April 1983. Clear, challenging and well written.

Beyer, Stephen, *The Buddhist Experience, Sources and Interpretation* (Belmont, California: Dickenson Publishing Company, Inc., 1974). Beyer writes, edits and translates with great good sense and humor. A grand introduction to the feeling and aesthetics of the Buddhist experience.

The Buddhacarita or Acts of the Buddha, Part II, translated by E.H. Johnston (New Delhi: Oriental Book Reprint Corporation, 1972/1936). Still one of the finest available works about the life of Gautama the Buddha by the great Aśvaghoṣa.

Buddhism: A Modern Perspective, edited by Charles S. Prebish (The Pennsylvania State University Press, 1975). An excellent anthology by a group of brilliant contemporary Buddhologists.

Buddhism, A Religion of Infinite Compassion. Clarence H. Hamilton, editor (The Liberal Arts Press, Inc., 1952). Selections well translated from Pāli, Sanskrit, Chinese, Tibetan and Japanese sources.

Buddhism in Translations, translated by Henry Clarke Warren (New York: Atheneum, 1963/1896). A good introduction to the Pāli texts with Warren's quite enjoyable translations.

Buddhist Mahāyāna Texts, edited by E.B. Cowell (New York: Dover Publications, Inc., 1969/1894). An exemplary collection of Mahāyāna works in dated but still highly readable translations.

Buddhist Scriptures, selected and translated by Edward Conze (Penguin Books, 1959). A fine collection of translations from both Theravāda and Mahāyāna sources by one of the most gifted and prolific English Buddhist scholars of the 20th century.

Buddhist Texts Through the Ages, edited by Edward Conze (New York: Harper & Row, 1964). Conze with three other scholars, I.B. Horner, David Snellgrove and Arthur Waley, edits and translates important Buddhist texts from the Pāli, Sanskrit, Chinese, Tibetan and Apabramsa traditions. A very impressive and basic text in Buddhist studies.

Campbell, Joseph, *The Hero With A Thousand Faces* (New York: Bollingen Foundation, Inc., Pantheon Books, 1949). The best introduction yet written to the perennial myth of the hero and its meaning for 20th century man.

Chattopadhyaya, Debiprasad, *Lokāyata, A Study in Ancient Indian Materialism* (New Delhi: People's Publishing House, 1959). The author traces the roots of modern Indian Marxism and materialism back to the Buddhist period. A good study by a meticulous scholar.

Conze, Edward, *Buddhism: Its Essence and Development* (New York: Harper & Row Publishers, 1959). A very nice introduction to Buddhism by a fine scholar.

Conze, Edward, "Buddhist Saviors" in *The Savior God*, edited by S.G.F. Brandon.

Conze, Edward, *Buddhist Thought in India* (London: George Allen & Unwin, 1962). A great study of Buddhism in India by a first rate scholar of Buddhism. Required reading for all serious students of Buddhism.

Conze, Edward, *Buddhist Wisdom Books Containing the Diamond Sūtra and the Heart Sūtra* (London: George Allen & Unwin, 1958). A good translation and commentary on two of the most important texts of Mahāyāna Buddhism.

Conze, Edward, *Further Buddhist Studies* (Oxford: Bruno Cassirer, 1975).

Conze, Edward, *A Short History of Buddhism* (London: George Allen & Unwin, 1980). An extremely compact, but always readable, history in Conze's grand style.

Conze, Edward, *Thirty Years of Buddhist Studies* (London: Bruno Cassirer, 1967). A grand collection of brilliant and frequently acerbic papers and reviews on matters Buddhistic.

Cook, Francis H., "The Sūtra Piṭaka" in *Buddhism: A Modern Perspective*, edited by Charles S. Prebish.

Coomaraswamy, Ananda K., *Buddha and the Gospel of Buddhism* (New York: G.P. Putnam's Sons, 1916).

Coomaraswamy, Ananda K., "Yakṣas," Smithsonian Miscellaneous Collections, LXXX, No. 6 (Washington, D.C.: Smithsonian Institute, 1928).

Dasgupta, Surendranath, *A History of Indian Philosophy*. Five Volumes (Cambridge: At the University Press, 1963/1922). Classic volumes in the history of Indian philosophy by one of the world's finest scholars. Required reading for all serious students of Indian philosophy.

Daye, Douglas D. "Major Schools of the Mahāyāna: Mādhyamika" in *Buddhism: A Modern Perspective*, edited by Charles S. Prebish. A brilliant, clearly written paper.

Deutsch, Eliot, *Advaita Vedānta: A Philosophical Reconstruction* (Honolulu: East-West Center Press, 1969). One of the best available reconstructions of advaita by a fine scholar and writer.

Developments in Buddhist Thought: Canadian Contributions to Buddhist Studies, edited by Roy C. Amore (Waterloo, Ontario: Wilfrid Laurier University Press, 1979). A sumptuous scholarly offering by Canadian Buddhologists. The articles are extremely well written. A spectacular volume.

The Dialectical Method of Nāgārjuna (Vigravyāvartani) translated by Kamaleswar Bhattacharya, critically edited by E.H. Johnston and Arnold Kunst (Delhi: Motilal Banarsidass, 1981).

Dialogues of the Buddha, Three Volumes, T.W. Rhys Davids, translator (London: Henry Frowde, Oxford University Press, 1899-1921). Still great, pioneering translations from early Buddhist scholarship.

Dutt, Sukumar, *Buddhist Monks and Monasteries of India* (London: George Allen & Unwin, Ltd., 1962). A grand study of Buddhist monasticism written with a particularly lively style.

Edgerton, Franklin, *The Bhagavad Gītā* (New York: Harper Torchbooks, 1964). A meticulously literal translation of this "New Testament of Hinduism" by a great scholar.

The Edicts of Aśoka, edited and translated by N.A. Nikam and Richard McKeon (The University of Chicago Press, 1959). A translation of the edicts of the illustrious Buddhist emperor Aśoka following his conversion to Buddhism. The first written accounts of Indian Buddhism taken from the carved rocks and pillars throughout Aśoka's realm.

Ehman, Mark A., "The Pure Land Sutras" in *Buddhism: A Modern Perspective*, edited by Charles S. Prebish.

Ehman, Mark, "The Saddharmapuṇḍarīka-Sūtra" in *Buddhism: A Modern Perspective*, edited by Charles S. Prebish.

Encyclopedia of Indian Philosophies, Advaita Vedānta Up to Śaṁkara and His Pupils. Edited by Karl H. Potter (Princeton University Press, 1981). An excellent introduction to those Hindu philosophers and their philosophies that became the chief critics of Buddha, Buddhists and Buddhism.

The English Philosophers From Bacon to Mill, edited by E.A. Burtt (New York: The Modern Library, 1939). Burtt's choices and his editing have made this collection the most popular work on the develoment of British empiricism to date.

Further Dialogues of the Buddha translated by Lord Chalmers in *Sacred Books of the Buddhists*, VI (Oxford University Press, 1927), in *A Source Book in Indian Philosophy*, edited by S. Radhakrishnan and C.A. Moore (Princeton University Press, 1957). Early translations of Buddhist texts; dated but good.

Gombrich, Richard, *Precept and Practice, Traditional Buddhism in the Rural Highlands of Ceylon* (Oxford: Clarendon Press, 1971). A brilliant study of modern Buddhism in Śri Laṅka.

Herman, A.L. "Ah, But There is a Paradox of Desire in Buddhism - A Reply to Wayne Alt" in *Philosophy East and West* 30, No. 4 (October 1980).

Herman, A.L., *An Introduction to Indian Thought* (Englewood Cliffs, NJ: Prentice-Hall, Inc., 1976). A basic introduction to Indian, particularly Hindu, thought that attempts to raise and solve the myriad philosophical problems that originate in that thought.

Herman, A.L., *The Problem of Evil and Indian Thought* (New Delhi: Motilal Banarsidass, 1976). An exploration of this classic philosophic problem in both Western and Eastern sources.

Herman, A.L., "A Solution to the Paradox of Desire in Buddhism" in *Philosophy East and West* 29, No. 1 (January 1979).

Hume, David. *A Treatise of Human Nature* (Oxford: At the Clarendon Press, 1888). This 18th century classic tries, among other things, to develop the phenomenalistic interpretation of the self. Great reading for the young philosopher.

Inada, Kenneth K., *Nāgārjuna* (Tokyo: The Hokuseido Press, 1970). A good, terse translation of the *Mūlamādhyamika-kārikā* with an extremely interesting commentary by Inada.

James, William, *Principles of Psychology*, Two Volumes (New York, 1890). The first professional psychologist in the United States writes a classic first study of psychology.

Jayatilleke, K.N., *Early Buddhist Theory of Knowledge* (London: George Allen & Unwin, Ltd., 1963). A marvelous discussion in some 500 pages of early Theravāda Buddhist thought with frequent references and comparisons to Western philosophic literature.

Kalupahana, David J., *Buddhist Philosophy, A Historical Analysis* (Honolulu: The University Press of Hawaii, 1976). A grand introduction to the historical background and philosophical implications of Theravāda and Mahāyāna thought.

Kalupahana, David J., *Causality: The Central Philosophy of Buddhism* (Honolulu: The University Press of Hawaii, 1975). A singularly important work on causality by a brilliant scholar written in a tight, prose style.

Keith, Sir Arthur Berriedale, *The Philosophy and Religion of the Veda and Upanishads*, Two Volumes (Delhi: Motilal Banarsidass, 1970/1925). Required reading for all serious students of Indian thought.

Kirk, G.S. and J.E. Raven, *The Presocratic Philosophers* (Cambridge University Press, 1963).

Klostermaier, Klaus J., "Hindu Views of Buddhism," in *Developments in Buddhist Thought*, edited by Roy C. Amore.

Kuklick, Bruce, *The Rise of American Philosophy*, Cambridge, Massachusetts, 1860-1930 (Yale University Press, 1977). The history of philosophy at Harvard presented in a lively and provocative manner.

Lancaster, Lewis R., "Doctrines of the Mahāyāna" in *Buddhism: A Modern Perspective*, edited by Charles S. Prebish.

Lancaster, Lewis R., "The Prajñāpāramitā Literature" in *Buddhism: A Modern Perspective*, edited by Charles S. Prebish.

Lancaster, Lewis R., "The Rise of the Mahāyāna" in *Buddhism: A Modern Perspective*, edited by Charles S. Prebish.

Locke, John, *An Essay Concerning Human Understanding*, edited by Alexander Campbell Fraser. Two Volumes (New York: Dover Publications, 1959).

Maslow, Abraham, "Lessons From the Peak-Experience," *Journal of Humanistic Psychology*, Vol. 2, 1962. A modern psychologist explores mysticism in the daily lives of ordinary people - a fascinating paper with vast implications for both believers in, and sceptics of, mystical experiences.

Mill, John Stuart, *Autobiography* in *The Harvard Classics*, Charles Eliot Norton, ed. (New York: P.F. Collier & Son Company, 1909).

Murti, T.R.V., *The Central Philosophy of Buddhism* (London: George Allen & Unwin, Ltd., 1955). Another classic work in the history and philosophy of Mahāyāna Buddhism; in this instance Murti takes up the study of Nāgārjuna and Mādhyamika Buddhism. Required reading for all serious students of Buddhist thought.

Nakamura, Hajime, *Indian Buddhism* (Kansai University of Foreign Studies, 1980).

Organ, Troy Wilson, *Hinduism, Its Historical Development* (Barron's Educational Series, Inc., 1974). A fine introduction to Hinduism and Indian thought, in general, by a fine scholar.

Origins and Doctrines of Early Buddhist Schools: A translation of the Hsüan-Chwawng Version of Vasumitra's Treatise by Jiryo Masuda (Leipzig: Verlag der Asia Major, 1925).

Pap, Arthur, *An Introduction to the Philosophy of Science* (The Free Press of Glencoe, 1962).

The Pocket World Bible, edited by Robert O. Ballou (London: Routledge and Kegan Paul, Ltd., 1948). A compendium of the world's religious literature with several very good and hard to find translations of Buddhist scriptures.

Potter, Karl H., *Presuppositions of India's Philosophies* (Englewood Cliffs, NJ: Prentice-Hall, Inc., 1963). A book that is rapidly becoming a modern classic in the interpretation of the systems of thought of early India. Required reading for all serious students of Indian philosophy.

Poussin, L. De la Vallée, "The Buddhist Councils," *The Indian Antiquary*, Volume XXXVII, 1908. Dated but exciting, pioneering account of the Councils.

Poussin, Louis De la Vallée, *The Way to Nirvāṇa* (Cambridge, 1917). A great and controversial work by one of the finest scholars of Buddhist thought.

Prebish, Charles S., "Buddhist Councils and Divisions in the Order," in *Buddhism: A Modern Perspective*, edited by Charles S. Prebish.

Prebish, Charles S., "Major Schools of the Early Buddhists: Sarvāstivāda" in *Buddhism: A Modern Perspective*, edited by Charles S. Prebish.

Prebish, Charles S., "Major Schools of the Early Buddhists: Theravāda" in *Buddhism: A Modern Perspective*, edited by Charles S. Prebish.

Prebish, Charles, "A Review of Scholarship on the Buddhist Councils," *The Journal of Asian Studies*, 33, 2 (February 1974). Required reading for anyone interested in the tangled web of council scholarship.

The Problem of Two Truths in Buddhism and Vedanta, edited by Mervyn Sprung (Dordrecht, Holland: D. Reidel Publishing Company, 1973). A well-written, handsomely edited work.

Radhakrishnan, S., *Indian Philosophy*, Two Volumes (New York: The Macmillan Company, 1929). Still one of the best introductions to Indian philosophy despite its date of publication and its rather strong bias towards advaita Vedānta.

Rahula, Walpola, *What The Buddha Taught* (New York: Grove Press, Inc., 1974). An interesting but polemical work written from a Hīnayāna point of view. A good antidote to the Sangharakshita volume, below.

Robinson, Richard H., *Early Mādhyamika in India and China* (Madison: The University of Wisconsin Press, 1967). An interesting and informative study for the advanced student written in Robinson's terse prose style.

Robinson, Richard H. and Willard L. Johnson, *The Buddhist Religion, A Historicl Introduction*, Second Edition (Belmont, California: Dickenson Publishing Company, Inc., 1977). A reworking of Robinson's early text has turned this book into a handy and well-written introduction to the Buddhist religion for the modern student.

Rhys Davids, T.W., *Buddhist India* (New Delhi: Motilal Banarsidass, 1971/1902). Lively style and a wealth of little known facts highlight this delightful volume.

Russell, Bertrand, *Our Knowledge of the External World* (The New American Library, 1960/1914). Russell's Lowell Lectures of 1914 in which he wrestled magnificently with this perennial problem of East-West philosophy.

Ryle, Gilbert, *The Concept of Mind* (London: Hutchinson & Company, Ltd., 1949).

Sangharakshita, Bhikshu, *A Survey of Buddhism* (Boulder: Shambala, 1980/1957). An interesting work written from a Mahāyāna point of view. A fair alternative to the Rahula volume, above.

The Savior God, edited by S.G.F. Brandon (Manchester University Press, 1963). An outstanding collection of studies about "Saviors" in various world religions.

Schumann, H. Wolfgang, *Buddhism, An Outline of Its Teachings and Schools* (Wheaton, IL: The Theosophical Publishing House, 1973). A very fine introduction to Theravāda and Mahāyāna Buddhism presented in clear and accurate language.

Sidgwick, Henry, *The Methods of Ethics* (London: Macmillan & Co., Ltd., 1963/1874). A classic in the field of Western ethics by a first rate philosopher.

Skinner, B.F., *About Behaviorism* (New York: Alfred A. Knopf, 1974). A work which attempts to clarify behaviorism; well written by its leading American exponent.

Skinner, B.F., *Beyond Freedom and Dignity* (New York: Alfred A. Knopf, 1971). An exciting book by a fine writer and exponent of behaviorism on several of the implications of behaviorism. Mandatory reading for all serious Buddhists.

Smart, Ninian, *Doctrine and Argument in Indian Philosophy* (London: George Allen & Unwin, Ltd., 1964). One of the best introductions to the use of argument, logic and reasoning in Indian thought,and written with Smart's good sense of style.

Some Sayings of the Buddha According to the Pāli Canon translated by F.L. Woodward (New York: Oxford University Press, 1973). Woodward's translations from the Pāli Canon of Theravāda Buddhism are well done and readable. For its size it is probably, as Edward Conze has said, "the finest anthology of the Pāli Canon ever produced."

A Source Book in Indian Philosophy, edited by Sarvepalli Radhakrishnan and Charles A. Moore (Princeton University Press, 1957). A collection of decent but often dated translations from various ancient Indian sources (Hindu, Jain, Buddhist, etc.) and several selections from modern Indian sources (Aurobindo and Radhakrishnan).

Stcherbatsky, F. Th,. *Buddhist Logic,* Two Volumes (New York: Dover Publications, Inc., 1962/1930). A classic study of Buddhist logicians and their logical endeavors, with grand translations from the original sources.

Stcherbatsky, Th., *The Central Conception of Buddhism and the Meaning of the Word Dharma* (New Delhi: Motilal Banarsidass, 1974/1923). Two classic works by one of the leading 20th century interpreters of Buddhism.

Stcherbatsky, Th., *The Conception of Buddhist Nirvāṇa* (Leningrad: Academy of Sciences of the USSR, 1927). A classical work by a great scholar.

Streng, Frederick J., *Emptiness, A Study in Religious Meaning* (Nashville: Abingdon Press, 1967). A beautifully written work on an extremely difficult subject: Śūnyavāda.

Sullivan, J.W.N., *Beethoven, His Spiritual Development* (New York: Vintage Books, 1927). A fine work by a philosopher of science about the genius of Beethoven, which explores suffering and its relation to that genius. A great book even after sixty years.

Suzuki, D.T., *The Field of Zen* (London: Buddhist Society, 1969). A splendid book by the scholar who brought Zen to the modern Western world.

Suzuki, D.T., *Outlines of Mahāyāna Buddhism* (New York: Schocken Books, Inc., 1963/1907). A fine study of Mahāyāna with essays by the world's greatest interpreter of Zen Buddhism.

Suzuki, Daisetz Taitaro, *The Laṅkāvatāra Sūtra* (London: George Rutledge and Sons, Ltd., 1932). A translation of the text from which Zen Buddhism derives much of its influence.

Thomas, Edward J., *Buddhist Scriptures* (London: John Murray, 1931). Fine translations by a great scholar.

Thomas, Edward J., *The History of Buddhist Thought* (London: Routledge & Kegan Paul, Ltd., 1951/1933). Thomas' book is still the best introduction to Buddhism on the market today despite the fact that it was written nearly 50 years ago. Required reading for all serious students of Buddhism.

Thomas, Edward J., *The LIfe of Buddha as Legend and History* (London: Routledge & Kegan Paul, Ltd., 1949/1927). Again, despite its date it is still the best introduction to Buddha and his life and times avaiable to students today. Required reading for all serious students of Buddhism.

Toffler, Alvin, *Future Shock* (New York: Bantam Books, 1971). A book that is all about change and its effects on human beings. The applications to Buddhism abound.

The Vedānta Sūtras of Bādarāyana With the Commentary by Śaṁkara translated by George Thibaut, Two Volumes (New York: Dover Publications, Inc., 1962/1896). The principal text of advaita Vedānta with a still readable translation.

Viṁśatikā of Vasubandhu: *Wei Shih Er Shih Lun* or *The Treatise in Twenty Stanzas on Representation - Only*, translated by Clarence H. Hamilton, American Oriental Series XIII (New Haven: American Oriental Society, 1938). A decent translation, but dated, of the principal text of the Yogācāra School of Mahāyāna Buddhism.

Vivekananda, *Complete Works of Swami Vivekananda*, 8 Volumes (Calcutta: Advaita Ashrama, 1962/1907). The writings of the modern representative of ancient Vedānta, the greatest disciple of the Bengali mystic, Paramahaṁsa Ramakrishna.

Vogel, Claus, *The Teachings of the Six Heretics* (Wiesbaden: Kommissionsverlag Franz Steiner BMBH, 1970). A translation of the known sayings of the six heretics encountered by Buddha in his ministry, in a clear and accurate translation.

Warder, A.K., *Indian Buddhism* (New Delhi: Motilal Banarsidass, 1970). A great study of Buddhism in India in some 600 delightful and informative pages.

Watts, Alan, *The Way of Zen* (New York: Pantheon Books, Inc., 1957). The modern master of Zen Buddhism in the West has written one of the best historical and doctrinal introductions to Zen available. Required reading for all serious students of Buddhism.

Welbon, Guy, *The Buddhist Nirvāṇa and Its Western Interpreters* (The University of Chicago Press, 1968). An engrossing history of the concept of nirvāṇa as understood by Western thinkers.

Wheeler, Sir Mortimer, *Civilizations of the Indus Valley and Beyond* (New York: McGraw-Hill Book Company, 1966). A splendid account of archaeological India.

Winternitz, M., *A History of Indian Literature*, Two Volumes (New York: Russell & Russell, 1971/1933). A classic commentary with rather good translations of Indian philosophic literature.

Wolfe, Thomas, *Of Time and the River, A Legend of Man's Hunger in His Youth* (Garden City, New York: The Sun Dial Press, 1944). A splendid book about youth, manhood, change and suffering.

Woozley, A.D., *Theory of Knowledge* (New York: Barnes & Noble, Inc., 1966/1949). A standard introduction to epistemology in a short and compact form: An excellent beginning for students of knowledge.

Zimmer, Heinrich, *Myths and Symbols in Indian Art and Civilization*, edited by Joseph Campbell (New York: Bollingen Foundation, Inc., Pantheon books, Inc., 1946). A classic work by one of the world's greatest Indian scholars and a renowned student of mythology.

Zimmer, Heinrich, *Philosophies of India* (Princeton University Press, 1969). Lectures by one of the world's foremost Indologists.

INDEX - GLOSSARY

A

G

H

Mūlasarvāstivāda Vinayavibhanga, fn. 29
Müller, F. Max, 142, fn. 277
Muṇḍaka Upaniṣad (*see* Upsaniṣads)
Murti, T.R.V., 289-90, 293, fns. 14, 26, 85, 115, 273, 276, 277, 280, 281, 290, 291, 292, 295, 297, 318, 335, 340, 344, 348
Mystical rationalism (*see also* Intuition, prajñā, Rationalism), 208
Myth (any story, legend or account that is true according to the mythic theory of truth), 2, 3-6, 18, 21, 170, 315, fns. 7, 159
Mythic theory of truth, the (a story, legend or account is true if and only if hearing and believing the story, legend or account leads to liberation"), xiv, 4-10, 70, 136, 239, 277, 306, 315, 345-46, 362, fns. 233, 241, 298, 328, 376

N

Nadī, 75
Nāgārjuna (2nd century C.E. founder of Mādhyamika), 280-325 *passim*, fns. 64, 280, 303, 318, 356
Nāgasena, 158-60, 169, 170, fn. 146
Naive realism (the view that things are exactly the way they seem or appear), 168-69, 195, 329, 330
Nakamura, Hajime, fn. 218
nāma (psychic phenomena), 187
Nanda, 78
Naturalism, 119-22, 161, 353, 354-55
neti, neti ("not this, not that"; the only possible way of describing the Indescribable) (*see also* avyākṛta, Brahman, śūnya), 38, 279, 303
Newton, Isaac, 69
Nidānakatha, fn. 2
Nigaṇtha Nataputta (Mahāvīra, the founder of Jainism), 52
Nihilism ("nothing-ism"), 141
Nikam, N.A., fn. 80
Nikāyas (collections of Buddhist compositions; the canonical, or orthodox, texts of Hīnayāna Buddhism), 87, 89, 90-94, 109, 113, 122, 124, fns. 14, 69, 166
nirmāṇakāya (the physical body of the Buddha) (*see also* trikāyavāda), 223-24, 225, 226, 228, fn. 215
nirvāṇa (Pāli nibbāna) ("blown out", extinguished; enlightenment, liberation) (*see also* Metaphysical realization, mokṣa), 7, 8, 9, 45, 46, 55, 58, 64, 66, 70, 77, 90, 99, 111, 112, 116, 117, 128, 129, 134, 136, 138-47, 148, 149, 150, 151, 159, 162, 180, 182ff., 190, 191, 193, 206, 209, 229-33, 236, 240, 241, 244, 248, 252, 253, 255, 256, 258, 262, 269, 271, 276, 281, 290, 291, 294, 295, 303-04, 307, 308-25, 353, 357, 362, fns. 40, 43, 134, 183, 186, 201, 217, 227, 244, 316, 352, 353, 360, 374;
annihilation in, 249;
gradual, 148;
positive and negative, 45, 46, 55, 141-43, 144, 359;
signs of, 148-49;
unconditioned, 145
Noble Eightfold Path (*see also* Four Noble Truths), 62-66, 74, 91, 129, 147, 224
Nominalism, Buddhist ("name-ism"; the view of Nāgasena that names do not designate or refer to objects; the view that only particulars exist

and that names do not point to them), 158-59, 160, 161, 162, 174, 199-200, fns. 145, 184
Northern Buddhism (*see* Mahāyāna Buddhism)
Nyāyabindu, 362-63, fn. 378
Nyāyapraveśa, fn. 378
Nyāya-Vaiśeṣika, fn. 180

O
Objective idealism (the view that only Mind is ultimately real), 177
Ockham's razor, 199
O'Flaherty, W.D., iii
Old Testament, 126
Organ, Troy Wilson, fn. 261
Original Buddhism (*see* Pristine Buddhism)
Ostensive (defining a term by pointing to an instance of it), 19-20

P
Pakudha Kaccāyana, 51, 177
Pāli Buddhism (*see* Hīnayāna Buddhism)
Pap, Arthur, fn. 294
Paradox of desire, 308, 319, 320-24, 347, fns. 310, 313, 330
Paradox of hedonism, 322, fn. 331
Pararox of mokṣa fn. 312
Paradox of nirvāṇa, 293, 307, 320, 324-25, fn. 329
Paradox of śūnya, the, 307-08, 320, 324-25, fn. 329
Parallels between Buddhism and Hinduism, 125, 132, 207-08, 209, 216, 250, 254, 264, 279-80, 302-04, 346, fns. 14, 188, 253, 277, 278, 304, 340
paramāṇuvāda (atomism), 195,203
Paramārtha (499-569 Yogācāra biographer of Vasubandhu), 326
pariṇāmavāda (transformationism), 284
Parmenides (5th century B.C.E., Greek philosopher who held that the real is that which never changes), 13, 115
Peak experiences, fn. 134
Perception of physical objects (*see also* Perceptual realism), 180, 181, 185, 188, 189-91, 200-03, 206
Pereptual idealism (the view that objects and their properties are mind-dependent) (*see also* Yogācāra), 175-76, 179, 330, 348-52
Perceptual realism (the view that objects and their properties exist independently of minds) (*see also* Direct Realism , Idealism, Indirect realism), 175-76, 179, 180, 206, 208, 328ff.
Personalists (*see* Pudgalavāda)
Phenomenalism (the view that talk about physical objects can be reduced to or translated into talk about individual sense experiences or sense data), 161-62, 177, 197, 270, 331, 335, fn. 345
Philosophic history, xii-xiii, xvi-xvii, 119, 187, 208, 282, 345-46, 362, fns. 101, 334, 372
Philosophic problems (the kinds of problems that philosophers attempt to solve - of course it's circular!) (*see also* Philosophic history, Philosophy), xvi-xvii
Philosophical nihilism (the view that philosophy is impossible), 179
Philosophy (that a discipline which attempts to set and solve philosophic problems -

Robinson, Richard H., fns. 40, 280
Ṛta (the Vedic principle governing the natural and moral order in the universe), 41, 225, 261, fn. 23
rūpa (material phenomena; body), 182, 186, 187, 196
Russell, Bertrand, 179, fn. 294
Ryle, Gilbert, fn. 144

S

Saddharmapuṇḍarīka Sūtra, 216-18, 230, 231-33, 237ff., 241, 244, 246, 280, fns. 205, 206, 221, 222, 223, 229, 230, 231, 232, 277
Saint Hilare, Jules Barthelemy, 142
St. John, 138, 139
St. Paul, 100
Sakka (the leader of the Gods), 124
Sāmaññaphala Sutta, fn. 29
Samantapāsadikā, fn. 64
Samayabhedoparacanacakra, fn. 64
saṁbhogakāya (the heavenly, or divine, body of the Buddha) (*see also* trikāyavāda), 224, 225, 226
Saṁgabhedavastu, fn. 29
saṁjñā (perception), 182, 186
Śaṁkara (Hindu advaita Vedāntist, 693-725 C.E.), 164-67, 328, 329, 348-52, fns. 152, 155, 180, 267
Sāṁkhya philosophy (a non-Buddhist, dualistic metaphysical philosophy), 281, 282, 283, 326, fn. 26
Sammitīya school (the second great heretical movement in Buddhism) (*see also* Heresy, Mahāsaṅghika), 102-03, 104, 107, 197, 207, 216, 269
saṁsāra (rebirth, suffering, this world) (*see also* duḥkha, Reincarnation, Transmigration), xiv, 29, 34, 35-36, 40, 41, 42, 48, 117, 168, 172, 249, 255, 280, 281, 290, 303, fns. 23, 92, 360
"Saṁsāra is nirvāṇa and nirvāṇa is saṁsāra" (meaning "there is no difference between saṁsāra and nirvāṇa") 117, 281, 297, 313-19, 361, fn. 368
saṁskāras (Pāli samkhāras) ("traces, impressions"; psycho-physical forces; conditioned or caused states and things), 111, 155-56, 162, 163, 167, 169, 171, 174, 182, 186, fn. 182
saṁtāna ("pattern" of dharmas) (*see also* prāpti), 154, 156, 158, 163, 169, 171, 174,182, 184, 185, 193, 269, 328, fns. 266, 270, 360
Saṁyutta-Nikāya, 91-92, 153-54, 294, fns. 32, 34, 72, 118, 133, 135, 139, 288
Sandaka Sutta, fn. 28
Saṅgha (the Order of monks and nuns of Buddhism; a monastic community), 75, 86, 88, 99, 129, 140, 150, 151, 251, 357, fns. 67, 136
Sangharakshita, Bhikshu, fns. 186, 227, 255
Sañjaya Belaṭṭiputta, 51-52
Śāntarakṣita (8th century Mādhyamika), fn. 97
Śāntideva (7th century C.E. Bodhisattva), 234-35, 257, fn. 255
Śāriputra (Pāli Sāriputta), 76, 218, 231-32, 237, 239, 240, 244, 247
Sarnath (the place where Buddha preached his first sermon), fn. 62
Sarvāstivāda school, xvii, 104, 107, 119, 154, 162, 174, 180, 181-95, 196, 197, 206,

T

V

Yogācāra), 182, 186, 189, 327
Vijñānavāda school (*see* Yogācāra school)
Vijñaptimātra (Pure Consciousness) (*see also* Yogācāra), 207, 278, 327, 346, 347, fns. 353, 357
Vijñapti-mātratā-siddhi, fn. 336
Viṁśatikā, 326, 328, 331-45, 348, 349, fns. 336, 346, 347
Vinaya (the texts of the rules of the Saṅgha of early Buddhism) (*see also* Saṅgha, Tripiṭaka), 82, 87, 88-89, 94-95, 129
Vinaya Mahāvaggya, fn. 116
Vinaya Piṭaka,88, fn. 64
viśiṣtadvaita Vedānta (*see* Vedānta)
Viṣṇu (the Vedic God who measured out the earth; and the Hindu God who now preserves it), 34, 114, 131, 178, 218
Visuddhi-Magga, 171, fns. 160, 161, 162, 163
Vivekananda, Swami (1863-1902, Hindu advaita Vedāntist), 361, 364, fn. 361
Vogel, Claus, fn. 29

W
Warder, A.K., fns. 253, 378
Warren, Henry Clarke, fns. 25, 138
Watts, Alan, 381, fns. 321, 322
Welbon, Guy, 142, fn. 127
Wheeler, Sir Mortimer, fn. 13
Wine, 88, 95
Winternitz, M., fns. 58, 64, 69, 72, 73, 74, 84, 280, 337
Wolfe, Thomas, fn. 95
Women, 78-79, 88, 92, 235, 250, 280, fn. 58
Woodward, F.L., fn. 11
Woozley, A.D., fn. 241

Y
yāna (career, vehicle), fn. 216
Yasa, 75, 94-95, fn. 51
Yoga (way, path or discipline), 29, 290, 291, fn. 353, 360;
bhakti yoga (devotion to a personal God or Being), 29, 255-58, 307, 315, 353, 357-58, fn. 360;
dhyāna yoga (meditation) (*see also* Meditation), 29, 63-64, 66, 145, 147-48, 224, 255, 307, 346, 357, fns. 40, 311, 360;
jñāna yoga (intuitive or mystical knowledge), 34, 40, 42, 99, 255, 280, 303, fns. 23, 360;
karma yoga (action without bondage), 72-73
Yogācāra school, xvii, 177, 180, 223, 268, 269, 278-279, 317, 325-52, 359-60, fns. 266, 336, 344, 349, 353, 356

Z
Zen Buddhism, xii, 85, 315, 317, 325, fn. 150
Zimmer, Heinrich, 306, 361, fns. 4, 308, 373

About The Author

A.L. Herman is Professor of Philosophy at the University of Wisconsin-Stevens Point. Educated at Stanford University, Harvard University and the University of Minnesota, he is the author of *India Folk Tales*(1968); *The Bhagavad Gītā, A translation and Critical Commentary* (1973); *Problems in Philosophy: West and East* with R.T. Blackwood, co-editor (1975); *The Problem of Evil and Indian Thought* (1976); and *An Introduction to Indian Thought* (1976).